THE MOULDING OF UKRAINE

THE MOULDING OF UKRAINE

The Constitutional Politics of State Formation

BY
KATARYNA WOLCZUK

CEU PRESS
Central European University Press

Published by

Central European University Press

Nádor utca 15
H-1051 Budapest
Hungary

400 West 59th Street
New York, NY 10019
USA

An imprint of the
Central European University Share Company

Distributed in the United Kingdom and Western Europe by
Plymbridge Distributors Ltd., Estover Road, Plymouth PL6 7PY
United Kingdom

ISBN 963 9241 24 5 Cloth
ISBN 963 9241 25 3 Paperback

Library of Congress Cataloging-in-Publication Data
A CIP catalog record for this book is available upon request

Printed in Hungary by Akaprint

To discover the rules of society that are best suited to nations, there would need to exist a superior intelligence, who could understand the passions of men without feeling any of them, who had no affinity with our nature but knew it to the full, whose happiness was independent of ours, but who would nevertheless make our happiness his concern, who would be content to wait in the fullness of time for a distant glory, and to labour in one age to enjoy the fruits in another. Gods would be needed to give men laws.

Jean-Jacques Rousseau
(*The Social Contract,* London: Penguin Group, 1968, p. 74)

TABLE OF CONTENTS

LIST OF TABLES

LIST OF ABBREVIATIONS

ARC	The Autonomous Republic of Crimea
CNDF	The Congress of National-Democratic Forces
CPU	The Communist Party of Ukraine
DPU	The Democratic Party of Ukraine
IBRB	The Interregional Bloc for Reforms
MDG	The Interregional Deputy Group
PDPU	The People's Democratic Party of Ukraine
SDPU(U)	The Social-Democratic Party of Ukraine (United)
SelPU	The Peasant Party of Ukraine
SPU	The Socialist Party of Ukraine
UNR	The Ukrainian People's Republic
URP	The Ukrainian Republican Party
ZOUNR	The Western Ukrainian Oblast of the Ukrainian People's Republic
ZUNR	The Western Ukrainian People's Republic

ACKNOWLEDGEMENTS

This book would not be possible without support from a number of people. Dr Judy Batt from CREES was a constant source of encouragement and advice. The research and revision of this book was facilitated by three research projects generously funded by the Economic and Social Research Council: 'The Political Economy of New States in Central and Eastern Europe and the Former Soviet Union' (ref.: R000 23 5650), 'The Quality of Democracy in Ukraine: Representation in and after the March 1998 Ukrainian Elections' (ref.: R000 22 2380), and '"Fuzzy Statehood" and European Integration in Central and Eastern Europe' (ref.: L213 25 2001). During my fieldwork in Ukraine, over various visits between 1995–1999, my interviewees were generous with the time they devoted in unveiling to me the intricacies of the constitutional process. Valentyna Dorozhkina and Anatoliy Zaiets from the Supreme Council and Anatoliy Tkachuk from the Parliamentary Development Project provided access to crucial primary sources. The staff of the Pylyp Orlyk Institute of Democracy and the Parliamentary Development Project, especially Valentyna Telychenko and Natalia Melnychuk, offered invaluable support on many occasions. Many other people from the Supreme Council, the Presidential Administration, and the Central State Archives of Civic Organisations of Ukraine facilitated the research process at various stages. Special thanks to Iryna and Joachim, as well as Luda for creating a homely feel in Kyiv. Back at CREES, conversations with a fellow traveller, Sean Hanley, provided an opportunity to air many ideas (and frustrations). I am indebted to Sarah Birch, who read and commented on the draft. Frances Millard and Richard Sakwa examined the PhD thesis on which this book is based, and provided valuable comments and kind words of encouragement. Needless to say, I am alone responsible for all the shortcomings. The final thanks go to Roman for being so refreshingly down-to-earth and keeping me on the 'straight and narrow'.

PREFACE

The collapse of communist federations in Eastern and Central Europe radically reshaped the political map of the region. Beside the states that regained their independence, such as Latvia or Estonia, a number of new states were created, such as Ukraine, Belarus or Moldova, which had no or very limited previous experience of sovereign statehood. Even in 'old', established states, such as Poland or Hungary, the process of redefining the political, social and economic profile of the state after communism was hardly straightforward. Yet, in new states, the task was considerably more onerous. They had to simultaneously undertake an unprecedented array of essential tasks such as the political transformation of the state, socio-economic restructuring and redefinition of national identity within the context of the overarching project of state formation. As the new states emerged from the rubble of their respective federations, pivotal decisions had to be made on the shape of the polity: Who are the 'sovereign people'? On what terms do individuals belong to the political community? What form of government best ensures efficiency and representation? What should the distribution of power in the centre-periphery relations be? What socio-economic goals ought the state to pursue? In seeking answers to these questions, the state-builders did not have tried-and-tested models to fall back on, as the pre-communist past offered few or no guidelines on how to organise and run the state. At the same time, seeking answers by looking to long-established states was hardly less fraught with difficulties. This was not only because of the plethora of alternative models available, but also because of the advanced insight needed into how foreign models might work in indigenous circumstances.

In light of the magnitude of the task of state formation, the aim of this book is to trace the key decision-making moments in the process of creating the blueprint of a new state, using Ukraine as a case study. Constitutional politics in post-Soviet Ukraine are examined with the aim of shedding light on the origins and consequences of the adopted model of statehood. This study of constitution making traces the process of working out the conception of statehood in the new constitution, while the analysis of post-constitutional developments highlights the ramifications of the adopted institutional design.

In embarking on a study of state building through the prism of the constitutional process, the book adopts the premise that the function of a written constitution is not necessarily limited to that of a pre-requisite for liberal constitutionalism. Following the collapse of communism, Central and Eastern Europe experienced an upsurge of constitution making, and one state after another promulgated new fundamental laws. The evident trust in the value of written constitutions tends to be explained by the yearning for constitutionalism, that is a limited government that respects individual rights and freedoms, after years of communist 'constitutionalism'. Yet it is not the only purpose of the constitutions. Notwithstanding the aspirations to constitutionalism, the constitution is a founding document of a state. Not only does it symbolically affirm newly acquired sovereignty; it also defines the institutional, territorial and cultural parameters of the polity.

The framing of new constitutions is rarely accompanied by consensus on the model of the state, which the constitution is to assert and define. Being a profoundly political act with a pivotal bearing on the future life of a polity, constitution making in polities with at least some degree of pluralism and democratic contestation is bound to elicit conflicting ideas and interests. In the case of Ukraine the achievement of such a consensus proved to be a truly formidable task because political actors, who engaged in constitution making, lacked even the minimal common depository of ideals, values and beliefs to build on. The roots of this disagreement can be found in Ukraine's history, which was marked by a circumscribed tradition of statehood. The past saddled Ukraine with diverse political experiences, levels of national awareness and adherence to different ideologies by the various segments of Ukrainian society. Therefore, despite the seemingly widely desired and almost uncontested passage to independence in 1991, orchestrated by the communist elites in tandem with the democratic opposition, the actual meaning of independence in Ukraine was far from understood and shared. Independence was gained before the essential thinking was done on the shape of the new state. This was reflected in the procrastination on constitution making in the first years of independence. But once the task could not be postponed any longer, it proved to be onerous. Divided by their interpretations of the pre-Soviet and Soviet past, some actors put forward different normative conceptions of statehood, while others, more narrowly mindedly, sought to take advantage of the opportunity to mould the institutional framework to their own liking. Therefore, constitution making engendered the contestation and reconciliation of different models of statehood, which were anchored in diverse interpretations of Ukraine's history, as well as numerous individual and group interests. The difficulties in their reconciliation account not only for the delay in the promulgation and the mode of passage of the constitution—Ukraine was the last amongst the post-Soviet states to adopt a new constitution in 1996 in a dramatic although peaceful climax—but also for the shortcomings of the constitutional design.

By removing the ideological and institutional residuals of the Soviet state model, the new fundamental 1996 law 'constituted' Ukraine as a modern, European nation-state with its homogenising aspirations and uniform institutional set-up. The passage of the constitution was heralded as a landmark victory for the 'European option' in post-Soviet Ukraine. In this context, the constitution functioned as a political manifesto. That the conservative Left failed in its attempt to preserve most of 'Soviet constitutional achievements' can be attributed to the informal alliance of the moderate right-wing and the president, who discovered much synergy in their views on the need to consolidate the state. In particular, the agenda of nation- and state building made the former democratic opposition pursue constitutional choices that it would otherwise eschew.

However, the constitution did not lead to greater political stability, a necessary precondition for the realisation of the professed goal of Ukraine's integration with Europe. The design of the legislative-executive relations put the branches of government on a collision course, something, which jeopardised the constitutional order by inducing conflict and uncertainty. Most of all, the hope for a strong presidency as an institution conducive to the consolidation of the state and implementation of the reforms has proved exaggerated. The aggrandisement of the institution has stifled the progress of democratisation and 'rule of law', while not delivering the promised economic recovery. The case of Ukraine demonstrates the discrepancy between the role of the constitution as a symbol and attribute of sovereign statehood, and its actual role in organising the machinery of the state, which is not necessarily conducive to the consolidation of a constitutional, democratic state.

The book consists of eight chapters. The first chapter examines the conceptual framework for the study of state building through the prism of the constitutional process in new states. It puts forward an argument that the role constitutions perform varies in different polities: in new states, notwithstanding possible aspirations to constitutionalism, constitutions also play a state-building role. Chapter 2 surveys Ukraine's past in order to provide both a historical overview of the circumscribed tradition of statehood and explain the reasons for the lack of clear-cut pre-communist models, which could have been restored in post-Soviet Ukraine, even if there was agreement on such a 'restoration'. Chapter 3 takes a closer look at the pivotal years, which witnessed the end of the Soviet Union and emergence of independent Ukraine. It is argued that Ukraine's passage to independence in 1990–1991 was a result of the confluence of factors amongst which the re-orientation of the key section of the Ukrainian communist elite stands out. However, the rapid pace of disengagement in Kyiv–Moscow relations is contrasted with the reluctance of the national communist elites to abandon the Soviet model, both in institutional and ideological terms, as a template inspiration for the constitutional framework of 'sovereign Ukraine'. Chapter 4 scrutinises the dismal record of constitutional reforms in the chaotic first years of Ukraine's independence. Chapters 5 and 6 deal with the re-launched constitution-making process in the aftermath of the 1994 presidential and parliamentary elections. Apart from analysing the impact of the elections on the constellation of political forces, chapter 5 examines the preferences for the model of the state—that is the form of government, the territorial—administrative model and the concept of the political community—put forward by the main political forces. While the models advocated by the Left and Right were diametrically opposed to each other, the presence of the president and the centrist forces added to the complexity of the matrix of preferences. Chapter 6 investigates the process of the contestation and reconciliation of the preferences. The dynamics of constitution drafting over 1995–1996 are examined in order to account for the peaceful passage of the constitution, despite the underlying tensions, and explain how actors' strategies either enabled or prevented them from shaping the content of the constitution. The product of the seven-year project, that is the conception of statehood that was enshrined in the new constitution, is analysed in the penultimate chapter. It is argued that not only did the passage of the constitution itself symbolise a critical threshold in the formation of a polity, but also that the content of the constitution was driven by the imperatives of state building. Thanks to the final dismantling of the Soviet model, the constitution contains the blueprint of Ukraine as a modern, European nation-state. But as chapter 8 argues this was achieved at the price of adopting institutional choices, which contributed to political instabilities and handicapped the process of democratisation. By examining the protracted legislative–executive conflict since the passage of the constitution, the chapter draws attention to the unforeseen consequences of the constitutional choices, insofar as the form of government was concerned.

CHAPTER ONE

INTRODUCTION: CONSTITUTIONS AND STATEHOOD

In Western political theory the concept of the constitution is closely linked with constitutionalism, the doctrine that strives to protect individual freedoms and prevent tyranny by putting legal limits on arbitrary powers of the government. However this doctrine is far from a coherent set of normative propositions. Rather it consists of a dynamic but loose cluster of ideas and principles formulated in the course of the eighteenth century, the diverse interpretation of which spawned different institutional arrangements in national contexts. These conceptual ambiguities surrounding constitutionalism obfuscate the diverse meanings of the constitution. While the constitution has been traditionally regarded as an emanation of constitutionalism, their symbiotic relationship was far from evident in the second half of the twentieth century. This parting of company led to the 'devaluation' of the written constitution as a meaningful defence against abuses of power. A proliferation of written constitutions without an accompanying intent to embrace the ideas of constitutionalism in new states provoked anguish amongst constitutional theorists. This disillusionment, however, reflected a lack of understanding of the multiple role constitutions play in different polities. In new states, the constitution is developed not only to limit but also to create and organise the state. The key premise of this chapter is that constitutions in new states have to be also considered through the prism of state formation. They 'constitute' the state. This function of the written constitution will be elaborated in this chapter in order to guide the empirical analysis of the constitution-making process in Ukraine.

This chapter, first of all, analyses the 'traditional' approach to constitutions as an expression of constitutionalism. Secondly, it will briefly discuss the relationship between the doctrine of constitutionalism and constitutions, and then outline the diverse meanings of the constitution. Thirdly, the 'state building' role that the written constitution can play in addition to constitutionalism will be discussed. The final section will summarise the key themes of the study and sketch out the layout of the book.

CONSTITUTIONS AND CONSTITUTIONALISM: THE ANGLO–SAXON AND EUROPEAN CONTINENTAL PERSPECTIVES

Preuss believes that constitutionalism avoided (unlike many other 'isms') a fall into oblivion.[1] However, due to its rich connotations and diverse strands the doctrine became a somewhat incoherent cluster of concepts and propositions; the relationships between them can be contradictory or even mutually exclusive.

The idea of the legal limitation of the state lies at the heart of Anglo–Saxon constitutionalism. Towards the end of the eighteenth century, when popular sovereignty supplanted absolutism in Western Europe as 'the state was the consciously contrived creature of the people',[2] liberalism, inspired by the political philosophy of such thinkers as John Locke, promoted individual liberty and freedoms derived from the doctrine of natural law. Locke divided societal interactions into two distinct and separate domains: private and public, and advocated confinement of government to the latter. Thus, parallel to the transfer of the locus of sovereignty from monarchs to people limits were imposed on the arbitrary rule of absolutist monarchs to prevent them from trespassing on the private domain of their subjects.[3]

But power is not only circumscribed (i.e. subjected to limitations to prevent encroachment into the private realm of the individual), it is also prescribed.[4] Constitutionalism is concerned not only with the relationship between the state and the body of citizens, but also with relations within the state. Procedures, rules and directives are set forth to formalise the making and implementation of decisions within the public domain. The arbitrary goodwill of the ruler is replaced by government *through* laws (laws are the only legitimate 'acts of domination') and *by* laws (government itself is subject to those laws).[5] Thus, governmental institutions are established and their functions, powers and interrelationships are delineated and formalised. Although no one specific institutional matrix was advocated by constitutionalism, structural provisions of 'mixed government', 'checks and balances', 'separation of powers',[6] 'power sharing', 'judicial review' and so on, were the key instruments created to contain and structure state power.[7] Institutional mechanisms were devised to constrain government but not to emasculate it to the point of inefficiency or anarchy. American constitutionalism born with the 1787 constitution was designed to avert the 'tyranny of powerlessness' after a period of weak and inefficient government; it strove to create limited but effective government. In order to constrain the state, a transparent and stable normative order was deemed indispensable.[8]

To this point, constitutionalism, in its most basic meaning, has been equated with a system of limited government, while its liberal component entails restricting the scope of politics in order to safeguard the individual's liberties and freedoms.[9] Liberal constitutionalism not only imposes limits on government but also on *the sovereign people* in order to protect the individual. The original drive to impose constitutional government aimed to prevent the tyranny of the absolutist monarch. Yet, the advent of popular suffrage presented dangers of a tyrannous democratic majority oppressing individuals belonging to a minority by infringing their civic liberties. The distrust of a vacillating majority was expressed by the American 'founding fathers'. Although the people became the bearers of sovereignty ('we the people'), they nevertheless had to be constrained, firstly by delegating power to representative bodies, so that there was limited scope for irresponsible shifts in popular will and, secondly, that they be limited by the provisions of the constitution. Therefore, constitutionalism with its commitments to rules and procedures also advocates the 'fencing off' of certain areas, such as civic rights, from majoritarian control.[10] This aspect features prominently in Preuss' understanding of constitutionalism:

> Constitutionalism embraces the idea of the normative penetration of the polity to the effect that its institutions continue and operate irrespective of changing majorities and of the vacillations of politics in general—it is the idea of normative supremacy and continuity.[11]

Individualism and the negative conception of liberty (with the stress on the judicial protection) is the essence of American (and to a more limited extent Anglo–Saxon) constitutionalism. This, however, has been challenged by continental strands of constitutionalism. In Europe, the republican French constitutional tradition has been centred on priority of the collective will and unity at the expense of the ideals of liberal, individualist constitutionalism. In accordance with the Jacobin universalist vision of republican democracy, popular sovereignty of the people required a special link between the state and its citizens; the former defines the general interest, while the individual's role as citizen took precedence over private interests.[12] In contrast, nineteenth century Germany witnessed the development of legal positivism, which prioritised the formal-dogmatic method and glossed over the ethical, political and economic underpinnings and applications of law. German positivism spawned the idea of *Rechtsstaat*, in which legality was interpreted as adherence to the formally adopted law, which fulfilled the criteria of procedural legitimacy rather than the demands of more elusive natural law.

Notwithstanding the republican strand of constitutionalism and German positivism, in Europe constitutional principles have been increasingly perceived as a vehicle used in the pursuit of the 'public good': advancing human welfare, happiness and prosperity alongside defending the liberty of individuals. As a result, striving for 'the common good' is not only facilitated by but also reaches beyond narrow negative constitutionalism, which rests on the conception of government that is exclusively devoted to the protection of individual liberties. In particular, Western Europe has experienced long-standing friction between liberal constitutionalism and 'other traditions in which a paternalistic view of the role of government and a notion of the state as the political expression of a solidaristic society were powerful factors'.[13] Throughout the twentieth century the provisions of welfare state have been gradually expanded (with strong support from democratic majorities) on the understanding that the universality of political rights cannot be fully achieved without a greater degree of equality in socio-economic status. With the expansion of the state's role in re-distributive policies, material benefits acquired the status of socio-economic rights to the effect of—what the German jurists called—the 'positivisation of natural rights'.[14] Effectively, elements of liberal constitutionalism have been supplemented by policies that served broader aims than just upholding liberties against the arbitrary use of power. This utilitarian and communitarian notion of Western European constitutionalism draws upon the political philosophy of Aristotle and Kant, rather than Locke or Montesquieu. (At the same time, the U.S. generally maintains its allegiance to the individualist bias in the interpretation of constitutional norms,[15] while Britain remains a somewhat hybrid case.) Today, the liberal versus utilitarian/communitarian notion of rights divides contemporary theorists of constitutionalism. And as Bellamy points out these disparate conceptions of liberty are ultimately rooted in radically different and, as such incompatible understandings of political realms.[16] To add to the conceptual and normative opaqueness, lately, political theorists have challenged modern constitutionalism for its exclusionary and discriminatory nature and advocated a radical renewal of constitutional politics through the development of novel forms of recognition and inclusion.[17] The key goal is to secure political recognition of identity either within the constitutional frameworks or—as some advocate—by overturning them.[18]

The above sketchy outline of constitutionalism, although far from exhaustive, illustrates the origins and strands of the doctrine that has featured prominently in the political transformation in the West over the last three centuries.[19] Even if constitutionalism is far from a coherent set of propositions itself, the picture is even more compounded by conceptual ambiguity about the relationship between constitutionalism and constitutions.[20] In principle, the former came first. Constitutionalism pre-dated constitutions: 'limited government was emblazoned upon the political consciousness of the West as "constitution" long before there were written constitutions'.[21] However, America set a powerful and influential example that the principles of constitutionalism are best embodied in and implemented through formal, written constitutions.[22] And although the English case shows that constitutionalism is possible without a formal written constitution, Britain's lack of a documentary constitution, despite being the cradle of constitutional government, has been put down to its particular historical evolution.[23] In other words, Britain is the exception rather than rule. Written constitutions have come to be identified with constitutionalism: 'there is a closeness between constitutionalism *per se* and the having of a constitution, a closeness that is behind the easy and frequent slippage from one to the other'.[24] This conceptual sloppiness, which has lead to the interchangeable use of constitution and constitutionalism, has important implications, because the concept of the constitution itself is far from unambiguous.

The survey of the literature on the subject reveals two basic meanings of 'the constitution': (1) the structure of government and (2) a written constitution containing the basic or fundamental law of a polity (*Grundgesetz*). Andrews recognised this duality of meaning by capitalising the term 'Constitution' to refer to the constitutional document or documents, whereas 'constitution' refers to the 'structure of government and its relationships'.[25] Finer adheres to the positivist definition of the constitution as 'codes of rules which aspire to regulate the allocation of functions, powers and duties among the various agencies and offices of government, and define the relationships between these and the public'.[26] Grey, in turn, stresses the legal character of the constitution and argues that constitutionalism is embedded in individual constitutional norms rather than written constitutions *per se*: 'a single system, a single constitution may contain written and unwritten, flexible, rigid norms' and it is effectively 'a cluster of institutions, rules, principles and practices gathered under the terminological umbrella of the term "constitution"'.[27]

From the above definitions, it cannot be deduced if the constitution denotes any political system or only those based on the principles of 'limited government'. In such a context, this slippage from constitutionalism to constitutions, as Sartori argues, is dangerous because the term 'constitution' began to denote 'the formalisation of government, *any* form of government in fact, whether "constitutional" or not'.[28] For Sartori constitution has an unambiguous aim (whether it is written or not is of secondary importance) to achieve *quarantissimo*—limited government', so the constitution is a fundamental set of principles and correlated institutional arrangements that would restrict arbitrary power.[29] As only this *telos* makes rules constitutional, Sartori advocates the re-conceptualisation of the term 'constitution' to return to the *quarantissimo* meaning and condemns the value-neutral, descriptive meaning of the constitution. Sartori rightly pointed out the original 'nuclear' meaning of the constitution and it is difficult to disagree with his powerful argument in favour of returning to and re-instating the narrower proper meaning. Yet, his plea captured the moment when the concept of constitution developed an inherently confusing diversity of meanings: a written document, a system of government and a *telos* of limited government.

Castiglione argues against and abandons the search for one absolute meaning of the constitution. Instead, he offers a taxonomy of the meanings of 'a constitution':

> This may be a document, the embodiment of either a norm, a command, a subjective will, or a practice; the organised form of a political society; or, finally, a series of devices through which independent normative principles are given institutional support within the political community.[30]

And he attempts to sort out and clarify the prevailing meanings by distinguishing: (1) a *positivist* meaning denotes a written Constitution regardless of any historical or traditional interpretation. Because this meaning includes any written document called 'a constitution'—whatever its origin, content, efficacy or legitimacy—it smacks of formalism and relativist bias. (2) An *absolute* meaning refers to a certain underlying normative order, which the constitution expresses. Purely formal and procedural characteristics (its written form, a strict amendment procedure) are not enough to constitute a normative order so the constitution must be based on a 'substantive norm-engendering principle'—some kind of ethical or meta-ethical preconception.[31] (3) A *functional* meaning focuses on the regularity and ordered functioning associated with constitutions and it plays down the normative aspect. Traditionally this meaning has epitomised the political form of the state. (4) An *instrumental* meaning subordinates the constitution to some 'external' principle. 'Constitution' is not an expression of the basic norm such as natural law (this would be normative meaning), but simply as an instrument to achieve autonomously defined ends. Those meanings often overlap, and yet have distinctive and even exclusive philosophical connotations. The differences lie in the view taken on the place of the constitution in the conduct of politics (a master or underlabourer) and whether the constitution has any intrinsic value or only instrumental role.

Having mapped the conceptual landscape (or rather minefield because of underlying controversies) of constitutionalism and constitutions we will look at the approaches to constitutions in the more specific cases of new states. The way out of this conundrum of diverse meanings, as suggested by Castiglione, will be to focus on the functions of the constitution.[32] It will be argued that the continuous world-wide popularity of constitutions can be attributed to their significance and functions in new polities.

FUNCTIONS OF THE CONSTITUTION

The relationship between democratic rule of the majority, and constitutions as a superior document binding that majority and committing it to principles of constitutionalism is tenuous. Nevertheless, despite inherent contradictions, constitutions are viewed as the keystone in building liberal constitutional democracies in Eastern and Central Europe.[33] The new post-communist constitutions are thus usually analysed as an instrument by which the usurping of power can be prevented, governments can be made accountable and human rights and freedoms enforced.[34] In that respect these constitutions seem to institutionalise the anticommunist 'revolutions', by imposing democratic restraints on governments after years of unconstrained rule by the communist parties.

This approach is inspired by the backlash against 'sham' constitutionalism in which the communist party as the supreme political authority was superior to—rather than subordinated to—the constitution and laws. Despite Marx and Engel's belief that 'state and law were repressive phenomena of the "superstructure" of class society and would disappear or "wither away" in direct proportion as the proletarian dictatorship evolved towards the classless communist society of the future',[35] the communist system did not dispose of the constitutions. Instead, it harnessed them to its own ends, disregarding the traditional link between constitutions and constitutionalism. The communist-era constitutions lacked the essential purpose of constitutionalism, namely that of imposing legal limits on the exercise of state power. While the constitutional doctrine in communist states adhered to the principle of 'popular sovereignty', the 'people' were equated with 'toilers' and united by the common aim of building a classless society. Therefore, the interests of the individual were subordinated to those of the collective endeavour to build socialism. Communist parties claimed to be the 'vanguard force' in the construction of socialism in the name and best interests of the people. This claim was enshrined in the communist states' constitutions as 'the leading role of the Party'. Wheare vividly described the decorative role of the constitution under communism: 'The Constitution is a mere skeleton; it is Party which provides the flesh and blood, which gives to the body politic its life and individuality'.[36] The Party oversaw the exercise of state authority, its institutional arrangements, political interactions and the decision-making process. It had a final say in resolving bureaucratic conflicts between different institutions of the state in the execution of policies set by the Party. Because of the belief that the exercise of state power is indivisible, no 'separation of power' nor 'checks and balances' were built in, which would have thwarted the Party's will, or, in the terms of the ruling political ideology, would have impeded moves towards the overriding goal, that of 'building socialism'. The lack of the limiting function of the constitution was reflected in the fact that control over constitutionality was assigned to the central political organs of the state and no separate constitutional review bodies existed. As the Party played a supervisory, co-ordinating and directing role, its structures were largely intertwined and merged with those of the state to the extent that communist states could be defined as 'party-states'. The ultimate supremacy of Party over state and the obvious contradiction between the formal provisions of the constitution and actual exercise of power made a mockery of the ideals of constitutionalism, the rule of law and popular sovereignty (see chapter 2).[37]

The experience of the monolithic, all-embracing Party-state precipitated the focus on the need to guard society against intrusive and arbitrary power in constitutions, and thus their defensive role has been brought to the fore once communism collapsed. As Holmes noticed 'constitution making was dominated by human lawyers who tended to assume that the main (and perhaps sole) function of the constitution was to de-ideologise the state, establish a bill of rights, limit the government, and outlaw abuses of power'. Negative constitutionalism—he argued—was 'the notion that constitutions have a primary negative purpose of preventing tyranny'.[38]

The focus on the constitution as a shield against the abuse of power reflects the original rationale behind the drafting of constitutions in the eighteenth and nineteenth century Western Europe. It was precisely because of the drive to limit government (by requiring those who govern to conform to laws, procedures and rules) that 'the history of modern European constitutionalism is the history of the progressive transfer of sovereignty from princes or kings, under whom state power had been centralised and consolidated, to the people and their representatives'.[39] So if we liken communist parties to absolutist, unconstrained kings, the constitution making drive to re-vest sovereignty with the people and their representatives in accordance with constitutional rules may indeed bear a resemblance, despite all the differences, to the advent of constitutional democracy in Western Europe.

This similarity, however, is deceptive; there is an important difference. During the era of absolutism in Western Europe, a centralised and territorially unified political system was established in which sovereignty was vested in the monarchs. Within such sovereign states new ideas incubated and were implemented. In the eighteenth and nineteenth century, the parallel development of the doctrines of constitutionalism, classic liberalism, popular sovereignty and democratic enfranchisement prompted the diversification of authority in order to defend fundamental values, such as liberty, equality and individual rights and to prevent absolutist tendencies of the monarchs. Institutional arrangements based on the principle of the 'separation of powers', 'checks and balances', and a 'balanced constitution' were devised to limit the ability of the rulers to use the state apparatus in an arbitrary manner and against the will of the sovereign people. Yet, while the locus of sovereignty shifted to the people, and institutional frameworks changed accordingly, the state remained intact: 'state power continued to exist in all its plenitude, but simply changed hands, residing now in the people rather than in kings'.[40] In Western Europe constitutionalism, popular sovereignty, and democracy developed over time within the framework of established states; constitutions reflected a qualitative change in the mode of governing within the *existing* polities, with few exceptions. These states were bound by law; written constitutions captured that moment and came to symbolise the new mode of governing.

Outside the established Western states, however, constitutions came to mark even more profound political changes. In considering why constitutions are adopted, Wheare points out that they demarcate a 'fresh start' and symbolise a break with the past.[41] The most radical break with the past is represented in the act of creating a new state, when not only the mode of governing changes but also new territorial boundaries are delineated, new institutions are incubated, and a new political community of citizens is created. In the United States, the creation of new and distinct institutions for governing coincided with a creation of the state in terms of the territory and body of citizens. This coincidence became *sine qua non* for any newcomers to the international community. Loewenstein perceptively observed that, as in the nineteenth century most 'old' states constitutionalised themselves, in the twentieth new states could not emerge unless they had a constitution announcing it.[42] 'This has been the practice certainly since 1787 when the American Constitution was drafted, and as the years passed no doubt imitation and the force of example have led all countries to think it necessary to have a constitution'.[43] The act of passing of the new constitution became a universally recognised rite of passage for new states. As Andrews put it: 'A newly-independent nation may have its birth registered through admission to the United Nations, but a Constitution is normally required as a baptismal certificate'.[44] Be it in Africa, Asia or more recently in Eastern Europe, the emergence of a new state has almost uniformly involved the adoption of a new constitution as a way of defining the distinctive, sovereign body politic and its operative rules, institutions and procedures. However, having a constitution was not synonymous with adopting constitutionalism; more often than not the original *telos* got pushed to one side. The net result was—as Sartori put it: '*Every* state had a "constitution", but only *some* states were "constitutional"' (emphasis added),[45] that is, utilise their constitutions as an effective tool for regulating political interactions between the state and the individual. This gulf between constitutions and political practice prevailing in many states has been condemned as the devaluation of constitutions in the modern world. As Finer bitterly admitted: 'in view of the stark contrast between the rights declared here and the exact opposite, that actually obtains in practically all the states on the globe, one does not know whether to howl with laughter or with anguish'.[46]

The disenchanted view stems from an assessment of other countries through Western lenses, which leads to the glossing over additional context-specific ends which constitutions serve. The fixation with the notion of constitutions as an emanation of constitutionalism obscures the wider imperatives for 'having a constitution' prevailing outside 'old' nation-states. The role of constitutions cannot be reduced to that of promoting constitutionalism, although this role cannot be ruled out either; rather the proliferation of constitutions can be accounted for and attributed to the multiplicity of their functions.

According to Castiglione, a constitution in broad terms performs three main functions: it constitutes, structures and limits. First of all, constituting a polity is 'the act of giving origin to a political entity and of sanctioning its nature and primary ends'.[47] Providing an identity through the constitution has a primary symbolic and integrative dimension as the constitution defines a people who as a community aspire to their own way of governing: the state. The second function is concerned with providing an institutional and procedural framework for a political community. This allows the state power not only to be organised, but also for this power to be exercised on the basis of order and regularity. Finally, the third function of the constitution is to limit state power and protect an individual from state interference. The limiting function is associated with the bill of rights and freedoms, which is an integral part of any written constitution, as well as the limits that the constitution imposes in exercise of state powers by its agencies. It is this last function that the doctrine of modern liberal constitutionalism emphasises as it focuses on constitutions as mechanisms of constraining government, although 'this does not seem to follow from any particular property of the constitution in general'.[48] As was pointed out, the limiting function is central to the doctrine of constitutionalism, yet the constitutional guarantee of rights and freedoms is not a sufficient condition for constitutionalism; it can only be a starting point, because constitutional norms only acquire social relevance when they are embedded in and supported by a legal culture. No legal norms, however perfectly designed, can prevent abuses of power, if no cultural expectation develops either in society or the state apparatus, that the state's organs have to conduct their functions in accordance with formal constitutional norms.

Therefore, the focus on the role of constitutions as a pre-condition for liberal constitutional democracy is too narrow to encapsulate all the ends that the constitutions play in different socio-economic, political and cultural contexts. Hence, the main conclusion of this section is that constitutions matter, but it may be for reasons additional to the pursuit of freedoms, democracy or 'rule of law'. These reasons need to be appreciated in order to grasp the role of the constitution and the significance of the constitution-making process in a new polity.

CONSTITUTION AND STATE FORMATION

Limiting functions alone cannot explain the world-wide appeal of written constitutions. Constitutions do not merely limit the state; they are instruments used in the process of setting it up. In the first place new states have to be constituted and the purpose of constitutions is to create, organise and legitimise the existence, structures and goals of the state rather than merely protect society from it. And in this context, the role of the constitution as a foundation of statehood, nationhood and sovereignty in Eastern Europe needs to be examined, as newly independent states which are being built on the rubble of the communist federations, have been saddled with the task of defining themselves in territorial, cultural and institutional terms. In order to consider the role of the constitution in the state-building process, the nature of the state as a particular form of political organisation needs to be reflected upon.

Defining a social phenomenon is the daily bread and butter of social scientists. Yet arguably none of the phenomena posed them more difficulties than that of the state, despite its centrality to social life. Historical and geographical variations made the state notoriously resistant to endeavours to single out its defining attributes.

From a historical perspective, the Greek *polis* is identified as the antecedent of the modern state, as the *polis* had a defined territory, a specific population, an idea of citizenship and legal system. Yet, the *polis* embraced the totality of life; institutions were not distinguished from the society in which they were embedded, and ethics were integral to politics. In a similar vein, political organisation in the Middle Ages cannot be easily compared with modern states, albeit for reasons different to those of the *polis*. Medieval principalities and kingdoms not only lacked a clearly defined territory, but also the monopoly over the use of force, because of the Pope's jurisdiction over the Christian world. Moreover, such principalities and kingdoms were based on kinship and patronage rather than a depersonalised and specialised state apparatus. Thus, the prevailing view is that these polities were 'pre-modern governing systems'.[49] Even those who argue that some forms of state can be discerned in the Middle Ages disagree on the exact time of their inception.

The emergence of the state can be traced back to the sixteenth century Europe. The drive to concentrate political power, to strengthen the capacity of rulers to conduct war and control disorder spawned the modern state in its fullness.[50] At that time the idea of sovereignty, that is the supreme, united, indivisible concentration of authority, developed by such thinkers as Bodin and Hobbes, became a conceptual linchpin of the state.[51] The Peace of Westphalia of 1648 consecrated the system of states in which 'each state is a self-organising, self-empowered unit operating exclusively in pursuit of its own interests'.[52] During the absolutist era, the role of the church and ecclesiastical supremacy declined, giving way to the divine right of monarchs; they embodied the living law and came to be personally identified as the source of state authority. Even if in practice absolute power proved impossible to install and absolutism 'was always in the making but never made',[53] the 'fuzziness' of political organisations in feudalism came to an end: the state exercised a sovereign authority over a delineated territory through a system of administrative–legal institutions.[54] As the state apparatus expanded, it became more differentiated, specialised and depersonalised. As pointed out above, in the nineteenth century such centralised and unified states became bound by the principles of constitutionalism: the use of state power was prescribed and limited by law.[55] Also, at that time the state, which operated in its own territory as the sole exclusive fount of all powers, developed national forms: its subjects were moulded into nations.[56] The history of Western European states demonstrated that nation building was contingent upon institution building and *vice versa*, as the institutional framework and policies of the state acted as a powerful agent in the process of forging an 'imagined community'.[57] By the early twentieth century common culture and national identity came to characterise the state as much as integrated and centralised state apparatus.

What is then the essence of the state, the core characteristics that remained constant throughout history? The elusiveness, ambiguity and abstractness of the state prompted arguments that the state is either impossible to define (indefinability thesis)[58] or that it is only possible to define the modern state (limitation thesis). In principle, the classic 1918 Weberian definition falls into the latter category, although some argue that with some qualifications the definition may be applied to pre-modern states. Inspired by Trotsky, Weber identified the state in terms of the centrality of force, which is monopolised, legitimate and territorially focused,[59] and on the basis of it social scientists constructed a structural definition (which purports to define what the state *is* rather than what *it does*) according to which the state is a set of unified institutions that exercise monopoly over the use of force within a geographically bounded territory.[60] However, this definition poses more questions than provides answers.

First of all, the institutional boundaries of the state are contested, fluid and evolving: in historical terms the institutions of the late twentieth century European state differ diametrically from the seventeenth century state, and, in geographical terms, Germany's state apparatus and its functions differ from that of South Korea. Despite the fact that the modern (non-totalitarian) state does not aspire to conflate state and society, the expansion of educational and welfare provisions makes the question of which institutions belong to the state notoriously difficult to answer with any degree of trans-historical and trans-geographical certainty. Secondly, the state's monopoly over the legitimate use of force is tentative at best. This situation prompted post-Weberian theorists of the state to revise the original definition along the lines that 'the state *tends to* be successful in asserting monopoly' or 'that it is *more* successful *than* any other form of political association' in asserting monopoly over force.[61] Although the state purports to achieve a monopoly over the legitimate use of force, in order to generate obedience and loyalty of its own population the state cannot solely rely on coercion. The state does not merely rule the people, but also nationalises them and promotes a collective sense of identity.[62] In particular, in the European tradition the association of the state and nation spawned the notion of the nation-state—the state that is predominantly associated with one people. However, national identity is emotive and contested, and the nation-state continues to rely on the power of law and force to assert sovereignty. Thus, Hoffman concludes that the inherent logic of the state is essentially contradictory:

> To say that the state merely 'seeks' legitimacy, 'claims' a monopoly and is only 'more or less' successful is to acknowledge that the state's identity is troubled … A conflict exists between the assertion and the reality, the theory and practice of an institution, which has of necessity to strive towards a goal that it cannot possibly realise.[63]

The functional definitions, which endeavoured to describe the state in terms of what is does rather than what it is, did not fare much better in capturing the essence of the state.[64] Theorists try to overcome the problem of defining the state by narrowing their focus to 'the modern state', the 'modern European state', or 'a nation-state'; some, like for example, Easton, abandoned such an abstract concept and instead focused on 'the government' as a more tangible and observable phenomenon.[65] Making such historical and geographical qualifications absolves social scientists of the need to search for a universally valid definition. Hay abandons such efforts on the grounds that dynamism combined with the diversity and complexity of historical incarnations of the state render any generalisations difficult or even impossible. He argues that the state is not amenable to space- and timeless analysis; it is not a fixed and static object of enquiry. Instead of a futile search for a hard and fast definition, which would capture the elusive nature of the state, Hay proposes focusing on three *moments of stateness:* 1) the state as *nation*: the state of a national 'people', who develop a common identity and a sense of belonging through participation in practices, ceremonies, and rituals; 2) the state as a *territory*: the demarcated terrain within which the state claims sovereign jurisdiction; 3) the state as an *institution*: a differentiated, but co-ordinated set of institutions, which operates within the territorially-bounded area. Being inherently related, these three moments of stateness add up to a dynamic constellation of institutions, relations and practices, which characterise the modern state.[66] The focus on the moments of stateness overcomes the limitations of the Weberian definition, but at the same time, purports to capture the essence of the state in defiance of the 'indefinability thesis'.

In light of the above proposition, the formation of a state, therefore, amounts to establishing sovereign authority, which exercises jurisdiction over a particular terrain through a set of specialised institutions, such as the military, administrative, judicial, and which is recognised as legitimate by the body of citizens (nation) and the international community. What role does the constitution play in state formation? The state building properties of the constitution stem from its role in the creation and authorisation of the power of the state. Although the constitution forms a part of the legal framework of the state, its nature intersects politics and law. As an act of the expression of the will of a political community, the constitution sets up the normative order, which enables the state to exercise its function, that is to realise state's aspirations to a legitimate monopoly of coercive power on a demarcated territory over the people who inhabit it. In setting up the normative order, constitutional norms 'constitute' the state. Firstly, the constitution affirms a sovereign people, that is a population seeking the political expression of its distinctiveness in sovereign statehood.[67] (Undoubtedly, the act of constituting a sovereign people by passing a constitution is laden with conceptual difficulties in new states. The constitution, paradoxically, expresses the collective will of the 'people' while at the same time constituting the 'people'. In other words, the constitutional enactment is 'a hybrid between the free manifestation of an original political will and the capacity to give normative order to an already formed collectivity'[68]). The constitution (most often in its Preamble) defines the political community and asserts the attributes of the 'collective identity of the polity', which define the way individuals (citizens) are united into a political association, and the terms on which they participate in it.[69] Secondly, with regard to the state as a territory, the constitution sanctions the jurisdiction of state institutions within particular geopolitical boundaries. When borders are contested and/or territorial sovereignty endangered by external or internal forces, the text of the constitution may explicitly describe the territory as, for example, did the 1917 Constitution of Mexico.[70] As an expression of the political will of a people, the constitution lays down a moral and legal foundation for the territorial sovereignty of the new state. Thirdly, the organising function of the constitution stems from its role in identifying the basic powers of the state and providing a basis for the *de jure* spatial and functional organisation of the state. The constitution outlines the institutions and procedures governing the relations both between central authorities and between national and sub-national institutions, which allow the state to perform a range of functions, such as rule-making, redistribution and arbitration. On the basis of the written constitution, the 'political constitution' develops, that is a plethora of rules, customs and routines, which state institutions concoct in the process of carrying out their constitutional functions.

The role of the constitution as a supreme, fundamental law of the polity is usually sanctioned by the extraordinary procedural legitimacy. Being elevated above ordinary laws, it forms the pinnacle of the state normative order. Therefore, the word 'constitution' tends to be used interchangeably with fundamental or basic law, and refers to the properties of the written constitution that transcend its formal attributes, and make it the *fundamental law of a polity (Grundgesetz)*.

Being an axiological self-expression of the polity, the constitution contains its blueprint. Therefore, the conceptual proposition, which guides the empirical analysis of this study, is that constitution making in new states, first of all, requires the elaboration of the conception of statehood: the political community, goals of the state, and the institutional infrastructure. This study aims to analyse the constitution-making process in Ukraine, one of the Soviet successor states, in light of an *instrumental* meaning of the constitution. The constitution defines statehood and is one of the key attributes of sovereignty. Although instrumental meaning touches upon the functional meaning, the two are different: the latter denotes the description and functioning of the state (which could be, at least, partially probed by studying the written constitution), whereas the instrumental meaning focuses on the role of the constitution as a written document in the process of defining and asserting statehood. The study will examine to what extent state building became the autonomously defined purpose of the constitution, notwithstanding the aspirations to develop constitutionalism.

PLAN OF THE BOOK

This book aims to trace the dynamics of state formation in Ukraine by examining the constitutional process between 1990–2000. The overarching thesis of the book is that the length of the constitution-making process and intensity of conflict surrounding the process in Ukraine reflected fundamental divisions over the blueprint and, indeed, even the sheer desirability of Ukrainian statehood. This conflict overshadowed constitution making and pushed other possible aims of constitution making aside. As a result in Ukraine, the primary role of the constitution lies in its state building functions rather than its organising and limiting qualities. This role is amply illustrated by post-constitutional developments, which exposed the shortcoming of the institutional design adopted.

The book adopts a case study approach, as there are no general theories of constitution making, and comparative studies are few and far between. A diachronic account captures the dynamics of a complex process, which involved decision making on a large number of issues of very different natures; these issues were deliberated in a variety of institutional settings over a prolonged period of time. These conditions necessitate an integrated, time- and space-bound history,[71] as no monocausal explanation could give justice to the intricacies of the process and account for the outcome. By linking ideas, interests, structures and constraints, the book aims to show how long-standing ideological traditions are filtered through a series of political contingencies. The inductive logic of the study and the actor-centred approach allows the development of an in-depth empirically grounded, context-sensitive understanding of the origins and some of the consequences of the constitutional model of statehood adopted in post-Soviet Ukraine.

In its folds of 'thick description', the study develops several themes, which capture the idiosyncrasies of state building in Ukraine. The first theme is that independence took place before serious thought was given as to what it entailed. Ukraine proclaimed independence in August 1991 and confirmed it in a referendum in December of that same year. Yet this unexpectedly speedy passage to independence precluded a thorough reflection on the nature, or even desirability, of sovereign statehood. In particular, independence took place in a kind of a historical vacuum as when the republic exited the Soviet Union, no symbolic 'restoration' of pre-communist statehood was proclaimed. Even if the framing of constitutions in new states rarely reflects pre-existing beliefs as to the political structure of the state, a 'fresh start' as a new state has to be preceded by a broad agreement on the faults of the past, which justify the creation of the new constitutional association. In Ukraine this would require a symbolic rejection of the Soviet past and a basic agreement on the desirability of moving away from its institutional, economic and cultural legacies. Yet, despite opting for independence, there was no such rejection and agreement. This lack of shared understanding of independence stemmed largely from Ukraine's complex past and societal heterogeneity. Being divided and ruled by neighbouring empires for centuries, Ukraine's society diverged in terms of linguistic, cultural, religious and economic characteristics. Only after the Second World War were the various ethnically Ukrainian regions, for the first time, united in a single administrative unit, the Ukrainian Soviet Socialist Republic. Ukraine emerged in 1991 as an independent polity with multiple 'grand narratives' of its past; this multiplicity was, most of all, reflected in the diverse evaluation, condemnatory and glorifying, of Soviet rule in Ukraine.

The second theme is that this ambivalence about the meaning of independence amongst the former communist elites, who remained at the helm of the state, accounts for much of the initial inertia and preservationist attitudes towards the Soviet constitutional model. Preserving the 1978 Soviet constitution, albeit with some modifications, compensated for the dearth of any positive inspiration for constitutional reform. During the first years of independence, the elites' procrastination on the constitutional reform, despite their tinkering with institutional prerogatives, led to a constitutional paralysis, which unfolded into a crisis of statehood.

The third theme is that when the political actors finally engaged in constitution making after the 1994 elections, the lack of a minimal common platform to build a consensus on the political, national and socio-economic structure of the state became fully apparent. The constitutional process revealed profound fault lines, the sheer number of which turned constitution making into an unprecedented challenge for the elites' ability to work out any kind of compromise. This accounts for the delay in the promulgation of the constitution, despite the urgent need to deal with the prevailing legal disarray in the country. Indeed, Ukraine was the last amongst the post-Soviet states to adopt the new constitution in a dramatic although peaceful climax. This lack of a minimal consensus and intensity of conflict until the very passage of the constitution created a sense of profound uncertainty and resulted in a perception of threat to statehood. Therefore, the consolidation of statehood became the proclaimed priority of constitution making. This objective came to overshadow the constitutional process and it inspired some actors to pursue choices which otherwise may have been eschewed. In particular, amongst those choices, which were endorsed with the view to strengthening the state, were that the institutional framework should be centred on a strong, executive presidency and based on a centralised territorial–administrative model. Only a detailed analysis of the shifting constellations of political forces and changing priorities and strategies of individual and collective actors allows a coherent account for such an outcome to emerge.

The fourth theme is that the Basic Law became a manifesto for Ukrainian state building. The aim of the constitution was not so much the protection of a pre-existing structure of the economic, political and cultural life but the creation of this very structure. This intention shaped the provisions on the institutional framework of the state, the notion of the 'sovereign people' and the socio-economic commitments of the state. With the overarching aim of integrating society and consolidating the state, constitution-makers drew inspirations from a variety of sources. The Ukrainian constitution was an endogenous product rather than a wholesale transplant of any particular exogenous constitutional model.

The fifth theme is that during post-Soviet constitution making highly circumscribed use was made of pre-communist statehood tradition. Undoubtedly, it is difficult to talk about a tradition of a polity, such as the Ukrainian People's Republic (UNR), which did not even have a chance to function in an orderly fashion. The brief spell of independent statehood under the UNR did not last long enough to leave any lasting imprint on the political organisation of society. Nevertheless, the UNR embodied a particular model of statehood centred on parliamentarism, decentralisation and a pluralistic concept of a political community. Yet little of this found favour when the state building project was embarked on again at the end of the twentieth century. Even the moderate right-wing forces, which asserted the continuity of the pre-communist statehood tradition, especially the UNR, distanced themselves from it. As chapters 5 and 7 will demonstrate, the strongest traits of the pre-communist tradition, namely parliamentarism, decentralisation, and, in particular, federalism, were eschewed for the sake of the consolidation of the state. The pre-communist state tradition was used as a symbolic weapon in the struggle to eradicate Soviet legacies but was not deemed a suitable template for the renewed project of state building.

The sixth theme is that the overarching agenda of the consolidation of statehood accounts for the limited role of the constitution as a power constraining mechanism. While the study does not aim to provide a comprehensive account of the discrepancies between the constitution as a written document, and the 'political constitution', as 'the actual political life of society',[72] it will draw attention to the way that the constitution structured political interactions. In the document, Ukraine was bequeathed an institutional framework that has perpetuated rather than moderated a crippling conflict over power. In particular, the interactions between the legislature and the executive have been profoundly unsettled, something that stifled further institutional reforms and the progress of democratisation. The symbolic power of the constitution was not matched by its organising and limiting functions. The multiple aims of constitution making could not be achieved simultaneously. This failure had grave consequences for the path of Ukrainian post-communist political and economic transformation.

The book examines the constitutional politics in Ukraine in a chronological-thematical way. As the dynamics of state formation in post-Soviet Ukraine can be only understood against the backdrop of Ukrainian history, chapter 2 offers a necessary historical introduction. The chapter surveys Ukraine's past in order to provide a historical overview of Ukraine's circumvented tradition of sovereign statehood. The pre-communist experience of statehood has bequeathed Ukraine with diverse and ill-defined institutional templates. In particular, while the UNR aspired to embody certain principles, such as decentralisation and parliamentarism, it was less successful in transcribing them into a workable institutional framework. Nevertheless, it is striking—as subsequent chapters will demonstrate—how little use was made of Ukraine's pre-communist political tradition, in particular by the moderate Right. Apart from discussing the non-communist statehood tradition, chapter 2 also surveys the Soviet model of statehood as a background to the issues addressed in later chapters, such as difficulties resulting from the improvised attempts to 'improve' the system of soviets in the early stages of the constitutional process and the views of the Left, which vehemently advocated the preservation of the Soviet state model.

Chapter 3 examines the events surrounding the end of the Soviet Union and Ukraine's passage to independence. Ukraine's emergence as an independent state in 1991 was made possible by the rapid re-orientation of the Ukrainian communist elite. The key role played by this elite explains the lingering reluctance to abandon the Soviet model, both in institutional and ideological terms, as a template for the constitutional framework of 'sovereign Ukraine', and the lack of a desire to embark on a radical overhaul of state structures. Separation from Moscow was not sought in order to eradicate the legacies of Soviet rule in Ukraine. This only became an objective later in the constitutional process. Even then it was not shared by all political forces, as the left-wing made the preservation of 'Soviet constitutional achievements' its primary goal until the very end of constitution making.

Chapter 4 examines the failure to enact constitutional reforms in the first years of Ukraine's independence under presidency of Leonid Kravchuk. With the communist elites still in the driving seat, the pre-independence ambiguities surrounding the meaning of independence were anything but resolved. Instead, the key actors opted for piecemeal institutional reforms on the grounds of the need to halt the political and economic drift of the new state. The net result was a political stalemate, which was only prevented from escalating by opting for pre-term elections. The lofty proclamations on state building contrasted with the dearth of actual determination and effort needed to pass a new constitution.

Chapters 5 and 6 scrutinise the decisive period of constitution making in the aftermath of the 1994 presidential and parliamentary elections. After analysing the impact of the elections on the constellation of political forces, chapter 5 examines the diverse conceptions of statehood put forward by the key political forces, namely the Right, Left, centrist factions and the president. Their views on the form of government, the territorial–administrative model and the concept of the political community are examined in detail. It is argued that the models advocated by the Left and Right were diametrically opposed to each other, above all because of their conflicting evaluation of Soviet rule in Ukraine. The presence of the president and the centrist forces, who were particularly interested in institutional prerogatives, added more complexity of the matrix of preferences. However, their shared opposition to the Left's objectives opened the way to an unlikely alliance of the Right, centrists and the president, which allowed for the constitution to be passed.

Chapter 6 outlines the dynamics of intensive constitution drafting over 1995–1996. The chapter demonstrates how actors' strategies either enabled or prevented them from shaping the content of the constitution and accounts for the peaceful passage of the constitution, despite the underlying tensions. The shifting and cross-cutting ideological and institutional cleavages account for the paradoxical outcome of constitution making. Despite the fact that it envisaged a strong presidency, the constitution was passed by a constitutional majority in parliament in defiance of the president. The long-standing line of conflict—between the president and the Right on the one hand, and the Left on the other—determined the content of the constitution, which—to a large extent—excluded the views of the Left. Yet, the passage of the constitution took place in a radically different context: the president and parliament were at loggerheads. The parliament closed ranks behind the relatively still pro-presidential version of the constitution as a 'lesser evil', when faced with the prospect of a referendum announced by the president.

The penultimate chapter examines the product of the seven-year project, that is the conception of statehood that was enshrined in the new 1996 constitution. It is argued that not only did the passage of the constitution itself symbolise a critical threshold in the formation of a polity, but also that the content of the constitution was driven by the imperatives of building a modern European nation-state. The constitution became a manifesto of state formation.

Chapter 8 deals with political developments under the new constitution. It analyses the role of the constitution in structuring interactions between the branches of power and draws attention to the unforeseen consequences of the constitutional choices. The creation of the semi-presidential system, in which the strong presidency shares power with the parliament over the cabinet of ministers, has proven a recipe for deadlock and a major source of ongoing political instability in Ukraine. The presidency, designed to compensate for a lack of consolidated political system during the testing years of state formation, has proven itself an obstacle to the creation of such a system. The omnipotent executive branch, headed by the presidency, has come to overshadow other state institutions, such as the legislature, judiciary and regional self-government bodies. The case of Ukraine demonstrates the discrepancy between the role of the constitution as a symbol and attribute of sovereign statehood, and its actual failure in securing the functioning of the state machinery, which is—in the longer term—conducive to the consolidation of a constitutional, democratic state.

NOTES

1 Ulrich K. Preuss, 'The Political Meaning of Constitutionalism', in Richard Bellamy (ed.), *Constitutionalism, Democracy and Sovereignty: American and European Perspectives* (Avebury, 1996), p. 11.

2 Gordon J. Schochet and John W. Chapman, 'Introduction: Constitutionalism, Liberalism, and the Study of Politics', in Roland J. Pennock and John W. Chapman (eds.), *Constitutionalism* (New York: New York University Press, 1979), p. 3.

3 In the wider context of the nation-state formation in Western Europe, the nation became a bearer of sovereignty. J. Habermas, *Facticity and Validity: Contributions to a Democratic Theory of Law and the Constitutional State* (Cambridge, Mass., 1993), p. 494.

4 William G. Andrews, *Constitutions and Constitutionalism* (Princeton: D Van Nostrand Company, Inc, 1968), p. 13.

5 Preuss, 'The Political Meaning', p. 16.

6 On the evolution of the doctrine of the separation of powers in America, France and Britain see M. J. C. Vile, *Constitutionalism and the Separation of Powers* (Oxford: Clarendon Press, 1967). The separation of state powers into the legislature, executive and judiciary provides four benefits: (1) it prevents arbitrary use of public power for private ends, (2) individual freedoms are easier to secure in a predictable environment, (3) efficiency gains are made thanks to the division of labour, (4) mutual accountability is promoted. Richard Bellamy, 'The Political Form of the Constitution: the Separation of Powers, Rights and Representative Democracy', *Political Studies*, Vol. XLIV (1996), p. 438.

7 Those principles have been embodied in a variety of institutional configurations, and the relationship between the head of state, legislature, executive and the judiciary does vary widely in Western constitutional states. Parliament-centred systems differ from the presidential system in terms of a mechanism of formation and control over the executive. In presidentialism two directly chosen agents of the electorate co-exist and are mutually independent in terms of their political survival and term of office. In a parliamentary system the executive is derived from and dependent upon the legislature. In the process of the formation of a parliamentary government the political parties play a pivotal role (rarely reflected in written constitutions), though their role is different in Westminster and PR parliamentarism. Presidentialism and two forms of parliamentarism are the ideal types of forms of government. See also Jan Erik Lane, *Constitutions and Political Theory* (Manchester and New York: Manchester University Press, 1996), chapters 5 and 6.

8 Neil MacCormick, 'Constitutionalism and Democracy', in Richard Bellamy (ed.), *Theories and Concepts of Politics: an Introduction* (Manchester: Manchester University Press, 1993), pp. 124–47.

9 However, the issue of the extent to which institutional provisions are merely instrumental in achieving this goal is contentious. Liberal rights-based constitutionalism of Anglo–Saxon origin is contrasted with a more republican conception of the constitution as a system of procedural politics rooted in popular sovereignty (Bellamy, 'The Political Form of the Constitution', p. 437). Those ways are rooted in historical trajectories and cultural predispositions of each polity. Castiglione argues that these diverse approaches demonstrate that there is no (and cannot be only) one way of restraining political power.

[Dario Castiglione, 'The Political Theory of the Constitution', *Political Studies*, Vol. XLIV, No. 3 (1996), p. 423]. However, Holmes rejects this dichotomy between liberal and republican strands of constitutionalism and strives to bridge the two by stressing the enabling and facilitating functions of the constitution rather than merely its limiting function. See Stephen Holmes, *Passions and Constraint: on the Theory of Liberal Democracy* (Chicago and London: University of Chicago Press, 1995).

10 As Kommers and Thompson argue constitutionalism is a precondition for liberal democracy as it guards an individual both against the state and democratic majorities. Donald P. Kommers and W. J. Thompson, 'Fundamentals in the Liberal Constitutional Tradition', in Joachim Jens Hesse and Nevil Johnson (eds.), *Constitutional Policy and Change in Europe* (Oxford: Oxford University Press, 1995), p. 38. For more on this issue see Jon Elster and Rune Slagstad (eds.), *Constitutionalism and Democracy* (Cambridge: Cambridge University Press, 1988), esp. the chapter by Cass R. Sunstein, 'Constitutionalism and Democracy: an Epilogue', pp. 327–56; MacCormick, 'Constitutionalism and Democracy', pp. 124–47; and Holmes, *Passions and Constraint.*

11 Ulrich K. Preuss, 'Patterns of Constitutional Evolution and Change in Eastern Europe', in Joachim Jens Hesse and Nevil Johnson (eds.), *Constitutional Policy and Change in Europe* (Oxford: Oxford University Press, 1995), p. 96.

12 Jeremy Jennings, 'French Constitutional Tradition', in Richard Bellamy, Victorio Bufacchi, and Dario Castiglione (eds.), *Democracy and Constitutional Culture in the Union of Europe* (London: Lothian Foundation Press, 1995), p. 23.

13 K. C. Wheare, *Modern Constitutions*, 2nd ed. (London: Oxford University Press, 1966), p. 50.

14 Bill Jordan, 'Constitutionalism and Social Rights', in Bellamy, Bufacchi, and Castiglione, *Democracy and Constitutional Culture,* pp. 121–36.

15 Wheare, *Modern Constitutions*, p. 52.

16 Bellamy, Bufacchi, and Castiglione, *Democracy and Constitutional Culture*.

17 Constitutional democracy is based on the representative system, which provides for equal participation for all within the political body. However, while its structural provisions recognise plurality of interests and ideologies and allow their mediation, they ignore identity as a locus of difference. See Judith Squires, 'Liberal Constitutionalism, Identity and Difference', *Political Studies*, Vol. XLIV (1996), pp. 620–34.

18 Tully, for example, condemns and rejects the imperial domination of universalist constitutionalism. Derived from a liberal, rational and individualistic Western culture rooted in the Enlightenment, constitutionalism marginalised and excluded minorities, such as for example, the Aboriginal people, who do not share this cultural heritage, but which had been imposed upon them, often by coercion. Thus the existence, needs and rights of such groups cannot be recognised and secured within prevailing constitutional frameworks. James Tully, *Strange Multiplicity: Constitutionalism in the Age of Diversity* (Cambridge: Cambridge University Press, 1995).

19 It has to be stressed that the doctrine's influence in other parts of the world has been more recent and its interactions with indigenous culture and traditions have always been complex and often strained. See, for example, Daniel P. Franklin and Micheal Baun J (eds.), *Political Culture and Constitutionalism* (Armonk and London: M.E.Sharpe, 1995). For an illuminating example of transplanting liberal American constitutional principles to Japan see K. Inoue, *MacArthur's Japanese Constitution: A Linguistic and Cultural Study of Its Making* (Chicago: University of Chicago Press, 1991).

20 This is not meant to be a criticism. As Giddens points out 'the chronic contestation or disputation of concepts and theories in the social sciences is in some part due to the fact that these concepts and theories are caught up in what they are about, namely social life itself'. Anthony Giddens, *Central Problems in Social Theory: Action, Structure and Contradiction in Social Analysis* (Houndmills and London: Macmillan, 1979), p. 89.
21 G. Maddox, 'Constitution', in T. Ball, J. Farr, and R. L. Hanson (eds.), *Political Innovation and Conceptual Change* (Cambridge: Cambridge University Press, 1989), p. 50.
22 Schochet and Chapman, 'Introduction', p. 11.
23 The lack of written constitution accounts for the fact that Britain's constitutional tradition is contradictory, as for example, the principle of the sovereignty of parliament has never been fully reconciled with the sovereignty of the people and the principles of the judicial review.
24 Schochet and Chapman, 'Introduction', p. 11.
25 Andrews, *Constitutions and Constitutionalism,* p. 21.
26 S. E. Finer, V. Bogdanor, and B. Rudden, *Comparing Constitutions* (Oxford: Clerendon Press, 1995), p. 17.
27 Thomas C. Grey, 'Constitutionalism: an Analytical Framework', in J. Roland Pennock and John Chapman W (eds.), *Constitutionalism* (New York: New York University Press, 1979), pp. 189–209.
28 G. Sartori, 'Constitutionalism: A Preliminary Analysis', *American Political Science Review*, Vol. 56, No. 4 (December 1962), p. 857.
29 On the basis of the extent to which constitutions limit government, Sartori distinguishes several types of them [criteria were put forward by Karl Loewenstein in 'Reflections on the Value of Constitutions in Our Revolutionary Age', in Harry Eckstain and David E. Apter (eds.), *Comparative Politics: A Reader* (London: The Free Press of Glencoe, 1963), pp. 149–63.] What that classification actually depicts is the relationship (or lack of it) between written constitutions and actual political practice of the state *through* and *by* law: (1) *garantiste* constitution (proper) when the *telos* adhered to; (2) nominal constitution—a collection of rules that organise but do not restrain the exercise of political power in a given polity. This could be called alternatively organisational constitutions. Although the *telos* of constitutionalism is disregarded the constitution describes the actual working of the system; (3) façade/fake constitution—contains no reliable information about the system.
30 Castiglione, 'The Political Theory', p. 421.
31 According to Castiglione, these can be of normative, positivist, voluntarist and organic character.
32 Castiglione, 'The Political Theory', p. 421.
33 For the concise argument on the need for constitutions to protect individuals rights from excesses of democracy and the discussion of 'countermajoritarian', right protecting devices see Jon Elster, 'On Majoritarianism and Rights', *East European Constitutional Review*, Vol. 1, No. 3 (Summer 1992).
34 On this approach to constitutions and an expression of disappointments with the slow pace of constitutionalisation in post-communist states see Istvan Pogany, 'Constitution Making or Constitutional Transformation in Post-Communist Societies?', *Political Studies*, Vol. XLIV, No. 3 (1996), pp. 568–91.
35 Unger L. Aryeh, *Constitutional Developments in the USSR: a Guide to the Soviet Constitutions* (London: Methuen, 1981), p. 4.

36 Wheare, *Modern Constitutions*, p. 75.

37 On constitutions and constitutionalism under communism see, for example, Robert Sharlet, *Soviet Constitutional Crisis: From De-Stalinization to Disintegration* (Armonk, New York: M.E.Sharpe, 1992); and Teresa Rakowska-Harmstone, 'Communist Constitutions and Constitutional Change', in Keith G. Banting and Richard Simeon (eds.), *The Politics of Constitutional Change in Industrial Nations* (London and Basingstoke: Macmillan, 1985), pp. 203–31.

38 Stephen Holmes, 'Conceptions of Democracy in the Draft Constitutions of Post-Communist Countries', in Beverly Crawford (ed.), *Markets, States and Democracy: The Political Economy of Post-Communist Transformation* (Boulder, San Francisco, Oxford: Westview Press, 1995), pp. 75. See also Preuss, 'Patterns of Constitutional Evolution', pp. 95–126.

39 Kommers and Thompson, 'Fundamentals' p. 27.

40 *Ibid.*

41 Wheare, *Modern Constitutions*, p. 6. France exemplifies this well as each of its republican incarnations was born with a new constitution. In England, the lack of desire to start afresh only partially explains the absence of a written constitution, as after 1688 'the development of the doctrine of the sovereign parliament ruled out any possibility of a Constitution which could control the legislature' (*ibid.,* p. 11)

42 Loewenstein, 'Reflections on the Value of Constitutions', p. 152.

43 Wheare, *Modern Constitutions*, p. 6.

44 Andrews, *Constitutions and Constitutionalism*, p. 24.

45 G. Sartori, 'Constitutionalism: A Preliminary Analysis', *American Political Science Review*, Vol. 56, No. 4 (December 1962), p. 856.

46 Finer, Bogdanor, and Rudden, *Comparing Constitutions*, p. 31. Schochet similarly commented: 'There is hardly a modern state that does not have a formal constitution that purportedly establishes and defines its governmental institutions. Thus, there is little point in discussing constitutionalism as a significant and distinct political concept; its apparent universality has rendered it vacuous'. Schochet and Chapman, 'Introduction', p. 5. Accidentally, the proliferation of constitutions—but not constitutionalism—added weight to the claim of behaviouralists that constitutions are irrelevant to study of 'real life' politics.

47 Castiglione, 'The Political Theory', p. 422.

48 *Ibid.* Pruess distinguishes a number of functions that a constitution can perform, such as a constitutive, creating sovereign authority, organising, limiting, power-sharing, authorising, legitimising political authority, and integrative. However, it remains a kind of a laundry list as these functions are only vaguely sketched out and lack conceptual precision. Preuss, 'Patterns of Constitutional Evolution', p. 98. The approach adopted by Castiglione whereby he rolls up numerous functions into three main ones, constituting, organising and limiting, is more transparent and at the same time more conceptually refined. Elster put forward another classification, and in his views the functions of the constitution are: 1) to define and protect the rights of citizens, 2) to establish the machinery of government and 3) to regulate changes to the constitution. [Jon Elster, 'Constitutionalism in Eastern Europe: an Introduction', *The University of Chicago Law Review*, Vol. 58 (1991), pp. 445–82.] However, the classification juxtaposes the description of the content of the constitution with the function it serves.

49 Patrick Dunleavy and Brian O'Leary, *Theories of the State* (London and Basingstoke: Macmillan, 1987), pp. 3–4. However, Michael Mann, 'The Autonomous Power of the State: Its Origins, Mechanisms and Results', in John A. Hall (ed.), *States in History* (Oxford: Basil Blackwell, 1986), pp. 109–96 does not reserve the concept of the state to modern times.

50 On the development of the state in Western Europe see Charles Tilly (ed.), *The Formation of National States in Western Europe* (Princeton: Princeton University Press, 1975); Gianfranco Poggi, *The Development of the Modern State: A Sociological Introduction* (London: Hutchinson, 1978), pp. 60–116; Andrew Vincent, *Theories of the State* (Oxford and New York: Blackwell, 1987), pp. 45–118; Kenneth Dyson, *The State Tradition in Western Europe: A Study of an Idea and Institutions* (Oxford: Oxford University Press, 1980).

51 Vincent, *Theories of the State*, p. 51.

52 Poggi, *The Development of the Modern State*, p. 88.

53 D. Parker, *The Making of French Absolutism* (London: Edward Arnold, 1983), p. xvi cited in Vincent, *Theories of the State*, p. 47.

54 Michael Mann, *The Sources of Social Power* (Cambridge: Cambridge University Press, 1995), Vols. 1 and 2.

55 On the constitutional theory of the state see Vincent, *Theories of the State*, pp. 77–118.

56 Poggi, *The Development of the Modern State*, p. 92.

57 On the role stressing the role of politics and the state in nation building see John Breuilly, *Nationalism and the State*, 2nd ed. (Manchester: Manchester University Press, 1993).

58 See, for example, D. Easton, *The Political System* (New York, 1953).

59 J. Hoffman, *Beyond the State: an Introductory Critique* (Cambridge: Polity, 1995), p. 35.

60 John A. Hall and G. John Ikenberry, *The State* (Open University Press, 1989), pp. 1–2.

61 *Ibid.*, p. 2 and Anthony Giddens, *The Nation-State and Violence* (Cambridge: Polity, 1985), p. 1.

62 Bhikhu Parekh, 'The Concept of National Identity', *New Community*, Vol. 21, No. 2 (April 1995), pp. 255–68.

63 Hoffman, *Beyond the State*, p. 66.

64 For an example of such an approach see Poggi, *The Development of the Modern State*.

65 Easton, *The Political System*.

66 C. Hay, *Re-stating Social and Political Change* (Buckingham and Philadelphia: Open University Press, 1996), chapter 1.

67 While the term 'political community' tends to be used interchangeably with 'the people', it was not to be found within a portfolio of concepts of classic Anglo–Saxon constitutionalism, which was inspired by individualism and contractual relations rather than any notion of collectivity. The concept of the community, which implies a shared identity of its members, was injected into constitutional terminology at the end of the eighteenth century in Germany, and was used by state theorists to boost the moral authority of the state in addition to its purely procedural and legalistic foundation. Vincent, *Theories of the State*, p. 27.

68 Dario Castiglione, 'Contracts and Constitutions', p. 68. On the linkage between constitution making and nation building see Ulrich K. Preuss, 'Feature: Constitution Making

and Nation Building: Reflections on Political Transformations in East and Western Europe', *European Journal of Philosophy*, Vol. 1, No. 1 (April 1993), pp. 81–92.

69 The term 'collective identity of the polity' was proposed by Parekh as a substitute for national identity to avoid conscious and unconscious connotations with the terms 'nation' and 'national'. Bhikhu Parekh, 'The Concept of National Identity'.

70 Ivo D. Duchacek, *Power Maps: Comparative Politics of Constitutions* (Santa Barbara: ABC–Clio Press, 1973), p. 25.

71 Johan Galtung, *Theory and Methods of Social Research* (New York: Columbia University Press, 1969), pp. 22–25.

72 Nor is it the aim of the study to elaborate a normative stance of what it takes to write a good constitution and what good constitution ought to be like. For the latter approach see Elkin and Soltan (eds.), *A New Constitutionalism.*

CHAPTER TWO

IN SEARCH OF A TRADITION: DISCONTINUITIES OF STATEHOOD IN UKRAINE'S HISTORY

The dynamics and challenges of state formation in post-Soviet Ukraine can only be understood and appreciated in the context of the history of Ukraine. Its history, like many other nations of Eastern and Central Europe, was marred by failed or circumscribed statehood. Since the period of Kyiv Rus', Ukraine witnessed two attempts to build an independent polity, both of which to some degree succeeded in establishing an institutional infrastructure, controlling territory, winning the allegiance of its population and gaining international recognition.[1] However, there was hardly any temporal or symbolic continuity between those historical reincarnations of statehood; they differed radically in terms of the form of government, territory, and the conception of 'the people'. The first, the Cossack Hetmanate, was a pre-modern formation, while, the second, during the Ukrainian Revolution, 1917–1921, not only lasted for a short period of time, but also spawned several different embodiments of the Ukrainian state. Under Soviet rule, Ukraine possessed all of the nominal trappings of sovereign statehood, most notably, a full set of republican institutions, like all other Soviet republics. Yet in reality, the Ukrainian Soviet Socialist Republic was only a hollow institutional caricature of a sovereign state.

In the light of discontinuity and diversity of legal and political institutions, Ukraine's history does not lend itself to configuration as linear national history modelled on the Western historical narratives of a nation-state, which tend to be centred on dynastic, institutional–administrative and/or territorial continuities. Post-soviet Ukraine lacks the 'historical legitimacy' derived from distinct and 'identifiable' institutional traditions and stable territorial boundaries. Moreover, there is not much else to pin national history onto, because the church, elites, language, and culture were all damaged, disrupted or destroyed and thus could not serve as firm pillars of national history. As von Hagen asserted, 'today's Ukraine is a very modern creation, with little firmly established precedent in the national past'.[2]

As a result of its history, Ukraine emerged as an independent state in 1991 with incompletely articulated and competing 'grand narratives' of its past, which glorified conflicting political traditions and historical periods, either pre-communist or Soviet. While few states in Central and Eastern Europe have an unblemished historiographical legitimacy by (ethnocentric) Western standards, the case of Ukraine is particularly complex and interesting because of, firstly, the multiple historical ruptures and, secondly, the advanced erosion of memories of pre-communist statehood. Both of these issues raised the vexed question of what exactly the indigenous political tradition was that Ukraine should embrace upon gaining independence in 1991. History left the elites in post-Soviet Ukraine with a Pandora's box of constitutional choices when it came to defining the conception of statehood in institutional, territorial and national terms. In particular, the significance of the Soviet rule in Ukraine's history proved difficult to define with any degree of consensus.

The chapter aims to provide an overview of the circumvented tradition of statehood. It will highlight the sources of diversity of political models that were confronted and had to be reconciled in the process of elaborating the conception of statehood in independent Ukraine. It will also help to illustrate the very limited use of the historical reservoir of political ideas on statehood from the pre-communist period during post-Soviet state building.

The chapter is structured chronologically and divided into three parts. The first provides a brief overview of the pre-modern history of Ukraine with a focus on the Cossack period. The second part examines the origins of the national movement in the modern era and the attempt to create a state in 1917–1921. This section also examines the form of government, the territorial model and the conception of nationhood as defined in 1917–1921. The third section will analyse the Ukrainian Soviet Socialist Republic as a quasi-sovereign formation, and focus on the institutional framework, territorial changes and the concept of the 'people'.

FROM KYIV RUS' TO THE HETMANATE

The meaning of the name Ukraine, literally 'borderland', reflects its location on the borders of other states, which dominated that part of Europe over the centuries after the disintegration of the first state on the territory of today's Ukraine—Kyiv Rus'. In the tenth century the Kyivan Rus' patrimony fostered contacts with Byzantium and converted to Christianity. After the schism within Christendom in 1054, Rus' became confined to a domain of Orthodox Slavic people. Following the death of Prince Yaroslav the Wise, Kyiv Rus' disintegrated into many principalities, amongst which the Galician principality to the west was the most powerful. After its demise in 1340 Galicia was incorporated into the Polish state. At the same time, the remaining territory of Kyiv Rus' fell pray to a Mongol invasion. Undoubtedly, the topography of Ukraine—the flat steppes, which posed no natural boundaries—accounts for the ease and frequency with which the territory of Ukraine was plundered and conquered over centuries, as Ukraine turned into a battle ground for domination by the states which surrounded it, such as the Grand Duchy of Lithuania, the Ottoman Empire, the Polish–Lithuanian Commonwealth, the Crimean Tatar Khanate, Moscovy, the Russian empire, and the Habsburg empire.

Apart from the Mongol devastation, in the fourteenth centuries Ukraine was incorporated into the Grand Duchy of Lithuania to the north, which was simultaneously coming closer to Poland. The dynastic union of Krevo in 1385 between Lithuania and Poland was followed by the 1569 Union of Lublin, which created the Polish–Lithuanian Commonwealth (*Rzeczpospolita*). The exposure to the gentrified republic resulted in Ukraine's polonisation and conversion to Catholicism. This conversion was institutionalised in the Union of Brest in the 1596 when the Uniate Church was created, which recognised the authority of the Pope, but retained Eastern rites. However, as Poland was not strong enough to defend its eastern borders, it had effective control only of the Right Bank of Dnieper. The Left Bank, the so-called 'wild fields', witnessed the rise of a distinctive socio-political formation—the Zaporizhian Host. The ranks of free Cossack warriors swelled from the influx of peasants who had run away from their masters against encroaching serfdom from Polish Ukraine; as Subtelny pointed out: 'in newly colonised Ukraine, some of Europe's most exploitative feudal lords confronted some of its most defiant masses'.[3] In 1648, Cossack Hetman Bohdan Khmelnytskyi staged a Great Revolt against Polish landlords, inspired also to defend Orthodoxy again Catholic expansion and the autonomous political formation—the Cossack Host—was established on both banks of the Dnieper. Unable to win the war with Poland without help, Khmelnytskyi looked for an ally and in 1654, the Union of Pereiaslav was signed between the Cossack Host and Russia, according to which the Cossacks recognised the authority and obtained the protection of the tsar and the Host joined Russia as an autonomous entity. However, more military struggles followed, and the Treaty of Andrushevo of 1667 split Ukraine: the Left Bank—the so-called Hetmanate—went to Russia, while Poland retained the Right Bank.

In eighteenth century Russia, the Hetmanate developed a separate political identity underpinned by a unique system of government, liberties and rights, which facilitated an emergence of a distinctive Little Russian identity.[4] However, the Hetmanate could not survive the strengthening and centralisation of the Russian state and political and cultural differences between Little and Great Russia were gradually ironed out. In 1720 Peter the Great prohibited the publication of books in Ukraine other than religious ones. In addition to halting the development of Ukrainian national culture, which had thrived in the sixteenth and seventeenth centuries, this retarded Ukraine, in comparison to Russia, in the development of a modern secular culture. In 1775 the Cossack *Sich* on the Dnieper was destroyed, followed by the abolition of the Hetmanate in 1783 by Catherine the Great.[5] The subsequent integration of the Ukrainian elites (*starshyna*) into the Russian nobility led to the loss of their distinct Little Russian identity, as they took advantage of new career opportunities within the Russian states. By 1820s, the *starshyna*—the main carrier of a Little Russian identity—was Russified and the peasantry was fully enserfed. By the early nineteenth century, Ukraine's role as a bridge between the West and Russia came to an end, and Ukraine effectively turned into a province within the Russian empire.

Although the Cossack *Sich*—in the form of the Hetmanate—could survive only under protectorate of a more powerful state, Ukraine developed a distinct political and administrative entity, which survived the best part of the eighteenth century. The *Sich* and the Hetmanate served as a fertile ground for cultivating glorifying myths of a national liberation struggle and a concerted aspiration for national autonomy, which were apparently frustrated by the tsars' breach of the Pereiaslav Agreement.[6] However, the legacy of Cossackdom cannot be easily moulded into the 'tradition of statehood'. The stabilisation of the Hetmanate associated with the transformation of the Cossack *starshyna* into gentry contrasted with the anarchistic-individualistic tradition of the *Sich* and the Haidamak movements, which exemplified a rebellion against the emergence of the modern, centralised state.[7] The Cossack tradition did not provide an equivocal design for the institutional framework of a modern state. The Hetmanate combined republican and monarchical traits, as a collective deliberative body (*Heneralna Rada*, and then *Rada Starshykh*) co-existed with powerful *Hetmans*. As such this form of government has been interpreted both as a precursor of a presidential system, in which powers are concentrated in a chief executive, and the government by assembly (see chapter 5). But even if mythologised as 'the tradition of state building', the Russification of the Cossack *starshyna* and the strangling of the autonomy of the Hetmanate meant that this episode in the history of Ukraine did not provide the basis for modern Ukrainian statehood. Beyond the realm of myths and symbols, the actual impact of the Cossack state on the future make-up of the Ukrainian state, in terms of institutional and legal traditions was minimal, with the exception of the intermittent conservative regime of Hetman Skoropadskyi in 1918 (see below). In the context of the discontinuity which followed the Cossack period, the intellectual aspirations to political trappings of statehood in Ukraine cannot be traced back firmly beyond the mid-nineteenth.[8]

THE UKRAINIAN REVOLUTION

UKRAINE'S NATIONAL 'AWAKENING' IN THE NINETEENTH CENTURY

Following the partitions of Poland in 1772, 1793 and 1795, the political subordination of Ukraine changed once again. Right-bank Ukraine (Kyiv, Podila, Volynia) was transferred to Russia, hence 're-joining' Left-bank Ukraine, while Galicia became part of the Habsburg Empire. As the modern Ukrainian national movements incubated in parallel in two empires, they developed different traits as a result of diverse political, cultural and socio-economic conditions. The rise of the modern

Ukrainian national movement in the tsarist empire can be conceptualised by using the scheme developed by the Czech historian Miroslav Hroch.[9] Despite its shortcomings,[10] for the purpose of this study, the scheme serves as a useful analytical tool for succinctly outlining developments. Hroch distinguished three phases in the process of national awakening of non-dominant ethnic groups in Eastern Europe: academic, cultural, and political. In the academic stage, from the 1820's onwards during the so-called Ukrainian Revival, scholars developed an interest in the culture and language of the peasantry, albeit without any defined and articulated political goals. In the second, cultural stage, a new type of activist embarked on agitation of the 'ethnographic masses' in order to win them over to the national cause. In Ukraine, the populists, who rejected the primary historical role of the nobility (especially as by then the Cossack *starshyna* had been assimilated into the Russian landlord class)[11] focused on the masses as an engine of human progress. The work of artist Taras Shevchenko (1814–1861), a redeemed serf, played a pivotal role in this phase. In his writings, Shevchenko used the Ukrainian vernacular to tell of past glories and the present ignominy of Ukraine and its people under foreign yoke. By the middle of the nineteenth century, the predominantly cultural activities of the populists had developed a political vein. The clandestine Cyrillo–Methodian Society of 1846–1847 and the *Hromady* in the 1850–1860's combined populism with demands for cultural autonomy.

These political ideas, however moderate, had little resonance beyond a narrow group of urban intellectuals. According to the 1897 census, 93 percent of Ukrainians were peasants, in Kyiv 54 percent of the population were Russians, and only 22 percent Ukrainians. There was hardly any Ukrainian bourgeoisie in Left-bank (that is territories to the east of the Dnieper) Ukraine. While the nascent working class was predominantly Russian and Jewish, ethnic Ukrainians—impoverished, peasant, illiterate, passive, and parochial—were not receptive to ideas of national revival and the assertion of cultural rights.[12] The cultural stage of the development of national consciousness was frustrated by the slow modernisation under tsarist rule and political repression. The process of raising the national awareness of the masses was given a crushing blow in the 1860–1880s in the form of the banning of the Ukrainian language in the public domain, including schools and publishing.[13] Thus, economic backwardness, the repressive policies of the tsarist regime, and the underdevelopment of the educational and cultural infrastructure seriously thwarted the emergence of third stage—the politicisation of the masses in support of national autonomy.

Throughout the second part of the nineteenth century, the nascent intellectual elites in tsarist Ukraine grappled with the conception of 'the Ukrainian people'. They oscillated between the assertion that Ukrainians were a branch of one people (*Russkiy narod*), who developed a distinct culture because of their different historical experiences (Mykola Kostomarov, 1817–1885), and the more radical assertion that Ukrainians had distinct roots from Russians (Mykhailo Hrushevskyi, 1866–1934). Despite these differences, the intellectuals adhered to the federalist model of statehood, in which Ukraine would be one of the constituting units. This model was most fully formulated in the writings of Mykhailo Drahomanov (1841–1895) who advocated the transformation of the Russian Empire into a democratic, constitutional republic composed of twenty states; the territory of Ukraine was to be organised into four states. As a committed socialist-anarchist Drahomanov doubted the role of the state in securing individual freedoms, and thus rejected the Western European model of a centralised nation-state for democratised Russia in general and Ukraine in particular. In Drahomanov's view, federalism would ensure not only the optimal conditions for Ukraine's national emancipation, which the centralised tsarist state hampered, but would also realise the universal principle of the individual freedom and autonomy. In contrast to the proponents of federalism, by the turn of century, the advocates of separatism, that is supporters of outright independence for Ukraine (*samostiinist*), such as Mykola Mikhnovskyi, Viacheslav Lypynskyi and Dmytro Dontsov were in a minority in 'Russian' Ukraine, although they were stronger in Galicia.

The obstacles to the development of national movement, however, were not as pronounced in Galicia, which was incorporated into the Habsburg Empire at the end of the eighteenth century, where Ukrainians were known as Ruthenians.[14] Although the level of socio-economic development was the same or even lower than in tsarist Ukraine, the Crown provinces of Galicia and, to a lesser extent, Bukovina, benefited from the fledging practices of parliamentarism (after 1867), an educational system in Ukrainian, religious freedoms, the right to use Ukrainian in state institutions, they also developed specifically Ukrainian institutions such as economic co-operatives, reading societies, newspapers, etc. In Eastern Galicia ethnic and religious divides coincided with the key social cleavage, as the Polish landlords ruled the Ukrainian peasantry. As a result, the Ukrainian national movement developed in fierce opposition to Poles (but in loyalty to Vienna).[15] Despite some confusion over the issues of identity in Eastern Galicia, independent statehood (*samostiinist*) was declared the objective of the Ukrainian national movement once Austria–Hungary crumbled, and Ukrainian nationalists encountered competing Polish claims to Eastern Galicia.[16]

THE UKRAINIAN REVOLUTION, 1917–1921: AN OVERVIEW

The collapse of the empires in the course of the First World War presented the Ukrainian elites with a long-awaited chance to realise their socio-economic and political ideals. Yet the international context and the divisions between the elites led to a creation of a string of successive governments: the Central Council, the Hetmanate, the Directory in Dnieper Ukraine, and the Western Ukrainian People's Republic in Galicia (Halychyna). While all of them claimed to embody Ukrainian statehood, the relations between them were often full of tensions. The period of the Ukrainian Revolution will be briefly presented below in order to argue that the political, military and social context impacted on the attempt at state building to the extent that it is difficult to define the pre-communist tradition of statehood with a high degree of precision.

Taking into account the ideological profile of the Ukrainian elites, separatism was not on the cards, when in the aftermath of the February revolution, in March 1917, the Central Council (*Tsentralna Rada*) was created in Kyiv by the prominent Ukrainian populist and socialist intellectuals and activists, such as Mykhailo Hrushevskyi, Volodymyr Vynnychenko, Serkhiy Yefremov, and Semen Petliura.[17] The *Rada,* which turned itself into a representative body in the summer of 1917, competed for power with the Bolsheviks and the Provisional Government in Ukraine.[18] In April 1917 the Ukrainian elites called for the federalisation of the Russian state with Ukraine as one of its autonomous units. Following the October Revolution, in its Third Universal (November 1917), the Central Council proclaimed the creation of the Ukrainian People's Republic (UNR) which was to be joined by federal ties to democratic Russia. It was only the military offensive of the Bolsheviks on Kyiv that forced the Ukrainian elites to accept that 'a complete breakup of the Russian imperial state was a more realistic goal than its democratisation and federalisation, and that for Ukraine the alternatives were, indeed, either independent statehood or national annihilation'.[19] In

January 1918 in its Fourth Universal the *Rada* proclaimed full independence of Russia. However, this accelerated radicalisation of the Ukrainian national movement was not backed by the institutional and human resources necessary to turn proclamations into reality. In particular, the Ukrainian leaders, inexperienced and idealistic as they were, failed to appreciate the need for establishing state institutions and an army to defend its territory. This proved to have pivotal consequences as soon as Ukraine became a theatre of numerous military interventions.

Despite the fact that the Bolsheviks lacked popular support in Ukraine (their power base was limited to the Russian working class),[20] they had a competitive advantage over the *Rada* thanks to their military, industrial, and organisational superiority.[21] The Bolsheviks refused to recognise the 'bourgeois-nationalist' UNR as a legitimate government of Ukraine and staged a war against the new Ukrainian state. In turn, the Central Powers (Germany, Hungary, Bulgaria and Turkey) recognised the UNR and signed a separate peace treaty in Brest in February 1918. Under the pretext of assisting the UNR against the Bolsheviks, the Germans entered Ukraine in April 1918 and triggered the fall of the *Rada* on 30 April 1918 (on the very day when the Constitution of the UNR was debated). Under German tutelage power was taken over by the conservative Hetmanate led by a descendant of a Cossack Hetman, General Pavlo Skoropadskyi, who was supported predominantly by Russified and Russian landowners. Having announced the creation of the 'Ukrainian State' (*Ukrainska Derzhava*), he assumed the role of the Hetman. However, following the defeat of Germany and Austro–Hungary and Skoropadskyi's decision to enter a federal treaty with (non-Bolshevik) Russia, the Hetmanate was overturned seven months later.

The UNR was restored when a new Ukrainian government, the Directory (*Dyrektoriat*), emerged in November 1918 led by, among others, social-democrats Volodymyr Vynnychenko and Symon Petliura. Soon Petliura assumed the role of Chief Otaman of the republican army in order to lead a military struggle on several fronts. However, mass support for the UNR and revolutionary vigour of the peasantry had evaporated by early 1919, and anarchy and chaos swept Ukraine, with the Bolsheviks, Whites, Denikin, anarchist Makchno and the Ukrainian troops moving across and fighting on its territory.[22]

In Western Ukraine, in November 1918, the collapse of Austro–Hungary prompted the creation of the Western Ukrainian People's Republic (ZUNR), under the leadership of Yevhen Petrushevych. The ZUNR immediately clashed with Poles who voiced competing claims to

Eastern Galicia, and the resulting war with Poland engulfed the larger part of the province. Apart from military actions against the ZUNR, the Polish army simultaneously fought the army of Petliura in Volynia. Thus, before the Directory's troops were expelled from Kyiv by the Bolsheviks in January 1919, Ukrainian forces consolidated to fight the common enemies. On 22 January 1919 unification of the UNR and the ZUNR was proclaimed in Kyiv in the 'Act of Unity' (*Akt Sobornosti*). The concept of *Sobornist'*, which until then referred to the ecclesiastical unity of the Orthodox Church, came to denote the unification of all historical Ukrainian territories into one state. The enlarged Ukrainian state was to be a quasi-federal as Galicia was to maintain its autonomy as a Western Ukrainian Oblast of the UNR (ZOUNR). Yet the scope of this autonomy remained undefined, as actual unification never took place, because of the military struggle on the one hand, and the profound ideological and cultural rift between the revolutionary Dnieper elites and more conservative, legally-minded and nationalist Galician leaders, on the other.[23]

The weakness of Ukrainian forces and their military defeats against the Bolsheviks prompted Petliura to enter an alliance with Poland at the cost of conceding Galicia. According to the Treaty of Warsaw in April 1920, the UNR renounced its authority over Eastern Galicia in favour of Poland in exchange for military help against the Bolsheviks, which by that time had instituted their government in Kharkiv.[24] The treaty was interpreted as treason by Western Ukrainians, who, in retaliation broke off their alliance with Petliura. The joint Ukrainian–Polish forces failed to win their war with Bolshevik Russia, and the Treaty of Riga of 1921 between Poland, Russia and the Soviet Ukraine confirmed the division of Ukraine along the lines defined in the Treaty of Warsaw, which conceded Eastern Galicia and Volynia to Poland.[25] The bitter disillusionment with the failure to secure independence over 1917–1921 steered some sections of the Ukrainian elites towards an indigenous strand of integral nationalism, the leading ideologist of which was Dmytro Dontsov.[26]

It is beyond the scope of this section to debate the causes of the ultimate failure of a state building project. In general, this failure has been attributed to a lack of social basis and incompleteness of the sociological nation;[27] a lack of experience, procrastination, indecisiveness and internal divisions amongst the revolutionary elites;[28] and the ideology of the elites, and neglect of institution building coupled with a lack of international support.[29] Yet the UNR, the existence of which was punctuated by the regime of Hetman Skoropadskyi in 1918, represented not only the first consolidated effort to organise a Ukrainian state in the modern era, but also a particular framing of statehood, which was nurtured by the conjunction of particular historical, political, socio-economic and cultural circumstances. In contrast to a centralised, autocratic tsarist regime, the UNR embodied aspirations to radical parliamentarism, decentralisation, and the pluralist conception of a political community. And the socio-economic plight of Ukrainian society shaped the socialist and social-democratic ideas on the state's role in the socio-economic transformation. However, the latter ideas were not shared by the Western Ukrainian elites, something that prevented the coming together of the elites from Galicia and Dnieper Ukraine to build a *Soborna Ukraina*. The conceptions of statehood, embracing an institutional framework, territorial model and notion of the political community, which were put forward in the period of 1917–1921, will be analysed in more detail below. It will be shown that even if any particular institutional design is difficult to pin down because of disruptions, the overarching principles guiding the Ukrainian leaders can be asserted with some clarity. The principles, however, did not find much support when the renewed state building project was embarked on in 1991.

THE UKRAINIAN STATE, 1917–1921

THE POLITICAL COMMUNITY

The UNR embodied a civic, pluralistic conception of nationhood with institutional provisions for minority representation. The *Tsentralna Rada* transformed itself from an organ of the Ukrainian national movement into an authoritative, territorial legislative body by including the local Russian, Jewish and Polish minority. In the 'Law on National Unions' of January 1918 national minorities were given the unique right to national-personal autonomy organised in the form of National Unions (*Natsionalni Soiuzy*), which could claim authority over and represent all members of the national minority, regardless of their place of residence in the UNR. The draft Constitution of the UNR, 'The Charter of State System, Rights and Freedoms of UNR' (which was never promulgated because of Skoropadskyi's coup in April 1918), proclaimed that 'sovereignty lay with the people of Ukraine, that is the body of citizens of the UNR' (art. 2) and the right of the ethnic groups inhabiting Ukraine 'to manage their cultural affairs within the state boundaries' (art. 6). National-personal autonomy was provided for the biggest groups (Russians, Poles and Jews) by direct norm in the Charter, whereas other minorities had to collect at least 10,000 signatures of the members of the minority in order to obtain that right.[30]

The Skoropadskyi government also adhered to the territorial conception of nationhood (although it seems that as Ukraine was envisaged as a monarchy, the concept of popular sovereignty did not apply), and the 'Law on Citizenship' of June 1918 automatically granted citizenship to all of those who lived in Ukraine at that time and would take an oath of loyalty to the Ukrainian state.[31] However, being more representative of the Russian and Russified Ukrainian gentry and tsarist *apparatchiks*, the Hetman did not continue the progressive policy of the *Tsentralna Rada* towards national minorities, and in July 1918, the institution of the personal-national autonomy was abolished. The brief 'Law on the Temporary Organisation of State Power of Ukraine' of April 1918 was silent on the rights of minorities and only declared that Orthodoxy was the state religion, while religious freedoms were to be guaranteed for other denominations (art. 10).

The *Dyrektoriat* returned to the tradition of the *Tsentralna Rada.* However, more ethnic undertones could be detected in the way the link between the state and the eponymous, Ukrainian majority was defined. The institution of national-personal autonomy was restored but only for the Jewish minority. Greater emphasis on the role and status of the titular majority was evident in the draft 'Basic Law of the UNR' prepared and debated in 1920 amongst the exiled members of the Ukrainian government. State territory was defined in accordance with the ethnographic principle: 'all territories, where the Ukrainian people constituted the majority' (art. 4) and Ukrainian was defined as the state language (art. 8). The trident was recognised as the state emblem, and blue and yellow defined as state colours (arts. 9 and 10), (these state symbols were then invoked by the national-democratic opposition on the eve of independence as the legitimate state symbols of Ukraine). Nevertheless, the *Dyrektoriat* did not essentially depart from a pluralist notion of nationhood. The ZUNR also advocated a civic conception and granted the national minorities the right to be represented in the legislature on the quota principle,[32] (although elections to parliament, the National Council, did not take place because of the war with Poland).

Overall, during the Ukrainian Revolution the political community in Ukraine was framed predominantly in inclusive, civic terms, which spawned a pluralistic model of statehood as minorities were granted cultural autonomy and political representation. This reflected the moderate democratic nationalism of the Ukrainian intellectuals, and the weakness of ethno-national awareness in Ukrainian society. The Ukrainian national movement developed in the shadow of the 'Great Russian' nation and tsarist autocracy, and at the beginning of the twentieth century, the strength of cultural and psychological bond between Ukrainians and Russians was reflected in the preoccupation with individual freedoms and equality, rather than the assertion of the position of the titular ethnic majority.

THE INSTITUTIONAL FRAMEWORK

Institutions at the Centre

Overall, the Ukrainian elites did not pay much attention to a rapid establishment of the institutional framework, with the notable exception of the ZUNR. According to Rudnytsky:

> The inadequate political and legal training of the *Rada*'s leaders was reflected in the drafting of Universals. These major state papers, which possessed the significance of fundamental laws, were wordy and overloaded with secondary matters, while the formulation of the salient points often lacked precision.[33]

Moreover, due to the profound political instability and military struggle, which by early 1919 engulfed the territory of Ukraine, the institutional arrangements changed with kaleidoscopic speed and diverged from the form of government envisaged by the constitutional acts. Therefore, institutional arrangements over 1917–1921 were essentially provisional, ill-defined, and were never properly tested in practice.

Even if the form of government was insufficiently elaborated, the parliamentary form of government was the unanimous choice of the UNR and ZUNR elites,[34] whereas Hetman Skoropadskyi opted for a monarchy. The Central Council, by transforming itself into the first legislature of the new state and appointing a coalitional government (*Heneralnyi Sekretariat*) (as was announced in the second Universal of July 1917), created a parliamentary system. In particular, amongst the Ukrainian elites, Mykhailo Hrushevskyi, who was elected the head of the *Tsentralna Rada,* was an ardent supporter of parliamentarism. According to the Fourth Universal of January 1918, the *Heneralnyi Sekretariat* was transformed into the Council of People's Ministers (Rada

Narodnykh Ministriv). The draft UNR constitution 'Charter of State System, Rights and Freedoms' of April 1918 proclaimed the principle of the separation of powers, (which was interpreted in a functional way), and envisaged a pure parliamentary form of government. Legislative power was to be vested in the directly elected National Assembly (*Vsenarodni Zbory*), which appointed the collective executive—the council of ministers and the general court (*Heneralyi Sud*), which was the highest judicial review body. There was neither prime minister nor head of state; these functions were combined with the headship of the National Assembly. However, at the meeting when the draft was debated Hrushevskyi was elected president of the UNR, even though this post was not envisaged by the Charter, something which indicates the largely improvised approach.

After the short-lived regime of Skoropadskyi, the UNR was reconstituted and became known as the Directory. In principle the parliamentary system was reinstated, yet in practice it did not function. The Congress of the Workers (*Trudovyi Congress*) acted as a parliament, which temporarily delegated all state powers to a narrow body—the *Dyrektoriat* led by Vynychenko and Petliura. The body soon came to be dominated by Petliura, who adopted the title of *Otaman*, and, in the face of military threats to Ukraine, assumed dictatorial powers. Also, the *Dyrektoriat* continued to exist beside the council of people's ministers and the powers of these two bodies overlapped. The draft Constitution, which was prepared in exile, defined the UNR as a 'sovereign and independent state with a democratic-republican, parliamentary system' (art. 1). Legislative power was to be vested in the State Council (*Derzhavna Rada*), whereas the executive was to consist of the head of state and the council of ministers (art. 106).

Finally, the ZUNR also adhered to a parliamentary form of government. The legislature, the National Council (*Natsionalna Rada*), appointed the government (*Derzhavnyi Sekretariat*), and the leader of Council acted as the head of state. However, in June 1919 as military pressures on the ZUNR mounted, the National Council granted its head, Yevhen Petrushevych, dictatorial powers.

In marked contrast, in 'Russian' Ukraine, in April 1918 Hetman Skoropadskyi broke with republican parliamentary traditions of the UNR by establishing a monarchy, thereby invoking the tradition of the powerful Cossack Hetman, exemplified by figures such as Khmelnytskyi and Doroshenko. However, the actual nature of the regime—whether constitutional or absolutist monarchy—was never clarified. In the initial 'Address to the Ukrainian People', apart from the Hetman, who appointed the cabinet of ministers, an assembly (*Seim*) was mentioned. Its composition, role and powers, however, were not defined. The brief 'Law on the Temporary Organisation of State Powers' of June 1918 vested all powers in the hands of the Hetman, who assumed the role of an absolutist monarch.

The Ukrainian revolutionary elites who embarked on the project of state building in 1917 had predominantly populist, socialist and sociodemocratic ideological roots. While the national movement was humanistic, libertarian and committed to democratic socialism, it lacked legalistic, constitutional awareness and rigour. Despite the progressive ideals, the insufficient constitutional know-how was exposed in imprecise and ill-thought institutional designs in the draft constitutions. Moreover, while parliamentarism was clearly the chosen form of government, the practice diverged from the constitutional proclamations, and Ukraine witnessed a succession of different provisional governments, which were a result of profound external vulnerability as well as splits within the elites themselves. Thus, in contrast to Western Ukraine, which had prolonged experience of parliamentarism since 1867, in 'Russian' Ukraine, parliamentarism was not consolidated and tested in practice.[35] As military struggles intensified, individuals were granted extraordinary powers. Therefore, the figure of a strong leader also featured in the precommunist Ukrainian political tradition. The Hetmanate of Pavlo Skoropadskyi even more forcefully exemplified this trait.

The Territory and Territorial–Administrative Model

In a similar vein, the spatial organisation of state power remained ill defined and open to conflicting interpretations, although overarching support for decentralisation, a revolutionary idea at the early twentieth century Europe, characterises the UNR. In the nineteenth century, within tsarist Russia, Ukraine was divided into nine *gubernias*. The latter served only as territorial–administrative units, and, prior to the revolution, 'Russian' Ukraine lacked tradition of territorial self-government. In contrast, Eastern Galicia and Bukovina in Austro–Hungary participated in parliamentary institutions and local Diets (whereas the Ukrainians in Transcarpathia were denied autonomy under Hungarian rule).

Nineteenth century political thinkers in Dnieper Ukraine saw the future of Ukraine in a federalised Russia, with extensive territorial self-government.[36] Drahomanov in the 'Free Union' (1884) outlined a federalist model for the Russian empire, which was to be divided into territorial units (*oblasts*) in accordance with their ethnic, economic and geographical profile. Ukraine was to be divided into Kyiv, Kharkiv and Odesa oblasts.[37] In a similar vein Hrushevskyi in the 'The Constitutional Question on the Ukrainian Issue in Russia' (1905) drafted plans for the division of Ukraine into 27 *zemli* (lands) and 3 autonomous cities (Kyiv, Odesa and Kharkiv). Yet, the long-standing federalist ideals were thrown into disarray in the course of 1917, because of the reluctance of the Russian elites to recognise the right of Ukraine to autonomy, let alone to federalise the remnants of the tsarist empire.

The Third Universal of July 1917 declared that the UNR would consist of the gubernias of Kyiv, Podila, Volynia, Chernihiv, Poltava, Kharkiv, Katerynoslav, Kherson, and Taurida (excluding Crimea). The future of other territories where the majority of population was Ukrainian was to be decided in a referendum. According to the draft Constitution of April 1918 'the Ukrainian People's Republic shall provide its lands (*zemli*), *volosti* [administrative division of Tsarist Russia] and communities (*hromady*) with the right to extensive self-government, abiding by the principle of decentralisation' (art. 5).[38] Therefore, self-government was to be institutionalised in a three-tier territorial division: *zemlia, volost'* and *hromada.*[39] But while the largest unit (*zemlia)* was to have a regional self-government, it was not explicitly defined as a federal component of the state.[40] The UNR, thus, was to be a decentralised and not federal state. The Act of Unification between the UNR and ZUNR of January 1919 envisaged that Galicia would become an autonomous part of the Ukrainian state, as the Western Oblast of the UNR (ZOUNR). However, the scope of spatial division of power and territorial autonomy were never clearly spelled out, as the Act of Unification between the UNR and ZUNR was effectively nullified by November 1919.[41]

Ultimately, the Ukrainian Revolution did not represent a culmination of the state-building process, but the first steps in that direction. At the time when the UNR was proclaimed, the elites in 'Russian' Ukraine were striving for (and would probably be satisfied with) territorial autonomy within Russia. They were animated by a vision of a just, social, democratic order and a Ukrainian state was instrumental in the creation of that order rather than a goal in itself. The pace of events forced the elites to 'think the unthinkable' and to opt for radical solution—independent statehood, which they neither contemplated, wished or prepared for, and which could not be sustained due to the prevailing internal and international context. While the UNR embodied progressive aspirations and scored some spectacular achievements, the Ukrainian Revolution witnessed a daring attempt to carve out some kind of Ukrainian state from the failing empires under profoundly adverse conditions. In Dnieper Ukraine the Ukrainian leaders aspired to create a parliamentary republic with a social-democratic profile, a decentralised territorial model and a civic notion of nationhood. Despite these progressive ideals, the elites' procrastination and military struggle prevented the institutional consolidation of the new state, as it came under attack from several directions.

Thus, the essentially improvised nature of the institutions diverged from the constitutional provisions and opened the way to conflicting interpretations.[42] Moreover, during the Revolution the pronounced differences in the political experiences, ideological outlook and chosen strategies of the leaders from Dnieper Ukraine and Galicia, became stumbling blocks on the path of unification of Ukraine. The UNR effectively functioned as a state for less than a year, and its leaders procrastinated on institution-building, which ultimately—at least to some degree—contributed to the UNR's demise. The institutional arrangements were provisional, and to a large degree remained in the form of declarations, never fully refined by being tested in practice.

THE UKRAINIAN SOVIET SOCIALIST REPUBLIC: 1919–1991

Despite the unmitigated failure to set up an independent state in 1917–1921, the endeavour advanced the cause of Ukrainian statehood; it compelled the Bolsheviks, who from 1919 onwards consolidated power in Ukraine, to recognise these aspirations. The strength of the centrifugal forces unleashed in the peripheries of the tsarist empire prompted the Bolsheviks to take on the federalist principle of Austro–Marxism; they first set up an 'alliance' and then a 'union of states', which in addition to Russia included national republics created of former borderlands of the Russian empire. In order to accommodate the fledging national sentiments of non-Russians in the new state, amongst others Ukrainians were granted their own ethno-territorial homeland—a Soviet Socialist Republic—as:

> [T]he embodiment of a compromise between Ukrainian nationalism and Russian centralism—of course not in the sense of a formal, negotiated agreement but rather of a *de facto* balancing of antagonistic social forces, neither of which was strong enough to assert itself completely.[43]

After two unsuccessful attempts to gain control over Ukraine in 1918 and 1919, the third Soviet Ukrainian government was established in December 1919. The 1919 constitution passed by the Soviet Ukrainian government in Kharkiv guaranteed the sovereignty of Soviet Ukraine and the right to conduct an independent foreign policy. Although the 1920 Treaty between Soviet Ukraine and RSFSR established an economic and military union, and Ukraine surrendered some commissariats to RSFSR, it was still defined as a sovereign and independent republic with rights to maintain direct diplomatic relations with other states. On the basis of the 1919 constitution, the Ukrainian SSR acted as a constitutive member of the Soviet Union in December 1922, when the treaty was signed by the representatives of the Russian, Belarussian, Transcaucasian and Ukrainian Soviet Socialist Republics, as a result of which the Union of Soviet Socialist Republics came into being.

Alongside many ethnic groups in the borderland of the tsarist empire, Ukrainians were endowed with all the nominal trappings of statehood but denied sovereignty. The subsequent republican constitutions of 1926, 1937 and 1978 defined Ukraine as a 'sovereign republic', while the constitutions of the USSR declared that 'every union republic shall retain the free right to secession from the USSR' (article 13 of the 1936 constitution and article 72 of the 1977 constitution of the USSR). The republic was equipped with a complete set of legal and administrative institutions. Moreover, perpetuating the façade of independence, together with Belarus, Ukraine was also granted membership of the United Nations in 1945.

Like all other republics, Ukrainian sovereignty was a constitutional figure of speech. The new constitutions of the UkrSSR of 1926, 1937 and 1978 were duly adopted after the passage of the Constitutions of the USSR (in 1924, 1936 and 1977),[44] and all the constitutional texts were drafted under the instructions from the centre. Moscow provided all Soviet republics with an almost identical template of administrative, economic and cultural institutions, such as ministries, academy of sciences, writers' unions, etc. The republican sovereignty was circumvented by removing decision-making powers from the republican institutions and vesting them with the Communist Party of Ukraine, which constituted an integral part of the Communist Party of the Soviet Union in accordance with the principle of democratic centralism. But quite apart from the omnipotent role of the Communist Party, the constitutional provisions explicitly asserted the supremacy of the Union centre over the republics. Republican institutions, including the Supreme Council, were subordinated to All-Union institutions, which had authority to override the decisions of the republican institutions. The 1936 and 1977 constitutions of the USSR included a provision that 'in the event of divergence between the laws of the union republics and a law of the Union, the Union law prevails' (arts. 20 and 74, respectively), while the 1978 constitution of the UkrSSR asserted that 'the economy of UkrSSR forms an integral part of one economic system, which encompasses all aspects of social production, distribution and exchange on the territory of the USSR' (art.16). The constitutional subordination of Soviet Ukraine to the Union, and the monopolisation of decision-making process in the Party rendered Ukrainian sovereignty a constitutional fiction.

Because of the largely nominal character of the constitutions of the Ukrainian Soviet Socialist Republic, Sliusarenko and Tomenko, the editors of the post-Soviet compilation of Ukrainian constitutional acts, concluded:

> All four constitutions of the Soviet Ukraine were political documents and were drafted in the ideological departments of the Central Committee of the CPSU. Taking this into account, as well as Ukraine's status of quasi-state these [Soviet] constitutional acts can be included in the category of the fundamental laws of the state only with great caution.[45]

Nevertheless, even if the Ukrainian SSR can be defined as a pseudo-state at best, it shaped the identity of independent Ukraine in institutional, territorial and national terms. While the Ukrainian Revolution lasted effectively for 4 years, Soviet rule in Ukraine spanned seven decades and left an enduring imprint on society and its political structures. Therefore, the socio-economic development and cultural change which took place in Soviet Ukraine will be outlined in the next chapter in order to help explain for the dynamics of Ukraine' passage to independence and the subsequent path of state building. The remaining part of this chapter will examine the legacy of Soviet rule in Ukraine in terms of the institutional model, the concept of political community, and territorial changes insofar as they became a baseline against which the new Ukrainian state was defined.

THE INSTITUTIONAL FRAMEWORK: THE SYSTEM OF SOVIETS

An analysis of the institutional structure of a Soviet republic tends to be preceded by the qualification that it reveals rather little about the nature of the political regime as the written constitution differed radically from the 'political constitution', which actually conferred power in the CPU. Yet, the demise of the Party on the eve of the breakup of the Soviet Union turned the soviets into an institutional fulcrum of the Soviet republics. Thus, the essential features of the institutional structures, with which Ukraine entered independence, will be outlined below.

The nominal institutional structure of the Soviet republic consisted of 'a single system of organs of state power' which is a hierarchy of layers of government—the soviets of people's deputies (*rady narodnykh deputativ*). The system had humble origins according to Hamper and Thompson: 'in their mode of origins, in short, the soviets, by ordinary Western standards, were simply overgrown, though exceptionally militant, city-wide strike committees momentarily thrown up by the Russian workers in the unruly days of 1905'.[46] In the wake of the October Revolution, membership of the original soviets was broadened to include not only workers, but also soldiers and peasants, and institutionalised into a system of soviets. This way the conditions for involvement of the ordinary citizen in the running of the state were created (Lenin's oft-quoted remark was that 'under socialism the housewife will learn to run the state'). The councils provided an institutional locus for mass participation in politics, they consisted of 'people from various walks of life', who were not occupationally specialised or differentiated from the masses. In practice, the composition of the soviets was engineered to mirror societal structure. Deputies were released from their workplace to participate in the sessions of the soviets, which operated on a part-time basis. The soviets embodied the totality of state power. The Soviet approach deliberately discarded the separation of powers and 'checks and balances', as smokescreens behind which the bourgeoisie exercised unfettered power in Western countries.[47]

In the Soviet Union, the 'separation of powers' was replaced by the principle of the 'unity of power': the soviets combined not only executive and legislative powers at the republican level, but also state power and self-government at the local and territorial level (which was based on the so-called state theory of self-government). The Supreme Soviet, which was the peak of the hierarchy of Soviets, was the highest state body in the republic with exclusive legislative powers and the prerogative to decide on any matter within the republican jurisdiction. All other state organs were in theory under the control of and accountable to the Supreme Council. The council of ministers was the 'highest executive and administrative body of state powers' and 'responsible and accountable' to the Supreme Council (art. 115 of the 1978 constitution of the UkrSSR). However, in practice this supreme position was not backed by any constitutional sanctions as no effective means of control were

Table 2.1. A Comparison of the System of Soviets and Western Parliamentarism

	The System of Soviets	*'Western Parliamentarism'*
Ideological Underpinnings	the principle of 'unity of power': the Soviets embodied state power in its totality and combined legislative, executive and judicial powers, although specialised bodies were delegated the task of the execution of those powers	the principles of 'limited government', the (functional) 'separation of powers' and 'checks and balances' and distinction between central state authorities and self-government at sub-state level
Functions of Parliament	combined legislative, executive and judicial functions	mainly law making and overseeing of the executive branch
Sphere of Competencies and Powers of Parliaments	could take over or delegate any prerogative (apart from the legislative function)	defined by the constitution
Separation of Personnel	a mandate of deputy can be combined with a mandate in another council or state apparatus	as a rule, a parliamentary mandate cannot be combined with a civil service post or position in local self-governing bodies (although it happens, for example, in France and Italy)
Type of Representative	part-time deputies released from their workplace to attend infrequent sessions of the Supreme Council	predominantly professional politicians
Role of Internal Bodies of Legislature	pivotal as they took over specialised functions (in particular the Presidium, with its extensive prerogatives, substituted for the Supreme Council between the sessions of the Council)	facilitating role
Type of Link between the Electorate and Their Representative	imperative mandate (the legal obligation of the deputy to carry out his/her electoral mandate in accordance with the wishes of the electorate,	free mandate (member of parliament is not bound by the wishes of the electorate after the elections)

which has the right of recall at any time)[1]

[1] The institution originated in the Paris commune. However, as it was not conducive to the development of representative democracy and party system, it did not take root in Western Europe. The Soviet Union revived the institution in order to emphasise the people's rule and the supremacy of the will of 'the people' over that of elected representatives. For the discussion on the imperative mandate see Petro Martynenko, 'Parliamentarism: the World Practice and Ukraine's Searches', *The Ukrainian Quarterly,* Vol. LII, No. 4 (Winter 1996), p. 318.

placed at the Supreme Council's disposal. Although the Supreme Council had the exclusive right of law making, the hierarchy of the normative acts of the state lacked clarity and transparency. The council of ministers issued 'resolutions and dispositions' (art. 120), while the Presidium of the Supreme Council had the vaguely defined right to issue decrees (art. 110). Remaining under the close tutelage of the CPU, the Presidium was delegated specialised functions and, as a result, assumed the key powers of the Supreme Council (and the Council tended to confirm the Presidium decisions in its brief sessions). Indeed, Soviet parliamentarism—based on the omnipotence of the popularly elected assembly, free from any checks and balances—lent itself perfectly to rule by a single party.[48]

However, once the CPU lost its hegemonic powers in 1991, the Supreme Council could assume its constitutional powers. The supreme role of the assembly led some to refer to the soviet system as 'Soviet parliamentarism', which implied that it was a variation of Western parliamentarism. However, despite the appearance of parliamentarism, the structure, functions and theoretical underpinnings of the system of soviets differed diametrically from those that characterised Western parliamentary systems. These differences are spelled out in Table 2.1 (although gross generalisations were necessary to construe an 'ideal type' of Western parliamentarism), and they will be referred to in the following chapters.[49]

THE TERRITORIAL CHANGES AND ADMINISTRATIVE DIVISION

The Soviet Union created a highly centralised model of statehood. Under Soviet rule, the bulk of ethnographic Ukrainian territories were unified for the first time within the boundaries of the Ukrainian SSR. The republic was initially made up of nine *gubernias* of the Russian empire: Kyiv, Podila, Volynia, Chernihiv, Poltava, Kharkiv, Katerynoslav,

Kherson, Taurida, but without Crimea (that is the territory claimed by the UNR in the Third Universal of July 1917), and it also included some western districts of the Don Army province. In 1924 the Autonomous Socialist Republic of Moldova was created of several *raions* adjacent to the border with Romania, while some territorial adjustment in favour of the Russian SFSR were made in 1925.[50] In September 1939 Western Ukraine was annexed by the USSR, as a consequence of the Ribbentrop–Molotov pact, and on 1 November it was officially incorporated into the Ukrainian SSR.[51] In 1940 Northern Bukovina and Southern Bessarabia became part of the UkrSSR, while the rest of Bessarabia formed the Moldovan SSR. In 1945 Transcarpathia (also known as Subcarpathia or the Carpathian Rus') was conceded to Ukraine in a treaty with Czechoslovakia. As result of the 1939–1945 border changes the following oblasts were created: Lvivska, Volynska, Rivenska, Ivano-Frankivska, Chernivetska, Ternopilska, Akermanska (Izmail), and Zakarpatska.[52] The formation of present day Ukraine was completed with the transfer of the Crimean Oblast (which until 1945 was the Crimean Autonomous Socialist Republic) in 1954.

After 1954, the Ukrainian SSR consisted of 25 oblasts and 2 cities of republican subordination—Kyiv and Sevastopol. Oblasts were purely territorial–administrative units and did not correspond to historical regions. Oblasts were further divided into districts (*raion*), cities (which were further divided into *raiony*), and rural settlements.[53] Each of those territorial units was represented in a soviet (*rada*). As pointed above, there was no conceptual distinction between local, territorial and central government as the Soviet Union adhered to the so-called state theory of self-government, and the local and territorial governing bodies formed an integrated part of the state apparatus. In contrast to the Western state tradition of self-government, the councils combined the functions of self-government with state powers, something that effectively denied their autonomy from the central authorities.

THE POLITICAL COMMUNITY

The Soviet regime in Ukraine constructed a complex, but essentially contradictory notion of the political community in attempt to reconcile class, ethnicity and territory as the markers of the political community in each republic. The four constitutions of the Soviet Ukraine (1919, 1926, 1937 and 1978) adhered to territory and class rather than ethnicity as the main criteria: 'Ukraine (was) a state of all people, expressing the will and interests of the workers, peasants and intelligentsia: the working people of all nationalities of the Republic' (1978 Constitution of the UkrSSR). At the same time, ethnicity was recognised as an important social category by the very formation of the UkrSSR, as Ukrainians were a titular nationality of a national–territorial administrative unit, after which that unit was named, and enjoyed some privileges conferred by the centre on titular majorities in the Soviet republics. Nationality was also institutionalised at a personal level as an ascriptive, legal category. It was fixed regardless of the place of residence, and, as such, acquired an extra-territorial, ethno-cultural dimension. Thus, as Brubaker argues the Soviet Union institutionalised two distinct models of nationhood: territorial/political and personal/ethnic.[54] While these categories were overlapping, they were never made fully congruent, as representatives of one nationality did not reside only in their 'titular' republics. The UkrSSR was not inhabited exclusively by Ukrainians, and Ukrainians lived in other Soviet republics. Yet the lack of congruence between the ethno-cultural and territorial models did not matter because of the largely symbolic nature of the republican, territorial boundaries. The constitutional fiction of sovereignty made Ukraine's political community only nominally 'national' and fully submerged in the wider community of the Soviet People (*Sovietskyi narod*). However, once the republican boundaries acquired political significance, this dual conception of a political community could not be sustained and a choice had to be made. The question of what united and turned citizens of independent Ukraine into 'the people', and the related questions of attributes of the state, such as state language, symbols, minority rights, proved to be highly sensitive and contentious.

CONCLUSION

When new states emerge, their apparent newness tends to be underplayed by stressing the historical roots of a new polity; any preceding tradition of statehood, however short and circumstantial, is flagged up in order to boost the historical legitimacy of a new polity and dissipate an image of an artificial construct. Thus, the national past becomes a cognitive point of reference in the renewed process of state building and is often explicitly evoked (most tangibly in the Preamble of constitutions). The predicament of Ukraine was that its different parts had different pasts. As it was variously ruled by other states, such as the Polish–Lithuanian Commonwealth, the tsarist Russia, the Habsburg empire, inter-war Poland, Hungary, and Czechoslovakia, prior to 1954 Ukraine did not exist as a state within its current borders under a uniform set of institutions. Moreover, the indigenous tradition of Ukrainian statehood in the pre-communist period was multivocal as was seen by the Ukrainian People's Republic, Skoropadskyi's Hetmanate, and the Western Ukrainian People's Republic. Their existence was cut short by the formation of the Ukrainian Soviet Socialist Republic. The UkrSSR was nominally conceived as a sovereign state, with a fully blown institutional edifice, yet it was a skeleton state with no life of its own and was animated by Moscow. And despite their temporal succession, the UkrSSR was cut off from the traditions of the UNR. Any historical continuity was denied and throughout Soviet rule, the UNR was depicted as a creation of the 'Ukrainian bourgeois nationalists', in spite of the socialist and social-democratic orientation of its leaders. Also, in terms of institutional design and Marxist–Leninist ideology, Soviet rule spelled a marked departure from the parliamentary, decentralised, and pluralistic traditions of the UNR. Thus, the twentieth century developments were marred by the kind of discontinuity, which characterised Ukraine's earlier history. With its multiple and disjointed pasts, there were multiple sources of cognitive reference for constitution-makers in post-Soviet Ukraine. The demise of the USSR posed the question of the historical pedigree of the new state, and made any kind of restoration of pre-communist models in post-Soviet Ukraine onerous. Thus, Ukrainian state building, as reflected in the constitution making which started on the eve of independence, entailed the contest and reconciliation of alternative visions of an idealised political order, which were inspired by different interpretations of the Ukrainian pre-communist and communist past.

NOTES

1 The most comprehensive treatment of Ukraine's history in English can be found in Orest Subtelny, *Ukraine. A History* (Toronto: University of Toronto Press, 1988) and Paul Robert Magocsi, *A History of Ukraine* (Toronto–Buffalo–London: University of Toronto Press, 1996). A short overview is provided in Roman Szporluk, *Ukraine. A Brief History* (Detroit MI: Ukraine Festival Committee, 1979), while selected themes are treated in Ivan L. Rudnytsky, *Essays in Modern Ukrainian History* (Alberta: Canadian Institute of Ukrainian Studies, 1987). For a compound survey of

some writings on Ukraine see David Saunders, 'Modern Ukrainian History', *European History Quarterly*, Vol. 21, No. 2 (1991), pp. 81–95.

2 Mark von Hagen, 'Does Ukraine Have a History?', *Slavic Review*, Vol. 54, No. 3 (Fall 1995), p. 667.

3 Subtelny, *Ukraine. A History*, p. 123.

4 Zenon E. Kohut, 'The Development of a Little Russian Identity and Ukrainian Nation Building', *Harvard Ukrainian Studies*, Vol. 10 (1986), pp. 559–76.

5 Zenon E. Kohut, *Russian Centralism and Ukrainian Autonomy: Imperial Absorption of the Hetmanate 1760s–1830s* (Cambridge MA: Harvard Ukrainian Research Institute, 1988).

6 See, for example, Frank E. Sysyn, 'The Khmelnytsky Uprising and Ukrainian Nation-Building', *Journal of Ukrainian Studies*, Vol. 17, No. 1–2 (Summer–Winter 1992) and 'The Reemergence of the Ukrainian Nation and Cossack Mythology', *Social Research*, Vol. 58, No. 4 (Winter 1991), pp. 845–64. pp. 141–70. See also, Andrew Wilson, 'Myths of National History in Belarus and Ukraine', in Geoffrey A. Hosking and George Schopflin (eds.), *Myths and Nationhood* (London: Hurst and Co, 1997), pp. 182–97 and Igor Torbakov, 'Historiography and Modern Nation-Building', *Transition* (6 September 1996). For an example of a study stressing the significance of the Cossack period in the process of Ukrainian state building in post-Soviet Ukraine see Valerii Shevchuk, *Kozats'ka derzhava: etiudy do istorii ukrainskoho derzhavotvorenia (The Cossack state: essays on the history of Ukrainian state building)* (Kyiv: Abrys, 1995). On the Ukrainian historiography see Stephen Velychenko, *National History as Cultural Process* (University of Alberta: Canadian Institute of Ukrainian Studies, 1992).

7 Rudolf Mark, 'Social Questions and National Revolution: The Ukrainian National Republic in 1919–1920', *Harvard Ukrainian Studies*, Vol. XIV, No. 1/2 (June 1990), p. 116.

8 See Ralph Lindheim and George S. N. Luckyi (eds.), *Towards an Intellectual History of Ukraine: An Anthology of Ukrainian Thought from 1710 to 1995* (Toronto–Buffalo–London: University of Toronto Press, 1996) and David McDonald, 'Nationhood and its Discontents: Ukrainian Intellectual History at Empire's End. A Review Article', *Journal of Ukrainian Studies,* Vol. 23, No. 2 (Winter 1998), pp. 105–16.

9 Miroslav Hroch, *Social Preconditions of a National Revival in Europe* (Cambridge: Cambridge University Press, 1985). For a succinct typology of nationalist movements see Miroslav Hroch, 'From National Movement to the Fully-formed Nation: The Nation Building Process in Europe', in Gopal Balakrishnan (ed.), *Mapping the Nation* (London, New York: Verso, 1996), pp. 145–74 and for a comparative table of the developments in national movements see Miroslav Hroch, 'Nation Self-determination from a Historical Perspective', *Canadian Slavonic Papers*, Vol. XXXVII, Nos. 3–4 (Sept 1995), pp. 283–98.

10 See the book review by Roman Szporluk in *The Annals of the Ukrainian Academy of Arts and Sciences in the United States*, Vol. 14, (1978–1980), p. 270.

11 The impact of the 'Little Russian' identity on the formation of modern Ukrainian identity is ambiguous. Kohut argues for a dialectical approach: when the Little Russian identity—defined in political terms—disappeared, the newly formed intelligentsia turned to the masses and focused on cultural activities, a synthesis of political and cultural strands took place. This laid the foundation for a modern Ukrainian nation building. This synthesis was exemplified, according to Kohut, by the writings of

such thinkers as Kostomarov, Maksymovych and Kulish. See Kohut, *Russian Centralism and Ukrainian Autonomy*. For developments in nineteenth century Ukraine in the context of European history see Omeljan Pritsak, 'Prolegomena to the National Awakening of the Ukrainians during the Nineteenth Century', in Roland Sussex and J. C. Eade (eds.), *Culture and Nationalism in Nineteenth Century* (Columbus, Ohio: Slavic Publishers, Inc., 1983), pp. 96–110.

12 Krawchenko, 'The Social Structure', pp. 97–112.

13 On the process of language development in Ukraine see George Shevelov, 'The Language Question in the Ukraine in the Twentieth Century (1900–1941)', *Harvard Ukrainian Studies*, Vol. X, No. 1/2 (June 1986), pp. 71–170.

14 'Western Ukraine' can be understood as 'Eastern Galicia' under Austro–Hungary, or more broadly including also Bukovina and Transcarpathia. The second meaning is usually used when denoting parts of Ukraine excluded from the Russian state in the nineteenth and the first half of the twentieth century. John-Paul Himka, 'Western Ukraine between the Wars', *Canadian Slavonic Papers*, Vol. 34 (December 1992), pp. 391–412.

15 On the formative influences of Poland (and Russia) on the formation of the modern Ukrainian nation and state see Roman Szporluk, 'Ukraine: From an Imperial Periphery to a Sovereign State', *Daedalus*, Vol. 126, No. 3 (1997), pp. 85–119.

16 On developments in Galicia in the nineteenth century see, for example, Andrei Markovits and Frank Sysyn (eds.), *Nationbuilding and the Politics of Nationalism: Essays on Austrian Galicia* (Cambridge, Massachusetts: Harvard University Press, 1982); Paul Robert Magocsi, 'A Subordinate or Submerged People: The Ukrainians of Galicia under Habsburg Empire', in Richard L. Rudolph and David F. Good (eds.), *Nationalism and Empire: The Habsburg Empire and the Soviet Union* (New York: St Martin's Press, 1992), pp. 95–108; Theodore Bohdan Ciuciura, 'Galicia and Bukovina as Austrian Crown Provinces: Ukrainian Experience in Representative Institutions, 1861–1918', *Studia Ucrainica*, Vol. 5 (1984), pp. 175–95; John-Paul Himka, 'The Greek Catholic Church and Nation Building in Galicia, 1772–1918', *Harvard Ukrainian Studies*, Vol. 8, No. 3/4 (December 1984), pp. 426–52; and John-Paul Himka, *Galician Villagers and the Ukrainian National Movement in the Nineteenth Century* (Alberta: Canadian Institute of Ukrainian Studies, 1988).

17 The *Rada* represented Ukrainian parties, the most important of which were the peasant-oriented Ukrainian Party of Social-Revolutionaries, the Marxist Ukrainian Party of Social Democrats, and the Ukrainian Party of Socialist-Federalists, which grouped liberal intelligentsia.

18 In the Declaration of July 1917, the Provisional Government recognised Ukrainian autonomy, although its August 'Instruction' limited the autonomous territory of Ukraine to five provinces and circumvented the powers of the *Rada's* executive body *Generalnyi Sekretariat*.

19 Ivan L. Rudnytsky, 'The Fourth Universal and Its Ideological Antecedents', in Taras Hunchak (ed.), *The Ukraine, 1917–1921: A Study in Revolution* (Cambridge, Mass.: Harvard University Press, 1977), p. 201.

20 On the strength of the Bolshevik forces in Kyiv during the revolution see, for example, Leszek Podhorodecki, *Dzieje Kijowa (A history of Kyiv)* (Warsaw, 1982), pp. 209–235.

21 For an account of the revolution in Ukraine see John Resheter, *The Ukrainian Revolution, 1917–1920* (Princeton: Princeton University Press, 1952); Taras Hunchak (ed.), *The Ukraine: 1917–1921: A Study in Revolution* (Cambridge, Mass.: Harvard Ukrainian Research Institute, 1977).; Richard Pipes, *The Formation of the Soviet Union: Communism and Nationalism, 1917–1923* (Cambridge, Mass.: Harvard University Press, 1957).

22 Rudolf Mark, 'Social Questions and National Revolution: The Ukrainian National Republic in 1919–1920', *Harvard Ukrainian Studies*, Vol. XIV, No. 1/2 (June 1990), pp. 114–31. S. Guthier, 'The Popular Basis of Ukrainian Nationalism in 1917', *Slavic Review*, Vol. 38, No. 1 (March 1979), pp. 30–47; and Krawchenko, 'The Social Structure', pp. 97–112.

23 On the fate of the unified Ukrainian state see Jan Jacek Bruski, 'Miedzy sobornoscia a separatyzmem. Funkcjonowanie i rozpad Ukrainiskiej Federacji Galicyjsko-Naddnieprzanskiej, 1918–1919 (Between sobornist' and separatism: the functioning and fall of the Galician-Dnieper Federation, 1918–1919)', in Irena Stawowy-Kawka and Wojciech Rajka (eds.), *Ku zjednoczonej Europie* (in Polish) (Krakow: Wydawnictwo Uniwersytetu Jagiellonskiego, 1997), pp. 37–52. On the ideological differences between the leaders of the UNR and ZUNR see Alexander J. Motyl, *The Turn to the Right: The Ideological Origins and Development of Ukrainian Nationalism, 1919–1929* (Boulder: East European Monographs, 1980).

24 The Ukrainian Soviet Socialist Republic was proclaimed in January 1919 in Kharkiv on the basis of the short-lived Kryvyi-Rih–Donbas Soviet republic.

25 The Council of Foreign Ministers of the Allies sanctioned the temporary right of Poland to Eastern Galicia (up to the river Zbruch) under the condition that Poland would grant territorial autonomy to Galicia, protect religious and political freedom and that the final decision will be taken on the basis of a plebiscite. In November 1919, Poland was granted the right to Galicia for 25 years and the newly formed League of Nations was to decide about the future of Galicia. Soon however, this decision was changed and status of Galicia was finally decided only in March 1923, when the sovereignty of Poland was confirmed. On the inter-war period see John-Paul Himka, 'Western Ukraine between the Wars', *Canadian Slavonic Papers,* Vol. 34 (December 1992), pp. 391–412 and Volodymyr Kubijovych, *Western Ukraine within Poland, 1920–1939* (Chicago: Ukrainian Research and Information Institute, 1963).

26 Motyl, *The Turn to the Right* and John A. Amstrong, *Ukrainian Nationalism*, 2nd ed. (Engelwood, Colo: Ukrainian Academic Press, 1990).

27 This view was most fully elaborated in a collection of essays, Hunchak, *The Ukraine: 1917–1921* and Guthier, 'The Popular Basis of Ukrainian Nationalism in 1917'.

28 For works stressing this factor see the essay on Vynnychenko in Rudnytsky, *Essays in Modern Ukrainian History*. On the divisions amongst the Ukrainian parties see also Motyl, *The Turn to the Right*. While a plethora of parties, movements and groupings emerged in revolutionary Ukraine, the Ukrainian elites were divided themselves on the question of the priority of the national *vis-à-vis* the social cause. Giving priority to social revolution, the left-wing of the social-democrats was willing to side with the Bolsheviks, whereas the right-wing refused to sacrifice the national liberation.

29 Alexander J. Motyl, *Sovietology, Rationality, Nationality: Coming to Grips with Nationalism in the USSR* (New York: Columbia University Press, 1990), chapter 7. On the general discussion of the causes see also Yaroslav Hrytsak, *Narys istorii Ukrainy: formuvania modernoi ukrains'koi natsii XIX–XX stolittia (A brief history of Ukraine: the formation of a modern Ukrainian nation)* (Kyiv, 1996), pp. 159–165.

30 The texts of the constitutional documents for the period 1917–1920 were published in *Konstytutsiini akty Ukrainy, 1917–1920 (The constitutional acts of Ukraine)* (Kyiv, 1992) and A. Sliusarenko and M. Tomenko (eds.), *Istoria ukrains'koi konstytutsii (A history of Ukrainian constitutions)* (Kyiv, 1997).

31 Hrytsak, *Narys istorii Ukrainy*, p. 129.

32 Seats in the parliament would be allocated in the following way: Ukrainians 70 percent, Poles 14.6 percent, Jews 11.9 percent, and Germans 2.7 percent.

33 Rudnytsky, 'The Fourth Universal', p. 208.

34 A parliamentary republic was advocated by all left-wing and centrist parties, including the Ukrainian Party of Social-Revolutionaries and the Ukrainian Social-Democratic Party which were the main parties of the *Tsentralna Rada*, while the latter dominated the *Dyrektoriat.*

35 'Being tested' is the criterion which for Sokolewicz determines the (in)desirability of restoring pre-communist models. See Wojciech Sokolewicz, 'The Relevance of Western Models for Constitution Building in Poland', in Joachim Jens Hesse and Nevil Johnson (eds.), *Constitutional Policy and Change in Europe* (Oxford: Oxford University Press, 1995), p. 251.

36 On the ideas of Mykhailo Drahomanov see 'Drahomanov as a Political Theorist' in Rudnytsky, *Essays in Modern Ukrainian History*, pp. 203–254.

37 An English language translation of the 'Free Union' was published in Ivan L. Rudnytsky (ed.), *Mykhaylo Drahomanov. A Symposium and Selected Writings* (The Annals of the Ukrainian Academy, New York, 1952), pp. 193–205.

38 Sliusarenko and Tomenko, *Istoria ukrainskoi konstytutsii,* p. 105.

39 The *Tsentralna Rada* essentially retained the tsarist territorial division, although gubernias were renamed *zemli.* Skoropadskyi reverted to the gubernias, the *Dyrektoriat* reinstated the *zemli.*

40 However, the territorial model envisaged in the draft Constitution of 1918 was interpreted also as federal. See for example, Oleksandr Kopylenko, De shukaty koreni? (Where to find the roots?), *Uriadovyi Kurier,* 30 April 1996, p. 6.

41 Bruski, 'Miedzy sobornoscia a separatyzmem', p. 51.

42 Mykola Tomenko, *Ukrainska perspektyva: istoryko-politolohichni pidstavy suchasnoi derzhavnoi stratehii (A Ukrainian perspective: the historical-political foundation of contemporary state strategy)* (Kyiv, 1995), p. 47.

43 Rudnytsky, *Essays in Modern Ukrainian History*, p. 464.

44 L. Aryeh Unger, *Constitutional Developments in the USSR: a Guide to the Soviet Constitutions* (London: Methuen, 1981).

45 Sliusarenko and Tomenko, *Istoria ukrains'koi konstytutsii*, p. 174.

46 Samuel N. Harper and Ronald Thompson, *The Government of the Soviet Union*, 2nd ed. (Toronto: D.Van Nostrand Company, 1952), p. 101.

47 Archie Brown (ed.), *New Thinking in Soviet Politics* (Houndmills and London: Macmillan, 1992), p. 20.

48 Loewenstein, 'Reflections on the Value of Constitutions in Our Revolutionary Age', p. 153.

49 Western parliamentarism is an ideal type system, as it takes different forms, as for example, the one based on proportional representation and the Westminster model. Thus, only the most general characteristics, which are intrinsic to parliamentarism in general, will be concentrated on.

50 In 1925 Southern Kursk and Voronezh, as well as Taganrog and Shaklty regions were transferred to Russia. Roman Laba, 'The Russian–Ukrainian Conflict: State, Nation and Identity', *European Security*, Vol. 4, No. 3 (Autumn 1995), pp. 457–87.

51 Yaroslav Bilinsky, 'The Incorporation of Western Ukraine and Its Impact on Politics and Society in Soviet Ukraine', in Roman Szporluk (ed.), *The Influence of East Europe and the Soviet West on the USSR* (New York: Praeger, 1976).

52 Before its annexation in 1939 Eastern Galicia's territorial division was inherited from the Habsburg empire, in Volynia the territorial units originated in the 1864 territorial reform in Tsarist Russia, while Bukovina became part of the Romanian territorial system.

53 The administrative structure of the Ukrainian SSR was defined in 'The Act on the Order of Resolving Issues of Administrative–Territorial Structure of the Ukrainian Soviet Socialist Republic' adopted by the Presidium of the Supreme Council of the Ukrainian Soviet Socialist Republic on March, 12, 1981.

54 Rogers Brubaker, *Nationalism Reframed* (Cambridge: Cambridge University Press, 1996), chapter 2.

CHAPTER THREE

INDEPENDENCE WITHOUT A VISION: CONSTITUTION MAKING IN 1990–1991

During the Ukrainian Revolution, the leaders of the Ukrainian People's Republic (UNR) were animated by the vision of a new, just, democratic political order. Their vision did not, at least initially, entail the creation of a sovereign state. The independence of Ukraine became instrumental in its realisation only once, in late 1917, it became clear that with the Bolsheviks at Russia's helm it was impossible to implement the vision in a centralised Russian state. In 1991, in contrast, the situation could be described as 'independence without a vision'. Ukraine was being propelled into independence by the cumulative effect of the disintegration of the centre and actions of the indigenous communist elites. Yet there was a dearth of positive inspiration behind the drive for independence. Constitution making reflected a lack of an overarching vision of a different political, socio-economic order and an enduring commitment to the 'old', Soviet ideology (even if only nominally) and institutions. This lack of reformist zeal found its reflection in the essentially conservative outlook of the communist elites, who 'appropriated' the Soviet political model as 'indigenous', while the democratic opposition lacked the strength to impose its ideas. Therefore, the attainment of statehood took place in 1991 before essential thinking was done about what kind of state Ukraine should become. This mode of the passage to independence—reality without vision—determined the idiosyncrasies of state building in Ukraine as was reflected in the protracted trajectory of constitutional reform.

In response to the loosening control of the centre over the periphery in the late 1980s, two distinct types of dynamic can be distinguished amongst the Soviet republics: 'bottom-up' and 'top-down' modes of mobilisation. In bottom-up cases, such as the Baltic republics, Georgia, Armenia, the popular pressure on the indigenous elites through mass demonstration and/or ballot box made them swiftly embrace the idea of independence. In top-down cases, most notably, in Central Asia, because of the weakness or absence of pro-independence mass attitudes, the elites did not face the same degree of pressure and took the route of bargaining with Moscow for greater economic sovereignty, and only gradually (and in some cases reluctantly) accepted the imperative of independence once the Soviet centre imploded.

Ukraine was a mixed case. The republic witnessed the late onset of perestroika, and despite some manifestations of popular mobilisation, by 1989, the fate of Ukraine (and the Soviet Union) was far from sealed. Yet, in the course of less than two years, 1990–1991, Ukraine transformed itself from a backwater of the reform-ridden Soviet Union to a reluctant participant and subsequently a staunch opponent of the renewal of the Soviet Union. In the context of the relative weakness of the mass nationalist awakening and limited bottom-up pressure, pro-independence sentiments spread from the opposition to the ruling communist elites (although mass politics affected the elites' strategic choices at turning points). Once the communist elite found itself empowered to re-negotiate the Union Treaty, which was to re-establish the Soviet Union as a voluntary federation, and to exercise the *pouvoir constituant*, the loyalty to the centre began to wane in its flanks. In the aftermath of the aborted 1991 August coup by the Soviet hardliners who aimed to reverse the reform process, the Ukrainian communist elites turned staunchly against the renewal of the Union and in tandem with the opposition opted for an exit from the Soviet Union. The referendum of December 1991, in which the elite-level choices were given a seal of approval by 'popular will', represented a culminating point in the passage to independence. Having orchestrated the pro-independence campaign and hardly challenged by numerically weaker opposition, the communist elites remained firmly at the helm of the state.

In 1990–1991 two distinct but interrelated processes can be singled out: the pursuit of sovereignty and defining the blueprint of the new Ukrainian state. The growing radicalism characterising the pursuit of sovereignty can be easily but mistakenly extrapolated onto the process of constitutional reform. Yet the analysis of the latter evidenced a lack of urgent desire to depart from Soviet constitutional 'achievements'. The constitutional debates on the eve of independence revealed the prevailing reluctance to depart from the Soviet institutions and ideology within sovereign Ukraine. Thus, the constitutional choices prior to independence hardly prepared Ukraine for existence as an independent entity. At the same time even if the constitutional reforms, initiated over 1990–1991, were not intended to create a functioning polity, they meant that Ukraine was already going down a particular path of constitutional reform, i.e. by introducing a directly elected presidency.

The aim of the chapter is to disentangle the two processes: the passage to independence and constitutional reforms. By examining them independently the chapter will demonstrate that the shift toward sovereignty and then independence did not entail a simultaneous rejection of the Soviet legacy by the key sections of the political elites. (As such this chapter does not aspire to offer a comprehensive, detailed account of republican developments over 1990–1991; this was undertaken elsewhere).[1] The first section offers a necessary historical background to the events of 1990–1991 by sketching out the process of socio-economic, political and cultural change in Soviet Ukraine in order to account for the relative weakness of popular pressure as a causal factor and to emphasise the significance of micro-political processes. The second part of the chapter focuses on elite-level politics in 1990–1991 and provides an overview of the key events in the process of elite realignment, which allowed the attainment of independence, such as the 1991 elections, the Declaration of Sovereignty, constitution making, the negotiation of the renewal of the federal framework of the Soviet Union, the Act of Independence and the December 1991 referendum. The third section will focus on the deliberations on the shape of the new polity and analyse the conception of statehood elaborated over 1990–1991.

UKRAINIAN SOCIETY UNDER THE SOVIET UNION: AN OVERVIEW

Soviet Ukraine, which was recognised as a territorial–administrative unit, developed a modern society with indigenous Ukrainian elites. Yet in terms of the self-identification of ethnic Ukrainians, the example of Ukraine testified to the considerable success of the Soviet nationality policy to drain nationalism of its vitality at the mass and elite level.

The Soviet Union addressed the problem of social modernisation, which pre-occupied and divided the Ukrainian elites prior to and during the Ukrainian Revolution. With forced industrialisation, which occurred at the cost of great human suffering and sacrifices,[2] a leap forward was made in terms of mass education, urbanisation and the raising of standards of living. These policies created sociologically complete structures of a nation, and in particular, for the first time in Ukraine's history a large stratum of an indigenous educated elites emerged.[3]

Gellner postulated that nationalism and the rise of national identity is a by-product of the specific conditions of industrialisation, mobility, mass literacy and public education. However, in the case of Ukraine the relationship between socio-economic advancement and the crystallisation of a national identity was distorted by the political and cultural context. After a brief, although intensive, spell of cultural and linguistic Ukrainisation during the period of *korenizatsia* in the 1920s,[4] from the 1930s onwards industrialisation went hand in hand with progressive Russification, which was greatly facilitated by Ukraine's cultural and linguistic proximity to Russia. In particular, in Eastern and Southern Ukraine, which became part of the Russian state in the seventeenth and eighteenth centuries, the high level of urbanisation (60–80 percent) coincided with a high degree of linguistic and cultural Russification.[5] The demographic processes further altered the ethno-linguistic profile of Ukraine. Throughout history, the territory of Ukraine witnessed the intermingling of cultures and migration of various ethnic groups: Russians, Poles, Germans, Jews, Greeks, Bulgarians, Crimean Tatars, Armenians; and according to the 1989 census, over 100 nationalities lived in Ukraine.[6] However Soviet Ukraine experienced an influx of ethnic Russians, and the expulsion of other ethnic groups, such as Poles and Tatars, so while Ukrainians constituted the majority with 72 percent in 1989, Russians emerged as the second largest ethnic group, accounting for 22 percent of the population, whereas other ethnic groups made up 6 percent.[7]

Whilst the ethnic identity of Ukrainians was ascribed by Soviet authorities, the large-scale encroachment of the Russian language in urban centres meant that the formal ethnic composition of the republic did not coincide with language use: the titular majority consisted both of Russophones and Ukrainophones. According to the official census in 1989, 66 percent of ethnic Ukrainians considered Ukrainian to be their 'mother tongue', yet the census underestimated the use of Russian, which effectively became the language of the public sphere and social advancement across the republic, with the notable exception of Western Ukraine. A study in the early 1990s found that over 50 percent of

Ukraine's population used Russian in daily lives as the 'language of convenience'.[8] Therefore, on the eve of independence in ethno-linguistic terms, Ukrainian society consisted of three main groups: Ukrainian-speaking Ukrainians, Russophone Ukrainians and Russians. However, the boundaries between those groups were fluid and overlapping; there was a continuum of language use with certain areas and people using a mixture of languages in different social contexts. Thus, no clearly identifiable, mutually exclusive and self-conscious groups of 'Russian speakers' and 'Ukrainian speakers' existed.[9]

In Ukraine, contrary to the sociological theory of nationalism, the process of modernisation under 'cultural colonialism' produced a literate, urban, educated society in Ukraine but simultaneously the Ukrainian 'ethnographic masses' were linguistically Russified, assimilated into 'high' Soviet culture, rather than, as Farmer claimed, becoming more aware of the 'national patrimony'.[10] Outside Western Ukraine, a significant number of Ukrainians lacked a sense of ethnic identity as defined by culture, language, religion, a sense of belonging and historical memories. This affected the will and capacity of society to respond to anti-communist and pro-sovereignty agitation by the opposition.

Apart from Western Ukraine and Kyiv, the majority of the population, despite accumulated grievances especially on socio-economic and ecological issues, did not engage in enduring collective action fuelled by nationalistic feelings in the wake of political liberalisation brought about by perestroika; in particular linguistic or cultural concerns played only a limited role. The uneven spread of organised anti-Moscow, anti-communist protests across Ukraine reflected the uneven erosion of faith in the existing political system. By 1991, Soviet rule was not de-legitimated across Ukraine to the same degree and for the same reasons. In Western Ukraine popular mobilisation stemmed from a commonly shared conviction that Soviet political rule was essentially illegitimate and did not have the moral authority to demand obedience from Ukrainians. In the rest of Ukraine, however, attitudes to Soviet rule remained much more ambiguous and far less condemnatory. There, the Soviet regime was not rejected on the grounds of its perceived original moral illegitimacy, but for instrumental reasons, namely that the political order was incapable of meeting the expectations of governmental performance. Anti-centre and pro-independence feelings, which came to the surface in 1990–1991, reflected, most of all, the protest against the regime's declining economic performance and its failure to fulfil its promises of economic prosperity, rather than culmination of long-cherished hopes for independent statehood.

No less complex developments took place at the elite level. The Soviet Union was organised as a federation of nominally autonomous ethnic homelands. A cadre of party and state officials drawn from the titular majority in each republic were given access to power and derived privileges from that access. As a result they developed a stake in maintaining the system and acted as gatekeepers by ensuring that the republican resources were not used for ends disapproved by the centre.[11] Centrifugal tendencies based on nationalist sentiments were controlled through the elaborated structure of incentives and deterrents, which weakened the propensity of the indigenous elites to identify with and advance the interests of their republican homeland, as opposed to those defined by the centre.

Nevertheless, despite spectacular successes in terms of suppressing ethno-nationalist sentiments in Ukraine, the Soviet system could not eradicate them altogether. As Motyl pointed out, the way that the Soviet state was set up was inherently contradictory. As a federation it consisted of ethno-territorial units, which were denied any autonomy, as political and economic power were concentrated in the Russian-dominated Communist Party.[12] Such a highly centralised state suffered from inefficiencies stemming from over-centralisation that periodically forced the centre to push for decentralisation. Yet decentralisation inevitably entailed a shift of decision-making powers to the republican level, which tended to loosen the centre's control over the periphery. Periodical decentralisation allowed republican cadres to promote republican interests rather than all-Union ones. This phenomenon was referred to as national communism, in line with the Austro–Marxist assertion that the path to communism had to be pursued taking into account national specificities in a federally organised state.[13] During the Ukrainian Revolution, national communism was represented by parties, such as *Borotbisty* and *Ukapisty*.[14] In Soviet Ukraine national communism was associated with figures such as Mykola Skrypnyk and Petro Shelest. Skrypnyk as the Commissar for Education ardently implemented the policies of '*korenizatsiia*' in the 1920s. As the first secretary of CPU in the 1960s, Shelest defended the economic interests of the UkrSSR, and tolerated dissent amongst the ranks of cultural intelligentsia.[15]

Nevertheless, the Soviet centre retained its ability to reassert its domination over the republics by suppressing the 'nationalist deviation'. The Union centre could always draw from the Russified cadres such figures as Volodymyr Shcherbytskyi, the first secretary of the CPU between 1972–1989, an apparatchik whose allegiance plainly was deposited in the centre rather than his republican homeland.[16] In the light of the sheer scale of involvement of the ethnic Ukrainian cadres in the governing of the Soviet Union, Armstrong described their role and position as that of 'younger brothers' of Russians.[17]

Under the hegemonic role of the Communist Party of Ukraine, the robust even if numerically weak dissident movement and, to a lesser extent, the state-sponsored cultural intelligentsia nurtured the ideas of democracy, human rights and cultural and linguistic revival. Under Shelest, young intellectuals, the so-called *shistydesiatnyky*, combined the promotion of the national rights of Ukrainians in the Soviet state with the cause of democratisation and defence of human rights. However, by early 1970s they were suppressed and driven underground (the *shistydesiatnyky* re-appeared in the public sphere in late 1980s and formed the core of the moderate right-wing, national-democratic parties).[18] Therefore, with access to institutional resources being eliminated or heavily circumvented until 1990, the opportunities for independent political mobilisation were scarce, and, thus, the resonance of the opposition's ideas at the mass level was limited.[19]

UKRAINE ON THE EVE OF INDEPENDENCE

Overall, by the mid-1980s Ukraine existed as a territorial–administrative unit with a modern society, elites and institutional resources. Yet, because of the tight cultural and political integration, anti-Moscow fervour was not an automatic response to the opening of public space initiated by Mikhail Gorbachev. At the grass roots level, informal groups, often instigated by the political dissidents who were released from Soviet prisons, sprang up in 1988. Yet, although they were not stamped out, they were barely tolerated and still depicted by the republican leaders as malignant deviants from 'socialist values'. By 1989 the republic was still living under the spell of Brezhnevism, and the republican elites, under the leadership of Volodymyr Shcherbytskyi remained staunchly resistant to the imperatives of perestroika. Frustrated by Ukrainian 'backwardness', the Ukrainian cultural intelligentsia appealed to Gorbachev to speed up reforms in the republic. The first signal that top-down perestroika had begun in earnest in Ukraine was the long-awaited removal of Shcherbytskyi in the autumn of 1989. He was replaced by Volodymyr Ivashko, who was equally loyal to the Soviet centre, but who, in contrast to his predecessor, was a genuine Gorbachevite, committed to allowing the winds of perestroika into Ukraine. Under his leadership the CPU permitted some pluralisation and adopted a more conciliatory policy style towards the opposition, yet without venturing beyond the range of policies and measures prescribed and sanctioned by the centre.

The Popular Movement for Perestroika in Ukraine (Rukh), which was created in September of 1989, championed the cause of perestroika, along with calls for the revival of the Ukrainian language and culture. The movement triggered an unprecedented mass political awakening and mobilisation. Yet the social base of Rukh remained limited, despite the fact that it served as an umbrella movement for the various oppositional groupings, which conveyed a wide range of political views ranging from mildly reform communism to integral nationalism. At the peak of its popularity, with over 600,000 members, Rukh was crippled by a regional bias in its membership, as the majority of its members were white-collar workers and ethnic Ukrainians from Western Ukraine and Kyiv, while its appeal and membership in densely populated Eastern and Southern Ukraine was limited.[20] As Rukh's localised and spontaneous mass protests lacked organisational backing, it failed to develop a genuinely national power base to organise popular unrest and challenge the hegemonic position of the CPU. Bottom-up mobilisation could undermine the legitimacy of the Soviet regime in Ukraine, but, as it failed to embrace the majority of the population (unlike in the Baltic states), it could not overturn the regime, without the support of the communist republican elites.

THE PASSAGE TO INDEPENDENCE

This section will examine the process of the reorientation of the key section of the communist elites towards sovereignty, in which they were assisted by the opposition, which took advantage of its newly found access to institutional resources to champion the case of independence. The focus will be on the milestones that over the course of less than two years paved the passage to independence: the republican elections (March 1990), the Declaration of Sovereignty (July 1990), the March referendum on the Union (March 1991), the Concept of the New Constitution (June 1991), the Act of Independence (August 1991) and the referendum on independence (December 1991).

The republican elections held in March 1990 were, at least in some parts of Ukraine, genuinely contested and marked the beginning of the demise of the hegemonic power of the Communist Party of Ukraine (CPU). Despite the obstacles created by the CPU in the process of opening the public space, a plethora of organisations emerged prior to the elections, with the Democratic Bloc being the largest one. The bloc united 43 organisations, including Rukh,[21] and its electoral programme in the main attacked the shortcomings of the Soviet system, passionately exposing the devastation and distortions it had caused by lasting totalitarian political practices, cultural and linguistic Russification, economic decline and ecological disasters. The bloc advocated political and economic sovereignty, political pluralism, constitutional reform, religious freedoms and national revival. In the elections, despite the CPU's control of the media and cases of intimidation, the Democratic Bloc returned 25–30 percent.

The election results reflected the uneven geographical distribution of support for the democratic opposition. Western Ukraine and Kyiv fell under the control of the opposition, especially as they also dominated local councils (*radas*) in Western regions—the first state institutions in Ukraine controlled by non-communist forces. But the CPU retained its stronghold position in the rest of Ukraine. Even if in Eastern Ukraine many of the candidates from the CPU establishment were not elected, the electorate favoured independent candidates (often also CPU members) rather than the Democratic Bloc. Southern Ukraine remained the bastion of the CPU.

As a result, over 85 percent of the newly elected deputies were members of the CPU (16.5 percent more than in the previous elections), while nearly one quarter of all deputies worked in the CPU apparatus.[22] Nevertheless, the membership of the Supreme Council was rejuvenated; 90 percent of its members were elected for the first time. This meant that it was a political debut not only for many opposition members, but also for the CPU majority with important consequences for its coherence in the nearest future. While the communists organised themselves into a faction 'For a Soviet Sovereign Ukraine' in the Supreme Council, the opposition formed its own faction the 'People's Council' (*Narodna Rada)*. This name not only reflected the opposition's claim to genuinely represent the electorate, but also had historical legitimacy stretching back to the nineteenth century proto-party, *Narodna Rada,* in Western

Ukraine.[23] In the newly elected Supreme Council, the *Narodna Rada* united 125 deputies, who represented 21 out of 25 Ukrainian oblasts. At this point, the CPU, despite remaining relatively monolithic, showed early signs of internal dissent and defection. The internal opposition within the CPU gathered into the 'Democratic Platform of the CPU', and joined the *Narodna Rada* on an associated status.[24] This was a prelude to the growing overlap between reform-minded members within CPU and moderate flanks of the opposition.[25]

The newly elected parliament was destined to play a greater role than its predecessor in line with the revived slogan 'All Power to the Soviets'. In June 1988 at the 19th CPSU Conference Gorbachev called for radical reform of the political system, and withdrawal of the Party from interference in state affairs as part of the process of revitalising the system of soviets as the fulcrum of the state. However, Gorbachev's vision of democratisation stopped short of challenging the 'leading role' of the CPSU, and he encouraged party members to become elected chairpersons of the rejuvenated soviets. In line with this 'recommendation', the first secretary of the CPU Volodymyr Ivashko was elected chairman of the Ukrainian Supreme Council in June 1990 although he did not remain in post long. Ivashko's unexpected despatch to Moscow to become Gorbachev's deputy in Moscow in July 1990 resulted in an important, yet at that time underestimated, change as a result of which the Politburo of the CPU lost its hegemonic control over the parliament. The position of First Secretary was separated from that of parliamentary chairman. The conservative Stanislav Hurenko was elected the head of the CPU; Vitalii Masol, another old-time apparatchik continued to serve as chairman of the council of ministers, while Leonid Kravchuk—the head of the CPU ideology department—was nominated by the CPU for parliamentary chairmanship. Kravchuk was perceived as a particularly suitable candidate to the post, capable of eloquently counterbalancing the opposition's highly charged anti-communist rhetoric. Despite the *Narodna Rada*'s boycott, Kravchuk was duly elected the chairman of Supreme Council by the communist majority (which, as a result of this voting, became known as 'the 239 group'). Kravchuk's post was regarded as the least prestigious amongst the three top positions according to the Soviet 'pecking order'. It seemed that the Communist Party of Ukraine remained in full control of the republic, and unshaken in its loyalty to the centre.

However, by taking advantage of institutional resources to defy the CPU, the opposition came to play a much greater role than might have been expected on the basis of its numerical strength. Despite the fact that the anti-communist opposition secured only one third of the seats in the Supreme Council in March 1990, it gained the institutional means to publicise their agenda and radicalise public attitudes in Ukraine. In the transition to sovereignty, the republican institutional structures—the product of Soviet nominal federalism—played a crucial role. This well illustrates the situation, where 'old' institutions are employed in changed circumstances to pursue different ends from those, which they were designed for. Republican institutions, which had been created to legitimise Soviet federalism, were used to undermine it.

Until the semi-free elections in 1990, the Supreme Soviet was hand-picked under the tutelage of the CPU to mirror the social breakdown of the population of the UkrSSR at large. While it used to meet twice a year for 3–4 days and ritualistically pass the laws, its Presidium was a permanently functioning body. And the newly elected Supreme Council was still not a professional parliament, and only one third were full-time politicians.[26] The '239' majority conformed to the long-term Soviet practice by treating its mandate in a routinely ceremonial way; the communists' work was marked by high level of absenteeism as they tended to prioritise their long-standing careers, for example, as enterprise directors or chairmen of collective farms, and fulfilled their deputy mandates mainly by attending and voting in plenary sessions. In contrast, the opposition treated their deputy mandates seriously and took maximum advantage of their presence in the republican institutions. Over half of the full-time deputies belonged to the opposition and the *Narodna Rada* was well represented in the powerful Presidium.[27] Undoubtedly, the sheer number of communists had a major impact when it came to voting (CPU members were issued with 'directives', the so-called *orientirovki*). But in practice, the majority enjoyed by the communists was not fully reflected in the actual workings of the parliament, as the opposition determined the content of many draft laws, thanks to their active work in the commissions. Yukhnovskyi—the leader of the *Narodna Rada*—noted: 'We [*Narodna Rada*] prepare draft laws, which the majority only passes.'[28] As it was also most active in plenary sessions, the opposition's highly charged speeches and superior oratorical skills were given publicity on television and in radio broadcasts of parliamentary sessions. Paradoxically, the institutional underdevelopment of the parliament allowed the opposition to turn it into a forum for contesting the idea of sovereignty by playing a key role in setting the agenda. In this institutional context the opposition could more effectively undercut the popular legitimacy of the Soviet regime and, crucially, pursue the 'battle for souls' of the CPU members.

The influence of the opposition was demonstrated when the 'Declaration on Sovereignty' was debated in parliament. The document was sponsored by the CPU, after in February 1990 its Plenum adopted a resolution on economic and political sovereignty. The CPU's initiative aimed to 'prepare' sovereign Ukraine for a new Union Treaty (which would replace the one signed in 1922). The Party did not allow the use of *derzhavnyi* (referring to 'state') and prescribed the use of 'Ukrainian SSR' rather than 'Ukraine'. Overall, the CPU's version was similar to the Russian Declaration of 12 June 1990, which, although asserted sovereignty, did so mainly in anticipation of the signing of the new Union Treaty. However, once the debates on the Declaration started in the Ukrainian parliament on 28 June 1990, the CPU's initiative was hijacked by the opposition, which radicalised the content of the Declaration in the course of the plenary session. Despite a much more radical content than had been envisaged by the Party, the document was passed by 335 votes in favour and only 4 against in July 1990. Apart from the interest in greater economic sovereignty, the uniform support of the communist majority undoubtedly stemmed from the fact that the Declaration was initiated by the CPU, despite the fact that the document was 'refined' by the oppositional *Narodna Rada*.[29]

The Declaration proclaimed 'the state sovereignty of Ukraine to be supreme; the autonomy, totality and indivisibility of the Republic's power within its territory, and its independence and equality in external relations'.[30] Moreover, 'any violent acts against the national sovereignty from political parties, civic organisation and individuals are punishable by law'. The Supreme Council asserted its constitutional powers by pointing out that 'only the Supreme Council can represent the nation' and de-legitimised the CPU's 'leading role' by stating that 'no political party, social organisation or any other association or person can represent the People of Ukraine'. The section on cultural development, while professing the cultural and spiritual revival of the Ukrainian ethnic nation (*natsiia*) as well as the functioning of the Ukrainian language in all spheres of life, also guaranteed free national-cultural development to all nationalities living in Ukraine. However, most space was devoted to economic sovereignty and relations with Moscow, which reflected the main concerns of the communist majority; on those issues their views began to coincide with the opposition.[31] Furthermore, the Declaration included provisions for a separate Ukrainian army and an independent foreign policy, which became a basis for adopting laws on Ukrainian external and internal security, something ruled out by the 1977 Soviet Constitution. Finally, the Declaration stipulated that it was to serve as a basis for a new republican constitution and that 'the principles of the Declaration are to be the basis of the new Union Treaty' and 'the relations of the Ukrainian SSR with other Soviet republics are to be based on the principles of equality, mutual respect and non-interference in internal affairs'. These references to the attributes of sovereignty were the boldest ventures beyond the CPU-approved agenda.

While the content of the Declaration was an outcome of the coincidence of various agendas, it broke new ground; it provided scope for co-operation between the opposition's and the part of communist majority. The debates unveiled cracks emerging in the monolithic Party. The top (the Politburo) continued to serve as 'a transmission belt' for the centre's directives, while the second echelon, mainly regional apparatchiks and economic nomenklatura (the so-called *haziaistvienniki)*, represented in parliament recognised the economic advantages stemming from greater republican sovereignty. They supported measures to give them more control over economic resources in the republic, and, thus, they were increasingly reluctant to follow blindly the CPU *orientirovki* (directives). The latter section of the communist nomenklatura came to be referred to as national-communists, a term derived from Austro–Marxism. The adjective 'national' distinguished this section of the Ukrainian communists from the 'imperial' communists who remained devoted to the ideal of communism within the framework of a centralised Soviet Union (although their ranks were dominated by hard-liners, they also included some reformers, who were, nevertheless, committed to the Gorbachev's vision of a strong, rejuvenated centre).[32] Nevertheless, the configuration of political forces was fluid and amorphous. The 'group 239' was never formalised, and the picture became even more blurred when internal splits began to appear within the communist majority.

Still in the autumn of 1990, beyond its symbolic significance, the tangible consequences of the Declaration were unclear. It appeared that the Declaration was little more than a fancy façade for the new Treaty, as the UkrSSR remained tightly integrated with the All-Union administrative machinery. Thus, while the Supreme Council's floor was a setting for the ideological deliberations over the nature of sovereignty, other republican institutions, such as the KGB or the army, remained aloof and largely untouched by claims to sovereignty.

After the Declaration, the push for further changes came from society. In October 1990 the students' hunger strike staged in the centre of Kyiv demanded greater political liberalisation and the implementation of the Declaration.[33] When after two weeks Kyiv workers threatened a general strike in support of the students' demands, the Supreme Council passed a resolution conceding to popular demands. This was not only the peak of mass mobilisation in Ukraine, but also the first successful attempt to force the communist elites to bow to popular pressure. As part of the concessions, Kravchuk dismissed the old guard chairman of the council of ministers Vitalii Masol, utilising this as an opportunity to emphasise the autonomy of the new parliament from the CPU. Moreover, parliament passed a resolution that the Treaty would be signed only after the passage of the new republican constitution, which would specify the powers Ukraine would concede to the centre. At this point Ukraine's participation in the renewed Union was made conditional on the passage of the new constitution; the two parallel processes were coupled and began to interfere with each other. And soon the need to draft the new constitution became a key argument for the delay in signing the Treaty.

Even if winter 1990 witnessed the last counter-offensive of conservative forces to suppress the anti-communist opposition across the Soviet Union, and in Ukraine, popular protest, which the opposition could mobilise to put pressure on the communist majority, tailed off, the political machine had by that time been set in motion. Two weeks after the end of the strike—at the end of October 1990, a Constitutional Commission was created. The Commission, which was a large, 59-member body, consisted of 49 deputies of the Supreme Council and 10 experts (mainly directors of research institutes of the Academy of Science) and was headed by the chairman of the Supreme Council, Leonid Kravchuk.[34] The Commission decided to outline general principles of the new constitutional order in the 'Concept of the New Constitution', which, after the approval of parliament, would be developed into a fully-fledged draft constitution. The Commission delegated the task to the smaller working group. Feeling less constrained by the CPU's 'directives', the group partially drew on the draft constitution of the Russian Federation, which was published in November 1990, and contained no references to the USSR. The first draft Concept of December 1990 was radical both in terms of relations with the centre (it did not mention the existence of the USSR), and its institutional innovations (it proposed a presidential system).

The debates on the draft in the Constitutional Commission in late 1990 and early 1991 revealed two opposing positions: the conservative Politburo of the CPU and the oppositional *Narodna Rada*. The Politburo was unshaken in its adherence to socialism as it asserted that 'the people of Ukraine remain loyal to the socialist choice and the Soviet system of *narodovladia,* and continued to support the voluntary and equal co-operation of people united within the Union of Soviet Sovereign Republics.'[35] The Party was aghast at the lack of any references to the Soviet Union and argued that Ukraine's firm commitment to the Union should be spelt out in the new constitution. In contrast, the oppositional *Narodna Rada* hoped to expand the provisions of the Declaration of Sovereignty and thus was not satisfied with the still cautious view on the Treaty in the draft Concept. The *Rada* insisted on removing all traces of the Soviet Union from the draft, and giving priority to Ukraine's international agreements and obligations as opposed to Soviet acts.

The debates within the Constitutional Commission evidenced the extent to which the members of the communist majority in the Supreme Council did not obediently follow the *diktat* of the Politburo. Kravchuk, as the chair of the Commission, while claiming that he only strove to reconcile the different viewpoints to speed up the process, actually pursued a more independent line from that of the Politburo.[36] He began to champion the idea of sovereignty on economic grounds:

> We have such an organisation as 'UkrInturist'—with the prefix 'Ukr'. It is ours! But I can tell you that Ukraine gets not a single unit of hard currency (*valuta)* from its own 'Ukr'. Here we've got our sovereignty ... If we want to be masters (*hospodari*), then there ought to be a sovereign Ukraine, so we have rights, duties and responsibilities both in relation to our people and to the Union, which we enter.[37]

Despite the CPU's insistence, Kravchuk argued that 'the relations with the centre are not an object for constitutional regulation. The Constitution of the state, as its basic law, deals with the relationships between society and the state and not its external relations.'[38] He opposed passing the Concept before the referendum on the renewal of the Treaty in March 1991. Taking into account the disparity of the positions, no consensus could be reached within the Commission, and the draft was tabled for further deliberations in the Supreme Council. After some inconclusive deliberations and further revisions, the parliament unexpectedly passed the Concept by a simple majority on 19 June 1991 thanks to Kravchuk's skilful steering of the parliament.

The Concept gave primacy to the republican interests, while still respecting the Soviet dogma of the 'socialist choice'. While the powers that Ukraine was willing to concede to the Union remained unspecified, the Concept re-stated the provisions of the Declaration of Sovereignty: 'the economic organisation of society is based on the tenet that the people of Ukraine have the exclusive right to all the national wealth of the republic'. And the new constitution was to outline 'the basic principles of financial, price, budgetary, banking, currency, tax, investment and customs systems of Ukraine'. The exclusion of a definition of relations between Ukraine and the centre acquired an anti-Union symbolism.

While the Politburo harshly criticised the approved Concept, it came up against the limits of its power. Without the disciplined communist majority in the Supreme Council, the CPU could no longer exercise its extra-constitutional powers and lacked the means to bring the 'unruly' Supreme Council and the Constitutional Commission under control. The Party realised that, according to the 1978 constitution, it did not have the right of legislative initiative. Thus, as did their counterparts in Russia,[39] the Ukrainian hard-liners decided to draft an alternative version of the constitution, which was to be tabled in parliament by a group of communist deputies as an ordinary draft law.

As the Supreme Council grew in prominence *vis-à-vis* the party structures, so did the assertiveness of the national communists under the consummate leadership of Kravchuk. Even if Kravchuk was careful not to alienate either the hard-liners or the increasingly radicalised opposition, and performed a balancing act between the two groups, his actions symbolised a growing split between the pro-Moscow and national communists and a narrowing of the gap between the latter and the opposition. Still, however, the coincidence was only partial: for the opposition the Concept was a step towards full independence, whereas the national communists still adhered to a vague formula of Ukraine as 'a state within the state'.

While the growing split between the national and imperial communists was kept away from the public eyes, it came out into the open in the course of the preparation to the referendum on the New Union Treaty in March 1991, which was set up by Gorbachev in order to exert pressure on the republican leaders to speed up the ratification process. The pro-Moscow Politburo limited itself to the agenda set by the centre, the national-communists emphasised their claims to sovereignty by adding an additional question, asking whether Ukraine should participate in the Union on the basis of the Declaration of Sovereignty. The 'All-Union' question received 70.2 percent votes in favour, whereas the second 'republican' question obtained 80.2 percent of the vote.

On the basis of the results of the referendum, Ukraine continued to participate in the process of renewing the Union (unlike the Baltic republics, Moldova, Georgia and Armenia) and its delegation attended the Novo–Ogarevo meeting (9+1) in April 1991, when the leaders of nine republics met with Gorbachev and agreed to sign the Treaty by August. However, even if Ukraine did not openly refuse to sign the Treaty, its hard bargaining for greater concessions slowed down the whole ratification process. When the revised draft Treaty was published in March 1991, Kravchuk criticised the proposed division of property, the delineation of power between the republics and the centre, and the republics' contribution to the all-Union budget. He favoured a 'union of sovereign states', a confederation rather than federation. On 27 June the Supreme Council dashed the CPU's and Gorbachev's hopes that the new Treaty could be signed in the summer by postponing consideration of the Treaty until 15 September 1991.[40]

In the spring and summer of 1991, Ukraine continued to assert its sovereignty in the legislation adopted by the Supreme Council. Bolstered by higher support for the second question in the March 1991 referendum, the Ukrainian parliament adopted over sixty laws in order to implement the provisions of the July 1990 Declaration of Sovereignty. The laws aimed at nationalising all-Union property on the territory of Ukraine, putting external trade under republican control, setting up a National Bank and establishing direct foreign relations.[41] These bold state-building measures would necessarily limit the prerogatives of the centre in the renewed federation. In addition, other laws, such as 'On National Guards', 'On the Referendum', 'On a National Army', were passed in July 1991. The process of cutting the 'umbilical administrative cord' between the centre and Ukraine began in earnest. In particular, the pro-sovereignty agenda was evident in design of the republican presidency, which was equipped with sweeping powers 'to suspend the action of decisions of the executive power of the USSR on the territory of the Ukrainian SSR if they contradicted the constitution and the laws of the Ukrainian SSR'.[42] The presidency was to symbolically legitimise Ukrainian sovereignty against the old Soviet centre, and more particularly against the Gorbachev presidency (created in March 1990), which although indirectly elected, was equipped with significant powers.

The pro-independence republican elite sought the additional authority that would derive from having a directly elected president; the popular mandate of the new institution was to be a tactical weapon with which the republic would oppose Moscow:

> An important role (perhaps at this stage—the most important), which the president has to fulfil, is to strengthen real sovereignty. The republic is unprotected, vulnerable to the attacks from the centre …The president, equipped with the right to adopt decisions operatively and independently, will undoubtedly better protect the republican interests.[43]

Kravchuk was especially supportive of a strong presidency, as by that time he had emerged as a leading figure in Ukraine and had this institution in mind for himself. The 'Law on the Presidency' scheduled the presidential elections for 1 December 1991.

However, even if over the spring and summer 1991 measures began to be taken to assert Ukraine's sovereignty, the national communists stopped short of embracing the idea of full independence, as they did not reject some kind of renewed Union with other Soviet republics. It was only the *coup d'état* of August 1991 that made the Ukrainian communists 'cross the Rubicon'. During the coup Ukraine remained inert as Kravchuk along with many national communists took an ambivalent stance, neither supporting nor condemning it, in contrast to Yeltsin's vigorous opposition. But once it was evident that the coup had failed on 22 August, Kravchuk abandoned the sinking ship and resigned from the CPU. On 24 August, under pressure from the *Narodna Rada*, the Supreme Council adopted the 'Act of Independence' (*Akt Nezaleznosti*) subject to confirmation in a national referendum in December 1991 (346 voted in favour, 1 against, 13 abstained),

The radicalising impact the coup had on the national-communist elites can be accounted for by several interrelated factors. Firstly, being largely composed of an economic nomenklatura, they were not interested in a renewed union with a pro-reform Yeltsin, who emerged as a key actor in Russia. Independence was a way of cutting themselves off from the reform process taking place in Russia. Secondly, had the coup succeeded, the Soviet conservatives would have clamped down on separatist republics. Thus the coup was straw that broke the camel's back as it persuaded the national-communists that Moscow was not to be trusted to respect republics' sovereignty. Thirdly, the *Putsch* ultimately discredited the CPSU in the eyes of the population. By proclaiming independence and dissolving the Communist Party of Ukraine (which until then had remained an integral part of the CPSU), the communists in Ukraine simultaneously avoided any recrimination on the part of the anti-communists in Moscow and—in the domestic context—from the opposition, while at the same time preserving their institutional power. As the coup finally discredited the idea of a 'state within a state', the republican communist elites turned into strident and uncompromising defenders of the 'national right to self-determination'.[44]

In preparation for the December 1991 referendum and the presidential elections, the republican apparatus agitated in favour of independence, while the pro-Moscow hard-liners' camp fell into disarray. In October, although the centre desperately tried to counteract the economic disintegration and preserve a common economic system, the Soviet republics proclaimed independence one after another. Ukraine refused to sign the Agreement on the Economic Union.[45] While the whole republican apparatus geared itself up for independence, Kravchuk's conciliatory style skilfully channelled popular discontent across Ukraine into almost uniform support for independence. Once such prominent members of the ruling elites as Kravchuk or his deputy in parliament Leonid Pliushch championed the idea of a Ukraine outside the Soviet Union, the population of Eastern and Southern Ukraine followed suit, something that the anti-communist, pro-independence opposition could never hope to achieve on its own, as these regions of Ukraine remained essentially distrustful of the nationalist ideas propagated by the 'Banderite' Western Ukrainians represented in the *Narodna Rada*.[46] In the context of accumulated grievances against the regime and the anti-Moscow campaign orchestrated by the Ukrainian media, independence was championed as a solution to all conceivable problems. Without any apparent alternative, over 90 percent of voters supported the Act of Independence in December 1991.

Undoubtedly, the concurrent vote for president made the choice for many easier. Kravchuk's unique appeal to many constituencies promised change, yet guaranteed a high degree of continuity, avoiding any extreme solutions. While large segments of society—as Kuzio put it: 'voted for independence and Kravchuk as a package',[47] many inhabitants of Ukraine remained essentially indifferent to the notion of independence. There was no opposition to Kravchuk from the communist quarters, and the national-democratic opposition arrived at the polls divided, competing with itself, which further split the votes for the option it represented (it put forward 4 out of the 6 presidential candidates: Ihor Yukhnovskyi, Viacheslav Chornovil, Levko Lukianenko and Petro Taburianskyi, while

Russophone liberal Volodymyr Hryniov stood independently). In the elections, Kravchuk received 61 per cent against 23 per cent of votes to Rukh's candidate Viacheslav Chornovil, 4.5 per cent went to Lukianenko, 1.7 per cent to Yukhnovskyi, and 4.2 per cent to Hryniov. The results of the referendum and the elections gave Kravchuk a mandate to state that 'under no circumstances would Ukraine have signed a Union treaty that presupposed a state within a state'.[48] Instead, on 8 December 1991 the leaders of Ukraine, Russia and Belarus, Kravchuk, Yeltsin and Shushkevich signed the so-called Belovezha Accord, which created the Commonwealth of Independent States (CIS) in place of the Soviet Union.

The Ukrainian communist nomenklatura accomplished the passage to independence, when in the course of 15 months, a key section moved from a position of unmitigated loyalty to Moscow to advocating Ukraine's right to self-determination. However, as the next section of this chapter will argue, this accelerated evolution was not matched by a vision of a political and economic order in the new state.

THE LIMITS OF CHANGE: CONSTITUTIONAL DEBATES AND INSTITUTIONAL REFORMS, 1990–1991

The previous section provided an overview of the passage to independence against the backdrop of re-alignment of the elites. The shift to sovereignty was reflected, as was pointed out above, in the Concept of the New Constitution and other constitutional acts, such as the 'Law on the Presidency'. Yet the analysis of these documents and the discussion preceding their adoption also demonstrate that the national-communists' increasingly radical stance on sovereignty contrasted with their essentially conservative outlook in the domestic context. They opposed the dismantling of the institutional and ideological pillars of the Soviet system within a sovereign Ukraine. Sovereignty was not sought as a precondition for wide-ranging reforms, but merely as a means of devolving decision-making power to the republic. The only major exception was the institution of the presidency, which, by claiming to represent popular sovereignty, was designed to challenge Moscow's authority in Ukraine. Therefore, despite the swelling support for Ukrainian sovereignty, the actual constitutional blueprint of the new Ukrainian state was essentially rooted in the old Soviet order.

This section will more closely analyse the vision of Ukrainian statehood on the eve of the passage to independence. Thus, three issues will be focused on—the institutional framework, notion of political community and ideological and socio-economic profile of the new state, as reflected in the key constitutional acts, the Declaration of Sovereignty (July 1990), the Concept of the Constitution (June 1991), the Law on Presidency (1991), the Declaration on Minority Rights (November 1991), and the Law on Citizenship (October 1991).

THE FORM OF GOVERNMENT

The onset of constitutional reform in Ukraine after seven decades of Soviet rule inevitably posed the fundamental question of the future of the system of soviets. This question involved not only the consideration of whether the system had the capacity to serve the needs of independent statehood, but—most of all—its historical legitimacy, having been installed in Ukraine by the Bolsheviks. However, the issue of the legitimacy of the system of soviets in Ukraine was pushed aside by the communist majority and no overhaul of the republican institutional setup was envisaged. The only major innovation was the republican presidency, which was *added* to the system of soviets in order to promote sovereignty.

Paradoxically, the first Ukrainian constitutional act, the Declaration of Sovereignty of July 1990, re-legitimised the system of soviets as a way to boost the standing of the republican institutions *vis-à-vis* the Party and the centre. The Declaration re-affirmed the supreme constitutional position of the *Verkhovna Rada* at the pinnacle of the state structure and its exclusive right to represent 'the people of Ukraine'. Although the Declaration also added that 'state power in the Republic is exercised according to the principle of its division into legislative, executive and judicial powers', this was not elaborated on sufficiently to undermine the principle of the 'unity of power' as the backbone of the Soviet system in Ukraine.[49]

The question of the future of the system of soviets soon re-appeared in the Constitutional Commission. The experts in the working group proposed to abolish the system of soviets: 'we have to abandon state-legal institutions, which have not passed the test of time, and courageously introduce the best achievements of world constitutional practice'.[50] The group advocated a radical shift towards the principle of separation of powers for the sake of establishing democracy and the rule of law. The proposed institutional overhaul for Ukraine was to include the creation of a professional, bi-cameral parliament; an executive presidency and vice-presidency; local self-government; and the abolition of other Soviet institutions such as the imperative mandate and the omnipotent *prokuratura*. The Supreme Council would be transformed into a professional legislature, which would operate on a permanent basis (so deputies could not combine their parliamentary mandates with seats on local councils or in the government). As its functions would be clearly delineated, the Supreme Council would cease to be the all-encompassing Soviet institution, which could delegate and/or take over functions of other state institutions. A second, upper chamber (*Palata Predstavnykiv*) would be created in order to improve efficiency (by dividing functions), install additional 'checks and balances' and provide representation for regional interests.[51] The executive powers would be vested in the directly elected president and vice-president, who would exercise power through representatives (*predstavnyky*) at the local and regional level. Local self-government at the municipal level would be guaranteed. The working group justified a wholesale replacement of the system of soviets with a presidential system in terms of the latter's superior efficacy and rule of law. The proposal of the working group, although at that stage still somewhat vague, offered the direction for far-reaching institutional reform in 1990-1991, inspired by the American and French constitutional models.

The oppositional *Narodna Rada* firmly supported this proposal, apart from bi-cameralism. The *Rada* believed that radical institutional reform was needed to dismantle the Bolshevik legacy—the system of soviets, especially as the soviets became the bastion of anti-reform, anti-sovereign forces in Eastern and Southern Ukraine. Also, facing the CPU's unmitigated loyalty to the centre, the democratic opposition strongly favoured a presidential regime, as it could offer both external and internal advantages. A directly elected presidency could act as a shield against the encroachment of Moscow on republican interests and would symbolise the republican sovereignty. In the domestic context, efficient decision making associated with the presidency was highly rated:

> A popularly elected president is a legitimate authority … it is a strong, decisive and mobile authority, which will be able to introduce radical economic reform and lead the country out of the crisis.[52]

The *Narodna Rada* also stressed the need for democratic accountability associated with the directly elected presidency, something missing from the Soviet system:

> Presidential power would personalise responsibility, and this is something that has been missing from our so-called collective leadership ... Under the Soviet system of *narodovladia* there was no separation of legislative, executive and judicial powers. There was 'joint' responsibility, and as a result a total lack of accountability. And the people were passive because they did not know whom to turn to. Only if we break that vicious circle by introducing direct elections, we will not only personalise the accountability of the president, but also make people responsible for their own choice.[53]

Yet the 'group 239', including both national and pro-Moscow communists, staunchly opposed the abolition of the system of soviets. Undoubtedly, the fate of *radas* was a matter close to the hearts of the communist deputies, many of whom combined their Supreme Council mandate with seats in local *radas* (in particular many oblast and district CPU first secretaries were elected heads of *radas*). The pre-occupation of many national-communists with their particular interests was reflected in the discussion on the mode of elections to local soviets. The communists advocated direct elections of heads of local *radas*, who would simultaneously become head of *rada* executive committees (*vykonkomy*) and acquire additional resources and power. The discussion on this issue ate up a lot of parliamentary time, although in the light of the gravity of questions under consideration the mode of the election was a detail of secondary importance. Kravchuk firmly asserted that 'the system of soviets in localities has to be maintained'.[54] Upon this directive the working group re-introduced the soviets as the pinnacle of the political structure in Ukraine in the Concept, before the Supreme Council approved the draft in June 1991.

However, despite the unity on the issue of soviets in the communist majority, on the issue of the presidency, the national communists parted company with pro-Moscow communists and sided with the national-democrats. Sensing its declining support, the Politburo opposed a directly elected presidency, as it feared the president's executive prerogatives, which could not only shift power away from the CPU but also to further champion the cause of sovereignty. Thus the hard-liners depicted the presidency as a prelude to a personal dictatorship and the destruction of the unique system of *narodovladia*.[55] They particularly attacked the institution of regional prefects as an executive arm of the presidency.[56]

The national communists, however, preferred the directly elected presidency, as was illustrated by Kravchuk's behaviour. As chairman of the Supreme Council, Kravchuk was instrumental in the approval of a directly elected presidency, as by that time, he had emerged as a key political figure in Ukraine and the most serious pretender to the office. As was pointed out above, Kravchuk skilfully avoided a direct challenge to the Party's position and portrayed himself as a conciliator of polarised views rather than an advocate of an openly anti-CPU line. However, in the debates on the presidency, he abandoned his 'non-bloc' status and actively lobbied in favour of a directly elected presidency with executive representatives in localities in defiance of the Politburo's stance. He criticised the unconstitutional nature of CPU rule, and argued that the president could not usurp powers because of 'checks and balances' in the new constitution, something —as he claimed to know from his own experience—the Politburo had never encountered.[57]

Kravchuk used his powers to steer debates in favour of a directly elected presidency, and to orchestrate voting accordingly. For example, immediately before the vote on the mode of presidential elections, he put pressure on the deputies to vote in favour of the directly elected presidency:

> After the parliament debate [on the directly elected presidency], we received so many letters proposing the personal vote on this issue in order to find out who amongst us trust the people and who doesn't. Some even suggest that we should publish the results of the vote in newspapers.[58]

Thanks to the alliance of the *Narodna Rada* and the national communists under Kravchuk's leadership, the popularly elected presidency and presidential prefects were approved in the Concept, with 313 deputies voting in favour. But the presidential powers *vis-à-vis* the Supreme Council were curtailed, and the institution's external purpose as a defender of sovereignty was emphasised. Nevertheless, the presidency was the only major innovation proposed by the working group that won approval in parliament, apart from a less contentious issue of professionalisation of parliament and the creation of the Constitutional Court. Despite favouring a directly elected presidency, Kravchuk insisted that 'the way to combine the soviets with presidential powers has to be found'.[59] Therefore, the scope of institutional reform elaborated by the working group of experts was substantively narrowed in parliamentary debates, as the communist deputies refused to abolish the system of soviets.

The issue of uni-cameralism fostered a consensus in parliament, and a bi-cameral legislature was rejected, when only 81 deputies voted in favour of it.[60] The CPU Politburo opposed the creation of the upper chamber as an erosion of the system of soviets. It defended uni-cameralism by arguing that it was in line with the Declaration of Sovereignty. Many national communists openly expressed their anxiety on the fate of the then current parliament and their career as deputies. They feared that voting in favour of creating a second chamber would mean voting themselves out of office; in the prevailing political uncertainty, they were cautious to embark on reform that would provide a justification for pre-term parliamentary elections. Deputies from Eastern oblasts—the most densely populated part of Ukraine—opposed the upper chamber that would not reflect the relative size of the population of Eastern Ukraine, and thus would favour less populated (and more radical) Western Ukrainian oblasts. The opposition was divided on the issue. Only the liberal Party of Democratic Revival (which originated in the CPU's Democratic Platform) consistently supported this innovation, while others feared bi-cameralism as a means of creeping federalisation of Ukraine. The vote in June 1991 was the first attempt to provide regional representation in the Ukrainian legislature, and since then the proposal then repeatedly resurfaced and was systematically voted down by the Supreme Council.

Overall, preferences on the institutional framework of the state as reflected in the constitutional debates in 1991 can be summarised as follows:

The Politburo	*The National Communists*	*The Opposition*
The System of Soviets	The System of Soviets	Local Self-Government
Indirectly Elected Presidency	Directly Elected Presidency	Directly Elected Presidency
Uni-cameralism	Uni-cameralism	Uni-cameralism

The form of government endorsed in the Concept was a hybrid combining the system of soviets and some vaguely specified elements of presidentialism and judicial review. In an attempt to justify this innovation, an ambiguous distinction was made between the directly elected bodies of state: the Supreme Council was to represent 'the popular will', whereas the president would represent 'the state'.[61] The preservation of *radas* alongside the directly elected presidency resulted in confusion amongst the deputies on whether the form of government should be called presidential, soviet, or soviet-presidential. The question was even posed as to whether the president (and vice-president) should be a deputy in parliament. The Concept also retained a number of unmistakably Soviet traits, such as an imperative mandate,[62] a powerful *prokuratura,* and instruments of direct democracy, while at the same time downplaying the role of political parties. Despite the Concept's references to the multi-party system (*bahatopartiinis't*), no mechanisms were proposed for consolidating the party system, such as for example, the reforms of the electoral law. If anything, the debates revealed the lingering distrust in parties. As one member of the working group argued: 'Multi-party relations should be multi-party relations. However, political and economic stability is in the interests of the republic and thus the mechanism of exercising state power should work like clockwork'.[63] The executive presidency was perceived as a safety valve for withstanding the 'destabilising' influences of party politics by ensuring the steadiness of the new state.

The Concept's lack of both a clear conception of the actual nature of the presidential powers, and a mechanism for its co-existence with the system of *radas*, was reflected in the 'Law on the Creation of the Institution of the President of UkrSSR', which was passed on 5 July 1991, two weeks after the approval of the Concept.[64] The law focused mainly on the presidency's external role. The Ukrainian president was given sweeping powers 'to suspend the action of decisions of the executive power of the USSR on the territory of the UkrSSR if they contradicted the constitution and the laws of the UkrSSR' (art. 7). The popular mandate of the new institution would be a tactical weapon with which the republic was to resist the centre's encroachment on its sovereignty. In a domestic context, however, the popular legitimisation of the head of the executive branch, which could challenge parliament's monopoly of power, was offset by the division of powers that gave the upper hand to parliament. The president, to be elected directly for 5 years in double ballot elections, was 'the highest state official in Ukraine and the head of the executive branch', who 'exercises executive rights through the cabinet of ministers' (art. 1). However, the president had to obtain parliamentary consent both for appointment and dismissal of prime minister (art. 114-6 of the revised 1978 Constitution). On the recommendation of the prime minister, the president could appoint and dismiss ministers, but in the case of the appointment of key ministries, parliament's approval was necessary. The government would be required to resign in the event of a no-confidence vote by parliament. Furthermore, the parliamentary chairman retained the right to suspend decisions of the executive branch under certain circumstances. The president had the right 'to issue decrees (*ukazy*) to implement the constitution and laws' and to veto parliamentary laws by returning them for renewed consideration within 14 days (art. 5). However, a simple parliamentary majority would be enough to override the presidential veto, as well as to veto presidential *ukazy* (art. 114-8). By contrast, the president could not dissolve parliament and call for new elections if the government resigned. Overall, the president was given few powers independently of parliament or the prime minister, who was subordinated to parliament. Thus, the presidency was designed as an addendum to 'Soviet parliamentarism'. Nevertheless, these initial presidential prerogatives, even if crudely grafted onto the system of Soviets, opened the door for the gradual extension of the role of the president within the next few months.

While the law on the presidency marked the beginning of *ad hoc* institutional changes, constitutional reform became chaotic and slowed down. Despite the fact that the law was adopted only two weeks after the approval of the Concept, it had already diverged from its provisions—no presidential representatives and vice-president were envisaged in the law. Also, little care was taken to harmonise the internal consistency of the 1978 constitution. While the Act of Independence on 24 August 1991 radically changed Ukraine's external situation and marked the kaleidoscopic demise of the Soviet Union, it did not accelerate the constitutional reform. Before the referendum on independence, parliament transformed the 1978 constitution into the basic law of independent Ukraine.[65] This was simply done by deleting all references to socialism, the Communist Party, and the Soviet Union. At the same time, the parliament resisted further institutional reforms: it voted against transforming itself into a professional legislature—something that had already been agreed in the Concept—and deputies were allowed to retain their positions in state institutions and in local soviets. Within a few months the tinkering with the odd bits of the institutional framework led to a paralysing confusion on the delineation of power between state institutions at the centre and local level.

SOCIALISM IN SOVEREIGN UKRAINE: IDEOLOGY OF THE NEW STATE

The debates on the place of ideology in sovereign Ukraine provide further evidence of the conservatism of the dominant section of the Ukrainian political elites, who even by 1991 were far from admitting the bankruptcy of ideology of Soviet socialism. Symptomatically, this issue attracted more attention than did the matter of the protection of the individual against the abuses of state power.

The issue of rights and freedoms (and mechanisms to safeguard them) hardly evoked any discussion during the debates in the Constitutional Commission and the Supreme Council. For the democratic opposition, the bill of rights, while an emanation of constitutionalism, could only acquire proper meaning on independence once Ukraine freed itself from Moscow's domination. For the communist elites, the enumeration of rights and freedoms in the new constitution represented a continuation of Soviet ritualistic practice in this sphere without real commitment to the curbing of the powers of the state *vis-à-vis* an individual.

The communist elites, however, did not show the same indifference to the issue of the 'de-ideologisation' of the state. The removal of the adjectives 'soviet' and 'socialist' from the name of the state and the constitution, as advocated by the working group, sparked heated debates. The *Narodna Rada* wholeheartedly supported the proposal of the working group, as it vehemently denied the communist system in Ukraine any legitimacy:

> To be honest, this choice was not made by the Ukrainian people in December of 1917, but by the Bolshevik party, which then imposed that choice on the people of Ukraine. Today, the CPU attempts to impose that choice for the second time in the history of the people of Ukraine.[66]

It was pointed out that the people in Ukraine actually made a different choice at that time:

> The socialist choice of the people of Ukraine is historically illegal (*nepravomirnyi*). Who knows the history of 1917–1920 realises that we had a Ukrainian People's Republic and Western Ukrainian People's Republic, which on 22 January 1919 proclaimed unification in Kyiv. This was the choice of our people. And after this there was only annexation and aggression.[67]

As Ukraine's aspirations to independent statehood, which were exemplified by the European, republican, democratic, parliamentary tradition of the UNR, were ruthlessly shattered by the seizure of Ukraine by Bolshevik Russia, Soviet rule amounted to foreign occupation. As one of the Soviet-era dissidents, Levko Lukianenko, argued 'We have to reject the system of slavery which existed and we have to transform colonial Ukraine into an independent Ukraine'.[68]

The opposition also argued that the 'socialist choice' was incompatible with multipartism and the ideological pluralism which the Concept preached, and that an ideology of only one of the political parties should not be appended to the name of the state.[69] Yet the opposition's arguments did not diminish the communists' declared commitment to socialism. Both national and pro-Moscow communists proved reluctant to drop the 'socialist choice' from the Preamble of the constitution. The Politburo furthermore insisted on including the adjectives 'socialist' and/or 'soviet' in the name of the state (on the basis that this name was fixed in the Declaration of Sovereignty). As usual, Kravchuk took the middle ground and attempted to reconcile those polar views by arguing that the name of the state should be 'neutral', but 'the goals and nature of our society should be expressed in the Preamble'.[70] As a result, the 'socialist choice' was endorsed and defined as 'an intention to build a society of social justice through work' in the Preamble, the title of the Basic Law was to be the 'Constitution of Ukraine', while the name of the state was to be decided by a referendum.

The issue of the transformation to a market economy and the revision of the role of the state in the economic sphere hardly featured in the constitutional debate. Although the Concept affirmed economic pluralism and protection of all forms of property, there was no explicitly stated intention to develop the market economy. The Concept only included ambiguous statements such as that the state was to 'defend the property owners against administrative-command methods of the state leadership' (*sic*). At the same time, according to the chairman of the cabinet of ministers, Vitaliy Fokin, the state's role in running the economy, if anything, was to be expanded:

> In ensuring equality of all forms of property and implementing processes of denationalisation and privatisation, we nevertheless firmly support the preservation of the state sector, and even more—its strengthening. We will take special measures to achieve this. Also, we are in favour of the dominance of the collective form of property in industry ... We will implement stabilisation and improve the system of social welfare.[71]

Despite some general declarations of greater constitutional protection of private property, the constitutional debates revealed no overarching commitment for the wholesale transition from the command economy to a market economy in Ukraine on the eve to independence. Rather some kind of liberalised, centrally administered economy seemed to command favour amongst the elites.

DEFINING THE 'SOVEREIGN PEOPLE'

As argued above, being concerned with their immediate interests, the communist elites displayed largely preservationist attitudes to the Soviet 'constitutional achievements'. That the pursuit of sovereignty from Moscow was driven by particular interests rather than animated by any particular vision of Ukrainian statehood inspired by pre-communist history, yet alone that of a Ukrainian nation-state was evidenced in their overwhelming indifference to the so-called 'national question', that is who and on what terms constituted the 'nation'. The hard-liners' attempted to discredit the idea of Ukrainian independence by spreading alarm on the dangers of raising the phantom of ethno-nationalism of the titular majority. Yet an analysis of the main constitutional acts passed in 1991 amply reflected the weakness of ethno-nationalism on the eve of independence, and the prevailing support for a territorial, multi-ethnic notion of the political community.

The 'national question' received relatively little attention in parliamentary debates on the Concept of the new constitution, especially in comparison to issues such as the presidency, the 'socialist choice' or the *prokuratura*. In principle, the text of the Concept most often referred to the sovereign subject as the 'people of Ukraine' (*narod Ukrainy*),[72] which was the most general and neutral description of the body of citizens. The Concept merely re-stated the provisions of the Declaration of Sovereignty by defining Ukraine as 'a sovereign national state', which promoted the cultural, spiritual and linguistic revival of the Ukrainian ethnic nation (*natsiia*), as well as guaranteeing free national-cultural development to all nationalities living in Ukraine. The distinction between national minorities and the titular majority, the Ukrainian *natsiia,* was the only departure from the Soviet conceptual canon. This innovation was opposed by CPU hard-liners, who argued that it would open the way to discrimination on ethnic grounds by dividing nationalities into the more and less equal. The CPU portrayed this as an attempt to spread the Western Ukrainian strand of integral nationalism across Ukraine, and pointed to developments in the Baltics, Moldova and the Caucasus as a warning of the potentially dire consequences of ethnic strife. The opposition, however, argued that there was nothing 'nationalistic' about singling out national minorities, as the term was widely used and recognised in international law. As the majority of the national communists did not object, the term 'national minorities' remained in the Concept.

The implementation of the 'Law on Language' confirmed the lack of zeal in the linguistic and cultural assertion of the position of the titular majority. The law, which was adopted in 1989, established Ukrainian as the sole state language, and stipulated that Ukrainian was to be introduced in higher education and state administrative bodies within 10 years (although it did not specify the mechanisms for its implementation).[73] In 1989 the passage of the law was a symbolic gesture towards the disgruntled cultural intelligentsia in order to subdue the raising tide of protests about linguistic Russification. As such, the law did not lead to a systematic change in republican language policy, and did not become a political issue prior to the referendum on independence in December 1991.[74]

The definition of Ukrainian citizenship and the Declaration of the Rights of National Minorities also reflected a non-ethnic notion of the political community.[75] The 'Law on Citizenship', which was passed 8 October 1991, adopted a territorial definition of citizenship and membership of the new state was granted automatically to almost everyone who was living in Ukraine at the time the law was passed (the so-called 'Zero Option'). As no category of the population was formally excluded from the political community, citizenship based on *ius soli* became one of the fundamental attributes of the new political community. The assertion was that inclusive citizenship would lead to the consolidation of the political community as 'a new civic nation-state based on territorial, not ethnic grounds'[76] was backed by the 'Declaration of the Rights of National Minorities', granted minorities far-reaching collective rights. The Supreme Council passed the Declaration on 1 November 1991, just a month before the referendum on independence, when the campaign to secure the support of all national groups for secession from the USSR was launched. In particular, the Declaration was designed to subdue any fears aroused by the CPU hard-liners' warnings of ethnic exclusion modelled on the Baltic republics. The Declaration reasserted the territorial principle of Ukraine's political community, stating that 'over 100 nationalities live on the territory of Ukraine, who together with ethnic Ukrainians make up the 52 million people of Ukraine (*narod Ukrainy*)'.[77] The Declaration promised far-reaching rights for minorities and emphasised the government's commitment to provide equality to all citizens of Ukraine, regardless of their nationality. In areas of dense settlement of a national minority it allowed for the language of that minority to function as a state language (art. 3).[78] It also explicitly permitted free use of the Russian language.

In 1991 profound ambiguity surrounded the iconographic symbols of Ukraine. The opposition promoted the trident and blue-and-yellow flag, as the legitimate symbols of the Ukrainian state, both of which—as was argued—had been used since 'time immortal' and were rooted in the tradition of Kyiv Rus', Cossack *Sich* and the UNR. These symbols were depicted throughout the Soviet period as symbols of bourgeois nationalism. In 1991 the proposal to restore these symbols by the *Narodna Rada* was not only rejected outright by the Politburo but also by part of the national communists. As there was no chance of obtaining the two-thirds majority in parliament, the issue of symbols was left out of the Concept and was to be decided by a constitutional referendum. Yet even without official endorsement, these symbols increasingly found their way into the public domain, especially in Western and Central Ukraine. After the referendum on independence, it became evident that the new state needed some form of iconographic representation. The new article 166 was added to the 1978 constitution stating that the 'symbols of Ukraine as an independent state are the state emblem, flag and anthem' without describing them. Then, the blue and yellow flag and the trident were approved in a resolution of the Supreme Council in January and February 1992. As they were approved by 253 and 264 votes, respectively, the symbols were introduced with a simple rather than constitutional majority, and hence were used by the state institutions without being legitimised by procedural legality.[79]

Overall, a pluralist, civic approach to the conception of a political community prevailed on the eve of independence. Calls for sovereignty were framed not in terms of ethnic rights of the titular majority, but economic efficiency, democratisation and rights of civil society. In that respect, in line with Brubaker's distinction, a political-territorial conception of nationhood prevailed on the eve of independence, as opposed to a personal-ethnic one (see chapter 2).[80] The limited constitutional debate on nationhood reflected the peaceful and harmonious character of interethnic relations in Ukraine, despite the Politburo's alarmist rhetoric. Even the opposition, despite its concern for the fate of Ukrainian culture and language, did not champion the rights of Ukrainians in ethnic terms. However, the 'national question' was anything but resolved. The questions of relations between the state and the titular nation, on the one hand, and the provisions for minorities on the other, turned out to be the pivotal and most divisive question in independent Ukraine.

CONCLUSION

Over 1990–1991 Ukraine witnessed an accelerated drive for sovereignty and then independence. Yet, even if by autumn 1991 Ukraine was engulfed in the 'all-out' campaign for independence, overwhelmingly supported in the referendum on 1 December, this fervour was not matched by systematic efforts to erect a solid constitutional foundation of the new state. This would require, first of all, the rooting out of the ideological and institutional pillars of the Soviet constitutional edifice. There was no evidence that there was a will for this to occur.

When the Union centre began to show signs of weakening and decay, the communist, republican elites were bequeathed with unprecedented freedom to pursue autonomy from the centre. The oppositional elite, who lacked strength to unseat the communists, as the March 1990 elections in Ukraine only dented rather than dismantled the hegemonic position of the CPU across Ukraine, played a role of 'allies of convenience' in this process. Yet the appreciation of the role of the elite-level alliance cannot paper over profound differences in motives, visions and ultimate goals. The anti-Moscow alliance was more of a coincidence than a meaningful convergence of goals pursued by the national communists and the democratic opposition. This was reflected in political discourses in Ukraine over 1990–1991, which conveyed a whole range of meanings of 'sovereignty', 'autonomy', and 'independence'. For the opposition 'sovereignty within the USSR' was far from an end in itself, but was a stepping-stone on the way to independent statehood, something that the national communists remained ambiguous about until the events of August 1991, which finally discredited the imprecise formula for Ukraine as a 'state within a state'. In this context, the significance of the Declaration of Independence in August 1991—as one author pointed out—lay in the fact that 'the [communist] majority officially declared its shift to the ideological position of the minority'.[81] But this new-found stance only applied to independence from Moscow and not to the internal ordering of the state.

Being focused on loosening and then severing relations with Moscow, the alliance did not extend to agreement in the domestic arena. For the opposition independence was a necessary pre-condition of far-reaching political and economic reforms, as well as cultural revival in Ukraine. However, the national communists, who emerged as the key, yet amorphous and unorganised political grouping, did not share this agenda, as was evidenced by their views on the new constitutional order discussed in the second section of this chapter. Taking into account that by June 1991 there were hardly any ideological constraints prevailing in the Soviet Union, the limited exploitation of this newly found liberty is only too evident. Even the 'socialist choice' (already dropped from the Russian draft constitution by 1991) was still preserved, along with the main pillars of the Soviet institutional framework. (The Ukrainian opposition found itself in the unhappy predicament of having to invoke the example of Russia—from which it wanted to separate Ukraine—in order to propagate internal reforms.) Because of the national communists' fixation with sovereignty, external radicalism was often extrapolated to the domestic situation, yet the analysis of the constitutional debate amply demonstrated the extent to which the national communists were reluctant to embark on reforms in the republic and limited the scope for political reforms to some changes justified by demands of sovereignty. And the major innovation—the presidency—was more of a functional arrangement for decision making against the centre, rather than a part of a radical overhaul of the existing institutional framework. At the same time, many national communists concentrated on changes affecting their immediate circumstances, and thus the secondary issue of elections of heads of *radas,* or status of village *radas* featured prominently in the debates. Numerous votes during the constitutional debates vividly reminded the opposition not only of the conservatism of their communist allies, but also of their own relative weakness, despite their strategic inroads on many issues. The alliance was not one of equal partners: the pro-reform forces were clearly in a minority.

The passage of the August 1991 'Act of Independence' by the elites, and its sanctioning in the December 1991 referendum on independence by the population at large, symbolised the rejection of the old order (negative legitimacy) of Ukraine being ruled by Moscow. Yet, as Beetham points out, negative legitimacy, in order to have a transforming potential, must be bolstered with 'the imagination to conceive of a different set of rules and relations for the fulfilment of basic social needs from the existing ones'.[82] Even if the old regime was discredited, this second condition was not fulfilled in Ukraine. There was no shared vision of an alternative order, which would be defined as superior and exemplary. In other words, there was no ubiquitous 'positive' inspiration to embark on change.

The opposition and the communist elites diverged diametrically in their evaluation of the communist and pre-communist past. The opposition's highly charged rhetoric on the Soviet occupation fell on deaf ears, as the national-communists refrained from condemning communism and reflecting on the origins of Soviet rule in Ukraine, which was illustrated by their continuous commitment to the 'socialist choice of the people of Ukraine'. The scope of any reform was ultimately determined by the strength of belief in the need for change. As Offe points out, 'the institutions to be replaced by the newly designed institutions must have been totally discredited (i.e. have failed in congruent socialisation) and must also have lost, perhaps partly due to de-legitimisation, their ability to cope with functional problems in their environment'.[83] And they do not require revision as long as they can 'pass a dual test of "making sense" and "being fit" for the mission'.[84] As the constitutional debates revealed, the Soviet institutional framework 'made sense' to the communist majority, including the national-communists. However, it was not 'fit' to secure sovereignty, which was best served by the presidency, which, thus, was *added* to the system. So while the opposition principally repudiated the Soviet legacy on moral grounds, the Soviet ideological and institutional model—anchored in the cognitive framework of the communist elites—provided a baseline for defining the constitutional framework of the 'sovereign' Ukraine. Other models played a subsidiary role. This resulted in the hybrid (presidential-soviet) institutional framework envisaged by the Concept of the new constitution and was followed by half-hearted and inconsistent institutional reform.

In the context of the continuity of elites, institutions and ideas, a 'thick' line could not be easily drawn between the Ukrainian SSR and independent Ukraine. Ukrainian independence could not be equated with a break from the past and the 'restoration of normality' through a 'return to Europe', the metaphor which encapsulated the transformation embarked on in East–Central Europe, including the Baltic states.[85] (There was an element of myth involved, of course, as the pre-communist inter-war period can in most cases hardly be classified as a 'golden past'.) There could be no 'restorative revolution' in Ukraine in

1991, because of the paucity of collective historical memories which treasured a vision of a 'golden past' and the template of a 'normal' social and political order. Without such cherished historical memories being widely shared, it was not possible (or necessary) to depict Soviet rule in Ukraine as an occupation. For the national communists, Soviet Ukraine was an integral and legitimate part of the state building process rather than a distortion and/or interruption of this process; it was the indigenous tradition of statehood. Therefore, the Preamble of the new Ukraine's constitution—the part of the constitution, which justifies changes to the constitutional order—was to be devoid of any emotion-laden condemnation of the communist regime, let alone any claims of oppression by a 'foreign' regime.

To this end, in the case of Ukraine the breakup of the Soviet Union was not precipitated by a new order, as the past could not provide a shared meaning of independence and a sense of direction for the future. While Ukrainian communist elites effectively signed the death sentence of the Soviet Union with their conversion to independence, the dilemma of defining of what was meant by a 'fresh start' in a new state was largely postponed to the post-Soviet era. In the protracted constitutional process extending over six years an eclectic conception of statehood was to be hammered out, which finally elaborated the meaning of independence.

NOTES

1 The comprehensive study of perestroika in Ukraine and the passage to independence is presented in Taras Kuzio and Andrew Wilson, *Ukraine: Perestroika to Independence* (London: Macmillan, 1994) and Bohdan Nahaylo, *The Ukrainian Resurgence* (London: C. Hust & Co, 1998).

2 The famine of 1933–1934 destroyed the Ukrainian peasantry, while the Stalinist purges of the 1930s and the 1940s decimated the ranks of the Ukrainian intelligentsia. See, for example, David R. Marples, *Stalinism in Ukraine in the 1940s* (London: Macmillan, 1986); Yurii Boshyk (ed.), *Ukraine during World War II: History and Its Aftermath* (Edmonton, Ont.: CIUS, 1986); Bohdan Krawchenko, *Social Change and National Consciousness in Twentieth-Century Ukraine* (Houndmills and London: Macmillan, 1985); J. E. Mace, 'Famine and Nationalism in Soviet Ukraine', *Problems of Communism,* Vol. 33, No. 3 (May–June 1984), pp. 37–50; Andrew Wilson, *Ukrainian Nationalism in the 1990s. A Minority Faith* (Cambridge: Cambridge University Press, 1997), pp. 114–5; Robert S. Sullivant, *Soviet Politics and the Ukraine 1917–1957* (New York: Columbia University Press, 1962); E. Mace, *Com-*

munism and the Dilemmas of National Liberation: National Communism in Soviet Ukraine, 1918–1933 (Cambridge, Mass.: Harvard University Press, 1983).

3 Bohdan Krawchenko, 'The Impact of Industralisation on the Social Structure of Ukraine', *Canadian Slavonic Papers*, Vol. 22, No. 3 (September 1980), pp. 338–57.

4 On the 1920s in Ukraine see, for example, George Liber, *Soviet Nationality Policy, Urban Growth and Identity Change in the Ukrainian SSR, 1923–1934* (Cambridge: Cambridge University Press, 1992).

5 Regional differences were not only eradicated but actually exacerbated. Western Ukraine was persistently depicted as a hotbed of Ukrainian nationalism, and thus portrayed as irreconcilably different from the rest of Soviet Ukraine, which had spent a much longer period under Tsarist and Soviet rule. Thus, opinion polls since independence have reflected these profound regional differences in world outlook. See, for example, Dominique Arel and Valeri Khmelko, 'The Russian Factor and Territorial Polarization in Ukraine', *The Harriman Review,* Vol. 9, Nos. 1–2 (Spring 1996), pp. 81–91.

6 According to the 1989 census, the biggest ethnic groups in Ukraine were: Ukrainians 37.4 million, Russians 11.4 million, Jewish 490,000, Belarussians 444,000, Moldovans 325,000, Bulgarian 234,000, Polish 219,000, Hungarian 160,000, Romanian 135,000, other 596,000 (total 51.5 million).

7 For a brief overview of Ukraine under the Soviet Union see Alexander J. Motyl and Bohdan Krawchenko, 'Ukraine: From Empire to Statehood', in Ian Bremmer and Ray Taras (eds.), *New States, New Politics: Building the Post-Soviet Nations* (Cambridge: Cambridge University Press, 1997), pp. 235–75. On the nation-building effect of the Soviet rule on ethnic groups in the USSR see Ronald Griogor Suny, *The Revenge of the Past: Nationalism, Revolution and the Collapse of the Soviet Union* (Stanford, California: Stanford University Press, 1993).

8 Instead of relying on 1989 census data, which appeared not to accurately reflect the use of Russian in Ukraine, Arel and Khmelko adopted the category 'language of convenience' in public opinion surveys in order to determine the size of the linguistic groups. The 'language of convenience' was defined as the language that respondents use in a survey interview at home when they are asked to use the language that they are most comfortable with. It was found that in eastern and southern Ukraine 81.5 percent of the population uses Russian as their language of convenience, that is the language, in which the people chose to communicate, even if they could understand or speak Ukrainian. See Arel and Khmelko, 'The Russian Factor and Territorial Polarization in Ukraine', p. 81.

9 For example, a hybrid Russian–Ukrainian (*surzhik*) is widely spoken within Kyiv. For a detailed discussion on identity in Southern and Eastern Ukraine see Paul S. Pirie, 'National Identity and Politics in Southern and Eastern Ukraine', *Europe–Asia Studies*, Vol. 48, No. 7 (November 1996), pp. 1079–104.

10 Kenneth C. Farmer, *Ukrainian Nationalism in the Post-Stalin Era: Myth, Symbols and Ideology in Soviet Nationalities Policy* (The Hague–Boston–London: Martinus Nijhoff Publishers, 1980).

11 Philip G. Roeder, 'Soviet Federalism and Ethnic Mobilization', *World Politics*, Vol. 43, No. 2 (January 1991), pp. 196–232.

12 Alexander J. Motyl, *Sovietology, Rationality, Nationality: Coming to Grips with Nationalism in the USSR* (New York: Columbia University Press, 1990).

13 T. Bottomore and P. Goode (eds.), *Austro–Marxism* (Oxford: Claredon, 1978). On the application of this concept to the Soviet republics see Motyl, *Sovietology, Rationality, Nationality.*

14 Jurij Borys, 'Political Parties in the Ukraine', in Hunchak (ed.), *The Ukraine, 1917–1921,* pp. 128–59.

15 On national communism in Ukraine see Wilson, *Ukrainian Nationalism in the 1990s,* chapter 4; Yaroslav Bilinsky, 'Mykola Skrypnyk and Petro Shelest: An Essay on The Persistence and Limits of Ukrainian National Communism', in *Soviet Nationality Policies and Practices* (1981), pp. 105–42; L. Tillet, 'Ukrainian Nationalism and the Fall of Shelest', *Slavic Review*, Vol. XXXIV, No. 4 (1975), pp. 752–68; and, a more restrained assessment, Grey Hodnett, 'The Views of Petro Shelest', *The Annals of the Ukrainian Academy of Arts and Sciences in the United States*, Vol. XIV, No. 37–38 (1978–1980), pp. 209–43. For a criticism of Soviet nationality policy in Ukraine by a prominent member of the Ukrainian cultural intelligentsia see Ivan Dzyuba, *Internationalism or Russification?* (London: Wiedenfeld and Nicholson, 1968).

16 On the role of Shcherbytsky in the highest echelon of Soviet political elites see Yaroslav Bilinsky, 'Shcherbytsky, Ukraine and Kremlin Politics', *Problems of Communism*, Vol. 32, No. 4 (July–August 1983), pp. 1–26.

17 John A. Amstrong, 'The Ethnic Scene in the Soviet Union: The View of the Dictatorship', in Eric Godhagen (ed.), *Ethnic Minorities in the Soviet Union* (New York: Praeger, 1968), pp. 14–21. See also John A. Amstrong, *Ideology, Politics and Government in the Soviet Union*, 3rd ed. (London: Nelson, 1974), pp. 176–80.

18 See, for example, Michael Brown, *Ferment in the Ukraine* (London and Basingstoke: Macmillan, 1971); L. Tillett, 'Ukrainian Nationalism and the Fall of Shelest', *Slavic Review*, Vol. 34, No. 4 (1975), pp. 752–68; Peter J. Potichnyj (ed.), *Ukraine in the 1970s* (Oakville, Ont: Mosaic Press, 1975). On the profile of the dissident movement see 'The Political Thought of Soviet Ukrainian Dissidents' in Ivan L. Rudnytsky, *Essays in Modern Ukrainian History* (Alberta: Canadian Institute of Ukrainian Studies, 1987), pp. 477–490, George S. N. Luckyi, 'Polarity in Ukrainian Intellectual Dissent', *Canadian Slavonic Papers*, Vol. 14, No. 2 (Summer 1972), pp. 269–79 and (during perestroika) Taras Kuzio (ed.), *Dissent in Ukraine under Gorbachev* (London: Ukrainian Press Agency, 1989).

19 On the situation in the early 1980s see Roman Solchanyk, 'Moulding the "Soviet People": The Role of Ukrainians and Belorussians', *RFE/RL Research Report*, No. 382 (9 November 1982).

20 85 percent of Rukh's members represented Western and Central Ukraine, 9 percent came from Southern Ukraine and 6 percent from the Eastern part of the republic. However, over 100 nationalities were represented at the First Congress. See David R. Marples, 'A Sociological Survey of Rukh', *Report on the USSR*, Vol. 2, No. 2 (1990), p. 19.

21 The main oppositional organisation Rukh was officially registered only in February 1990, just four weeks before the elections, what prevented it from campaigning under its own banner. In February a Central Committee Plenum in Moscow recommended the amendment of art.6 on the leading role on the CPSU, which was then legislated by Congress of People's Deputies in March.

22 Only 68 deputies were not CPU members in the 450-seat Rada. In terms of its Communist Party membership in newly elected Supreme Rada, Ukraine lagged only behind Central Asian republics and Azerbaidzhan. See Darrell Slider, 'Political Elites and Politics in the Republics', in David Lane (ed.), *Russia in Flux* (London: Edward Elgar, 1992), p. 43.

23 The *Narodna Rada* was the name of the first political organisation in Ukraine, which was created in 1885 in Lviv. The *Narodna Rada* then was incorporated into the Ukrainian National-Democratic Party in 1890, which had amongst its leaders a historian Mykhailo Hrushevskyi and, a distinguished poet and writer, Ivan Franko.

24 The *Narodna Rada*, despite its formalised status, was not consolidated in organisational and ideological terms and consisted of three internal factions: the most radical nationalistic flank, consisting mainly of members of the Ukrainian Republican Party, formed 'Independence' (*Nezalezhnist*), moderate members of the cultural intelligentsia gathered into the faction of the Democratic Party of Ukraine, while the Democratic Platform, which transformed itself into the Party of Democratic Revival of Ukraine made up the third faction.

25 David R. Marples, 'The Ukrainian Election Campaign: The Opposition', *Soviet Analyst*, Vol. 2 (9 March 1990) and 'The First Session of the Ukrainian Parliament', *Report on the USSR*, Vol. 2, No. 39 (28 September 1990), pp. 15–7.

26 In line with the Soviet tradition, people's deputies were merely delegated from their workplace and many of them combined two deputy mandates (as they sat on councils at different levels). Out of 449 deputies, only 129 worked full time, while the rest remained on 'part-time' basis. [*Biuletyn Verkhovnoi Rady Ukrainy* (Bulletin of the Supreme Council of Ukraine) (Third Session), 1991, No. 11, p. 37–8].

27 The *Narodna Rada*'s members headed 7 out of 23 commissions, while the hardliners controlled only 6.This overrepresentation of the *Rada*, which was the result of Ivashko's generosity, further added to the opposition's relative weight in the powerful Presidium. Wilson, *Ukrainian Nationalism in the 1990s*, p. 107.

28 The Ukrainian State Archive of Civic Associations (formerly the Archive of the Communist Party of Ukraine), FOND 1, OPYS 11, Delo. 2278, Stenographic transcript of the Meeting of Politburo on 2 July 1991, p. 14. By the spring of 1991 the CPU fully realised that it needed to boost its standing in the Supreme Council by sending more of the communist deputies to work on a professional basis. However, the Party still opposed the idea of a professional parliament on the basis that it would 'spend more time not only on laws but on politics' (*ibid.*).

29 Ivashko's untimely departure to Moscow further radicalised stances. It was interpreted in Ukraine as reflecting the supremacy of the All-Union posts in Moscow and belittled the republican ones. Thus, this career move, following a seemingly normal course of affairs in the Soviet Union, antagonised the Ukrainian Supreme Council, which at that very time began to assert its newly found importance as the highest republican institution. As Ivashko's departure coincided with the debates on the Declaration, it fuelled anti-Moscow sentiments.

30 For the English language translation of the Declaration see, Alexander Dallin and Gail W. Lapidus (eds.), *The Soviet System: From Crisis to Collapse*, Revised Edition (Boulder, San Francisco, Oxford: Westview Press, 1995), pp. 405–10.

31 In fact, the Declaration elaborated the law on economic sovereignty that was adopted two weeks prior to it, and created a legal basis for the organisation of the financial,

budgetary, credit, and monetary system of the state, and taking control over the economic enterprises, which until then were subordinated to All-Union ministries. The Declaration and the numerous laws adopted to implement it marked the growing segmentation of the Soviet economic space, that is moving from the 'uniform economy' to more independent economic policies.

32 The Communist Party of Ukraine remained torn between the need to boost its republican standing, now somewhat undermined by the opposition's rhetoric, and its loyalty to the Soviet centre and the principle of 'democratic centralism'. In contrast to the communist parties in the Baltic republics, the CPU refused to exit the Communist Party of the Soviet Union. Instead, the 27th Congress decided that the CPU as an autonomous organisation be registered by the republican Ministry of Justice, while at the same time remaining within the CPSU.

33 Students demanded: 1) the resignation of Vitalii Masol, chairman of the Council of Ministers, 2) a law stipulating that the military service would be performed in Ukraine, 3) the withdrawal from the negotiations on the Union Treaty, 4) nationalisation of Party property and 5) the holding of genuinely competitive new elections to the Supreme Rada. Also 8 radical deputies from the *Narodna Rada* joined the students. Roman Solchanyk, 'The Uncertain Road to Independence', *Report on the USSR*, Vol. 3 (4 January 1991), p. 22–24.

34 The members of the commission were predominantly state officials in Ukraine (86 percent) as 46 members were deputies of the Supreme Rada, 16 members worked in the executive branch, judiciary and *prokuratura* and 8 worked for other state agencies (the numbers do not add up as one person could combine several various posts). *Politychna Dumka*, No. 2, 1994, p. 214. Within the Commission, a smaller working group, consisting of 35 professionally qualified members, was created under the leadership of a distinguished academic, Professor Yuriy Yuz'kov. In practice, only 12–15 of them were directly involved in drafting. The Commission provided a general direction but never proposed ready-made articles to the working group.

35 CSAOCOU, FOND 1, OPYS 11, Delo 2316, p. 2.

36 Kravchuk had already loosened his links with the CPU. He was released of the position of Second Secretary of the CPU in September 1990, on the grounds that he needed to focus on the parliamentary chairmanship, which, in addition to other functions, involved representing Ukraine in external relations. Roman Solchanyk, 'The Changing Political Landscape in Ukraine', *Report on the USSR* (14 June 1991), pp. 21–22.

37 *Biuletyn Verkhovnoi Rady Ukrainy* (Third Session), 1991, No. 50, p. 35.

38 *Biuletyn Verkhovnoi Rady Ukrainy* (Third Session), 1991, No. 50, p. 32.

39 H. J. Berman, 'The Rule of Law and the Law-Based State (*Rechtsstaat*) (with special reference to development in the Soviet Union)', *The Harriman Institute Forum*, Vol. 4, No. 5 (1991), pp. 5–6.

40 This decision was partly due to popular pressure, as students threatened with another hunger strike, and partly to dissatisfaction with the content of the new draft Treaty. Although by June 1991 the draft of the Treaty envisaged a Union of Sovereign States, many central institutions, such as the presidency, Supreme Soviet, and Union ministries, were still preserved, which would necessarily limit the political and economic autonomy of Ukraine. Roman Solchanyk, 'Ukraine and the New Union Treaty', *Report on the USSR*, Vol. 3, No. 30 (26 July 1991), pp. 22–24.

41 Also, the parliamentary agenda for spring 1991 included laws on the structure of the Council of Ministers, relations between the Council of Ministers and the Council of Ministers of USSR, relations between the Council of Ministers and the Supreme Council (at that time the council of ministers was re-organised and it renamed the cabinet of ministers). These measures aimed to place the republican administrative institutions under the jurisdiction of the Ukrainian parliament rather than the Council of Ministers of the USSR. *Biuletyn Verkhovnoi Rady Ukrainy* (Third Session), 1991, No. 37, p. 23.

42 Art. 7 of the 'Law on the Creation of the President of the Ukrainian Soviet Socialist Republic and Changes to the Constitution of UkrSSR', which was published in *Pravda Ukrainy*, 1 August 1991.

43 'K voprosu ob uchrezdzeni posta prezydenta' (On the Question of the Presidency), *Archives of the Constitutional Commission*, Second Meeting, (4 December 1990).

44 But the CPU did not defect wholesale to the national cause. It was outlawed (30 August 1991), and its property nationalised (7 September). As by 1991, the CPU remained 'unconverted', and committed to 'democratic centralism', the party that was to re-emerge as its successor in 1993 would inherit a virtually unchanged ideological platform of Marxism–Leninism).

45 The last draft of the new Treaty was published in November 1991, which envisaged a looser confederation based on a Union parliament and the State Council as a central governmental body composed of the republican leaders. However, by this time the Ukrainian elites were not satisfied even by the centre's willingness to devolve far-reaching powers to the constituent subjects of the confederation.

46 Under the Soviet Union Western Ukraine was depicted as a hotbed of Ukrainian nationalism with fascist leanings, which were epitomised by the figure of the leader of the Organisation of Ukrainian Nationalist, Stepan Bandera.

47 Taras Kuzio, 'An Independent Ukraine—but Still Communist?', *Soviet Analyst* (28 August 1991), p. 1.

48 Bohdan Krawchenko, 'Ukraine: the Politics of Independence', in Ray Taras and Ian Bremmer (eds.), *Nations and Politics in the Soviet Successor States* (Cambridge: Cambridge University Press, 1993), p. 93.

49 The provisions for the political institutions were scanty in the Declaration. Apart from the Supreme Council, only two institutions were mentioned as key instruments in championing the cause of economic sovereignty, the National Bank and the *prokuratura*. Yet, the Declaration of Sovereignty unmistakably affirmed the Soviet institutional framework, as it re-stated the position of the Supreme Council, as envisaged by the 1978 constitution of the Ukrainian SSR. This allowed the defenders of the old order to use the Declaration in their struggle to preserve the system of soviets in Ukraine. Effectively, the Declaration turned into an obstacle to constitutional reform in Ukraine, and the reformers faced the task of justifying the bypassing of the Declaration's idiosyncrasies without undermining its symbolic significance.

50 Minutes of the second meeting of the Constitutional Commission, (4 December 1990), p. 2.

51 The upper chamber would consist of representatives of oblasts (each oblast would have 3 representatives). The draft concept of the Ukrainian Constitution as of March 1991 (in author's possession). The lower chamber was to be called *Narodna Palata*.

52 *Biuletyn Verkhovnoi Rady Ukrainy* (Third Session), 1991, No. 52, p. 10.

53 *Biuletyn Verkhovnoi Rady Ukrainy* (Third Session), 1991, No. 51, p. 75.
54 *Biuletyn Verkhovnoi Rady Ukrainy* (Third Session), 1991, No. 50, p. 39.
55 CSAOCOU, FOND 1, OPYS 11, Delo 2278, Stenographic transcript of the Meeting of the Politburo, 2 July 1991.
56 CSAOCOU, FOND 1, OPYS 11, Delo 2316, p. 133. Yet the CPU did not rule out the presidency altogether. It favoured a 'parliamentary system with an indirectly elected president', a system which, as argued, would 'combine the specific conditions and political traditions of Soviet Ukraine with the contemporary experience of foreign state–legal institutions'. The Party accepted that the presidency might perform some executive functions, but only under the condition that: 'granting the president with extraordinary powers and the right to interfere in the executive branch has to be seen only as a temporary measure, which parliament can adopt in extreme situations for a limited, clearly defined period'. CSAOCOU, FOND 1, OPYS 11, Delo 2314, pp. 3–4.
57 *Biuletyn Verkhovnoi Rady Ukrainy* (Third Session), 1991, No. 50, p. 45.
58 *Biuletyn Verkhovnoi Rady Ukrainy* (Third Session), 1991, No. 58, p. 35.
59 *Biuletyn Verkhovnoi Rady Ukrainy* (Third Session), 1991, No. 50, p. 39.
60 *Biuletyn Verkhovnoi Rady Ukrainy* (Third Session), 1991, No. 58, p. 41.
61 *Biuletyn Verkhovnoi Rady Ukrainy* (Third Session), 1991, No. 50, p. 19.
62 The imperative mandate was not abolished as 279 deputies voted in favour of its retention [*Biuletyn Verkhovnoi Rady Ukrainy* (Third Session), 1991, No. 58, p. 42].
63 The Minutes of the Third Meeting of the Constitutional Commission (14 February 1991), Archives of the Constitutional Commission, p. 12.
64 The law was published in *Pravda Ukrainy,* 1 August 1991. Curiously, the 'Law on the Creation of the President of the Ukrainian Soviet Socialist Republic and Changes to the Constitution of UkrSSR' was adopted at the same time and included presidential prerogatives, which did not appear in the 'Law on the Creation of the Institution of the President' itself.
65 *Biuletyn Verkhovnoi Rady Ukrainy* (Fourth Session), 1991, No. 10, pp. 4–49.
66 *Biuletyn Verkhovnoi Rady Ukrainy* (Third Session), 1991, No. 53, p. 48.
67 *Biuletyn Verkhovnoi Rady Ukrainy* (Third Session), 1991, No. 51, p. 55.
68 *Biuletyn Verkhovnoi Rady Ukrainy* (Third Session), 1991, No. 53, p. 79.
69 *Biuletyn Verkhovnoi Rady Ukrainy* (Third Session), 1991, No. 52, p. 33 and No. 53, p. 48.
70 *Biuletyn Verkhovnoi Rady Ukrainy* (Third Session), 1991, No. 50, p. 37.
71 *Biuletyn Verkhovnoi Rady Ukrainy* (Third Session), 1991, No. 37, p. 30.
72 The Concept of the constitution used 19 different names of the political community, such as the Ukrainian people, Ukrainian nation, citizens of Ukraine, citizens of the Republic. Volodymyr Butkevych, 'Proiekt Konstytutsii Ukrainy u Verkhovnii Radi (Drafts Constitutions in the Supreme Council)', *Nova Polityka*, No. 3(5) (May–June 1996), pp. 10–19.
73 For the full text of the law see: *Radianska Ukraina*, 3 November 1989.
74 See Dominique Arel, 'Language Politics in an Independent Ukraine: Towards One or Two State Languages', *Nationalities Papers*, Vol. 23, No. 3, (September 1995).
75 When the new 'Law on Citizenship' was drafted in September 1991, the issue of dual citizenship (with other post-Soviet republics states) was the main stumbling block in the passing of the law, as the national-democrats opposed this provision, while the

communists were divided on the issue. Without a prospect for agreement, a compromise was reached, whereby the law rested on the principle of sole citizenship but provided for the possibility of dual citizenship if corresponding bi-later agreements were made with other states. For the debates surrounding the passage of the law see *Biuletyn Verkhovnoi Rady Ukrainy* (Fourth Session), 1991, No. 7, pp. 30–96 (first reading) and No. 18, pp. 3–64 (second reading), the text of the 'Law on Citizenship' was published in *Pravda Ukrainy*, 10 October 1991.

76 Serkhiy Tolstov, 'Dimensions of Inter-ethnic Relations in Ukraine', *The Ukrainian Review*, Vol. XL, No. 2 (Summer 1993), p. 29.

77 For the texts of the 'Declaration of Nationalities' Rights' and the 'Law on National Minorities' see *Informatsiinyi Biuletyn*, No. 2 (June 1995), the Ministry for the Affairs of Nationalities, Migration and Cults.

78 Also, within administrative–territorial units, which were densely populated by members of several nationalities, a language acceptable to the population (i.e. Russian) was to be allowed to function at a level equal to the state language (art. 3) and the state authorities were to create 'conditions suitable for the development of all national languages and cultures' (art. 2).

79 *Biuletyn Verkhovnoi Rady Ukrainy* (Fifth Session), 1992, No. 2, p. 19 and *Ukrainian Reporter*, Vol. 2, No. 5, May 1992, p. 9. The law, which was supposed to properly define the form of symbols, never materialised, presumably because of controversy surrounding the issue.

80 Rogers Brubaker, *Nationalism Reframed* (Cambridge: Cambridge University Press, 1996). p. 41.

81 Valentyn Domoroslyi, 'Deklaratsiia pro Derzhavnyi Suverenitet Ukrainy: Vytoky i Naslidky (The Declaration of the State Sovereignty of Ukraine: the Origins and Consequences)', *Viche*, No. 51 (June 1996), p. 144.

82 Beetham, *The Legitimation of Power*, p. 109. See also Ágnes Heller, 'Phases of Legitimation in Soviet-type Societies', in T. H. Rigby and Ferenc Fehér (eds.), *Political Legitimation in Communist States* (London and Basingstoke: Macmillan, 1982), pp. 45–63.

83 Claus Offe, 'Designing Institutions for East European Transitions', in Jerzy Hausner, Bob Jessop, and Klaus Nielsen (eds.), *Strategic Choice and Path Dependency in Post-Socialism: Institutional Dynamics in the Transformation Process* (Aldershot: Edward Elgar, 1995), pp. 47–65.

84 *Ibid.*, p. 48.

85 Even if in the majority of East–Central European states the demise of communism was equated with the 'restoration of normality', which entailed the re-legitimisation of non-communist statehood traditions, the wholesale restoration of the pre-communist constitutional order proved impossible and/or undesirable. Apart from Latvia, which essentially restored its 1922 constitution, the 'restorative revolution' was confined to the symbolic sphere. It was most fully reflected in changes to the names of the state and institutions, symbols, state holidays and celebrations, rewriting of history, etc.

CHAPTER FOUR

SIMULATING REFORMS AMIDST CONSTITUTIONAL DISARRAY: UKRAINE UNDER KRAVCHUK'S PRESIDENCY

Despite the momentous demise of the USSR, the Ukrainian political landscape was hardly affected by independence; not only were no first democratic elections to the parliament announced, there was not even a change of prime minister or the government. The only innovation, albeit a major one, was the election of a president: the office went to a prominent member of the communist elites, Leonid Kravchuk. At the same time, constitutional reform became a matter of urgency not only for legitimising the new polity, but also in dealing with the pragmatic and urgent task of governing a newly sovereign state and coming to terms with the consequences of the breakup of the Soviet Union. Yet hardly any sense of urgency could be detected amongst the elite; a master plan for constitution making was missing. The unreformed agency, post-communist elites, having abandoned their commitment to socialism in the very final days of the Soviet Union, proved unable to show the way out of the growing constitutional chaos. The search for some kind of transitional institutional formula came to dominate the period after the 1991 presidential elections. The search became even more frantic as the economic collapse deepened in 1993. Yet, despite repeated tampering with the constitutional framework, the pre-independence dilemmas about the form of government were not resolved. As in Russia, the origins of the constitutional paralysis, which engulfed Ukraine in 1993, can be traced directly to the half-baked reforms of 1991, as a result of which the system of soviets was married to the popularly elected presidency.

While the former opposition, organisationally weak and divided on the issue of strategy, lacked the muscle to push the process forward, the communist majority in parliament lost any remaining cohesion. By early 1992 the pre-independence divisions dissolved and political blocs and groupings, however informal, fell into disarray; they could not provide lasting support for any particular configuration of actors and powers. Even if individual office holders exploited the ample opportunities to expand their institutional competencies under the banner of state building, they could not turn their temporary gains into permanent solutions. The constitutional process reached a blind alley by 1994.

The aim of this chapter is to examine the political interactions as a result of which Ukraine slid into a constitutional vacuum during the first years of independence. The first section sketches out the main ideological orientations in Ukraine, and the main political groupings, which represented them in order to highlight the essential volatility and confusion brought about by independence and abolition of the Communist Party of Ukraine. It is followed in the second section by an analysis of executive–legislative relations, which demonstrates how the key actors, the president, prime minister and chairman of parliament, failed in their attempts to re-assign powers to their own advantage on a more permanent basis under the banner of reforms and state building. Piecemeal institutional reforms were undertaken while the new constitution was being slowly drafted so that the two processes became intertwined. Hence, the third section traces the progress of drafting a 'proper' constitution and reveals the extent to which the content of the drafts closely reflected the interests of the incumbents.

THE POLITICAL SCENE AFTER INDEPENDENCE

The passage to independence was not followed by free, democratic elections. While the amorphous mass of former nomenklatura stayed at the helm of the new state, they avoided the test of a ballot box. The fledging political parties, which could not enter the political space on new terms, lingered on the fringe of politics, and, as a result, played a relatively modest role in constitutional reforms in 1992–1993. Despite the fact that the situation had changed radically since the semi-free elections in March 1990, political parties had no opportunity to contest the popularity of their ideological platforms.[1]

Nevertheless, in early 1992 the broad ideological orientations of post-Soviet Ukraine began to crystallise: the left, the national-democrats, and the liberal/socio-democratic centre. The latter two orientations emerged from the disintegrated *Narodna Rada*, which over 1990–1991 united various groupings in a broad platform of anti-communism, reforms and independence. After the passage of independence the all-embracing, democratic opposition was not sustainable, as the members of the opposition divided on the priorities of the new state, and the *Rada* disintegrated by January 1992 into centrist New Ukraine and the so-called national-democratic bloc.

However, in organisational terms those orientations were represented in a number of fluid, overlapping and fast changing factions, parties, alliances, and *ad hoc* initiatives. In particular, the Supreme Council still did not make much progress in transforming itself from a gathering of delegates of the amorphous *trudiashchykh mass* (working masses) to a structured parliament. It was populated by a plethora of fuzzy caucuses as the parliamentary rules allowed deputies to belong to two factions simultaneously.[2] The fluctuation and overlapping membership in factions does not make it possible to break parliament neatly down into factions, which would represent the three orientations.[3] It is estimated that out of 450 deputies, 244 (54 percent) were former communists with preservationist views on economic and political reform, 129 (29 percent) were national-democrats and only 77 (17 percent) were liberal/social-democratic centrists.[4] The remainder of this section will provide an overview of these three blocs in terms of their membership, organisational structures, strategies and ideologies.

THE NATIONAL-DEMOCRATS[5]

Even if during 1990–1991, the anti-communist opposition worked towards a split within the communist majority, the speed with which the national communists embraced the cause of independence and the subsequent demise of the USSR took the national-democrats by surprise. The swift passage to independence was organised by their former adversaries, who, as a result, retained their positions in the political and economic institutions of sovereign Ukraine. Thus, the national-democrats faced an unhappy predicament: either to assist the old ex-communist elites in consolidating independence or remain in the opposition, and try to dismantle the old regime by pushing for political and economic reforms. The question of strategy towards the former nomenklatura, in general and the concentration of power in the hands of the ex-communist president, in particular, threatened the unity of Rukh as the umbrella oppositionist movement.[6]

The presidential elections of December 1991 left the national-democratic bloc weakened and divided. By borrowing their pro-independence slogans in the electoral campaign, Kravchuk took the edge off their distinctive and easily identifiable agenda. Moreover, an internal rift developed within the bloc as several of its prominent members, Chornovil, Yukhnovskyi and Lukianenko, competed against each other in the presidential elections. Unable to agree on the support for Kravchuk, Rukh splintered in the summer 1992, when the Congress of National-Democratic Forces (CNDF) was created by the Ukrainian Republican Party (URP), the Democratic Party of Ukraine (DPU), and several smaller right-wing parties (also many individual members of Rukh joined it).[7] Overall, nationalism took the upper hand over anti-communism in the Congress as its platform was based on the premise that opposition to the popularly elected president would jeopardise independence and the acceptance of the need for a 'stronger hand' in order to strengthen the state.[8] In contrast, Rukh under the leadership of Chornovil declared 'constructive opposition' to Kravchuk, which meant support for presidential policies as long as they did not contradict Rukh's priorities, which, apart from the consolidation of statehood, included political and economic reforms. At the fourth congress in December 1992 Rukh finally transformed itself into a fully-fledged political party with 50,000 members.

Nevertheless, in spite of organisational divisions and divergence on strategies, the national-democrats shared the ideological platform, which included pro-Ukrainian language and cultural policies, market-oriented reforms, abolition of the system of soviets, anti-Russian/CIS foreign policy orientation, and integration with European institutions. However, cultural issues took priority over economic ones. While, because of the urgent desire to boost popular support for independence, their economic proposals remained vague and often bordered on populism, they concentrated heavily on promoting the state's security, and cultural and linguistic 'de-colonisation' of Ukraine. Their own numerical weakness forced them to rely on the ex-communists to pursue these goals. Similar to the CNDF, Rukh felt compelled to support Kravchuk or at least to curb its criticism of the president.[9] At the same time, Kravchuk courted the national-democrats and called for support for his efforts to build an independent state through unity in order to boost his own popularity. The national-democrats were given minor ministerial posts (for example, of education, culture, ecology), made presidential advisers, presidential representatives at the local level, and were allocated diplomatic postings. Despite being largely symbolic, their co-optation into governmental positions created the impression of the tightening alliance between the national-democrats and the former communists, which blurred the pre-independence divisions between the conservatives and reformers.

CENTRE

This orientation was mainly represented by the liberal alliance 'New Ukraine', which had its roots in the cosmopolitan, pragmatically oriented wing of the Democratic Platform of the CPU. The Platform had transformed itself into the Party of Democratic Revival of Ukraine in 1991, and became a collective member of the oppositional *Narodna Rada*. New Ukraine was created in January 1992 by liberal and social-democratic politicians and entrepreneurs, once it became evident that the *Narodna Rada* could not contain ideological diversity within its ranks. The alliance was headed by Volodymyr Filenko, and its members included Russophone Volodymyr Hryniov, industrialist Vasyl Yevtukhov and pro-market reformer Volodymyr Lanovyi.[10]

New Ukraine prioritised economic liberalisation and protection of political freedoms and opposed their subordination to the project of state building as advocated by Kravchuk. As the creation of the market economy was a precondition for democracy, New Ukraine supported market-oriented reforms including privatisation, anti-monopoly measures, price liberalisation, foreign investment, and a free system of trade and supply. Economic co-operation with Russia and the CIS was supported insofar as it assisted in economic recovery; thus, New Ukraine opposed the rushed secession of Ukraine from the rouble zone in 1992, before steps had been taken to build an independent financial system capable of serving the national needs. Because of Kravchuk's ambivalent economic policy and increasingly isolationist, anti-Russian stance, New Ukraine declared its opposition to the president in June 1992. New Ukraine's pre-occupation with economic issues meant that to a large degree it remained a one-issue alliance.

In parliament, the centrist bloc was the smallest; New Ukraine consisted of 56 deputies in February 1992, while the total number of centrist deputies was about 70–80. However, because of its high-profile membership in the otherwise amorphous and fluid political structures in parliament, New Ukraine emerged as one of the key factions, even if it lacked internal organisation and voting discipline (for example, before parliamentary votes it used to give only recommendations to its members). Despite its influence New Ukraine did not transform itself into a political party and remained a loose grouping of liberal politicians, directors of state enterprises and fledging business circles in Ukraine. This catch-all membership and weak grass roots weakened its cohesion and strength as a political actor. By the time it held its second congress in March 1993, New Ukraine had already lost much of its initial vitality, despite the fact that one of its members—Leonid Kuchma—served as prime minister. It briefly enjoyed a new lease of life when Kuchma emerged as the main competitor to president Kravchuk in the June/July 1994 presidential elections.

THE 'FORMER 239' AND THE LEFT

After the banning of the CPU in August 1991, the ideologically motivated leftist forces consolidated around Oleksandr Moroz—the leader of the Socialist Party of Ukraine, which was created in October 1991. The party managed to attract only a small number (60,000) of the 2,700,000 members of the CPU. Nevertheless, the SPU emerged as the biggest party in Ukraine (while Rukh was still a civic movement until December 1992). The party's leadership represented a progressive, Gorbachevite strand of the CPU and accepted political pluralism and the multi-party system as pillars of the new order. Party leaders such as Oleksandr Moroz, Ivan Chyzh and Borys Oliynyk attempted to revive the Ukrainian social-democratic traditions embodied in the early twentieth century parties, such as the Ukrainian Social-Democratic Workers Party and the Ukrainian Party of Social Revolutionaries, which had striven to simultaneously resolve the 'national' and 'social' questions. While accepting the results of the referendum on independence, the SPU emphasised the pivotal role of the Soviet period and its social achievements in the formation of an independent Ukraine, and opposed the exclusive prioritising of the national question over socio-economic issues. Condemning the transition to capitalism as well as the isolation of Ukraine from other post-Soviet states and the CIS, it called for the creation of a common economic space within the territory of the former USSR. However, the party's rank and file had a more hard-line profile, as the SPU sheltered many disoriented, orthodox communists from Southern, Eastern and Central Ukraine. Because of this catch-all membership, the party oscillated between social-democratic and communist positions. In parliament, the socialists accounted for 30–40 deputies. The socialists' main ally was the Peasant Party of Ukraine (SelPU), which was created in Kherson in January 1992 (with Serhiy Dovhan as a leader) on the basis of the Soviet Peasant Union. Its parliamentary faction consisted mainly of chairmen of collective farms, and as such acted as an agricultural lobby, while on other questions its views coincided with those of the SPU.

However, the SPU with its social-democratic leanings did not replace the Communist Party of Ukraine. After the latter was de-legalised and its property nationalised after the coup in August 1991 in a resolution of the presidium of the Supreme Council, the Left continued to argue the unconstitutionality of this decision. The issue of re-legalisation of the CPU simmered throughout 1992, and finally came back on the parliamentary agenda in the spring of 1993, despite the vehement protests of the national-democrats. The party re-emerged (although it had to register as a new party) as a successor to the unreformed, hard-line stance of the pre-independence Central Committee, and had not relinquished the Marxist–Leninist ideology: a centrally administered economy and the restoration of the Union of Sovereign Soviet States were all part of the manifesto. The re-legalisation of the CPU in June 1993 reshuffled the leftist bloc by strengthening its conservative wing. Many traditional communists (in particular pensioners and war veterans) returned to the fold of the CPU. Although the SPU proved more attractive to the intelligentsia, it was the orthodox CPU that emerged by far the biggest party in Ukraine on the eve of 1994 elections.[11]

Even if the CPU as an organisation collapsed, the organisational disarray did not prevent the former communists from shaping the political developments of Ukraine, as by that time the higher echelons of CPU apparatchiks had *en masse* entered the state and economic structures. The communist 'group of 239', although it was often referred to as a parliamentary majority before independence, was never formalised. After August 1991, only the remnants of the 'group of 239' joined the left-wing parties, while the bulk of the central and regional bureaucrats, former party officials and economic nomenklatura (accounting for over half of all deputies in parliament) eschewed party membership and lingered unaffiliated. As argued in chapter 3, while overwhelmingly standing on the platform of independence, they had no ideological convictions on the future path Ukraine should take, and seemed predominantly pre-occupied with their immediate pursuits. Their influential positions and opportunistic attitudes earned them the nickname of the 'party of power'. The non-affiliated, ex-communist deputies consistently opposed holding pre-term elections to parliament, something Rukh and New Ukraine repeatedly called for. Although those deputies were not organised in a faction, the group retained some cohesion; when someone from their rank, Leonid Pliushch, was to replace Kravchuk as the chairman of the Supreme Council on the recommendation of the newly elected president, 261 deputies voted for Pliushch.[12] Overall, they backed the presidency, although their loyalty waned in the course of 1993, when Kravchuk's presidency hit the rocks.

EXECUTIVE–LEGISLATIVE RELATIONS: FROM IMPASSE TO CRISIS

Having surveyed the key ideological orientations, none of which was numerous and consolidated enough to set Ukraine on the path of constitutional reform, this section will examine the executive–legislative relations over 1992–1994. The period between the referendum on independence and the first free elections was characterised by a frantic search for a form of government capable of counteracting the economic decline. In this search three key stages can be distinguished: the first was marked by the growth in prominence of the president, the second was characterised by the strengthening of the prime minister, and the final one by the descent into a political crisis. Despite the urgency created by the worsening economic situation, the search for a quick fix solution to the institutional paralysis not only proved futile, but also interfered with, and hampered, the process of drafting the new constitution.

THE AGGRANDISEMENT OF THE PRESIDENCY

The formal affirmation of independence in the referendum on 1 December followed by the Belovezha Agreement prompted Kravchuk's calls for an immediate revision of the institutional framework. Having emerged as the key political figure, Kravchuk was well positioned to claim more institutional power. In December, he won a popular mandate, which made his standing stronger *vis-à-vis* the Supreme Council, as the latter had been elected in the semi-free elections in 1990, and, thus, lacked democratic credentials. Moreover, Kravchuk came first in the elections way ahead of any other candidate, as the three national-democratic candidates together won 31 percent of votes in comparison to Kravchuk's hefty 61 per cent. As argued in chapter 3, the presidency had essentially been designed as a buffer against Moscow and its powers in the domestic context were left ill defined and vague in the sketchy 'Law on the Presidency' (adopted in July 1991). Despite being named 'chief executive', the presidency hardly had any 'teeth', as the little executive powers it was granted were not backed by an effective mechanism to exercise them. To a large extent, this design reflected the concerns of the hard-line communists in 1991 that the popular legitimacy of the presidency could become a basis for an alternative to the parliament's monopoly of power.

To overcome this limitation, Kravchuk embarked on a rapid extension of presidential power along horizontal and vertical axes. In February 1992 he proposed a strengthening of the presidency on the grounds that 'without a strong executive branch, it would not be possible to implement economic and political reforms'.[13] Overall, Kravchuk did not encounter heavy opposition, as the Supreme Council acquiesced in the president taking direct control over the stabilisation and reform of the economy during the turbulent early days of independence for a lack of a better alternative. After scaling down some of the presidential powers proposed by Kravchuk (such as, for example, the right to appoint all judges of the Constitutional Court), parliament proceeded to adopt constitutional changes by a constitutional (two thirds) majority in February 1992.

According to the revised 1978 constitution, the president was made responsible for 'defending the rights and freedoms of citizens, the state sovereignty of Ukraine and implementation of the Constitution and laws of Ukraine' (art. 14-5.1) and was named the Commander-in-Chief of the Armed Forces (art. 114.5-2.1).[14] He was given new rights to 'lead and direct' the activities of the cabinet of ministers of Ukraine, to re-organise administrative structures and set up consultative bodies (art. 114.5-7.1), to issue decrees on economic matters (having the force of law, if they were not regulated by existing laws) (art. 114.5-6), to appoint and dismiss ministers and senior officials (although in the case of seven key ministries and committees the approval of parliament was still necessary), to propose the state budget in parliament and report on its implementation (art. 114.5-4.1). The president was also required to outline his policies to parliament in an annual report (art. 114.5-5). Despite obtaining new powers to create and reform the executive branch, the president did not gain any leverage against the Supreme Council. He was denied the right to dissolve parliament and call for new elections.[15] The parliament retained its right to override a presidential veto by a simple majority and the prime minister could only be dismissed by the president with parliamentary consent.

The constitutional amendments of February 1992 turned the president into a chief executive, yet his powers were confined to the centre. At the local level the soviets and their executive committees (*vykonkomy*), which united both state and self-governing functions remained the institutional backbone of the state after the demise of the CPU. Their inability to assume the self-governing functions and the perceived lack of control over the regional and local level fuelled demands for 'reinstating authority at the local level' and 'to increase the role and responsibility of the state in overcoming the crisis'.[16] Thus, the institution of presidential representatives (*predstavnyky*), which was envisaged by the Concept of the New Constitution but then dropped from the 'Law on the Presidency' (see chapter 3), came back to the agenda. Kravchuk argued that *predstavnyky* were to act as a transmission belt for reform from the centre to localities and to prompt local soviets to 'stand up to the conditions of independence'.[17] All political groupings—ranging from the Socialist Party of Ukraine, New Ukraine and the majority of national-democrats—supported this innovation.[18] After relatively minor changes to Kravchuk's draft, on 5 March 1992 the 'Law on the President's Representatives' was adopted by the Supreme Council with 280 votes in favour.[19] The law granted the president the right to appoint his representatives as heads of the local state administration, which were 'the highest body in the state executive structures' in oblasts and districts, and in Kyiv and Sevastopol (art. 1), and who were nominated for the presidential term (art. 2). Representatives' powers could be divided into two spheres: as the executive arm of local councils and as the agent of the centre in oblast and regions. Firstly, they were to implement local budgets and the programme of socio-economic development of the territory adopted by oblast and local councils (art. 6). Secondly, they were responsible for overseeing the implementation of laws, presidential decrees and resolutions of central state organs (such as ministries) by local self-government (art. 7). Also, the presidential representatives could suspend office holders, and challenge in court the decisions of local self-governing bodies, if they violated the law and the constitution (art. 12). Their decisions were binding in the respective oblast/regions for local administration, industry, organisations and institutions, and civic associations (art. 14). Presidential representatives were accountable upwards to the higher-level representatives and the president, and could only be recalled by the latter (art. 2). Also, the president could grant them additional powers in an emergency (art. 15).[20] The law created a unitary vertical executive structure, which was to co-exist with the local *radas* that were grossly emasculated and limited to mostly representative functions.

By the spring of 1992 Kravchuk had accumulated extensive executive powers. The Ukrainian presidency as defined in early 1992 encompassed four major prerogatives: to lead the activities of the cabinet (although parliament retained some appointive powers); to restructure the executive branch; to issue decrees with the power of law on economic issues, and to appoint state representatives at the local level. As Kravchuk's pursuit of more powers was indistinguishable from measures to secure independence and counteract the institutional inefficiency, the changes in the constitutional framework encountered hardly any concerted opposition. Therefore, in early 1992 Ukraine followed a pattern common across post-Soviet states, whereby the presidents were granted more authority on the grounds that this was indispensable for the consolidation of statehood. However, in contrast to other post-Soviet states, in the case of Ukraine the incumbent refrained from using the formal powers granted to the presidency.

KRAVCHUK AS THE CHIEF EXECUTIVE

Initially, Kravchuk set to use his constitutional powers to reform the executive arm of the state. By a presidential decree a State Council (*Duma*) was created in February 1992. The Council was conceived as a taskforce to establish the main directions for internal and international policy and to co-ordinate activities of executive agencies of the state.[21] Other *ad hoc* bodies proliferated (such as the Security Council and a special taskforce to oversee economic reforms), the creation of which was part of Kravchuk's declared agenda to strengthen the executive capacity of the state.

Kravchuk's reforms, however, provoked an immediate backlash. In particular, the former communists feared that the extra-constitutional

Duma—staffed by the national-democrats—had shifted decision making beyond the cabinet of ministers. They argued that:

> The creation of yet another high executive body will destroy the cabinet of ministers, which is accountable and subordinated (*vidpovidalnyi* and *pidzvitnyi*) to the Supreme Council, whereas the *Duma* takes over the function of the cabinet of ministers, and yet is accountable only to the president.[22]

Thus, the Supreme Council scrutinised the presidential decrees and debated whether the president had exceeded his constitutional rights.[23] Parliament re-asserted its exclusive constitutional powers to determine both the institutional infrastructure of the state (art. 80 of the revised 1978 constitution) and the general direction of policy making (art. 97). Even if the pro-reform lobby, the national-democrats and the New Ukraine, remained supportive of the presidential initiatives, the debates in parliament vividly reminded Kravchuk of the limits of his powers and volatility of parliament, which granted him the powers.

By the summer 1992, Kravchuk's focus drifted away from domestic affairs, as he began to closely co-ordinate foreign and military affairs, seeing the promotion of Ukraine on the international arena as a precondition for safeguarding Ukrainian independence. The far-reaching institutional reform announced by Kravchuk remained largely unrealised, apart from a half-hearted reshuffle of central administrative institutions in February and March 1992. The potentially influential State Council (*Duma*) was abolished at the end of 1992. Kravchuk also rejected calls from Rukh and New Ukraine for new parliamentary elections and for more active use of his powers at the local level. Presidential activity in the legislative arena dried up after the first few months.[24] When the reformers in parliament suggested that Kravchuk should take direct charge of the government, he stated that he 'will not act like Boris Yeltsin and, apart from being the head of state, he will not perform the function of the head of the government'. In Kravchuk's view, the president 'should construct the state while the economy should be the domain of the government'.[25]

Throughout 1992, in spite of the popular expectations of economic prosperity in independent Ukraine, the country's economy entered into a free fall. The heavy regulation of the economy, extremely soft and accommodative macroeconomic policy and the impact of external shocks fuelled inflation and caused a drastic worsening of all economic indicators.[26] Under such circumstances, the pro-reform forces (Rukh, 'New Ukraine' and even the pro-presidential CNDF) closed their ranks on the necessity to remove the Fokin government in June 1992, and proposed a vote of no confidence in the cabinet. The president, however, defended Fokin. The reformist forces succeeded in ousting Fokin in September 1992, and Kravchuk fulfilled his presidential duty by proposing a candidate for premiership—the little known Leonid Kuchma, a director of *Yuzhmash*, the biggest missile factory in the world in Dnepropetrovsk who, as a non-controversial, technocratic candidate, was swiftly approved by parliament. Being closely linked with the League of Ukrainian Industrialist and Entrepreneurs and 'New Ukraine', Kuchma was a representative of the so-called industrial lobby in parliament, who favoured an 'evolutionary', 'specifically Ukrainian' path towards a market economy. Kravchuk left the task of appointing the ministers and reforming the structures of the cabinet to Kuchma. Kravchuk's consent to Kuchma's ministerial appointments and plans to reform the cabinet hallmarked the president's tacit agreement to disengage from the direct leadership of the executive branch, several months after claiming executive powers.

In 1992, the presidential sphere of authority remained profoundly unsettled. The president as the head of state and chief executive could direct both the cabinet of ministers and the state administration at the local level. However, without a new constitution, the powers of the presidency were fluid, ill defined, and ultimately depended on parliament, which had the exclusive right to interpret and change the 1978 constitution. Striving to rise above politics as a non-partisan founder of the state, Kravchuk did not join or create any party in an attempt to widen his power base. This strategy, however, taking into account the polarised and fragmented nature of the Ukrainian political spectrum, resulted in chronic vacillation between various political agendas. As Wilson points out Kravchuk was elected in December 1991 by the same electorate that voted for the preservation of the USSR in March 1990 and the outlook of the unorganised ex-communist majority in parliament and the president coincided.[27] To placate this element, Kravchuk backed preservationist economic policies. He also tried to seduce the national-democrats by bringing some of them into the key positions. Yet the president lacked a consolidated power base in parliament. Out of 450 deputies, nearly half were conservatives, national-democrats had around one third of all seats, and only 77 (17 percent) were centrists;[28] none of them was strong enough to support him nor could he command their support on all issues. The fact that the boundaries of the presidential sphere of competence remained ambiguous allowed various political groups in parliament to bring the issue of presidential prerogatives back onto agenda, and summon the president whenever his policies infringed on their interests. Ultimately, the president's powers and policies depended on a vacillating majority in parliament, which necessitated building fragile coalitions on each issue. Despite securing an array of executive powers, Kravchuk eschewed using them in order not to estrange any element in his wide yet precarious coalition of support.

THE RISE OF THE PRIME MINISTER

The new prime minister, Leonid Kuchma, proved eager to take over responsibility for the executive branch, and despite the problem of garnering support in the Supreme Council for his cabinet in October 1992, he succeeded in the first overhaul of government in independent Ukraine. He quickly gained clout with his blunt and—as was seen by deputies—realistic assessment of the state of the economy: 'our state is bankrupt'.[29] On the grounds that 'critical focus of state building has moved to the economic issues',[30] Kuchma secured for his cabinet emergency law making powers for six months (until May 1993). The government was given the right to issue decrees on practically all economic matters, except the budget, while the presidential right to do so was simultaneously suspended. In sum, in November 1992 the prime minister undermined the powers of the president as chief executive. One of the key presidential prerogatives—the right to issue decrees with the force of law—was transferred from the president to the cabinet.

However, once again the *ad hoc* redistribution of powers failed to provide a solution to the crisis of ungovernability. Despite having been equipped with decree-making powers, the government failed to rescue the economy.[31] Not only was the decline of the GDP not halted but inflation grew into hyperinflation by June 1993. Kuchma blamed the Supreme Council and the president. Indeed, Kravchuk refused to dismiss his presidential representatives who, according to prime minister, obstructed economic reforms at the local level.[32] Also, parliament did not relinquish its constitutional prerogatives to issue resolutions on the economy, often in contradiction to the government's policy.

A STALEMATE

While the economic imbroglio deepened, the extraordinary powers of the cabinet of ministers expired on 17 May 1993, and the issue thus again appeared on the parliamentary agenda. Arguing that a minimum period of two years should be allowed for economic stabilisation, Kuchma proposed not only the extension of decree-making powers, but also demanded additional authority.[33] The president's role was to be confined to outwardly directed representative and symbolic functions. Kuchma argued that the economy was the key to the consolidation of the Ukrainian state, and his remarks such as 'a flag, anthem and emblem, this is not yet statehood' ridiculed Kravchuk's fixation with symbolic attributes of independence.[34]

However, wary of Kuchma's growing appetite for authority and his own waning popularity, Kravchuk decided to re-establish his tarnished position as that of an active chief executive and even outlined a proposal to abolish the post of prime minister and to create a presidential council, which would replace the cabinet.[35]

There was no way out of the stalemate between Kravchuk and Kuchma. Even though in response to Kravchuk's proposal Kuchma backed off, and filed his resignation, parliament could not come up with a solution for the stand-off. It refused to extend extraordinary powers to the government, yet 223 deputies voted against releasing Kuchma from the premiership. At the same time only 90 deputies voted in favour of Kravchuk's draft law, which would allow the president to take over direct control of the cabinet. In mid-1993, the president and prime minister clashed in their attempts to become the sole heads of the executive branch. This was a result of the half-hearted incorporation of elements of the presidential system, which posed the vexed question of the division of powers between the two constituent parts of the executive branch. As Kuchma persisted in securing more decision making powers, Kravchuk attempted to restore his damaged authority. The unstructured parliament emerged as an arbiter in the intra-executive tussle, which presaged the deepening constitutional crisis in Ukraine in the second year of independence.

The impasse unfolded into a full-blown crisis. Triggered by consumer price rises, in June 1993, a miners' strike broke out in Donbas. By putting forward an overtly political platform, as well as making economic demands, the strike threatened further political destabilisation in Ukraine. The strike leaders (in close alliance with the regional state apparatus) demanded, apart from political autonomy for Donbas, referenda on confidence in parliament and the president. In order to deal with economic demands, Kravchuk brought the Mayor of Donetsk, Efim Zhviagilsky, to Kyiv to take up the influential post of first deputy prime minister. While the issue of autonomy moved onto the back-burner, the striking miners demanded a special session of parliament, which convened on 14–16 June. The debates fully unveiled the scale of paralysis at the centre. Parliament engaged in mutual recriminations; all main parties and factions declared themselves to be in opposition to each other and to the executive branch. Both the right- and left-wing accused the government of implementing the policies of their adversaries. At that time, Kravchuk once again hesitantly attempted to combine the presidency with the premiership by issuing a decree in which he allocated prime minister Kuchma the role of head of the Special Economic Commission, while he would be in charge of the 'power ministries' (interior, justice and security).[36]

Over the summer 1993 little was done to make the referendum happen, something which reflected both the president's and the parliamentarians' reluctance to undergo a test of popular support.[37] Instead, in September parliament resolved on pre-term parliamentary and presidential elections. The elections, scheduled for the autumns of 1994 and 1995, respectively, were brought forward to March and June 1994. Parliament's decision was undoubtedly prompted by Yeltsin's dissolution of the Russian parliament on 21 September 1993. Aware of its critically low popularity in society, the Supreme Council feared that the result of the referendum would not be favourable, so that the pre-term elections would have to follow anyway.

Nevertheless, the impasse between the branches of power continued. Shortly after Kuchma finally resigned in September 1993, Kravchuk issued a decree in which he subordinated government to the president, suspended the post of prime minister, and appointed a caretaker government with Efim Zhviagilskyi as acting prime minister until the spring 1994 elections. Having had second thoughts about the pre-term elections, Kravchuk began to put pressure on the Supreme Council to rescind its September 1993 resolution. However, parliament scorned pleas and even some threats by Kravchuk and pressed ahead with the presidential elections in June/July 1994 (see chapter 5).

Undoubtedly, the chairman of the Supreme Council, a prominent member of the national-communist nomenklatura and former colleague of Kravchuk, Leonid Pliushch, who was aiming at the presidential office, played a role in the unbending of parliament. Pliushch set about circumventing Kravchuk's powers by dismantling the presidential executive structure in the regions. Having developed presidential ambitions, Pliushch had a vested interest in preserving the structure of the soviets in order to use them as a vehicle for the presidency. With the support of the rejuvenated Left in parliament (see above), Pliushch mastered a growing coalition for the re-endowment of the soviets with executive authority, claiming that being highly democratic 'the system of soviets has to be given a chance'.[38] Thus, the presidential representatives were first weakened by parliament's measures (for example, by making the approval of a candidate by the local *radas* obligatory) and then the 'Law on Elections to Local Councils' adopted in February 1994 envisaged their abolition after the June 1994 local elections (which were held together with the first round of presidential elections).[39]

The first two years after Ukrainian independence witnessed a frantic search for quick fix solutions to the institutional disarray. By autumn of 1993, the collapsing economy and political stalemate forced the elites to resort to the ballot box as a way out of the crisis. The drafting of the fully-fledged constitution became caught in the same tug-of-war between the key members of the elites, and the content of the drafts mirrored the changing political fortunes of the main office holders. In contrast to the intra-executive conflict between president Kravchuk and prime minister Kuchma, constitution-drafting became a battlefield between Kravchuk and Pliushch.

CONSTITUTION DRAFTING, 1992–1993

Apart from its leadership, the composition of the Constitutional Commission hardly changed between 1990–1994. When its chairman Kravchuk was elected president, he proposed that the chairman of parliament Pliushch be co-opted as his deputy in order to make the Commission more representative. However, as the Constitutional Commission was a parliamentary commission, the Supreme Council insisted on Pliushch becoming chairman. A compromise emerged when Pliushch was appointed co-chairman with Kravchuk in April 1992. This leadership of the Commission to a large extent determined the form of government envisaged in the consecutive drafts, irrespective of the agreed provisions of the 1991 Concept. Initially, it was Kravchuk who was well positioned to turn the aggrandisement of the presidency in early

1992 into a pillar of the new constitutional edifice, whereas in 1993 Pliushch took over the initiative.

The first fully-fledged draft was published in June 1992, a year after the Concept of the new Constitution was approved in the Supreme Council. In terms of the form of government, the draft envisaged a presidential system. The wide-ranging powers granted to the president in the spring 1992 were not only copied in the constitutional draft, they were widened even further. The cabinet, for example, was to be 'subordinated to the president, accountable to him and in its activities guided by his programme and decisions', while the prime minister was defined as 'a deputy of the president' (art. 190). The issue of bi-cameralism, first raised in 1991, re-emerged on the agenda, but no agreement was reached. Thus two versions—one with a uni- and the other a bi-cameral legislature—were prepared (despite the fact that the Concept envisaged a uni-cameral parliament). According to the bi-cameral version, the legislature (*Natsionalni Zbory*) would consist of a *Rada Deputativ* (lower chamber) and *Rada Posliv* (upper chamber); the latter would consist of 5 representatives of each oblast.

The draft proposed a centralised model of the state, and stressed the territorial integrity of Ukraine, which was defined as a 'single (*yedyna)*, indivisible (*nepodilna*), inviolable (*nedotorkana*), and integrated (*tsilisna*) state' (art. 7). However, a major breakthrough was made as the system of soviets was finally abandoned. Despite the fact that the system of soviets (*radas*) was retained in the Concept, the 1992 draft envisaged a 'de-statisation' of the *radas*, that is they were only to embody self-governing functions, whereas 'state powers' would be performed by presidential representatives. Representatives at the oblast and *raion* level were to be appointed by the president from a list proposed by respective councils. The draft left the issue of the form of elections—whether direct or indirect—to councils at the oblast and *raion* level indeterminate (there were two variants in art. 228). Thereby the role of oblast and *raion* remained unclear. Self-government was explicitly guaranteed only at the community level (cities and villages). The Crimean Republic was defined as a state-territorial organisation of power and self-government of the population of Crimea (art. 110). However, because of the ongoing confrontation between Kyiv and Simferopol, its powers were not outlined in the constitution.

While the 1992 draft followed many proposals of the working group in 1991 (see chapter 3), the chapters on the form of government were specifically written with Kravchuk in mind. Yet the incumbent did not seek quick ratification of the constitution, perhaps realising the difficulties in mastering a constitutional majority for such a pro-presidential constitution in the Supreme Council where he lacked a stable powerbase. Public discussion and consultations on the draft took place in the second half of 1992, at a time when Kravchuk's authority began to wither away. Following the consultations a revised draft of the new constitution was ready in July 1993, debated in parliament on 5–8 September and finalised by the end of October 1993. By that time, Ukraine was engulfed in the political crisis and new constitution was anything but priority.

The October draft reflected the changed distribution of power: a weaker president and stronger chairman of parliament. The weakening of the presidency in the 1993 draft reflected not only the elites' reduced trust in Kravchuk's leadership skills, but also the presidential ambitions of the chairman of the Supreme Council, Leonid Pliushch. The latter utilised his position as a co-head of the Constitutional Commission to circumvent Kravchuk's powers and eliminate the main pretender to the presidential office in the 1994 presidential elections. The draft endorsed the superiority of the uni-cameral legislature (the name *Verkhovna Rada* was preserved). It was the only institution authorised to represent the people, with powers to decide on any issue that was not defined in the constitution as lying exclusively in the competencies of other state or self-governing institutions. The executive functions were concentrated in the hands of the cabinet of ministers, which was defined as a 'higher body of executive power' (presumably parliament was 'the highest').[40] The role of the directly elected president was defined as that of 'head of state' and confined to representative functions, especially in external relations. The cabinet was to carry out the programme of the president, but be accountable to the Supreme Council. Presidential law making powers were circumvented: decrees, which he had the right to issue, were defined as lower than laws (*pidzakonni*). The vertical structure of presidential representatives was abolished in the draft. The only major prerogative of the president was the right to veto laws, which could be overridden by a two-thirds majority. The draft put a heavy stress on the instruments of direct democracy (*narodovladia*), such as referenda, consultations, and people's right to propose laws. Even if the draft retreated from the presidential form government, it did not quite go back to the soviet system. The territorial division of power in the draft was a hybrid containing elements of the system of soviet and self-government. Oblast councils would embody both functions of territorial autonomy, which their executive committees were defined as 'bodies of state power'.

Despite publication of the October draft, the constitution-making process ground to a halt when it became evident that there was no possibility of adopting a new constitution before the 1994 elections, because of the prevailing disarray in the Supreme Council. After October 1993, the Supreme Council did not resume debates on the draft constitution. The last meeting of the Constitutional Commission in January 1994, to which also heads of oblast councils, presidential representatives, and representatives of political parties were invited, amounted to a last desperate attempt to find a way to pass the constitution. Whilst a constitutional conference, constitutional assembly, and a referendum were being considered, the total lack of direction for the constitutional process became only too evident. Kravchuk undoubtedly added to the confusion when he tabled the 'Law on Power' for the consideration of the Constitutional Commission, as a temporary solution to the constitutional crisis. The law was to reinstate his lapsed authority. By that time the Commission members were even unclear as to what was the purpose of the meeting and subject of the debate.

In sum, over 1992–1993, co-headed by Kravchuk and Pliushch, the Constitutional Commission proved itself unable to rise above the agenda of its co-chairmen. The constitutional lawyers ended up rewriting the constitutional draft to suit the aspirations of the power holders. With the key actors driven by narrowly defined self-interest, there was not much chance to re-think and elaborate on the broad principles of the new constitutional order. While pre-term elections were opted for in order to defuse the political stalemate in Ukraine, the 1993 draft constitution was put onto the backburner, and effectively forgotten, especially as it did not suit the new president. When in 1994 the process was re-launched it started virtually from scratch.

CONCLUSION

It has been widely noted that in post-communist countries, when the old political regimes crumbled, the political actors, such as individuals and political parties, were provided with a unique opportunity to mould the institutional framework to their own advantage. Yet such actions do not necessarily lead to lasting changes to the institutional structure. The case of Ukraine exemplifies a situation whereby actors fail to engineer the institutional outcomes by mutually 'neutralising' each other, despite their repeated attempts.

While the vast majority of post-communist states had already passed their new constitutions, in Ukraine institutional reform reached a dead end after a prolonged search for quick-fix solutions without a determined attempt to adopt a new constitution. This path of constitutional reform was a direct consequence of the mode of Ukraine's extrication from communism and the Soviet Union. Because of the abolition of the CPU in the aftermath of the August 1991 coup, the political class of communists—unlikely architects of a new order—came out unscathed from the turmoil of the collapse of the USSR, and found itself at the helm of a new state. Although the national-democratic forces campaigned for the 'de-communisation' of Ukraine through lustration modelled on states such as the Czech Republic, the issue of limiting the political rights of former communists has never seriously entered the political debate. Moreover, even if in 1991 the counter-elite advocated independence and extensive reforms as a package, independence 'tied their hands'. The tensions surrounding the Black Sea Fleet and denuclearisation fuelled the perception that both Russia and the West treated Ukrainian sovereignty as a temporary phenomenon, while Crimean separatism vividly demonstrated the fragility of the new state under the pressure of centrifugal forces. Under the circumstances, in what Wilson refers to as a 'Grand Bargain',[41] many national-democrats backed the former communists in their efforts to secure independence, rather than remaining in the opposition and exposing the misdeeds of their former adversaries. In any case, the former opposition could hardly act as an agent of reform, not only because its conflicting priorities, but also because of its relative numerical weakness.

As the members of the Soviet nomenklatura, who largely abstained from taking on political party affiliations, retained key positions in the political and economic structures of the state, they also took charge of constitution making, despite a lack of inspiration into how the new state should be constituted. In 1992–1993 institutional *Kompetentz* became the object of a 'tug-of-war' within the triangle of the president, the chairman of the Supreme Council, and the prime minister. They attempted to re-assign the *Kompetentz* on an almost daily basis, as a wealth of opportunities and dearth of constraints spawned a chaotic search for instant institutional powers. The members of the ex-communist elites, Kravchuk, Kuchma and Pliushch, attempted to reshuffle the prerogatives on the grounds of state building, a demanded strengthening of executive authority (which was to be vested in the president, government and parliament, respectively). In their hectic tinkering with institutional powers, the individuals focused only on particular prerogatives such as, for example, decree-making powers without an overarching vision of the form of government. As this frantic search failed to produce the outcome desired by any of the actors, they resorted to the ballot box to resolve the conflict.

At the same time, while playing with the individual pieces, there was little interest in putting the whole constitutional jigsaw together by passing a new constitution. While other states were busy promulgating new fundamental laws, the ritualistic public 'discussions and consultations' on the draft constitution in 1992–1993 and inconclusive debates in the Constitutional Commission could hardly be taken as a sign of a commitment to finalise the task in Ukraine. This diffidence comes as a surprise in light of the desperate need to counteract the growing political disarray and the economic crisis.

The net result of the piecemeal constitutional reform over 1992–1993 was that the 1978 constitution lost any internal consistency with its array of contradictory rules. It could not offer much of an organising framework and ceased to be respected by all political forces. This clumsy approach only worsened the problems stemming from the essentially hybrid nature of the institutional framework as initially amended in 1991. Ukraine's form of government over 1992–1993 did not match any recognisable ideal type and remained an amorphous and inherently contradictory combination of a system of soviets, and a parliamentary republic with elements of presidentialism. While the expanded presidency existed alongside the vertical of soviets subordinated to the Supreme Council, their respective domains of authority were unclear. The rushed and ill thought-out constitutional amendments resulted in numerous contradictions and loopholes.

Elster *at al* argue that 'a core symptom of failed consolidation is violence, which may take the forms of international war, civil war, violent repression, or "civic" violence of ordinary crimes'.[42] However, despite the unmistakable signs of breakdown in rules governing the polity, Ukraine avoided the escalation of conflict and eruption of political violence, in contrast to Russia, where a similar standoff resulting from extensive overlapping powers of parliament and the president culminated in a violent showdown in October 1993. Why did Ukraine escape such a scenario? Essentially, the key actors were not strong enough to impose their preferences. Fragmented elites and cross-cutting cleavages prevented any one individual or grouping from garnering lasting support and from being in control of the developments for a prolonged period. Moreover, the lesson from the Russian experience timely prompted the Ukrainian elites to search for a consensual way to diffuse the potentially explosive situation in the autumn of 1993. Thus, pre-term elections were opted for.

Over 1992–1993, the prevailing, lofty rhetoric of state building, in which, in particular, Kravchuk excelled, starkly contrasted with the limited actual transformation taking place in the domestic politics. The period illustrates the idiosyncrasy of the state-building processes. Not all planks of statehood could be erected simultaneously, and while the external dimension (embassies, army, currency, international recognition) was swiftly taken care of by the elites, other fundamental issues, such as deciding on the form of government, remained unresolved. Yet, despite the symbolic affirmation of unity, the inability to check the political and economic disarray led not only to a constitutional crisis, but also to a threat to the new state because of the intensification of centrifugal tendencies (see next chapter).

When the first free elections were held in 1994, the country had regressed almost to where it had started its constitutional reforms prior to independence. But by 1994 the necessary differentiation between the governing functions could be delayed no longer. The desperate need for economic stabilisation and the organisation of centre–periphery relations meant that the question of what kind of institutions Ukraine should be furnished with had to be resolved. Yet, while the early elections were opted for, Ukraine missed its 'window of opportunity', when the (relatively straightforward) question of the institutional powers dominated the constitutional debates and the left-wing bloc was still in disarray. As will be argued in the next chapter, the 1994 elections marked the revival of the Communist Party of Ukraine and the rejuvenated Left emerged as the strongest political orientation with the platform of restoring the *status quo ante*. Once constitution making got under way again, the Right and Left put forward diametrically different conceptions of statehood, and in particular, the highly charged problem of nationhood surfaced and got entangled with other issues, which further compounded the complexity of constitution making in Ukraine.

NOTES

1 For an overview of the Ukrainian political spectrum see Taras Kuzio, 'The Multi-Party System in Ukraine on the Eve of Elections', *Government and Opposition*, Vol.

29, No. 1 (Winter 1994) and Andrew Wilson and Artur Bilous, 'Political Parties in Ukraine', *Europe–Asia Studies,* Vol. 45, No. 4 (1993).

2 Because deputies did not win their mandates through party membership, factions of political parties did not generate much loyalty, and suffered from notoriously poor voting discipline. Party factions were denied formal recognition and material resources, and co-existed with groups of deputies created on the basis of profession, e.g. agrarians, industrialists and other *ad hoc* groupings. The Soviet-era *deputatsii (*groups of deputies representing the same oblast) remained the main organisational units in the Supreme Council, even if by that time members of the *deputatsii* belonged to different parties and/or had different ideological orientations. Representatives of the *deputatsii* were still granted the right to speak on a par with party-based factions.

3 In parliament the three orientations were represented by the following factions, groupings and alliances: *The Left:* 'Zemlia and Volia' (the faction of the Agrarian Party of Ukraine supported by about 76 deputies); the faction of the Socialist Party of Ukraine (30–40 deputies); the faction 'For Social Justice' (communist supporters under the leadership of Borys Oliynyk); *the Centre*: 'The Party of Democratic Revival' (37 deputies); 'New Ukraine' (58 deputies); *the Right*: the 'People's Rukh of Ukraine' faction (40 deputies); the group of 'Democratic Deputies', faction *Narodna Rada* (re-created in early 1993, consisted of 90 deputies); group 'Democratic Revival of Ukraine'; the group of the Ukrainian Republican Party (10–11 deputies), and the 'Independence and Democracy' group (pro-Kravchuk national democrats, mainly the URP and DPU, but also including some Rukh members, 70 deputies); the faction of the Democratic Party of Ukraine (about 25 people).

4 Andrew Wilson, 'Ukraine: two presidents and their powers', in Ray Taras (ed.), *Postcommunist Presidents* (Cambridge: Cambridge University Press, 1997), p. 78.

5 The term 'national-democrats' was derived from the name of the National-Democratic Party, which was formed in Western Ukraine in 1890 on the basis of the *Narodna Rada*. The national-democratic bloc encompassed a number of smaller parties and associations, such as the Peasant Democratic Party of Ukraine, Christian Democratic Party of Ukraine, Ukrainian Christian Democratic Party, the Ukrainian Language Society 'Prosvita' and the Union of Ukrainian Students. Further to the right were more radical, nationalist parties, which to a large extent remained outside parliament. On the ultranationalist parties and groups see Bohdan Nahaylo, 'Ukraine', *RFE/RL Research Report*, Vol. 3, No. 16 (22 April 1994), pp. 42–9 and Taras Kuzio, 'Radical Nationalist Parties and Movements in Contemporary Ukraine before and after Independence: The Right and Its Politics, 1989–1994', *Nationalities Papers,* Vol. 25, No. 2 (1997), pp. 211–42.

6 In organisational terms Rukh remained an umbrella 'civic' association, and, apart from individuals, it had also collective members, such as the Ukrainian Republican Party (the successor to a dissident Helsinki Union), and the Democratic Party of Ukraine (founded by the Soviet-era establishment cultural intelligentsia).

7 See *The Ukrainian Reporter*, Vol. 2, No. 9, September 1992, pp. 1–4.

8 Mykola Riabchuk, 'Authoritarianism with a Human Face?', *The East European Reporter*, Vol. 5, No. 6 (November–December 1992), p. 54. Apart from Chornovil, the majority of Rukh's parliamentary deputies, including Horyn and Lukianenko (leaders of the Ukrainian Republican Party, which was a collective member of Rukh) advocated support for Kravchuk's state building measures. Lukianenko complained at the 'bunker

psychology' of many national-democrats, who did not understand that 'since 24 August [1991] these are now our [Ukrainian] organs and we have to co-operate with them'. *The Ukrainian Reporter*, Vol. 2, No. 2, p. 5. Because of its unconditional backing for Kravchuk, the CNDF was even nicknamed the 'presidential party'.

9 To counteract the pressure from the Left to re-legalise the Communist Party of Ukraine, the *Narodna Rada* was briefly resuscitated in early 1993, with 90 deputies. *Biuletyn Verkhovnoi Rady Ukrainy* (Seventh Session), 1993, No. 10, p. 10.

10 By the end of 1992, New Ukraine consisted of the Liberal Democratic Party of Ukraine, the Green Party of Ukraine, the Social Democratic Party of Ukraine, the United Social Democratic Party of Ukraine, the Party of Democratic Revival of Ukraine, the Constitutional Democratic Party of Ukraine (Kuzio, 'The Multi-Party System in Ukraine', p. 125). None of those parties had any large following. New Ukraine was joined by people's deputies, some ministers, trade unions officials and directors of state enterprises, and enjoyed close links with nascent business circles, such as the Ukrainian League of Industrialists and Entrepreneurs.

11 The CPU claimed a membership of 130,000–140,000. Andrew Wilson, 'The Ukrainian Left: In Transition to Social Democracy or Still in Thrall to the USSR', *Europe–Asia Studies*, Vol. 49, No. 7 (1997), p. 1302.

12 Volodymyr Lytvyn, *Politychna arena Ukrainy (The Political Scene of Ukraine)* (Kyiv, 1994), p. 293.

13 *Biuletyn Verkhovnoi Rady Ukrainy* (Fifth Session), 1992, No. 1, p. 88.

14 Kravchuk took the first steps toward increasing his power in December 1991 when he made himself a commander-in-chief of the newly created Ukrainian forces by decree.

15 For the text of amendments see *Pravda Ukrainy*, 7 April 1992.

16 *Biuletyn Verkhovnoi Rady Ukrainy* (Fifth Session), 1992, No. 23, p. 16.

17 *Biuletyn Verkhovnoi Rady Ukrainy* (Fifth Session), 1992, No. 23, p. 80.

18 Overall, out of 24 deputies who spoke on Kravchuk's proposal on the first day of parliamentary debates, 22 were in favour, albeit some proposed modifications. Once again only Chornovil criticised the presidential aggrandisement and mocked Kravchuk's law as the 'Law on the Usurpation of Powers'; his objections were put down to his dashed presidential ambitions. *Biuletyn Verkhovnoi Rady Ukrainy* (Fifth Session), 1992, No. 23, p. 37.

19 *Biuletyn Verkhovnoi Rady Ukrainy* (Fifth Session), 1992, No. 30, p. 84.

20 *Vidomosti Verkhovnoi Rady*, No. 23, 1992.

21 The Council was headed by the president while the prime minister was deputy, with four collegia on economic, scientific–technical, humanitarian and legal affairs. Most importantly, three out of four collegia were headed by prominent *Narodna Rada* activists. The following people were appointed: Mykola Zhulynskyi (Culture/Education), Ihor Yukhnovskyi (Science/Technology), Oleksandr Yemets (Law), and Oleksandr Yemelianov (Economics).

22 *Biuletyn Verkhovnoi Rady Ukrainy* (Fifth Session), 1992, No. 45, p. 14.

23 The Presidential Administration (occupying the former CPU headquarters) not only did not supplant the cabinet, but it did not even emerge as a competing decision making centre, as it did not define the political course on domestic matters (in contrast to the international arena). *Biuletyn Verkhovnoi Rady Ukrainy* (Fifth Session), 1992, No. 45, p. 9–100. See also *Pravda Ukrainy*, 3 April 1992.

24 The Presidential Administration remained relatively small, in early 1992 it was about 150 people. This included the staff of two departments, which were transferred from the Supreme Council to the Administration (of Citizenship and Amnesty, and of Awards). See interview with the Secretary of the Administration of the President of Ukraine, H. G. Khomenko in *Pravda Ukrainy*, 29 February 1992, p. 2.

25 *Holos Ukrainy*, 5 June 1992.

26 The strategy of the government of prime minister Fokin relied on maintaining price controls despite increasing inflation, supporting the volume of production at any cost and relaxed fiscal and monetary policies, mainly because of the pressure of the powerful industrial and agricultural lobbies. Marek Dąbrowski, 'The Ukrainian Way to Hyperinflation', *Communist Economics and Economic Transformation*, Vol. 6, No. 2 (1994).

27 Wilson, 'Ukraine: two presidents and their powers', p. 71.

28 Wilson, 'Ukraine: two presidents and their powers', p. 78.

29 *Biuletyn Verkhovnoi Rady Ukrainy* (Sixth Session), 1992, No. 21, p. 14. On the condition of the Ukrainian economy in the autumn of 1992 see Simon Johnson and Oleg Ustenko, 'Ukraine on the Brink of Hyperinflation', *RFE/RL Research Report*, Vol. 1, No. 50 (18 December 1992), pp. 51–9.

30 See text in *Holos Ukrainy*, 19 November 1992 or *Biuletyn Verkhovnoi Rady Ukrainy* (Sixth Session), 1992, No. 21.

31 Dąbrowski, 'The Ukrainian Way to Hyperinflation', p. 6.

32 Kravchuk appointed local figures such as former heads of local councils or *vykonkomy* rather than outsiders as presidential representatives. The national-democrats criticised presidential representatives as throwbacks to the past, and cited plenty of examples of the former high-ranking members of CPU being appointed to those pivotal state positions. It was pointed out that only 11 out of 26 representatives could be considered democrats, and those were mainly confined to Western Ukraine. Out of 26 prefects, 12 were former heads of their respective oblast councils (or their executive committees), 5 were deputy heads and 3 were heads of city councils (*Ukrainian Reporter*, June 1992, Vol. 2, No. 6, p. 5). Furthermore, presidential representatives formed a new vertical structure parallel to that of *radas*, which resulted in dual authority and, as a result, fuelled tensions over the respective sphere of competencies between the presidential representatives and the disfranchised heads of the soviets.

33 He also demanded the subordination of the National Bank, Anti-Monopoly Committee, and the State Property Committee to the Cabinet, along with the dual subordination of the local state administration (to the cabinet of ministers and the president).

34 *Holos Ukrainy*, (20 May 1993).

35 See K. Mihalisko, 'Public Confidence in the Ukrainian Leadership', *RFE/RL Research Report*, Vol. I, No. 43 (1992) and K. Mihalisko, 'Ukrainians and their Leaders at a Time of Crisis', *RFE/RL Research Report*, Vol. II, No. 31 (1993), pp. 54–61.

36 Kravchuk cancelled the decree once parliament conceded to the miners' demands by resolving that a referendum on confidence in president and parliament was to be held on 26 September 1993.

37 By 24 September, two days before the referendum, it became evident that no preparations had been made for a referendum, as even voting slips were not approved by parliament and printed.

38 *Holos Ukrainy*, 18 March 1992.

CHAPTER FIVE

HOW TO ORGANISE THE STATE? CONSTITUTIONAL DEBATES AFTER THE 1994 ELECTIONS

The passage to independence in 1991 was not accompanied by an underlying consensus on what kind of state Ukraine should become, nor in what ways it should draw from the Ukrainian pre-communist and Soviet traditions, as well as foreign constitutional models. As had been only too evident in 1991, the members of the ex-nomenklatura, who remained in charge of the state, lacked a vision and commitment to embark on key constitutional reforms. Prior to and following the independence, the former opposition, the national-democrats, were not only too weak numerically, to push the process forward single-handedly, but also were afraid of 'rocking the boat' for their former adversaries, who called for unity in the interest of state building. The fear was that political confrontation in Ukraine would have created shockwaves, which the new state could not absorb. The orchestrated public appearance of unity, despite the ongoing conflict over the institutional division of power, was to cover up the fundamental disagreement over the meaning of independence. Yet a declarative affirmation of support for independence could not camouflage the fragility stemming from the profound ideological cleavages; during the 1994 elections signs of disunity could not be suppressed any longer. Constitutional debates, which resumed after the elections, soon illuminated the full scale of fundamental divisions running through the Ukrainian polity.

The parliamentary and presidential elections did not deliver a configuration of political forces conducive to a fast constitutional reform. Firstly, due to an ill-designed electoral law, a large contingent of independent deputies with nebulous ideological inclinations got elected to a new legislature. Secondly, with the left-wing orientation enjoying a new lease of life, two hostile ideological blocs emerged in parliament: the national-democrats and the Left. Thirdly, due to the failure of the liberal, centrist forces, the newly elected president lacked a stable power base in parliament, and his platform put him at odds both with the Left and the Right. The scene after the elections revealed the profound gulf between the actors' views on the optimal way to organise the Ukrainian state, which stemmed from their radically different interpretations of Ukrainian history and disagreement on the priorities of the new state, as well as diverse interests. And yet it was this parliament and presidency, which embarked on the constitutional reform, that would determine the blueprint of Ukrainian statehood. The fact that the constitution necessitated the simultaneous resolution of numerous issues pertaining to the shape of the state forced actors to prioritise some issues over others. This paved the way to an unlikely alliance between the president and the national-democrats, which not only allowed the constitution to be passed but also grossly affected the outcome, that is the conception of statehood elaborated in the new constitution (see chapter 7).

The aim of this chapter is twofold. First of all, to briefly discuss the results of the 1994 elections and the organisational and ideological profiles of the political actors after the elections. Secondly, to analyse the debates on the model of Ukrainian statehood amongst the new actors. The three clusters of issues are examined in detail: firstly, the form of government, that is the institutions and rules governing the relations between the legislature and the executive branch; secondly, the territorial distribution of power between the centre and the regions, which is usually framed in terms of federal, de-centralised and centralised unitary models of the state; and thirdly, defining the nature and attributes of the 'political community'. The chapter unveils a complex matrix of preferences that were intensely contested in the process of constitution drafting, which will be discussed in chapter 6.

THE 1994 PARLIAMENTARY AND PRESIDENTIAL ELECTIONS

THE NEW PARLIAMENT: AN UNDECIDED BALANCE

The parliamentary elections held in spring 1994 failed both to return the incumbents, and to clarify the balance of power in parliament.[1] This outcome was, to a large extent, put down to the ill-devised, majoritarian electoral law. The law was not only biased against nascent political parties, it also made it difficult to elect deputies at all, because of high requirements for turnout and voting threshold. The law favoured workers' collectives or groups of voters in nominating candidates while political parties faced much higher legal hurdles. The law also stipulated that a candidate in order to be elected had to obtain over 50 percent of votes cast, at the same time at least 50 percent of registered voters had to participate in the elections (otherwise the elections were declared invalid); this meant that a successful candidate had to obtain at least 25 percent of votes of the total number of citizens eligible to vote. If there was no candidate who fulfilled these stringent requirements, then the two highest candidates had to go to the second round, and again had to obtain the absolute majority of votes cast. Such an electoral system favoured parties with good organisation at the local level and/or well-known figures that could easily mobilise support at the local level.[2]

Table 5.1. Party Membership in Parliament (March/April 1994)

Left	
Communist Party of Ukraine	91
Socialist Party of Ukraine	14
Villagers' Party of Ukraine	21
Centre	
Labour Party	5
Civic Congress of Ukraine	2
Party of Democratic Revival of Ukraine	4
Social-Democratic Party of Ukraine	2
Christian Democratic Party of Ukraine	2
Party of Democratic Revival of Crimea	1
Right	
Rukh	22
Ukrainian Republican Party	10
Democratic Party of Ukraine	3
Radical Right	
Ukrainian Conservative–Republican Party	1
Congress of Ukrainian Nationalists	3
Ukrainian National Assembly	3
No Party Affiliation	218
Total	*405*

Source: Verkhovna Rada Ukrainy: paradygmy i paradoksy, Ukrainska Perspektyva, 1995.

Overall, the newly elected parliament was dominated by the left-wing parties and independent deputies (Table 5.1). The Left consisted of the re-registered Communist Party of Ukraine (CPU), the moderate Socialist Party of Ukraine (SPU), and the Peasant Party of Ukraine

(SelPU). The rejuvenated Communist Party, only six months after registration, emerged as the biggest party with 86 seats, and together with the socialists and peasants, the Left won 147 seats (43 percent). The leftist parties, consisting mainly of the lower echelons of the Soviet-era CPU, took advantage of their high degree of organisation and control inherited from the Soviet era in Eastern and Southern Ukraine (CPU) and Central Ukraine (SelPU). The CPU performed particularly well in heavily populated Donbas. While the leftist parties dominated small towns and rural areas of Central, Eastern and Southern Ukraine, in Donbas the CPU dominated both rural areas and large urban centres. Due to the mechanics of procedure, the left wing obtained one third of the seats, despite the fact that it won only one fifth of the actual votes.

Prior to the elections, the moderate nationalist parties and civic associations consolidated into the Democratic Coalition of Ukraine, in which Rukh and CNDF put aside the differences which split them under Kravchuk. Despite this alliance, the national-democratic parties gained only about one fifth of all seats. If some of the independents with national-democratic inclinations and the radical right-wing deputies are included, the right-wing bloc accounted for 27.2 percent of deputies in April 1994.[3] Its share of seats in parliament remained almost identical to that of the 1990 elections. The elections confirmed that their geographical base was limited to Ukrainian-speaking Western Ukraine and urban centres in Central Ukraine (mainly Kyiv).[4]

However, the biggest loser in the elections was the fledging liberal centre, which was almost squeezed out of the contest. The centre-liberal orientation was represented by the political alliance 'New Ukraine' with the Union of Industrialists and Entrepreneurs of Ukraine, which formed the Inter-Regional Bloc of Reform in January 1994,[5] co-led by Leonid Kuchma and Volodymyr Hryniov. The IRBR represented liberals from urban centres in Eastern and Southern Ukraine, and aimed to target the non-communist electorate in Eastern and Southern Ukraine, as it was both pro-reform and opposed to the anti-Russian foreign policy orientation of Kravchuk and the national-democrats. They also favoured federalism and linguistic autonomy for Russophone regions in Ukraine (see below). The Inter-Regional Bloc for Reform won only 6 seats, and together with other sympathising deputies, claimed 27 seats (6 percent) in the new parliament.[6]

There was a significant overlap between the centre and the national-democrats. Regarding the economic crisis the 'restorationists' (the Left) viewed the economic reforms as source of crisis, and advocated reverting to a centrally administered economy and economic integration with Russia/CIS. In contrast, the 'reformers'—the liberals and the national-democrats—saw the lack of reforms at the root of the economic crisis. However, there was a deep split among 'reformers', as the Eastern Ukrainian liberals advocated closer integration with Russia as a strategy to overcome the crisis. This strategy evoked insurmountable opposition from the national-democrats, who feared a reintegration of Ukraine into the 'Eurasian' as opposed to 'European space'. Although both liberals and national-democrats took a pro-reform and anti-Communist stance, pro-Russian tendencies among the IRBR leadership sparked a deep mistrust of them by the national-democrats, which continued throughout constitution making.

The independent candidates won over half of all seats. Many of them could be categorised as members of 'the party of power', the group of non-affiliated high- and middle-rank state officials, who relinquished their Communist Party cards in 1991, yet refrained from joining other political parties. While they had no single platform and strategy, they were characterised by their entrenchment in the state structures either at the local or central level, something that facilitated their election, as they developed clientalistic relations with the electorate. The single-member majoritarian electoral system put a premium on the constituency level and allowed the former nomenklatura to obtain a mandate by using informal networks at the local level.[7] They were strongest in Central Ukraine, especially in rural districts. However, not all of the independent candidates who got elected were without party affiliation; some of them stood as independents only because of the law biased against political parties (see Table 5.1). Nevertheless, the majoritarian electoral system was used by the state apparatchiks to obtain parliamentary mandates rather than boost the standing of political parties. Out of 405 deputies over half of the seats went to central and local government officials, directors of state enterprises and collective farm chairmen.

The structuralisation of parliament into groups and factions took place within a short space of time, even if some groups were ephemeral creations with no clearly defined social constituency. In principle, the parliament comprised three political blocs: Left, Right and the centre (Table 5.2). Yet only the factions on the left and the right, which were created on the basis of political parties, had a more or less clearly identifiable ideological orientation.

On the right part of the political spectrum, the faction of Rukh and Statehood (*Derzhavnist*) formed on the basis of the People's Movement of Ukraine (Rukh) and the Ukrainian Republican Party, respectively. The factions shared the main planks of their ideological orientation and closely co-ordinated their strategies. They were assisted by *Reformy* (Reforms), the faction that originated from the New Wave (*Nova Khvylia*) consisting of the younger generation of liberally minded politicians from Western Ukraine. The faction was joined by (mainly Ukrainophone) liberals from other regions of Ukraine and thus became the only faction in the new Supreme Council that drew its members from the majority of oblasts (the rest of the factions had a pronounced regional bias). Despite lacking a party basis, *Reformy* developed a consistently pro-reform line especially on economic issues, while on the 'national question' it tended to side with the national-democrats, though somewhat less consistently. Despite having a considerable intellectual capacity, the faction *Reformy* remained a loose grouping centred around several prominent personalities to the extent that it was referred to as a 'group of stars'.

Table 5.2. A Breakdown of the Ukrainian Parliament (December 1994 and May 1995)

	December 1994	*May 1995*
Left		
The Communist Party of Ukraine	84	90
The Socialist Party of Ukraine	25	27
The Peasant Party of Ukraine	36	47
Centre		
Inter-Regional Group of Deputies	25	30
Unity *(Yednist)*	25	31
Centre *(Tsentr)*	36	30
Independents	–	27
Right		
Rukh	27	28
Reforms	29	35
Statehood	27	28
Non-affiliated Deputies	88	29
Total	*403*	*405*

Source: 'Verkhovna Rada Ukrainy: paradygmy i paradoksy', *Ukrainsky Perspektyva,* Nos. 1 and 2, Kyiv, 1994).

The Left comprised three factions—Communist (CPU), Socialist (SPU) and Peasant (SelPU)—which were formed on the party principle, although in the case of the Socialist faction, the communists helped by 'lending' it several deputies, as the Socialist Party with only 14 seats could not form a faction on its own (the minimum was 17). However, despite being the biggest and best-organised parliamentary bloc, the Left was at odds with the former communists, who by then entrenched themselves in central and regional administration and eschewed political party affiliations. The election results cemented the split between the left-wing parties and the remnants of the nomenklatura's 'group of 239'. The latter representatives united in parliamentary groups such as *Yednist* (Unity), which represented the Dnipropetrovsk oblast, and *Tsentr* (Centre), which consisted of apparatchiks from central state structures. The group *Nezalezhni* (Independents) attracted a heterogeneous mass of deputies under the leadership of the former chairman of the Ukrainian National Bank, Vadym Hetman. The Inter-Regional Group of Deputies (MDG) emerged from the defeated centrist-liberal, Russophone Interregional Block for Reforms (IRBR) and contained the large contingent of Crimean deputies. Later, in June 1995 another faction, the 'Social-Market Choice' (*Sotsialno-Rynkovyi Vybir*), was created by taking away deputies from the MDG, *Yednist*, and the Independents; it mainly consisted of deputies from Donetsk and Dnipropetrovsk oblasts. There were also other *ad hoc* groupings, which cut across formal factions and groups.[8] Some deputies eschewed faction membership altogether.

In terms of party affiliations, the new Ukrainian parliament emerged polarised along party lines with better-articulated groupings at opposite ends of the political spectrum, yet with the overall balance, at least initially, favouring the communists and their allies, the socialists and the peasants (see Table 5.1). They represented a considerable force due to their disciplined internal decision making and unanimous voting in comparison to other factions (except *Derzhavnist'* and Rukh).

Even if the elections marked its grand comeback, the Left fell short of getting a majority in the legislature. The centrist deputies, the ideological preferences of a large section of which remained nebulous, held the balance. But as the 'centre' was merely a label for the space between the Right and the Left, rather than advocating any clear and coherent political option, the balance of power in parliament proved prone to unexpected shifting. The centrist deputies effectively sided with the party based factions (such as the Communists or Rukh) depending on the issue under consideration [such vacillation earned them the nickname *boloto* (swamp)]. The weakness of centrist, liberal parties was to leave the newly elected president with no power base in parliament. This weakness provides clues as to the shifts in Kuchma's preferences and strategies soon after the elections. At the same time, the presence of a large contingent of state officials, who were soon to become dependent for their posts on the president had a important impact on the balance of power within the Supreme Council and its relations with the executive branch during constitution making (see chapter 6).

THE NEW PRESIDENT: THE ECLECTIC ELECTORAL PLATFORM

The undetermined balance of power in parliament raised the stakes of the presidential elections. Apart from Kravchuk, several candidates were registered, including the leader of the Socialist Party of Ukraine, Oleksandr Moroz, the former prime minister and co-chairman of Interregional Bloc of Reforms, Leonid Kuchma, and Leonid Pliushch, the former chairman of the Supreme Council, who was of similar background to Kravchuk, though of a more nationalist provenience.[9]

The incumbent Kravchuk was the main candidate supported by the state-controlled media. His program on socio-economic issues advocated a gradual transition to a market economy. However, above all he kept emphasising Ukrainian independence and criticised Kuchma for his 'Russophile' tendencies and willingness to convert Ukraine into a neo-colonial state within the Russian domain, something which, Kravchuk warned, would lead to a civil war in Ukraine. Kravchuk portrayed the choices Ukraine faced in terms of survival of the polity, and thus stressed the need for peace and harmony in order to save the state. Indeed, the salience of the 'Russian question'—both in terms of linguistic policies and foreign policy orientation—turned the elections into a second referendum on independence.

Kravchuk's main competitor was the former prime minister, Leonid Kuchma, one of the leaders of the centre-liberal Russophone Interregional Bloc for Reforms (IRBR). While serving as prime minister, Kuchma became a well-known politician and by spring 1993 in public opinion surveys Kuchma's popularity began to reach that of Kravchuk. Although the latter continued to be viewed as the most authoritative figure in the country since independence, the regional distribution of support for Kravchuk became increasingly distorted: his popularity was highest in western and lowest in eastern oblasts. The support for Kuchma was more evenly spread around the country, and, taking into account the distribution of population in Ukraine, where clearly Eastern Ukraine sets the tone of the elections (the population of the Donetsk oblast alone was bigger than that of the three Galician oblasts together), it was a decisive factor in Kuchma's victory in the election. Overall, during the campaign, despite limited access to the state-controlled media, Kuchma portrayed himself as an efficient and decisive administrator, who, once in charge of the executive structures of the state, would be capable of leading the country out of its crisis. Kuchma convincingly blamed Kravchuk for hindering his economic policies when he was a prime minister. Kuchma rejected the full-of-pathos *Derzhavnist'* (statehood) rhetoric of Kravchuk and claimed to be a pragmatist who believed that the economy should take precedence over politics. Economic reform depended on political reform, which would bring about the separation of powers with 'a strong executive branch based on the principle of competency, order and responsibility'.[10] Devolution of power to the regions, especially greater financial autonomy, was the key to economic recovery. In contrast to the co-chairman of the IRBR, Volodymyr Hryniov, Kuchma stopped short of advocating federalism. But like the IBRB, he argued that the best economic strategy for Ukraine was to become 'a leader of an Eurasian region'. In the campaign Kuchma argued that during the 'controlled transformation' of the administrative economy toward the socially oriented market economy (including demonopolisation, liberalisation and privatisation), Ukraine should aim to renew economic ties with Russia and the former Soviet Union as well as enter into the CIS Economic Union. Furthermore, he emphasised populist 'law and order' issues, as well as the upgrading of the Russian language to 'official status' alongside Ukrainian. Incidentally Kravchuk also advocated the upgrade in the final stages of the electoral campaign, but belatedly and less convincingly.

Overall, in order to appeal to the widest sections of the electorate, Kuchma somewhat played down the issue of economic reform, while simultaneously proclaiming the need to end the economic drift and isolationism through re-establishing closer ties with Russia. He positioned himself to capture the Russophone electorate, that is the voters outside Western Ukraine, who favoured economic recovery via strengthening links with Russia, and were not preoccupied by threats to sovereignty, something which troubled the Western Ukrainian electorate.

In the first round Kravchuk won over Kuchma (38 to 31 percent). However, due to the re-alignment of votes, in the 'run-off' second round Kuchma won with 52 percent. Despite the fact that the national-democratic opposition reluctantly supported Kravchuk in the second round as 'the lesser evil', the alienation of the electorate from Kravchuk's 'nationalist platform' in the densely populated Southern and

Table 5.3. Results of the Second Round of the Presidential Elections (10 July 1994)

	Kravchuk (%)	*Kuchma* (%)
West		
Lviv	93.8	3.9
Ternopil	94.8	3.8
Ivano-Frankivsk	94.5	3.9
Volyn	83.9	14.0
Zakarpattia	70.5	25.2
Rivno	87.3	11.0
Chernivtsi	61.8	35.3
Centre		
Vinnytsia	54.3	42.3
Zhytomyr	55.6	41.6
Kyiv Oblast	58.3	38.4
Kyiv City	59.7	35.6
Kirvohrad	45.7	49.7
Khmelnytskyi	57.2	39.2
Cherkasy	50.8	45.7
Poltava	37.4	59.2
Sumy	28.9	67.8
Chernihiv	25.0	72.3
South		
Crimea	8.9	89.7
Sevastopol	13.5	92.0
Mykolaiv	44.7	52.8
Odesa	29.2	66.8
Kherson	32.0	64.6
East		
Donetsk	18.5	79.0
Dnipropetrovsk	29.7	67.8
Zaporizhzhya	26.8	70.7
Luhansk	10.1	88.0
Kharkiv	25.9	71.0
Overall Average	*45.0*	*52.2*

Source: Vybory v Ukraini (Kyiv, International Foundation for Electoral Systems, Kyiv, 1994).

Eastern Ukraine turned out to be decisive. The distribution of votes clearly split the country into two, as the majority of population in all but one oblasts east of the Dnieper voted for Kuchma (Table 5.3). The elections reflected the deeply ingrained cleavages rooted in different political histories of the regions in Ukraine. While these cleavages were not so evident during the referendum in 1991, when the idea of independence, albeit for different reasons, was supported more evenly across Ukraine, the two disillusioning years of Ukrainian independence made them more apparent. These divisions were readily exploited by the presidential candidates. For example, in the electoral campaign Kuchma capitalised on the resentment over the influence of Western Ukrainian elites on Kyiv's policies and called for an end to the 'reign of Galician nationalism'. This rhetoric put Kuchma on a collision course with the national-democrats during and immediately after the elections. However, while Kuchma's strategy of targeting the densely populated Russophone regions of Ukraine proved the key to success, the pronounced regional distribution of votes implied that the new president had to accommodate Ukraine's heterogeneity in his policies and bridge the gap between the East and West.

DEFINING UKRAINIAN STATEHOOD: THE CONSTITUTIONAL ISSUES AND PREFERENCES

The end of the electoral campaign and the swearing in of the new parliament and president immediately reintroduced the issue of the new constitution. As was argued in chapter 4, between 1992–1994 constitutional reform was animated by the interests of the key institution holders, namely the president, prime minister and chairman of the Supreme Council. This amounted to a permanent 'war at the top', as the key actors could not secure the lasting support of an unstructured and volatile parliament. By the time the new representative institutions were elected, their respective spheres of authority were overlapping, and rules defining their interactions were profoundly confused. The confusion extended to the regional and local level. In June 1994, the local councils and their heads were elected in accordance with the February 1994 'Law on the Election of People's Deputies'. Being in charge both of the local councils and their executive committees, the heads of councils encompassed two branches of power. In effect, 24 oblast governors and 2 mayors of Kyiv and Sevastopol acquired unconstrained executive power over their mandate territory (in accordance with the principle of the Soviet system that a higher level council could decide on any issue of the lower level council). Yet, it was unclear to whom they were accountable. The juxtaposition of the elements of the system of soviets with presidentialism meant that regional leaders could decide on their own allegiance: either to the president, the prime minister or the chairman of the parliament.

Moreover, the elections coincided with the intensification of centrifugal tendencies in regions such as Donbas. The first two years of Ukrainian independence proved disillusioning, as they failed to deliver on the pre-independence promises of the four D's: Democracy, *Dostatok* (Prosperity), *Dukhovnis't* (Spirituality) and *Doviria* (Trust). In particular, the impact of hyperinflation on people's standards meant that the unfulfilled promise of prosperity had a galvanising effect on the Eastern and Southern Ukraine, which felt duped by the tandem of Kravchuk and 'nationalist' Western Ukrainians. The regional elites hoped that Ukraine's independence would bring about greater autonomy for the regions. In reality, independence did not bring the end of the dictate of the 'centre' but boiled down to a mere geographical shift of 'centre', as Kyiv took over the role of Moscow with its powerful drive to control the periphery. As a result, regionalisation intensified in the run up to the elections with strengthened calls for devolution of power to the regions. In Donbas, a local referendum, which was held simultaneously with the parliamentary elections of 1994, teased out public opinion on a number of questions, including public support for federalism and Russian as the official language in the two oblasts.[11] Transcarpathia also continued to call for greater autonomy.[12] These tendencies put under strain the unitary model of state that Ukraine inherited from the UkrSSR, and raised the question of the territorial distribution of power.

In a similar vein, the elections marked an end of the placid acceptance of the notion of nationhood as defined by Kravchuk and the Western Ukrainian elites, who took charge of the cultural, educational and language policies within government between 1992–1994. The high profile of the 'Russian question' (the status of the Russian minority and language in Ukraine, and Ukraine's relations with Russia) during the electoral campaign indicated that the very notion of political community, national identity and geopolitical orientation was open to contestation. After two years of independence, the appearance of unity, which Kravchuk so keenly crafted, was all but gone and the divisive issues had to be tackled head on.

Even if the 1994 elections failed to deliver a structured parliament, they nevertheless highlighted two clearly identifiable orientations: the Left and the Right. In the context of the historical political cleavages, the protracted consolidation of the party system in post-Soviet Ukraine resulted in the partial crystallisation of the ideological spectrum at its opposing ends in 1994. Both the left- and right-wing factions were characterised by deep ideological commitments (perhaps with the exception of the more pragmatically disposed leftist agrarian lobby), and adhered to rigid and incompatible conceptions of statehood. However, apart from parliamentary blocs, the political scene also consisted of the presidency as a powerful institutional actor. Even if his electoral programme remained eclectic and nebulous, the president soon demonstrated a strong set of preferences.

As Ukraine had to reanimate the lapsed constitutional process, the breadth and diversity of views signalled that constitution drafting would perhaps become even more difficult in the presence of the consolidated Left and Right than it was under Kravchuk. Thus, the remaining part of this chapter will examine 'the bones of contention'—the issues that awaited resolution in the Fundamental Law—through the prism of actors' preferences. The chapter does not aim to examine the ideologies of the actors involved in terms of their morphological structure (completeness and coherence), origins or evolution. Instead, it will analyse the preferences on the main planks of statehood demonstrated by the key group and institutional actors involved in the constitution making after the 1994 elections, even if their preferences had only vague resemblance to any recognisable ideologies and/or were rooted in narrowly-defined (institutional, group or individual) interests. The chapter also aims to highlight the nature and scope of debates. While some issues were discussed at great length, other issues were barely touched upon. Thus, the chapter highlights the patchwork of preferences woven out of ideas and interests, which served as building blocks in the process of creating a constitutional blueprint of the Ukrainian state. Three clusters of issues will be focused on: the form of government (institutions at the centre), the territorial distribution of power and the definition of the political community and its attributes.

THE FORM OF GOVERNMENT

THE LEFT: NARODOVLADIA

In terms of the institutional framework of the state, the rejuvenated leftist bloc in the new parliament upheld the traditional Soviet-era motto of 'all power to the soviets' and aimed to reincarnate the Soviet system of *narodovladia* embedded in a hierarchy of people's soviets (*radas*). The communists fervently advocated a classic Soviet model, according to which *radas* combined the functions of state power and local self-government, with the Supreme Council at the pinnacle of the institutional framework. As a member of the Communist faction blatantly declared: 'we will not vote for a constitution that does not have a system of soviets. It is against our understanding of *narodovladia'*.[13] According to the model, the Supreme Council exercises and/or delegates executive functions, appoints and oversees the judicial apparatus. As the chairman and the Presidium of the Supreme Council performed representative functions of head of state, there was no need for a president. Neither was the Constitutional Court necessary, as the Supreme Council had the exclusive right to interpret the constitution. The communists were only too happy to abolish the institution of the presidency altogether, not only because it did not fit with their notion of *narodovladia*, but also because they held it responsible for the demise of the USSR under the leadership of the 'traitor nationalist Kravchuk'. Claiming that in 1991 the presidency was introduced as a temporary institution, they believed in the redundancy of the institution of the presidency in Ukraine. However, as a compromise they would allow a temporary extension of the institution in a circumscribed form, that is reduced to purely symbolic and ceremonial functions.

While stressing the unity of power as a key principle for the institutional framework of the state, the Left condemned a blind faith in the principle of the separation of powers. They criticised the consecutive drafts during 1995–1996 (see next chapter) for misunderstanding the essence of the separation of powers and taking it too literally:

> As a matter of fact, reference to this principle [in the draft], which is apparently the most fully implemented in the Constitution of the USA, is speculation. In the USA the separation of powers has for a long time been transformed into a system of 'checks and balances', the division of powers and functions in the exercising of united state authority (*yedynoi vlady*). The majority of prerogatives of state bodies in the USA are shared. Their carefully designed system of 'checks and balances', [and] well worked-out procedures secure the efficient functioning of the state mechanism, the balanced relations, despite unavoidable differences, and the business-like co-operation of the branches of power.[14]

In other words, the communists argued that the separation of powers was a lofty principle, and that even in the USA the unity of state power took priority over the separation.

Alongside the people's councils, instruments of direct democracy—most of all referenda and an imperative mandate—formed the cornerstone of the Soviet system of *narodovladia*. According to the communists, the people were to have the right to referenda on the most important and controversial issues: the name of the state, national symbols, form of government, socio-economic system of the state, changes to the territorial structure of Ukraine, and political unions with other states. *Narodovladia* would only be complete with the right of people's initiative to submit draft laws in parliament as well as to initiate the pre-term recalling of the mandate of the president and parliament. Moreover, because no single party had a majority in parliament, it was argued that the decision on key constitutional principles should be decided in the referendum, something which would allow the eliciting of the people's vision of the Ukrainian state before the final Basic Law of Ukraine was drafted. The Left stressed the binding nature of the 1990 Declaration of Sovereignty, which adhered to the system of soviets, and the 1991 Concept of the Constitution of Ukraine, which envisaged a referendum on the constitutional principles.

However, while the communists preferred a form of government which closely resembled the 1978 constitution, the socialists and peasants were open to 'revisionism' by accepting—what they perceived as—a modified version of the system of soviets which oscillated towards a Western parliamentary system with an indirectly elected, ceremonial presidency and the prime minister subordinated to the parliament. As such, they accepted functional (as opposed to institutional) separation of powers as a blueprint of the new system. In that respect, the socialists' stance reflected their hesitant evolution to Western-type of social democracy.[15] This readiness to embrace elements of a Western parliamentary system distinguished them from the communists, and made them more amenable to co-operation with the centrist factions, which generally favoured a system centred on a strong parliament (see below). However, having to choose between some kind of (semi-)presidential system—as advocated by the president and the national-democrats—or the classic Soviet model, the socialists and peasants fell back on the latter as it was much closer to their understanding of 'people's rule'.

Overall, the Left preferred the system of soviets as the form of government for independent Ukraine, but the possibility of compromise on Western parliamentarism was contemplated by the more moderate socialists and peasants. As was argued in chapter 2, these two institutional models, despite apparent similarities, are essentially incompatible, and the difficulties in marrying them were never fully acknowledged nor resolved. Insofar as the left-wing factions were concerned, both of them would secure the supremacy of parliament in the institutional edifice of the state.

THE NATIONAL-DEMOCRATS: AWAY FROM THE SOVIETS

While the Left advocated a relatively clearly defined model—the system of soviets, the national-democrats' views on the form of government were marked, most of all, by a deep abhorrence of the system of soviets, rather than a clearly formulated alternative. In essence, their preferences on the form of government were shaped by the political circumstances and the imperatives of state building. Thus they did not advocate the restoration or transplants of any form of government, whether derived from Ukraine's past or existing elsewhere, despite their insistence on the symbolic continuity of post-1991 Ukraine with the Ukrainian People's Republic of 1917–1920, and Ukraine's European identity.

In 1992, Rukh's programme document 'Conception of State Building in Ukraine' advocated an essentially parliamentary system with the president performing the role of the head of state on grounds of historical legitimacy:

> The form of government that in terms of [Ukraine's] historical traditions, theoretical thoughts on statehood at the beginning of the twentieth century, and the psychological traits of the Ukrainian nation is most appropriate is that of a parliamentary-presidential republic with the head of state, who is not the chief executive. Historically, this is confirmed by the forms of governments utilised in the Cossack Republic and the Ukrainian People's Republic.[16]

However, by 1994 parliamentarism was deemed unsuitable for Ukraine for a number of reasons. Firstly, as Sartori pointed out 'parliamentary democracy cannot perform (in any of its varieties) unless it is served by *parliamentary fit* parties, that is to say, parties that have been socialised (by failure, duration, and appropriate incentives) into being relatively cohesive or disciplined, into behaving, in opposition, as responsible opposition, and into playing, to some extent, a rule-guided fair game'.[17] It was evident that those pillars of parliamentarism were not present in Ukraine, especially as the 1994 electoral law was designed to discriminate against political parties. Secondly, the largest political party by 1994, the Communist Party of Ukraine, could not be even trusted to guard Ukraine's independence. The national-democrats feared that parliamentarism would favour the 'anti-state' Left and facilitate an alliance of the left-wing parties in parliament with the regional elites in Eastern and Southern Ukraine on the issue of a pro-Russian foreign policy orientation and state language. Thirdly, the national-democrats' growing aversion to parliamentarism stemmed from its connotations with the system of soviets (or 'Soviet parliamentarism' as the socialists referred to it) that was so advocated by the Left. The national-democrats feared that had they supported the parliamentary form of government (regardless of the lack of the functioning party system), this would simply result in leaving the system of soviets intact. And Ukraine would be stuck with the infamous Soviet 'cousin' of European parliamentarism, which would confine Ukraine to a bygone era and undermine its European credentials.

In contrast to the Left, for the national-democrats the principle of separation of powers epitomised the 'civilised' and democratic form of government. However, while they religiously embraced the principle as an antidote to the system of soviets, the concept itself did not provide any clear-cut guidelines on institutional designs, and came to be associated with diverse forms of government (see chapter 1).[18] The domestic predicament forced the national-democrats to carefully choose amongst the various models prevailing in the West; no wholesale foreign transplant commanded their favour. Instead they argued that the principle of the separation of powers would be best adapted to the Ukrainian conditions in a presidential system, which denoted a division of powers between the legislature and a directly elected, executive presidency modelled on the American system (but without bi-cameralism and federalism). The executive presidency, which headed the government, was perceived as having the potential not only to counterbalance the Left's continuous harking back to the past and obstruction of reform in parliament, but also to circumvent centrifugal forces through the vertical chain of the presidential representatives. Thus, the national-democrats pinned their hopes for the successful consolidation of the state on decisive leadership, something which, by 1994 they came to believe only an executive presidency could offer. However, the degree of support for a strong presidency was uneven across the right-centre political spectrum. Believing that the presidency had a prominent role to play, even if it smacked of a 'strong hand' approach, some national-democrats, i.e. the faction *Derzhavnist,* advocated a pure presidential system. The faction 'Reforms', in turn, while agreeing that the *Verkhovna Rada* could not propel economic reforms, still favoured the power-sharing system based on the balance between the legislature and strong yet not omnipotent presidency. However relying on the reformist zeal and patriotic feelings of future presidents, some national-democrats were not ready to place the fate of the country in one person's hands, and argued that the actual power-sharing arrangement between the parliament, president and prime minister had to be crafted carefully.

Nevertheless, overall the national-democrats were willing to support a stronger presidency for the sake of reform of the Soviet state structure (especially at the regional level which in Eastern Ukraine became a locus for entrenchment of reactionary pro-Soviet and anti-reform forces) as long as the bulk of the leftist bloc in parliament opposed political and economic reforms.

The legislature had to have sufficient power to counterbalance the authoritarian leanings of the president. But the national-democrats were divided on the issue of bi-cameralism, which was advocated by Kuchma (see below). In principle, they would welcome the additional 'checks and balances' that the upper chamber (*Senat*) could offer against the leftist forces, which dominated the lower chamber. The creation of the upper chamber would also be a radical departure from the uni-cameral Supreme Council. However, they feared that taking into account the need to speed up the legislative process, the upper chamber would make the legislative process even more cumbersome. In other words, the problems of the protracted legislative process resulting from the inexperience and lack of professionalism in the lower chamber would be exacerbated rather than eased by the introduction of the upper chamber. And because of the fear of federalisation by the 'back door', they only supported the idea of bi-cameralism if the upper chamber consisted of an equal number of senators from each oblast, rather than in proportion to the size of oblast population (something which was, in turn, rejected by regional leaders from Eastern and Southern Ukraine).

The arguments in favour of a strong, uni-cameral parliament appealed in particular to the centrist factions. Even if they accepted the need for an executive presidency and broadly accepted the separation of powers as the underlying principle for institutional reform, the centrists' preferences for a more parliament-centred form of government stemmed from their immediate circumstances—mainly their concern over their parliamentary mandates. Even if many of them simultaneously held parallel posts in the state administration, the Supreme Council remained a valued 'safe heaven' for them, because of the parliamentary immunity membership conferred. They feared that the fate of parliament would be sealed through the gradual emasculation of parliamentary powers by a president. Thus, they fiercely opposed both the creation of bi-cameral legislature and the right of president to dissolve parliament. They viewed the extensive 'checks and balances' between the president, prime minister and parliament as the guarantee of the viability of parliament.

THE PRESIDENT: IN PURSUIT OF EXECUTIVE POWERS

Unlike the national-democrats, the newly elected president Kuchma held clear-cut views on the preferred form of government, in which the most potent institution was to be the presidency. For Kuchma all Ukraine's economic evils stemmed from half-hearted political reform:

> An analysis of the situation in Ukraine leads to the conclusions that the degradation of the economy is not due to purely economic factors. The imperfect organisation of state power, the unfinished separation of powers ... are two of the main obstacles in the way to economic stabilisation.[19]

Thus, Kuchma advocated doing away with the collective responsibility of local soviets and their subordination to the Supreme Council, and proposed their replacement with a strong executive chain of command in order—as he argued—to overcome political resistance to the reform of the regional level. The aim of the constitutional reforms was, firstly, to concentrate decision making power in the executive branch, secondly, to introduce a rigid subordination of executive structures to the president, and, thirdly, to clearly delineate the legislature's functions to prevent it from interfering with the work of the executive. Kuchma blamed the lack of economic reform on the fact that 'the Supreme Council as a rule attempts to influence directly executive activities [and] takes decisions in matters which do not belong to its competencies', because 'the Supreme Council cannot get rid of the syndrome of direct control over the government'.[20] Also law making was not to remain the exclusive prerogative of the Supreme Council:

> Because of the slow legislative process and natural propensity of the legislature to be dominated by politico-ideological emotions, which are detrimental to the legislative work, especially when many questions (in the economic sphere) need urgent legislative decisions, it would be advisable to give the cabinet of ministers the right to issue normative acts with the power of law.[21]

To justify the creation of a strong presidency, historical tradition, spanning from Kyiv Rus' to UkrSSR, was invoked by the presidential entourage: 'we have to use world experience but let us not forget our own traditions. In the historical traditions of our land, [there is] single head of the executive branch, head of state: Prince (*kniaz'*), Hetman, Tsar and General Secretary (*sic*). Thus, there is no need to re-invent the wheel'.[22]

President Kuchma strongly favoured the creation of the upper chamber, the Senate, which would be elected in indirect elections and granted extensive appointive powers (to be shared with the presidency). The indirect mode of elections would provide the president with an instrument to control the composition of the upper chamber, as the president would have the upper hand in the appointment of regional representatives.[23] Such a pro-presidential Senate would not only provide a counterbalance for the left-leaning lower chamber, but would also weaken the autonomy of the legislature *vis-à-vis* the executive branch.

Kuchma's preferences regarding political reforms stemmed from his normative conception of efficient government, which was shaped by his previous managerial and, especially, prime ministerial experience. Kuchma repeatedly and persistently argued that the government could only do its job effectively when it was free from intrusion by parliament. Because the volatile majority in parliament could not sustain a coherent policy line, the position of the Supreme Council as the supreme authority of the state hampered the reform process. The parliament's powers were to be circumscribed and the presidency was to remedy the paralysis of the governing structures in Ukraine. According to Kuchma's argument, being directly elected, the presidency combined the popular legitimacy enjoyed by parliament with effective and steady leadership that the country needed during an acute economic crisis. Thus, while Kuchma enthusiastically embraced the principle of a separation of powers, he interpreted it as the means by which he could limit the powers of parliament over the cabinet of ministers. The executive branch was to be subordinated to the president, with parliament's powers being essentially nominal. However, unlike Kravchuk, at no point did president Kuchma propose to abolish the post of prime minister and the cabinet of ministers. When during constitution drafting, the national-democrats and some constitutional experts proposed to abolish the post of prime minister and subordinate the cabinet of ministers directly to the president, Kuchma categorically objected. He did not even insist on being named the 'chief executive', and was satisfied with the 'head of state'. This restraint can be explained by the reluctance of the president to take on direct responsibility for the performance of the executive branch, even when ultimately headed by the president, who could unilaterally dismiss the prime minister at any time. The role of the cabinet was to be designed as an intermediate link in the chain of executive authority allowing the prime minister rather than the president to shoulder the direct responsibility for socio-economic policies. As will be demonstrated in chapter 8, the opportunity to use prime ministers as scapegoats indeed proved to be a powerful instrument in the president's hands. However, the separation of powers, as perceived by Kuchma, was not designed to prevent the president from sharing his law making powers with parliament, as he was to be granted the right to issue decrees (*ukazy*).

To summarise, the main actors in the constitutional process advocated the following forms of government[24]:

The Left	*The Centre*	*The Right/President*
(Soviet) parliamentarism	parliamentary-presidential	presidential-parliamentary

However, it should be pointed out that although the above concepts were widely used in the constitutional debate, they served as labels for vaguely defined yet different forms of government in terms of the structure and status of the executive branch. The parliamentary-presidential system was to be centred around parliament rather than the president, although the latter would perform certain executive functions. The presidential-parliamentary system was characterised by the allocation of extensive executive powers to the president, with parliament retaining some control over the cabinet of ministers. With numerous competencies to be allocated and each of them being dealt with separately, the configurations of institutions could be moulded into diverse forms of government. When discussing the institutional framework a whole range of shades of preferences prevailed, which reflected the wide range of details in the institutional configurations to be decided by the constitution makers. The resulting mosaic of preferences lacked clarity and transparency, and led to cumbersome debates on a myriad of institutional powers, rights, competencies, and prerogatives. However, even if the overall matrix of interests and preferences was complex and opaque, the debates symbolised the clash between the incompatible ideals of the Soviet system of *narodovladia* favoured by the Left and Montesquieu's classical system of the separation of powers advocated by the centre, the national-democrats and the president. Yet, despite the consensus on the overarching principle of the separation of powers, the anti-left forces disagreed among themselves on the precise delineation of prerogatives between the parliament and the president, especially on the issue of control over the cabinet of ministers.

THE TERRITORIAL FRAMEWORK OF THE STATE

The rise of centrifugal forces and the failure of half-hearted institutional reforms under Kravchuk placed the vexed question of the territorial division of power at the top of the constitutional agenda. Thus, the constitution drafters faced the task of defining the up-to-now only broadly understood centre–periphery relations by choosing between the unitary or federal models of the state, determining the position of Crimea, and (in the case the unitary form was chosen) devising the form and competencies of local and regional self-governing bodies.

FEDERALISM VERSUS UNITARY MODELS

Federalism

In 1990–1991 the idea of the federalisation of Ukraine found a place in the programmes of several smaller parties, such as the Party of Democratic Revival of Ukraine, the Alliance of Social-Democratic Parties of Ukraine, the Liberal-Democratic Party of Ukraine, and the Constitutional-Democratic Party of Ukraine.[25] However, while in 1991 the working group of the Constitutional Commission considered proposals to federalise Ukraine by dividing it into historical lands (*zemli*), it opted for the preservation of the unitary structure of the republic (with the oblast as the main administrative unit). In the voting in the Supreme Council, only 49 deputies voted against the unitary system of state. Prior to the 1994 elections, the pro-federal camp was joined by liberal parties and leaders of eastern Ukrainian origin. Donbas politicians in favour of federalism or greater autonomy included, for example, Zviagilskyi (the deputy prime minister) and Valentyn Landyk, who were close to the Labour Party, (which represented the 'red directors' and leaders of the local state structures). These regional parties failed to win more than a few seats in the new 1994 parliament. However, the hopes of the federalists were pinned on a close political ally of the newly elected president Kuchma, Volodymyr Hryniov, who consistently propagated the federal model for Ukraine, and who was ideally placed to encourage the president to adopt this idea. Hryniov argued against the simplistic tendency to view the unitary state as strong and federal state as 'weak, tending towards disintegration',[26] and propagated the economic benefits of federalism. The economic autonomy of regions would provide incentives for better and more efficient use of the economic potential of Ukraine; it would stimulate bottom-up economic reforms, especially by fostering organic privatisation and entrepreneurship. In the particular case of Ukraine, federalism would counteract large regional disparities and deal with the economic grievances held against Kyiv's arbitrary redistribution of resources. According to Hryniov, 'the very idea of unitarism carries a threat to the statehood of Ukraine' as the deteriorating economic situation and the centre's drive to control the economic resources would lead to the intensification of centrifugal, separatist forces. He also pointed out that federalism would enhance the democratic credentials of the new state. Hryniov dismissed the arguments in favour of unitarism (see below) according to which 'the federal system is viewed as an invitation to separatism, while the unitary model—as a mechanism for suppressing it', by pointing out that the cause of separatism ultimately lays in the centralising tendencies of apparatchiks in Kyiv. Those policies forced regional elites to defend themselves and resort to 'federalism' as an instrument of curbing the powers of the centre.[27]

The arguments in support of federalism were coming from other quarters as well. While economic motives prevailed amongst the Eastern Ukrainian elites, the representatives of national minorities, such as the Romanian deputy from the Chernivtsti oblast, Ivan Popesku, suggested that a federal structure should be a long-term goal for Ukraine in light of its multi-ethnic composition. As a stepping-stone towards federalism, Popesku advocated territorial autonomy (*natsionalno-terytorialni utvorenia*) for national minorities, which lived in compact settlement.[28] However, any calls for territorial autonomy for national minorities fell on deaf ears both with the national-democrats and the Left because such autonomy interfered with their conceptions of nationhood (see below).

While the regional, pro-federal elites lacked representation in parliament, they looked to the president as a champion of their interests. Yet Kuchma's support for federalism, if it ever existed, proved elusive. Some argued that Kuchma never supported federalism.[29] Nevertheless, Kuchma's links (via IRBR) with Hryniov and his, even if vague, calls for decentralisation, put him in the camp of federalists. Many Ukrainian analysts argued that 'the popularity of the idea [of federalism] was skilfully used by the team of Leonid Kuchma during the electoral campaign'.[30] Yet even if Kuchma capitalised on his alignment with forces advocating the federalisation of Ukraine in the elections, once elected, he not only never openly supported federalism but advocated the centralised model of the state. Although Volodymyr Hryniov became the presidential adviser on regional issues, his progressive marginalisation within the presidential apparatus reflected Kuchma's distancing from the idea. Instead, the president began to argue that regions had to concede their autonomy for the sake of economic reforms. As a token gesture reminiscent of the idea of giving greater powers to the regions, the president set up an advisory Council of Regions (see chapter 6) and supported a bi-cameral legislature, in which the upper house would represent the regions. However, aimed at counterbalancing the left-dominated Supreme Council (which would become the lower chamber), those initiatives were predominantly designed to strengthen the presidency, rather than to give the greater representation for the regions.

Overall, federalist ideas enjoyed the support of the regional elites and parties rooted in Eastern and Southern Ukraine. However, because of their immediate circumstances, the proponents of federalism tended to focus on their narrow regional perspectives at the expense of forming a pan-regional alliance to promote federalism. They stopped short of elaborating a detailed and coherent federal model. Whilst the advocates of federalisation of Ukraine generally referred to the federal-land system (*federalno-zemelnyi ustriy*), they did not specify the units of the future federation and their respective powers. The Eastern Ukrainian elites failed to unite on the issue as they were internally divided between the (economic) reformist wing of local leaders and leftist parties. While the latter represented the regions in parliament, they rejected federalism.

Unitarism

As federalism gained prominence, the opposition, consisting of the president and national-democrats and Left, united against it, albeit the motives of each of those actors were different. Nevertheless, the range, intensity and sheer volume of arguments against the federal model evidenced the persuasiveness of federalist ideas in the Ukrainian constitutional debates. The opponents of federalism tried to discredit federalism and demonstrate its unsuitability for Ukraine.

The Left, in general, opposed even the use of the terms 'unitarism' and 'federalism'.[31] Federalism was at odds with the 'pyramid of soviets', as it would necessitate a bi-cameral legislature. The left-wing parties opposed reform of state institutions and territorial units that Ukraine inherited from the Soviet Union.

However, for a variety of reasons, federalism was also discarded by 'the reformers', i.e. those who insisted on the need to reform Soviet-era regional and local institutions. The national-democrats took the lead in dismissing federalism, assisted in their task by prominent constitutional lawyers. Other actors, such as the president and the centrist factions, tacitly accepted the validity of their reasoning. The national-democrats rejected federalisation on the grounds that Ukraine needed to become a single organism and integrate its regions into one political entity.[32] As the national identity was unevenly developed, granting the Russified regions substantive political, economic and cultural autonomy would deepen the already pronounced historical, cultural and linguistic cleavages.[33] As sub-state government tends to encourage territorial socialisation by the forging of distinct identities of political territories (through educational systems and the use of iconographic symbols such as a flag and emblem), central government would have to compete with federal sub-national governments in fostering allegiance. By institutionalising regional differences, federalism would not only perpetuate them, but would also mobilise centrifugal forces by providing them with a symbolic legitimacy and institutional resources. If the sub-national association grew too strong, this would encourage regional loyalties at the expense of the unity of the nation; regional interests would prevail at the cost of the consolidation of the new polity. The national-democrats insisted that first of all there had to be a strong national identity to resist centrifugal tendencies. As such an identity was lacking in Ukraine, the creation of sub-state units would jeopardise the nation-building process and endanger Ukrainian independence. The arguments of the national-democrats revealed the lingering lack of trust in the loyalty and allegiance of Eastern and Southern Ukraine's elites to the new Ukrainian state, who were believed to prioritise regional as opposed to national interests and to favour re-integration with Russia.

Instead, Ukraine's regions should be homogenised through a uniform system of local self-government. The exposure of regions to the unitary system of institutions would facilitate the integration of the new polity, in line with the classic European traditions of state building:

> The establishment of a modern nation-state requires a unitary political system that would allow for the implementation of a general methodology of state building and for the functional co-ordination of central and regional governmental mechanism. European constitutionalism dictates that a nation-state is built as a single, unitary organism.[34]

For the national-democrats, the concept of *soborna Ukraina* encapsulated the ideal of independent, united and integrated state.[35]

Arguments favouring federalism as a way of accommodating those political, ethnic, cultural and economic differences—in other words strengthening territorial integrity by weakening centrifugal drives—were discarded for two reasons. First, because of the pronounced centrifugal tendencies found in Donbas, Nova Rossiya, Transcarpathia and Crimea. Second, because of Russia's imperial ambitions and readiness to support separatist movements in Ukraine (like, for example, it did in Transdnistria). Thus, 'rather than promote the implementation of reforms, [federalism] would on the contrary be capable of leading to the intensification of separatist tendencies in certain regions of Ukraine, and, by the same token, would destabilise the situation in society'.[36] The breakup of the Soviet Union and separatist movements in the Russian Federation (including the war with Chechnia) were proof of the disintegrative potential of federalism.[37]

However, the national-democrats faced a dilemma. While they emphasised the tradition of Ukrainian state building and cherished the memory of the intellectual fathers of modern Ukrainian statehood, federalism featured prominently in the thinking of such key Ukrainian intellectuals, as Mykhailo Drahomanov and Mykhailo Hrushevskyi, whose political ideas and activities greatly advanced the Ukrainian national cause. These federalist ideas were dismissed as a product of *Zeitgeist*. According to professor Volodymyr Shapoval, one of the leading constitutional lawyers involved in constitution drafting, the federative ideas of Drahomanov and Hrushevskyi originated in the specific circumstances of Ukraine in a centralised Russian empire at the end of the nineteenth century, when federation of Slavic nations was viewed as a viable way of building a Ukrainian state. As Shapoval argued:

> In the second half of the nineteenth century, the idea of federalism was fairly popular among the progressively thinking Ukrainian intelligentsia. However, those who upheld the idea of federalism were attracted only by its external aspect, so the role and place of the Ukrainian nation and its land were considered in the context of a so-called federation of Slavic republics, rather than the territorial division of the authority of state bodies.[38]

In other words, while federalism was conceived as a means of carving out Ukrainian autonomy within the Russian empire, it was not to be regarded as a model for the internal organisation of the Ukrainian state. Federalism was predominantly viewed as a legacy of foreign domination: 'all foregoing forms of political life on Ukrainian land were in fact the state systems of *other* countries, not of Ukraine' (emphasis in the original).[39] Moreover, the deliberations of Ukrainian intellectuals could not guide the state-builders in post-communist Ukraine, because, as it was pointed out, Ukraine had never experienced a territorial division of state powers pursuant to the principle of federalism:

> There were no clear-cut principles to delineate the historical boundaries of the regions between the subjects of the federation and neither their number nor competencies were specified. Therefore, this justifies the cautious approach to the tendency to 'absolutise' the federal conception of statehood in Ukrainian political thought.[40]

The confining of federalist ideas to the dustbin of history by the political forces in independent Ukraine which claimed to continue state-building tradition initiated by such figures as Hrushevskyi signified the break with the indigenous intellectual heritage. As Rudnytsky pointed out:

> The strength of the old federalist concept was its breadth of vision. It placed the Ukrainian problem within a wide international context, organically connecting the goal of national liberation with the cause of political liberty and social progress of Eastern Europe as a whole.[41]

By the end of the twentieth century as new forms of co-operation and integration between states developed, the two currents of Ukrainian political thought, federalism and separatism appeared to no longer be mutually exclusive but, rather, complementary.[42] However, insofar as the national-democrats were drawing on the indigenous tradition, the attainment of *samostiinist* (independence) took primacy over more pluralistic forms of statehood advocated by their intellectual forebears.

The ideal of an integrated sovereign state permeated the constitutional debates. Once the state existed, the rationale for having a federation vanished. Federalism was understood as a mechanism for founding new states, but not reforming existing ones. Countries such as USA, Switzerland, and Canada 'evolved from confederations (a union of sovereign states) to federations (a united sovereign state) through choice, consent or convenant'.[43] In other words, federations are formed by autonomous territories wishing to become a single political system: 'federalism is a means of unifying separated regions, not decentralising the integrity'.[44] Ukraine had no separate territories to unite, because it already existed as a legally bounded territory. Thus, there was no need to draw the separate units together through federal arrangements. It was argued that in the case of the USA federalism was synonymous with centralisation. In contrast, in post-Soviet Ukraine federalism would amount to disintegration rather than integration. Curiously, examples of other federations, such as Germany and Austria, were viewed as 'of a more or less artificial character', as these states were 'artificially' federalised (although the historical roots of those federations in the nineteenth century German principalities and Austro–Hungarian provinces were acknowledged). In line with Soviet theory, only federations built on ethnic principles were genuine federations.

Instead, the national-democrats evoked the tradition of the Ukrainian People's Republic (UNR) of 1917–1921, which was defined as a decentralised unitary state (see chapter 2), to demonstrate the indigenous tradition, which was also more appropriate for an independent Ukraine. This model was viewed as sufficiently flexible to integrate Ukrainian 'ethnographic lands' with various political traditions. But while it was acknowledged that the 1918 draft constitution also envisaged 'national personal autonomy', that is the right to form national unions with self-governing competence in issues affecting the 'national way of life' of minorities, it was emphasised that national-personal autonomy was not to be confused with territorial autonomy for minorities.

The idea of federalising Ukraine never entered into the formal stage of constitution making; the second Constitutional Commission, which was created in 1994, flatly refused to consider it. Yet even if the federal model was rejected by the constitution drafters and did not find its way into the constitution, the debate on federalism highlighted the salience of regional diversity in Ukraine and the search for a formula to accommodate it.

However, the rejection of federalism as an option for state building in Ukraine did not mean that the elaboration of the unitary model was a straightforward matter. First of all, the case of Crimea had to be dealt with separately. Second, in a unitary model of state, the actual institutions of the state at the regional and local level had to be defined.

Crimea

While the federal model of the state was rejected by the unlikely coalition of national-democrats, the Left, the president and some centrists, the question of Crimea divided the 'unitarists'. All of them conceded that Crimea was a special case. However, the 'unitarists' differed in their views on the institutional means to deal with specificities of Crimea.

The Crimean peninsula was the only region of Ukraine with an ethnic Russian majority; it also had strong historical links with Russia. Crimea was incorporated into Ukraine in 1954 as an administrative–territorial unit (oblast) after the Crimean Autonomous Soviet Republic was abolished in 1945 (following the deportation of the Crimean Tatars in 1944).[45] In recognition of this distinctive character, on the eve of Ukrainian independence in the spring 1991 the status of the Crimean Autonomous Republic was renewed by the Supreme Council of Ukraine. However, these measures failed to placate the Crimean elites, and after the 1991 Ukrainian referendum on independence, the separatist tendencies intensified, exacerbated by the encouragement of Russia's political elites, who viewed Crimea as rightfully belonging to Russia. The issue was further compounded by the unresolved issue of the Black Sea Fleet stationed in Sevastopol. In May 1992 the Crimean leaders passed the Constitution of the Republic of Crimea, which proclaimed the peninsula to be a sovereign state that 'enters into the state of Ukraine and defines its relations with Ukraine on the basis of contract and agreements'.[46] In 1994 the separatist tendencies peaked with the elections of the pro-Russian Crimean president Yuriy Meshkov. This surge of anti-Ukrainian and pro-Russian attitudes in Crimea resulted in a clampdown by Kyiv. The first step was the 'Law on the Autonomous Republic of Crimea' of 17 March 1995, which reduced the autonomy of Crimea, abolished the Crimean presidency and cancelled the 1992 constitution. This was followed by Kuchma's decree, which put the executive institutions of Crimea under the direct jurisdiction of the 'executive authority of Ukraine'. In August 1995, the president issued a decree 'On the Bodies of State Executive Power of the Autonomous Republic of Crimea', which revised his March decree, and stipulated that the prime minister of the Autonomous Republic of Crimea (ARC) could be appointed and dismissed by the Supreme Council of ARC upon the agreement of the president of Ukraine. Also state administration at the *raion* level in ARC was formed and subordinated to the cabinet of ministers of ARC, the cabinet of ministers of Ukraine and the president of Ukraine. In November 1995 the Supreme Council of ARC adopted a new Constitution of the Autonomous Republic and submitted it to the Supreme Council of Ukraine. In April 1996, the Ukrainian parliament considered this Constitution, and rejected twenty articles that contradicted the laws of Ukraine, in such spheres as Crimean citizenship, state symbols, control over power ministries, property rights, and two state languages (Ukrainian and Russian).

It was a matter of urgency that the new Ukrainian constitution finally defined the scope of Crimean autonomy; the main 'bones of contention' included: the name; the law making powers of the Crimean parliament; the right to have a constitution, to establish diplomatic relations, to maintain separate security forces, establish Crimean citizenship and hold dual citizenship with other states, to control the budget and raise taxes, and the official language and property rights in the peninsula.

Although they rejected a federal model for Ukraine at large, Kuchma, the leftist and centrist factions made an exception for Crimea. They conceded that extensive autonomy was indispensable to placate the centrifugal forces and prevent separatism. In particular, the Left and the Inter-Regional Group of Deputies (MDG) supported the Crimean elites on a number of issues, such as the name 'Autonomous Republic', the constitution, the law making prerogative of the Supreme Council of Crimea, citizenship and language. Also, as an attribute of sovereignty they supported the creation of a permanent representative of the Crimean Autonomous Republic in Kyiv.

In contrast, the national-democrats vehemently opposed any far-reaching concessions on the grounds that the creation of the Crimean Republic would reinforce separatism in the peninsula. Any recognition of the sovereignty of Crimean institutions over the territory of peninsula would usurp the sovereignty of the Ukrainian state as a whole. While radical right-wing parties called for Crimea to be reduced to the status of an oblast, the two national-democratic factions, Rukh and *Derzhavnist'*, conceded that Crimea could not be equated with other oblasts and required tailor-made arrangements. Yet they stressed the imperative to integrate Crimea into Ukraine and prevent separatism by giving Kyiv the upper hand in the division of power. The national-democrats contemplated only limited Crimean Autonomy (*Avtonomia*) instead of the status of a 'republic' on the grounds that an autonomous republic would be incompatible with the unitary model of state. As an 'autonomy', Crimea would be denied the attributes of sovereignty, such as a presidency, the constitution, the right to pass laws and raise taxes.[47] Rather than a fully-fledged parliament with law making powers, the Supreme Council of Crimea was to be a regional representative organ issuing 'decisions and resolutions'. Moreover, Rukh, with its appreciation of ethnicity (see below), promoted the recognition of the Crimean Tatars as the 'indigenous people'. The Tatars, who were returning from Central Asia to Crimea after the deportation by Stalin in 1944, were viewed as the rightful, 'indigenous' people of the peninsula, in contrast to the recent migrants—ethnic Russians. However, in contrast to its stance in 1992, Rukh stopped advocating the Crimean Tatars' right to self-determination through the creation of territorial autonomy in Crimea. This would be a dangerous precedent for other minorities living in compact settlements, such as Romanians.

However, apart from the Inter-Regional Group of Deputies (MDG), which opposed the unitary model of state, the differences between the actors in Kyiv, the president and centre-right factions in parliament, were not irreconcilable, as there was broad agreement that Crimea would not be allowed to have its own (or dual) citizenship, security forces, or to foster diplomatic links bypassing Kyiv. Instead, the main 'bones of contention' were whether Crimea should be named 'republic' or 'autonomy', and whether the Crimean parliament should have the right to pass laws and adopt the constitution. However, it was firmly held that Crimea's situation was exceptional and no similar provisions were to be made for other regions of Ukraine, such as Donbas, Transcarpathia or Bukovina.

THE UNITARY MODEL: 'REFORMERS', 'RESTORATIONISTS' AND DECENTRALISATION

While 'unitarists' rejected federalism as an option for Ukraine for the reasons outlined above, they did not discard the idea of decentralisation, as long as it stopped short of territorial self-governments becoming the 'sub-units of the state'. Decentralisation was not to undermine the sovereignty and territorial integrity of Ukraine:

> In a decentralised form of autonomy, there exists at first an independent sovereign power, which then gives up a part of its rights and attributes to certain territories. Autonomy is the next developmental stage upon the establishment of the central power system, and does not contradict the unitary form of government.[48]

Yet, even if the prevailing view was that Ukraine should be a unitary decentralised state, precisely how it should be presented in the constitution was far from clear.

Apart from the leftist factions, there was a general preference for the abolition of the system of soviets, which was viewed as incapable of offering genuine self-government because of the underlying 'state theory of self-government' that defeated the idea of autonomy. In practice, after the demise of the Communist Party, the councils (*radas*) were associated with a lack of accountability at the local level, and were viewed as an impediment to economic reforms. The reformers, that is the centre-right factions and the president, shared the conviction that genuine local self-government at the level of villages and cities was needed, which would be responsible for the provision of services to local communities. In that respect, they took on board the obligations stemming from Ukraine's admission to the Council of Europe in November 1995, which, among other things, required the implementation of the European Charter on Local Self-Government. The Charter guaranteed local self-government and recognised the community as a basic unit of local government independent of the state.

Despite the broad support for genuine self-government at the level of communities, the intermediate, regional layer of institutions (*meso* level) proved more difficult to agree upon. The concept of decentralisation—which most political forces included in their blueprints on constitutional reforms—conveys a number of meanings and does not imply any particular scope of devolution of power to the regional level. The European Charter of Local Government was also less specific about regional autonomy than about the self-government at a municipal level. Overall, the issue of decentralisation raised three interrelated issues: 1) the formation of regional units; 2) the role and power of self-governing bodies at the *meso* level *vis-à-vis* the centre and regional bodies of state administration; 3) the representation of regional self-governing bodies at the centre. These issues will be dealt with in turn.

Regional Units

The fundamental issue was the type and size of units to be granted territorial self-government. In Tsarist Russia gubernia was the main administrative unit; the USSR replaced them with oblasts.[49] As the largest territorial units in the Ukrainian SSR, oblasts had directly elected councils (*rady*), which controlled the councils at lower levels (village, village-type settlement, cities, and *raion*). As the Tsarist and Soviet systems were highly centralised, there was no indigenous tradition of a self-governing territorial community. Moreover, as a purely administrative creation, oblasts did not coincide with historical regions. However, the quest for historically legitimate and self-contained regions was laden with difficulties, despite, or rather precisely because of, Ukraine's highly fragmented territory. Throughout Ukraine's history, regions, such as Transcarpathia, Galicia (Halychyna), Bukovina, Volynia, Podila,

Chernihiv, Sloboda Ukraine, Nova Rossiya, or Donbas, belonged to different states (for different lengths of time) prior to their incorporation into Soviet Ukraine, and as a result developed different cultural, economic and political profiles.[50] At the same time, because of the volatility of state boundaries, the geographical boundaries of regions were blurred, overlapping, and delineated differently depending on the context. The most important obstacle was the perception that the institutionalisation of historical regions (however difficult they were to delineate) would emphasise the patchy territorial composition of twentieth century Ukraine. In particular, the national-democrats faced a conundrum. On the one hand, oblasts could not be satisfactory territorial units, as they lacked legitimacy and cut cross 'historical' regions; on the other hand, the 'historical' regions proved not only difficult to delineate but their institutionalisation would highlight the weak territorial cohesion of independent Ukraine. The Left, however, did not have similar misgivings about the oblasts, as not only were they Soviet creations but also their preservation allowed the Left to retain their powerbase at the regional level. Similar motives prevailed amongst many centrists.

In the end, under the strain of the sheer number of issues to be dealt with, and the pressure to finalise constitution drafting, the task of elaborating territorial units, which would have greater historical legitimacy without emphasising their distinctiveness as former parts of other states, proved overwhelming. For the lack of viable alternatives, the Soviet-era oblasts came to be accepted as the *meso* level territorial units in Ukraine. However, oblasts' lack of historical legitimacy shaped the actors' views of their role in the spatial division of power.

The Role and Powers of the Regional Self-governing Bodies

Once the path of 'least resistance' was chosen, the key question then concerned the role of oblasts: how much autonomy should they have? Were they to implement the policies of the centre in the region or represent autonomous self-governing units? The problem boiled down to the balance of power between the agencies of the centre (state administration) and representative, directly elected institutions at the *meso* level.

The Right was prepared to devolve power only insofar as it would not subvert the territorial integrity of Ukraine; thus the national-democrats opted for the preservation of oblasts (despite their Soviet pedigree) as a lesser evil, but objected to granting them extensive powers. While favouring extensive self-government at a local level, they opposed the creation of the directly elected regional representative bodies, and instead advocated the indirectly elected oblast *radas,* the legitimacy of which would be weaker *vis-à-vis* the centre. In that respect the national-democrats abandoned their adherence to 'European tradition': directly elected regional self-government performing various functions of regional administration was—by the mid 1990s—the norm in the European Union. The national-democrats believed that in Ukraine, state building required the subordination of regional interests to those of the centre and thus necessitated the circumscription of regional autonomy. In particular, they feared that directly elected regional bodies could challenge the centre's policies in the sphere of language, education and cultural policies, as, for example, did Donbas, which voted in a local plebiscite in 1994 in favour of Russian becoming the official language of administration. The supporting argument in favour of indirect elections was that new people would be recruited 'to [new] *raion* and oblast *radas*, and not the nomenklatura of oblast and *raion* level'.[51] Overall, even if the national-democrats declared their support for decentralisation, in the proposal they strove to weaken the regional self-governing bodies as a safety precaution to prevent centrifugal drives, which could threaten the territorial integrity of the state.

President Kuchma, in turn, stressed the imperative of control and greater efficiency as a rationale for strengthening control over the *meso* level:

> Practically, [today] nobody rules Ukraine. [At the regional level] everybody is interested in his own welfare. The interests of the people and the practical issues of running the state are pushed to the side. There are the first signs of the disintegration of the state. Some oblasts and even districts (*raion*) have taken decisions on the level of their contributions to the state budget. This means that one of the most important laws of Ukraine is not being implemented.[52]

Stressing the lack of accountability and resistance to reform, Kuchma called for the creation of strong executive organs of the state extending to the regions in order to overcome the prevailing anarchy:

> The fully-fledged executive vertical structure is needed to end 'anything goes' (*vsedozvolennist'*), and cronyism, practised by a number of *raion* and city heads. At this level mismanagement prevails, and an ordinary person is left without any protection, support, or justice. We have to eliminate such manifestations of contemporary local feudalism, [and] take radical measures to restore order, [and] protect our citizens.[53]

In the president's view, as the regional self-governing bodies proved unwilling and/or incapable of combating the economic crisis, only the creation of a rigid vertical executive structure could alleviate the problem, with a simultaneous weakening of the oblast and *raion* councils. Kuchma thus favoured the shift to the indirect mode of elections, which would deprive the councils of their popular legitimacy and the re-creation of presidential representatives at the oblast and *raion* level. The chairpersons of such councils would simultaneously be presidential representatives (*predstavnyky prezydenta*) heading the executive body of the regions (the regional state administration). The strict subordination of the heads of local state administrations from the top down would allow the delegation of 'the important decision making, such as the management of state property, to the regional level'.[54] In other words, the decision making power would not be devolved to regions' representative bodies, but delegated to state officials subordinated to the president. Essentially, the president advocated the far-reaching circumvention of regional autonomy, and the creation of a highly centralised model of state. Nevertheless, like the national-democrats, he favoured 'de-statisation' (*vidderzhavlenia*) of the self-governing bodies: they were to cease to be part of the unified and integrated system of state organs, which existed under the Soviet Union (see chapter 2). Yet *vidderzhavlenia* was not to entail a loosening of control over the periphery; instead a reinstated system of French-style prefects, which was first created in the spring of 1992, was to carry out the decisions of the centre at the sub-national level.

As pointed out above, the Left aimed to restore the system of soviets and, to this end, adhered to the so-called 'state theory of local government', according to which representative institutions performed both the functions of self-government and those of state administration, and formed as uniform state structures. This way, the *radas* (soviets) would continue to be subordinated to the central state authorities:

> We support the preservation of the system of councils of the working masses with a clear division of functions between the various levels ... and the vertical subordination of the executive organs of councils to the higher level up to the Council of Ministers in matters of national importance.[55]

At the same time, according to the Left: 'Starting from the criteria outlined in the European Charter [on Local Self-government], there are sufficient grounds to conclude that the Councils of People's Deputies are one of the most powerful and effective forms of self-government'.[56] However, the Left did not reconcile the autonomy of local and regional self-government with the principle of 'democratic centralism', which denoted the hierarchical subordination of councils of lower levels to the higher level (for example, city to oblast). It glossed over the problems that traditionally the soviets could not be autonomous from the state, as they *constituted* the state. In particular, because of the strict financial subordination, the councils had no independent resources to perform their functions and the resources were instead allocated by the centre to the oblast, which then made further allocation to the lower level. The councils had no independent revenue-making sources, such as taxes or municipal property (in line with the Left's opposition to turning land into a commodity).

However, the Left, arguing that the councils combined functions of self-government and state powers, opposed the institutional 'duality of power' at the regional level, that is the co-existence of popularly elected councils with local state administrations headed by the presidential representative. In particular, the institution of a representative as an extension of centre at the regional level undermined their concept of *narodovladia*. Furthermore, the Left consistently argued in favour of the direct mode of elections to all levels of councils, including the oblast and district level, something the national-democrats and the president opposed. The Left even invoked the World Declaration of Local Self-government, which made explicit references to self-government of larger territorial units, while the national-democrats gave priority to the European Charter with its vague references to regional autonomy. Paradoxically, because of its support for directly elected oblast councils, the Left turned into a champion of decentralisation:

> [R]ejecting demagogy and politicking, and striving for democratic principles, there is no need to abolish Councils, but to clearly divide—most of all in the Constitution—the sphere of competencies between the centre, regions and the local level, between the representative and executive bodies, [and] to transfer the right to decide local matters to the local level, and give regions and localities maximum autonomy (*samostiinist*).[57]

Representation of Regions at the Centre

The final question that needed to be resolved was on the representation of the regions at the centre. As a norm, the representation of regional interests takes place through the upper chamber of legislature designed to give voice to the regions, rather than the entire body of citizens. Because of pronounced regional differences, the case for bi-cameralism was strong in Ukraine, and the idea of the upper chamber of parliament repeatedly reappeared during constitutional debates. In 1991 the Working Group of the Constitutional Commission argued that, firstly, bi-cameralism would allow for the division of labour: the lower chamber would focus on law making and financial questions, whereas the upper chamber would perform appointive powers, ratify international treaties and grant citizenship; secondly, it would serve as a forum for regional representation, which was needed in Ukraine because:

> Historically Ukraine was formed as a unitary state. However, the historical, regional and national-ethnic differences of its territories and oblasts remain pronounced. The preservation of the unitary system will be justified only if an effective mechanism for representation of those differences is created. This will be achieved through the representation in the Supreme Council of individual territories (administrative–territorial units).[58]

Amongst the political actors after the 1994 elections, the president supported the idea, yet parliament at large opposed it. The proponents of bi-cameralism consisted of individual deputies scattered across right-wing and centrist factions of parliament, who put forward a range of arguments in favour, most importantly stressing the need for the representations of regional interests at the centre and the need for additional 'checks and balances'.[59]

The arguments levelled against bi-cameralism were basically a repetition of arguments against federalism and regional autonomy. The most common argument against bi-cameralism was that upper houses were needed in federations, whereas Ukraine was a unitary state. Oblasts were purely administrative units and not historical regions, and as such they did not need to be represented at the centre. As Serhiy Holovatyi, the Minister of Justice, argued 'we have oblasts and not regions. Let's create regions and only then represent them'.[60] To the arguments that some unitary states such as Poland, had an upper chamber, opponents pointed out that bi-cameralism in Poland was sanctioned by tradition, whereas in Ukraine such traditions did not exist. In particular, some national-democrats feared the Senate would become a first step towards the federalisation of Ukraine 'through the back door'.

The Left principally objected because bi-cameralism was incompatible with the model of the system of soviets. However, it used the argument of territorial integrity to discredit the institution arguing 'it is necessary to take into account the fact that the creation of the Senate would stimulate separatist and centrifugal forces.'[61] Even the centrist MDG, while favouring the far-reaching devolution of power to the regions, rejected bi-cameralism on the grounds that it would 'split Ukraine' and 'because of the threat of instability, exacerbate regional differences and complicate the legislative process'.[62] However, the MDG's scepticism stemmed from its objection to the formula proposed by the president for the formation of the upper chamber in the November and March 1996 drafts (see chapter 6). As each oblast would have three Senators, the Senate's composition would not reflect the weight of the densely populated Eastern and Southern Ukrainian oblasts, thereby giving an undue prominence to Western and Central Ukrainian oblasts. Each oblast would be represented by three senators regardless of its population. The pivotal issue was that units that were unequal in terms of population were to be given equal representation. For example, in Donetsk one senator would represent 1,300,000 voters, as opposed to 226,000 voters in Chernivtsi. In face of the opposition from the centrist and leftist factions, the supporters of bi-cameralism, including the president, were in minority, and did not go out of their way to insist on the creation of the upper chamber.

To summarise, in term of the concepts of the territorial framework of the state, the main cleavage was between the 'restorationists', who simply favoured the restoration of the *status quo ante*, and the 'reformers', who advocated the abolition of the system of soviets. However, while not without its merits, this division is too simplistic and glosses over the sheer breadth of the issues at stake, such as federalism, regional and local self-government, Crimea, and bi-cameralism. While, the 'reformers' overwhelmingly agreed on the need for and the form of self-government at the local level, they differed in their views, firstly, on the appropriateness of the federal model for Ukraine, and, secondly, on the regional layer of institutions. In other words, while the 'reformist' orientation firmly advocated an end to the system of soviets, there was no agreement on either the concept of regions as territorial units, or their relations with the centre. Attention was focused on the rebuttal of the federal model and the system of soviets, rather than positively elaborating the details of the actual territorial model of division of powers. Even if the unitary decentralised model was advocated by the majority of forces, no essential principles were thought out and agreed upon.

DEFINING THE 'POLITICAL COMMUNITY'

Another dimension of statehood, which remained essentially contested and awaited resolution in the constitution, was the nature of the political community in the name of which the state exercised sovereign authority. In contrast to the institutional issues, where the numerous institutions and prerogatives were to be defined, the questions of nationhood generated two distinctive and opposing conceptions: the Left's 'people of Ukraine' and the national-democrats' 'Ukrainian people', both of which were rooted in and reflected the Soviet dual notion of nationality: politico-territorial and ethno-cultural (see chapter 2). These conceptions encapsulated different definitions of 'the people', its attributes, such as language and symbols, and different approaches to minority rights.

THE NATIONAL-DEMOCRATS: THE 'UKRAINIAN PEOPLE'

According to the 1989 census, ethnic Ukrainians constituted 72 percent of the population of Ukraine. For the national-democrats, the vexed question was: should ethnic Ukrainians be equated with and thus 'diluted' in the mass of over a hundred other nationalities living in Ukraine, or should the new constitution recognise the Ukrainian ethnicity, culture and language as the foundation of the new polity? The Right's key goal was the assertion of the position of the titular majority in the Ukrainian state, as a distinctive ethno-cultural collectivity, which had striven for a state: 'if there is no language and nation, there is no need for a president'.[63]

In their view, the Ukrainian ethnic nation originated in the mists of time from a common ancestry, and embodied a romantic notion of the pre-political community, in which ethnic identity denoted a primordial set of highly valued and unique qualities moulded in a long collective history. To depict this collectivity the national-democrats used the two interrelated concepts of '*natsiia*' and '*ethnos*'. As the development of the Ukrainian *ethnos* took place on the territory of Ukraine, even when it was ruled by other states, Ukrainians formed the indigenous nation (*korinnyi narod*), which exercised its right to self-determination in 1991 and created a nation-state. Nowhere could the fundamental 'ethno-cultural' rights of Ukrainians be realised and protected other than in Ukraine: 'Ukraine can be defined as a nation-state because only Ukrainians historically lived in a given territory and this is the only place in the world where they can realise their right to self-determination'.[64] Therefore, there is a special bond between the state and the titular majority:

> [T]he actualisation of the gamut of national rights of the various ethnic groups, which inhabit Ukraine, is inseparable from the acknowledgement of the fact that the Ukrainian nation (*natsiia*) holds the status of its historical master in the republic. Ukraine is the only territory in the world on which the fully valid existence and development of the Ukrainian *ethnos* is possible.[65]

As the Ukrainian state came into being primarily as a result of the self-determination of the ethnic Ukrainian nation, Ukrainian ethnicity served as the 'foundation' around which a political community was to be built. In other words, the *demos* was formed on the basis of the *ethnos*. For it was the ethno-linguistic collectivity—the Ukrainians—which spawned the political community, the new state was to assume a special responsibility *vis-à-vis* the titular majority.

> Ukraine is a nation-state (*natsionalna derzhava*), that is something that has been a titular nation, which compactly lives on a certain territory, exercising its basic right to political self-determination. The nation-state secures the appropriate conditions for the preservation and development of its [ethnic] nation and the mutual benefit and development of all ethnic groups, which live on its territory.[66]

In particular, the Ukrainian language was given a prominent place amongst the markers of Ukrainian national identity:

> An important integrating factor in ethnic communities is language and national consciousness. A national language is the foundation and the primary source of a culture, the basis of the national existence of a people, and a universal human value. When a national language dies, the people perish as a nation.[67]

The Ukrainian state had a special duty to embrace the Ukrainian language and culture after the centuries-long cultural and linguistic oppression of the Ukrainian *ethnos*. In order to instil feelings of kinship among ethnic Ukrainians and promote the 'linguistic rehabilitation of the citizens of Ukraine',[68] a 'national idea' needed to be implemented through state-sponsored cultural and language policies. The Ukrainian culture and language could be secured only if the legacy of Soviet domination—Russification—was reversed:

> The preservation and deepening of the linguistic *status quo* would deny the Russified Ukrainians their language and national roots ... Large numbers of assimilated people [Russified Ukrainians] remain of secondary importance in the large parts of their land—[this is] a specific phenomenon, which resulted from domination by foreign empires.[69]

According to the national-democrats, the new constitution had not only to assert the 'leading role' of the Ukrainian *ethnos* in the Ukrainian state by adopting their national symbols, but also 'to fix the right of the Ukrainian *ethnos* to a national revival in its land'.[70] In other words, the constitution was to put the state authorities under an obligation to protect and develop the Ukrainian language and culture.

Ukrainian was defined as the state language in the 1989 'Law on Languages' (and to this end article 73 of the 1978 constitution was amended). However, taking into account the widespread use of Russian, especially in Eastern and Southern Ukraine, it was suggested that Russian be granted the status of 'official' language (see below). For the right wing placing Russian alongside Ukrainian in the constitution would legitimise the centuries-long discrimination against the Ukrainian language and fix the *status quo,* which resulted from foreign domination that is the factual dominance of the Russian language in Ukraine. Thus, if the revival of the Ukrainian language was to take place, no provision for Russian was to be made in the constitution. Even if a large percentage of ethnic Ukrainians in Eastern and Southern Ukraine were Russophones, for the national-democrats the Russian language in Ukraine was only the language of the ethnic Russians, and, thus, it had to be 'rolled back' to coincide with the boundaries of Russian minority. The argument (factually incorrect) was that nowhere in the world was the language of a national minority elevated to the position of the state language. In those few states where bilingualism existed, such as Canada or Switzerland, it was because those states were constituted by several *ethnie*, each of which 'entered' the common state with their own territory and language territory.[71]

With granting the constitutional recognition to Russian, not only would past injustice not be redressed; the future of the state was also at stake according to the national-democrats. Independence could only be assured when bonds of mutuality, social solidarity and brotherhood developed on the basis of ethno-cultural ties embraced by the population of Ukraine. The national-democrats believed that a democratic political culture could not develop without some ethno-linguistic uniformity; the indigenous Ukrainian democratic political culture was destroyed by the Soviet Union and constitutional, civic patriotism could not be relied upon to secure the loyalty to the new state. In other words, the revival of the Ukrainian *ethnos* was to help to gel the population into a civic nation. The national-democrats argued that such a path was universally followed as 'nowhere in the world do there exist states created on a non-ethnic basis. Simply, they have been along that road a long time ago and simply forgot it'.[72] It was further argued that the constitution should adopt the attributes of the Ukrainian *natsiia* as its symbols: the trident, the 'blue and yellow' flag, and the anthem 'Ukraine Has Not Yet Perished'.[73]

Nevertheless, despite stressing the right of the Ukrainian *ethnos*, the right wing adhered to the pluralist notion of the nation.[74] By distinguishing between the ethnic Ukrainian nation (*natsiia)* and the national minorities (*natsionalni menshyny*), it recognised the presence and the rights of the latter.[75] Minorities were defined as distinctive ethno-cultural communities that inhabit the territory of Ukraine alongside ethnic Ukrainians. While seeing Ukraine as a 'pluralistic nation-state', the national-democrats advocated the creation of the Ukrainian political nation on the basis of the core ethnic Ukrainian nation (*natsiia*) with the national minorities incorporated as collective members of the 'Ukrainian nation'. To this end, the national-democrats' appreciation of ethnicity turned them into champions of the rights of national minorities, albeit according to the degree of 'indigenousness'. In line with the draft UN 'Declaration on the Rights of Indigenous People', the right-wing parties distinguished between the 'indigenous people' (*korinni narody*) of Ukraine, that was those minorities which did not have 'historical homelands' outside Ukraine, and other national minorities, such as Poles, Russians, Romanians, which had their 'host' states outside Ukraine. Symptomatically, apart from the Crimean Tatars and other small ethnic groups, the former category also included the titular majority, ethnic Ukrainians:

> In Ukraine there are no other nations because other national groups have their own states outside Ukraine, and [thus] they do not have objective and subjective reasons for the formation of a separate [ethnic] nation (*natsiia*) on Ukrainian territory. The exception is the case of the Crimean Tatars and, with some qualifications, the Karaims, Krymchaks and others, which survived only as an indigenous *ethnos*.[76]

According to the national-democrats, the possession of a homeland outside Ukraine conferred a different status and rights on ethnic groups in Ukraine, compared to those that lacked such homelands. Thus, non-Ukrainians were to be given collective rights according to their degree of 'indigenousness': those without homelands outside Ukraine—indigenous people—were assigned higher status (but Rukh retreated from its promise of territorial autonomy by 1994), whereas the national minorities were to be entitled to cultural autonomy. Rukh pointed out that its stance on minority rights fully met the European standards on human rights, because as a minimum Rukh advocated cultural autonomy.

Overall, the moderate Right advocated the conception of a political community defined as the 'Ukrainian people'. Nevertheless, while accepting the presence and rights of national minorities as 'state-forming communities', they believed that the indigenous rights of the Ukrainians made them the core *ethnos* around which the new civic nation was to be built. In order to guarantee the survival and development of that *ethnos*, its position was to be fixed in the new constitution, most importantly in the Preamble and articles on the state language and symbols.

THE LEFT: 'THE PEOPLE OF UKRAINE'

Although in Ukrainian the word *natsiia* denotes an ethnic notion of a nation, the Left interpreted the 'Ukrainian people' (*Ukrainskyi narod*) in exclusive, ethnic terms. For it the adjective 'Ukrainian' depicted ownership of the state by the Ukrainian *natsiia* and symbolised 'Ukraine for Ukrainians'—the slogan associated with the brand of integral nationalism propagated by the militant Organisation of Ukrainian Nationalists of the 1930s, which drew its supporters mainly from Eastern Galicia (*Halychyna*) in inter-war Poland. Thus, the Left claimed that 'the Ukrainian people' lacked a deeper resonance in Ukrainian society, apart from a narrow group of nationalists of Western Ukrainian stock. In particular, they vehemently opposed the notion that Ukraine emerged as a result of 'self-determination of the Ukrainian *natsiia*'.

Instead, the Left defined the political community of Ukraine as the territorial, supra-ethnic community 'the people of Ukraine' (*narod Ukrainy*). By defining 'the people of Ukraine' as the sum of people living on Ukrainian territory, Ukraine's multi-ethnic composition was to be asserted and preserved. On the one hand, 'the people of Ukraine' would emphasise both equality of all nationalities living in Ukraine, and, on the other the state's 'neutrality' in the sphere of language and culture. Ethnicity—as a state-validating factor—was rejected. Moreover, they opposed breaking 'the people' down into sub-components, the eponymous majority and national minorities, on the grounds that 'it was discriminatory and would practically exclude the tens of millions of citizens of Ukraine of other nationalities who build and support their state—Ukraine'.[77] In particular, as the communist leader Petro Symonenko declared, they opposed defining Russians in Ukraine as the national minority.[78] Instead, they favoured the definition coined by Kravchuk: 'When Leonid Kravchuk was running for the presidency [in 1991], he expressed a very applaudable (*slushnu*) idea that the Russians in Ukraine were not a national minority, but one of the two branches (*hilky*) of the one people of Ukraine (*narod Ukrainy*)'.[79]

The attributes of the political community—language and symbols—were to reflect and respect the multi-ethnic composition of Ukraine. While all languages could develop freely, Russian was to be become the state or at least the *official* language of Ukraine alongside Ukrainian, although the meaning of 'official' as opposed to 'state' language remained unclear. The examples of Finland and Switzerland, which recognise several languages as equal, were cited as a model for Ukraine. The Left feared that Russian would be squeezed out by the state-sponsored Ukrainisation policies aimed at linguistic and cultural revival of the titular majority. In a similar vein, what for the national-democrats were the legitimate historical symbols of Ukrainian statehood—the blue and yellow flag, the trident and the anthem 'Ukraine Has Not Yet Perished'—were depicted by the Left as exclusive and alienating. The communists particularly ardently opposed these symbols as they were used by the 'bourgeois nationalist' Ukrainian People's Republic (1917–1921) and, moreover, by the Ukrainian Insurgent Army, which waged a struggle against the Soviet Union in Western Ukraine in the 1940–50s. Using highly emotional rhetoric the Left insisted that the symbols adopted in 1991 played only an antagonising role outside Western Ukraine, in contrast to, for example, the Soviet hammer and sickle, which innocently 'signified the importance of labour'.[80] Thus the Left recommended that the choice of symbols be subjected to a referendum on the principles of the new constitution (as was the case in Belarus in 1995), or the symbols were to be left out of the constitution, and later defined by an ordinary law.

The Left's arguments for preventing the supremacy of one ethnic group—the titular majority—could give the appearance of the support for a pluralistic model of nationhood, especially in light of the fact that minorities constituted 28 percent of the population of Ukraine. But while claiming that the assertion of the position of the titular majority would set it against national minorities and open the door to discrimination and exclusion on ethnic grounds, the Left did not champion minority rights. By rejecting the very concept of national minorities, the Left rejected the need for collective rights of national minorities living in Ukraine. As Brubaker has reminded us 'minorities can only exist where there is an ethno-cultural majority'.[81] The Ukrainian Left denied recognition of ethnicity altogether; its concept of political community, the *narod Ukrainy* actually implied a homogeneous entity composed of individuals living on the territory of Ukraine. By denying ethnicity any formal recognition at the state level, the Left adhered to the 'purest' form of the territorial nation based on the universalist notion of citizenship: all individuals who were collectively subject to the same government and the same laws form a nation.

Rather than ethnicity, the Left stressed the role of socio-economic rights in forging the solidarity and unity of a political community. With their focus on class, the communists, in particular, adhered to the Soviet regime's assertion according to which 'Ukraine [was] a state of all people, expressing the will and interests of the workers, peasants and intelligentsia: the working people of all nationalities of the Republic' (1978 Constitution of the UkrSSR). And instead of interfering in the cultural domain, the Ukrainian state was to confine itself to the promotion of socio-economic progress, which was defined either in classic Marxist–Leninist terms (Communists) or more hybrid communist/social-democratic terms (Socialists). The role of the state lays primarily in ensuring socio-economic welfare and equality, and, thus, the Left insisted on the state's protection of collective property in the constitution, together with explicit state guarantees of free education, housing, work, holidays, health care and so forth. The constitution was to explicitly place the state under obligation to deliver an array of socio-economic 'goods'. (In contrast, the other actors favoured a vaguely worded 'indication of intentions' of the state to act in the socio-economic sphere.)

However, while the communists, socialists and peasants united in their vehement denial of an ethnic Ukrainian foundation of the new state, there was a pivotal split within the Left. The socialists and the peasants accepted the *status quo*, that is the new political community was legitimately constituted in a referendum vote on independence in December 1991. The Communist Party of Ukraine, however, did not recognise the results of the referendum and declared its aim to restore the Soviet political community through the voluntary creation of the equal (*rivnopravnyi*) Union of Soviet Sovereign States, because 'all historical experience demonstrates that it was the best, the optimal form for all-round development of former republics'.[82] The leader of the CPU, Petro Symonenko, argued that the CPU supported the Declaration of Sovereignty of July 1990 and the Act of Independence of August 1991, and in March 1991 the renewal of the Union. Therefore, the Act of Independence was entirely compatible with Ukraine's remaining within the Soviet Union, and 'the destruction of the Soviet Union was illegal, performed without the consent of the peoples of Union republics and the [Soviet] Union at large'.[83] As such, the CPU, the largest political party in the country did not come to terms with Ukraine's sovereignty and advocated the restoration of the *status quo ante*—'the Soviet people'. The 'people of Ukraine' (*narod Ukrainy*) were to serve as a stepping-stone in the rebuilding of the larger collectivity, the 'Soviet people'. The communists insisted on the right on a referendum to decide Ukraine's 'voluntary accession to political unions with other states which emerged on the territory of the former USSR'.[84]

To this end, the Left adhered to a strictly territorial definition of the political community encapsulated in the notion of a '*narod Ukrainy*' denying any recognition of the special position and privileges to the Ukrainian *ethnos* in post-Soviet Ukraine. As a consequence, the Left rejected 'nationalistic' symbols and insisted on the upgrading of the status of the Russian language to that of 'official' language. By rejecting ethnicity as a state-validating factor, the Left viewed the fulfilment of socio-economic rights as a primary responsibility of the state, rather than implementation of cultural and linguistic policies.

THE PARLIAMENTARY CENTRE AND THE PRESIDENT

While the Left and Right clashed in their conceptions of nationhood, the centrist factions were profoundly divided on the issue. Overall, the split in the centrist bloc was in line with the regional and linguistic composition of the factions. The Inter-Regional Group of Deputies (MDG) took the most consistent stance and sided with the Left in its opposition to the ethnicised notion of the *Ukrainskyi narod*, 'nationalist' symbols and the lack of recognition of the Russian language in the draft constitution. The 'Reforms' favoured Ukrainian as the only state language, and principally backed the right wing factions on the national question, although it paid less attention to the issue. Other Ukrainophone factions, such as the 'Centre', aligned themselves with the national-democrats. The 'Social Market Choice' faction was divided between the Russophone and Ukrainophone deputies.

Overall, the parliamentary centre failed to develop a coherent, alternative stance to that of the Left or Right. The majority of factions were divided internally, though the 'national question' did not feature prominently on their agenda. The centrists tended to be too preoccupied with sectoral, functional, or personal interests to engage in ideologically loaded discussions on the conception of nationhood, (which tended to be time-consuming and exhausting, yet brought few tangible benefits for the Right and Left). Hence, the centrists tended to side either with the Left or Right in their views on 'Ukrainian People' or 'People of Ukraine', state language and symbols, although the rationale underlying their stance often differed from their allies. For example, a liberal Russophone deputy, Volodymyr Aleksiiev, justified calls for granting 'official' status to the Russian language in Ukraine by invoking 'fundamental human rights'. The state's role was to serve its citizens rather than impose state language, and create an artificial division between the *korinni* and *nekorinni* (non-indigenous) nationalities.[85]

Taking into account the bi-polarity of parliament on this question, the stance of the president could decisively swing the pendulum. While the first president of Ukraine[86] Leonid Kravchuk was depicted as a nationalist by the left-wing parties, his successor, the technocrat Leonid Kuchma, came to power on an anti-nationalist platform. In that respect, Kuchma was representative of the anti-communist strand of Russophone elites. In the election campaign Kuchma rejected 'romantic Galician nationalism' arguing that the consolidation of the Ukrainian state had to take place in full recognition of the fact that Ukraine was a multinational state. In his inaugural speech, Kuchma asserted that:

> A Ukrainian state cannot be an end in itself. The state exists for the people and not the people for the state … Ukraine is not an icon, in front of which one has to pray. Ukraine is a multinational state. Any attempts to ignore this fact threaten to create a deep gulf in our society and crush the idea of the Ukrainian state … In the nearest future, I'm going to propose changes to the legislation in order to give Russian official status.[87]

To the outcry of the national-democrats, Kuchma's assessed 'the geopolitical realities' in the following way:

> Historically Ukraine is a part of the Eurasian economic and cultural space. Today, Ukraine's vital national interests are concentrated on the territory of the former USSR ... The self-isolation of Ukraine, its voluntary refusal to actively pursue its interests in the Eurasian sphere was a serious mistake, which caused significant damage, most of all, to the national economy.[88]

Shortly after the elections, Kuchma's declared intention of upgrading Russian to 'official' status and a pro-Russia foreign policy orientation seemed to put him firmly in alliance with the leftist bloc and in opposition to the national-democrats.

However, within several months, to the relief of the national-democrats, Kuchma turned into what was referred to as *derzhavnyk,* a firm supporter of Ukrainian sovereignty and territorial integrity. He distanced from his original proclamations in favour of re-integration with Russia:

> The objective political, economic and geopolitical analysis gives basis to the assertion that only an independent Ukraine is today the optimal form of preservation (*samovyzhyvannia*) of its people ... The point of no return has been passed, and in whatever direction the development of Ukraine will go, there can be no return to the past.[89]

In the recurring battle in the Ukrainian parliament between the Left and Right on the question of membership in the CIS Inter-parliamentary Assembly—the political arm of the Commonwealth—Kuchma sided with the Right. Ukraine remained a reluctant associate member of the CIS. He also firmly rejected the possibility of dual citizenship for Russians in Ukraine, which were still insisted on by Russia and the Communist Party of Ukraine in early 1995.[90]

Kuchma played down the sensitive and controversial issue of Russian as the second official language, despite it having been the cornerstone of his presidential campaign (significantly he himself switched from using Russian to Ukrainian). Although not keen on promoting the 'national idea' as the new state ideology through a 'top-down' Ukrainisation policy (something associated with, though not in fact pursued by, Kravchuk),[91] Kuchma continued the mission of moderated 'nation building' of his predecessor.[92] He soon came to appreciate the 'genealogy' of the Ukrainian state and glorified Ukrainian history as a sequence of national liberation struggles. Ukraine's history, as he suggested, 'can be understood only in terms of the achievements and frustrations of the nation'.[93] Kuchma celebrated the role of Cossack Hetman Bohdan Khmelnytskyi as that of a national hero, and asserted that 'today, carrying on Bohdan's work, we are realising the third attempt at the revival of our state'.[94] However, Kuchma stopped short of asserting 'state ownership' by the titular majority and argued that 'international peace and interethnic harmony is evidence that we adhere to the correct policy in a matter of such importance and sensitivity as the national policy of the state. In short, its essence is: Ukraine—is a common home, homeland for all its citizens'.[95] Having witnessed Kuchma's evolution many observers—with the benefit of hindsight—noted that his newly found 'patriotism' stemmed from the logic of his position as head of an independent state, though this was less than evident on the eve of and immediately after the election.[96]

To be sure, the presidential entourage did not speak with one voice. Dissenting voices originated even from the highest quarters, including presidential advisers. In two books published by Kuchma's associates in 1995, more 'cosmopolitan' views were projected, and the authors advocated 'integration into the Eurasian space', bi-lingualism, a pro-Russian foreign policy orientation, and openly doubted the 'historical distinctiveness' and even the viability of Ukraine as an independent state. However, those voices were swiftly muted and/or marginalised.[97]

Kuchma's transformation on the 'national question' prompted the opinions that 'instead of national romanticism [of Kravchuk], a new idea came to the fore—that of statehood as a call for a new, strong, paternalistic and—*within reason—national state'* (emphasis added).[98] However, how 'national' the state should be according to Kuchma was far from clear, and, as will be argued in the next chapter, it was a flexible item on the presidential agenda during constitution drafting. Nevertheless, Kuchma's credentials as a *derzhavnyk* and his decision to distance himself from the policy of granting Russian official status in Ukraine, even if accompanied by a cautious approach to cultural and language policies, sufficed for *a modus vivendi* with the national-democrats and opened the way for close co-operation during the passage of the constitution.[99]

CONCLUSION

Despite being designed to maximise the incumbents' chances of being re-elected, the electoral law returned few of them to their parliamentary seats in the 1994 parliamentary elections. Once again parliament was filled by a large contingent of independent candidates with nebulous ideological profile. While the centrist parties won a handful of seats, the re-legalised Communist Party of Ukraine emerged as the biggest winner. The national-democrats duplicated the 1990 election results gaining about one fourth of all seats. This meant that the new Supreme Council turned into a forum of contest between the two ideological blocs. As is clear from the constitutional debates, the Left and Right demonstrated two diametrically opposing conceptions of statehood (Table 5.4).

The leftist bloc, which was made up of Communist, Socialist and Peasant parties, that had their geographical power base is Eastern, Southern and rural Central Ukraine, was united by a shared idealised view of the Soviet past, its achievements, and its political and economic institutions. This was accompanied by a passionate rejection of 'Ukrainian bourgeois nationalism', which was equated with the constitutionally enshrined official status of the Ukrainian language and symbols. In its view, alongside Russians and Belarussians, Ukrainians belonged to the East-Slavic civilisation, which developed a distinctive mentality and traditions, which set these nations apart from the Western world. The preferred conception of statehood was ultimately a perpetuation of the Soviet model. Nevertheless, the bloc was not homogeneous and was split in terms of attitudes toward independence. While the socialists and peasants (and some communists) accepted Ukrainian independence and did not advocate the restoration of the Soviet Union (although they did favour close co-operation with Russia and the CIS), and thus preferred a socialist path of development *within* an independent Ukraine, the hard-line communists openly denied the legitimacy of Ukrainian statehood by calling for the reincarnation of the USSR.[100]

At the opposite end of the political spectrum, the national-democrats (represented in the Rukh and Statehood factions) derived their support from Western and urban Central Ukraine. This bloc saw itself as the avant-garde pushing for Ukraine's 'return to Europe' after centuries of oppression and exploitation suffered in the Russian empire. It was passionately anti-communist and equated Soviet rule with a foreign occupation, which brought about the genocide of the Ukrainian nation, the distortion of Ukraine's economic development and the degeneration of its social and cultural tissue. Rebuking the past meant repairing the damage done to the Ukrainian language and culture as a matter of priority in building a Ukrainian nation-state. The socio-economic transformation towards a market economy and the political reform leading to a strong and efficient democratic state also figured on their agenda, although it was defined in a much less precise way than the strategy on

Table 5.4. Positions of the Parliamentary Factions on Key Constitutional Issues (Spring 1996)

	Executive Presidency[i]	**Presidential Representatives in Regions**	**Crimean Republic**	**Guarantee of the Right to Private Property**	**National Symbols**	**Ukrainian Language as the Only State Language**
The Left						
Communists	-	-	+	-	-	-
Socialists	-	-	+	-/+	-	-
Peasants	-	-	+	-	-	-
Centrist Factions						
MDG	-/+	-	+	+	-	-
Independents	-/+	-/+	+	+	*	+/-
Agrarians for Reforms	+/-	+/-	+	+	+/-	+/-
Unity	+/-	+/-	+	+	*	+/-
Centre	+	+	+/-	+	+/-	+/-
Social Market Choice	+	+/-	+/-	+	*	+/-
The National-Democrats						
Reforms	+/-	+/-	-	+	+	+
Rukh	+	+	-	+	+	+
Statehood	+	+/-	-	+	+	+

Key: - 'opposed' + 'supported' +/- 'mostly in favour' -/+ 'mostly opposed' * 'undecided'

Source: Adapted from Artur Bilous *et al.*, *Proiekt Konstytutsii Ukrainy: stan, problemy, perspektyvy* (Kyiv, 1996).

[i] The president appoints the members of the cabinet of ministers.

the 'national question'. The institutional framework was to embody the democratic, European credentials of the new state, while ensuring the territorial integrity and progress of socio-economic reforms. Despite emphasising the symbolic continuity between the Ukrainian People's Republic (1917–1921) and post-Soviet Ukraine, the national-democrats took a cautious stance on the usefulness of the UNR's form of government for state building in independent Ukraine. The pure parliamentary model and far-reaching territorial decentralisation, which characterised the UNR, were rejected for post-Soviet Ukraine because of the fear that they would strengthen the anti-state left-wing forces, feed centrifugal tendencies, and hamper economic reforms. In other words, in order to successfully continue the state-building process initiated by the leaders of the UNR, the pre-communist traditions had to be carefully screened and reinterpreted.

The bi-polarity of ideas and visions between the Left and Right shaped constitution making. The aim of the Left was to prevent change and minimise the 'freshness of the start' by retaining the institutions and the goals of the previous regime in the Ukrainian state. Hence, the constitution was to preserve the essence of the Soviet system, and, hence, they only accepted some 'improvements' rather than a radical overhaul. Conversely, the national-democrats perceived the constitution as a vehicle for abandoning the Soviet past and a device for rooting-out the vestiges of the communist order on Ukraine's journey to 'the civilised world'. The 'indigenous way of life' was 'European', whereas the communist era was an aberration from the normal path of development initiated with the establishment of the UNR in 1917. However, Soviet communism in Ukraine left legacies, which necessitated a particularistic approach, to state building. Universal models had to be screened and adapted to indigenous circumstances, in order to leap from the post-Soviet 'here' to a European 'there'. These two blocs, which advocated the competing and mutually exclusive models of statehood, clashed head-on in the course of constitution drafting.

Being numerically underrepresented and organisationally weak, the liberals in parliament could hardly stand up to the role of mediator between the two hostile forces. Despite the formation of many self-proclaimed centrist factions, which grouped unaffiliated deputies (many of whom worked in the state apparatus), their ideological orientation was often nebulous and difficult to pin down. Nevertheless, in contrast to the previous parliament of 1990–1994, this pragmatically disposed group of deputies came to tacitly recognise the need to eradicate the institutional vestiges of the Soviet model and accept a separation of powers as the underlying principle for constitutional reform. This demonstrated a profound shift from the constitutional debates in 1991, when the majority (the 'group of 239') still adhered to the system of soviets as the legitimate form of government for sovereign Ukraine.

Moreover, the ideological cleavages in the Supreme Council were further compounded by the institutional divisions, as the two ideological blocs, which were represented in parliament, cohabited with an unaffiliated president. Initially, the views of the newly elected president, who lacked an independent power base in parliament, cut cross those two ideological blocs in the Supreme Council. On the one hand, Kuchma advocated radical political reform away from the system of soviets in order to pursue economic reforms, an agenda that the national-democrats firmly backed. On the other hand, he took an 'anti-nationalist' stance and advocated a foreign policy orientation aimed at re-integration with 'Eurasia', something that was also championed by the Left. However, within a short space of time, Kuchma underwent a remarkable double 'realignment'. Prior to the elections he moved towards championing the rights of the Russophone electorate and re-integration with Russia/CIS, which proved decisive in his victory. Yet after the elections the 'Russian question' was quietly dropped from the presidential agenda, as this proved to be a major hindrance to get support from his potential allies in parliament, the national-democrats, on political and economic reforms. Thus, even if before the elections, the agenda of 'anti-nationalist' and pro-Russian left-wing forces appeared to coincide more with Kuchma's platform, after the elections Kuchma himself shifted in favour of the position adopted by the national-democrats. As will be argued in the next chapter, this re-alignment opened a 'window of opportunity' to pass the new constitution of Ukraine by a constitutional majority, despite the diametrically opposed concepts of statehood prevailing in parliament.

NOTES

1 Out of 174 deputies who stood for re-election, only 49 won seats in the new parliament. Moreover, not all seats were filled in the new parliament. After several rounds of by-elections in 1994, parliament put a moratorium on further re-elections between December 1994 and December 1995.

2 Sarah Birch, 'Nomenklatura Democratization: Electoral Clientelism in Post-Soviet Ukraine', *Democratization*, Vol. 4, No. 4 (Winter 1997), pp. 40–62.

3 The radical right, which was not united in any formal electoral bloc, was represented by parties such as the Congress of Ukrainian Nationalists (KUN), the Ukrainian National Assembly, and the Union of Sovereign Statehood. As they obtained only 12 seats and accounted only for 0.5 percent of the composition of the Supreme Council, they played a marginal role in constitution making.

4 In Eastern and Southern Ukraine the national-democrats received on average 30 percent of the votes, although the percentage was much lower in the densely populated and more politically radical Donbas. Rukh proved unable to reach to rural Ukrainian-speaking constituencies in Central Ukraine, which tended to vote either for the Agrarian and Socialist Parties or independent members of local elites. In Western Ukraine the moderate nationalists lost some seats in favour of the radical right. Because of the lack of discernible mechanical effects of the electoral system, the right-wing parties received seats roughly in proportion to their share of the votes.

5 However, the 'liberal bloc' was most of all devised as an electoral machine, and, as such, represented an amalgam of pro-Russian, Slavofile, pro-Western parties, blocs and alliances, as well as being an association of industrialists and so-called red directors, etc. It was also joined by the Party of Democratic Revival of Ukraine, the Social Democratic Party of Ukraine. In western Ukraine, the 'New Wave' represented a local brand of liberalism. The IRBR had overlapping and fuzzy organisational structures, and failed to consolidate into a political party.

6 Other centrist parties, such as the Labour Party, which was pro-Russian, favoured federalisation and represented local Donbas elites, lost to the CPU.

7 Sarah Birch, 'Electoral Systems, Campaign Strategies, and Vote Choice in the Ukrainian Parliamentary and Presidential Elections of 1994', *Political Studies*, Vol. XLVI, No. 1 (March 1998), pp. 96–114.

8 For example, the bloc 'Soiuz' aimed to re-create the Union of the former Soviet republics. It was headed by a communist, Ivan Symonenko, and consisted of 35 deputies (24 communists, 4 MDG, 3 APU, 2 SPU, 1 Yednist, 1 Civic Congress) mainly from Eastern and Southern Ukraine. The list of names of the members was published in *Vechirniy Kyiv*, 2 November 1995.

9 Candidates could be nominated by political parties or blocs, which had to have a minimum of 1,000 members in order to propose a candidate (only one candidate per party/bloc). Also, candidates could be nominated by meetings of voters (a minimum of 500 voters had to be present). In order to be officially registered with the Electoral Commission, the candidates had to submit a list of 100,000 signatures of citizens with the right to vote, which had to include no less than 1,500 citizens in two thirds of the total number of the constituencies. (For an English-language translation of the electoral law see Yarpolok Kulchytskyi (ed.), *Presidential Election Guide* (Kyiv: International Foundation for Electoral Systems, 1994).

10 *Vybory v Ukraini (Elections in Ukraine),* (Kyiv, International Foundation for Electoral Systems, 1994), pp. 138–139.

11 Donbas (the region of Ukraine, which consists of two oblasts, Donetsk and Luhansk, in the Donbas basin, 15 percent of which is within the Russian Federation), have the highest proportion of ethnic Russians (apart from Crimea): 45 percent in Luhansk and 44 percent in Donetsk. Moreover, the majority of ethnic Ukrainians are Russian speakers. In 1990–1991 some attempts to establish an interfront organisation in Donbas were made, as well as to form a union of 12 eastern and southern Ukrainian

oblasts. Already before independence, calls for federal structure of Ukraine and making Russian the state language were made. A local referendum was held in Donbas during the parliamentary elections of 1994 . Four questions were asked regarding 1) full membership of Ukraine in CIS; 2) a federal structure for Ukraine; 3) the introduction of Russian as a second language; 4) the immediate introduction of Russian in Donbas as an official language alongside Ukrainian. Each of those questions obtained over 50 percent of votes. However, Donbas, in contrast to Crimea, did not push for secession from Ukraine.

12 Transcarpathia was incorporated into Ukraine in 1945 (it belonged to Hungary until 1918, and Czechoslovakia in the interwar period, followed by a brief spell of independence under the name of the Republic of Carpatho–Ukraine in 1939). In 1989 the population was 78 percent Ukrainian, 13 percent Hungarian, 4 percent Russian, 2.4 percent Romanian, and 1 percent Roma. However, the Ukrainian majority itself was divided, as part of it claims a Rusyn ethnic identity. On 1 December 1991, the oblast population voted in a referendum on the question 'Do you want Sub-Carpathia to receive autonomous status as a subject within an independent Ukraine?', which was approved by 78 percent of those who voted. Ethnic Hungarians voted in favour of creating a Hungarian Autonomous district in the Berehovo region of Transcarpathia, where the Hungarians form a majority of the population. *Ukrainian Reporter,* Vol. 1, No. 23, (1991), p. 3. On the history of Transcarpathia see V. Shandor, *Carpatho–Ukraine in the 20th Century* (HURI, 1996). On 22 June 1994, the Transcarpathian oblast *rada* asked the Supreme Council of Ukraine to grant it administrative autonomy.

13 Author's interview with Volodymyr Moiseienko, Kyiv, a member of the Communist faction, Kyiv, November 1995.

14 *Kommunist,* No. 49, December 1995, p. 4.

15 Ivan Chyzh, the leader of the Socialist faction in parliament linked the traditions of the SPU to the socialist and social-democratic parties of 1917–1920 such as the Ukrainian Social-Democratic Workers' Party, the Ukrainian Party of Social Revolutionaries, and the Ukrainian Party of Social(ist) Federalists. At the same time he asserted that 'Ukrainian socialists will be always more leftist than the [European] socialists and social-democrats', especially during the type of socio-economic collapse that occurred in Ukraine. However, while still broadly adhering to Marxism–Leninism, the SPU was open to and drew from the rich European socialist tradition (which set it apart from the CPU). Ivan Chyzh, 'Ukrainski sotsialisty zavzhdy budut' livishymy vid evropeiskykh (The Ukrainian Socialists Will Always Be More to the Left that Europeans)', *Viche*, No. 6, 1997, pp. 112–122.

16 '*Kontseptsia derzhavotvorenia v Ukraini (The Conception of State Building)*' (2–4 December 1992). The document was adopted by the Fourth All Ukrainian Congress of Rukh.

17 Giovanni Sartori, 'Neither Presidentialism nor Parliamentarism', in J. J. Linz and A. Valenzuela (eds.), *The Failure of Presidential Democracy* (Baltimore, London: The Johns Hopkins University Press, 1994), Vol. 1, p. 112.

18 See M. J. C. Vile, *Constitutionalism and the Separation of Powers.* (Oxford: Clarendon Press, 1967). Many post-communist constitutions refer to a 'separation of powers', as for example does the constitution of Bulgaria, even if the dominant form of

government in post-communist states—parliamentarism—could be characterised more precisely by the separation of functions rather than powers.

19 Kuchma's speech was published in *Uriadovyi Kurier*, 24 December 1994, pp. 1–3.

20 *Holos Ukrainy,* 24 December 1994, p. 3.

21 Artur Bilous *et al., Proiekt konstytutsii Ukrainy: stan, problemy, perspektyvy (The Draft Constitution of Ukraine: the Current Situation, Problems, Prospects)* (Kyiv, 1996), p. 17.

22 *Ibid.*

23 Later, the president conceded to the formation of a Senate in direct elections. However, the main candidates in direct elections tended to be state administration officials, who would be nominated by the president. With the Senate consisting of individuals subordinated to the president, it would become a pro-presidential organ.

24 The classification of forms of government used in the constitutional debate reflected the specific constellation of preferences in Ukraine, and as such was not based on any particular Western classifications.

25 For the arguments supporting federalism in Ukraine see the article by the leader of the Constitutional–Democratic Party of Ukraine, Volodymyr Zolotariov, 'A Federative System of Government as a Means of Resolving the Present Crisis in Ukraine', *Demos*, Vol. 1, No. 7 (28 November 1994).

26 Dominique Arel and Andrew Wilson, 'The Ukrainian Parliamentary Elections', *RFE/RL Research Report*, Vol. 3, No. 26 (1994). p. 28.

27 Volodymyr Hryniov, *Nova Ukraina: Yakoiu Ya Yi Bachu (New Ukraine: How I See Her)* (Kyiv, 1995), pp. 27 and 36.

28 Ivan Popesku, 'Ludyna v derzhavi: harmonia prava (An Individual in the State: the Harmony of Law)', *Holos Ukrainy*, 3 December 1996, p. 7.

29 Taras Kuzio, 'Issues of Voters Preferences during the 1994 Presidential Elections in Ukraine', Working Paper, Centre For Russian and East European Studies, 1995.

30 Mykola Tomenko, *Ukrainska perspektyva: istoryko-politolohichni pidstavy suchasnoi derzhavnoi stratehii (A Ukrainian Perspective: the Historical-Political Foundation of Contemporary State Strategy)* (Kyiv, 1995). p. 54.

31 CSAOCOU, FOND 1, OPYS 11, Delo 2278 (Stenographic transcript of the Meeting of Politburo on 2 July 1991), p. 10.

32 Interestingly, Viacheslav Chornovil, the then ex-chairman of the Lviv council, who became a leader of Rukh, advocated the idea of federalism before Ukraine became independent in order to maintain the special identity of Galicia and protect against pro-Russian, pro-communist attitudes prevailing in Kyiv in 1990–1991. Strong regions were intended to counteract the conservative centre. Yet, when the national-communists opted for independence, the idea of federalisation of independent Ukraine was not only discarded but labelled 'anti-state' by national-democrats, including Chornovil.

33 Yevhen Baltarovych, 'Ukraine: A Federal or Unitary State', *Demos*, Vol. 1, No. 7 (28 Nov. 1994), p. 3.

34 Baltarovych, 'Ukraine: A Federal or Unitary State', p. 3.

35 This term was derived from the *Akt Sobornosti* (unity) which proclaimed the unification of the Ukrainian People's Republic (UNR) and the Western Ukrainian People's Republic (ZUNR) in Kyiv on 22 January 1919 (see chapter 2). At that time, *sobornist* epitomised the integration of Ukrainian ethnic territories in one state. After the

first World War *sobornist'* acquired a meaning of not only an integrated, but also a centralised state model in order to prevent disintegration. See Alexander J. Motyl, *The Turn to the Right: The Ideological Origins and Development of Ukrainian Nationalism, 1919–1929* (Boulder: East European Monographs, 1980).

36 *Ukrainian Law* (1996), No. 1, p. 128.

37 M. Kornienko, 'Regional Autonomy: Federation or Decentralization', *Ukrainian Law*, No. 3 (1996), p. 141.

38 Volodymyr Shapoval, 'The State System of Ukraine: Political and Legal Aspects', *Ukrainian Law*, No. 3 (1996), p. 130.

39 Shapoval, 'The State System of Ukraine', p. 135.

40 Tomenko, *Ukrainska perspektyva: istoryko-politolohichni pidstavy*, p. 52.

41 Ivan L. Rudnytsky, 'The Fourth Universal and Its Ideological Antecedents', in. Taras Hunchak (ed.), *The Ukraine, 1917–1921: A Study in Revolution* (Cambridge, Mass.: Harvard University Press, 1977), p. 218.

42 *Ibid.*

43 Shapoval, 'The State System of Ukraine', p. 135.

44 Kornienko, 'Regional Autonomy: Federation or Decentralization', p. 141.

45 On the developments in Crimea in the early 1990s see Gwen Sasse, 'The Crimean Issue', *Journal of Communist Studies and Transition Politics*, Vol. 12, No. 1 (March 1996), pp. 83–100.; Ian Bremmer, 'Ethnic Issues in Crimea', *RFE/RL Research Report*, Vol. 2, No. 18 (Apr. 1993).; Andrew Wilson, 'Crimea's Political Cauldron', *RFE/RL Research Report*, Vol. 2, No. 2 (12 Nov. 1993).

46 The Constitution was published in the *Vedomosti Verkhovoho Sovieta Kryma (Information from the Supreme Soviet of Crimea)*, 1991–1992, No. 7.

47 The national-democrats proposed for Crimea to be granted a Charter (*Statut*) for Crimean Autonomy, which would be approved by the Supreme Council of Ukraine.

48 Kornienko, 'Regional Autonomy', pp. 139–45.

49 Ukraine inherited a multi-layered administrative division from the Soviet Union: village, village-type settlement, cities, *raion* and oblast with the latter two being intermediate level units. For an overview of the territorial division of post-Soviet Ukraine see *Ukrainian Law*, No. 3 (1996), p. 151.

50 For a detailed overview of territorial–administrative units and their historical names see Volodymyr Kubijovych (ed.), *Encyklopedia ukrainoznavstva (The Encyclopedia of Ukrainian Studies)*, Vol. 1, Reprint of the 1949 edition (Kyiv, 1994), pp. 119–24.

51 Roman Bezsmertnyi, 'Konstytutsiia garantuie samovriaduvania' (The Constitution Guarantees Local Self-Government), *Nova Polityka*, No. 5 (1996), pp. 25–8.

52 *Holos Ukrainy*, 24 December 1994, p. 3.

53 *Ibid.*

54 *Ibid.*

55 The speech of the leader of CPU, Petro Symonenko at the session of the Supreme Council on the constitution. *Kommunist*, No. 17, April 1996, p. 3.

56 *Kommunist*, No. 49, December 1995, p. 5. See also an article by a member of the Legislative Institute of the Supreme Council, Vasyl Bordeniuk in favour of the 'state theory of local government' in *Holos Ukrainy*, 9 August 1995, p. 12.

57 *Kommunist*, No. 49, December 1995, p. 5.

58 Materials from the Third Meeting of the Working Group of the Constitutional Commission, Archives of the Constitutional Commission (February–March 1991), p. 45.

59 For a summary of the arguments in favour of bi-cameralism see the text of the speech made by Volodymyr Butkevych, chairman of the Commission on Human Rights, National Minorities and Interethnic Relations of the Supreme Council, in *Holos Ukrainy*, 30 April 1996, pp. 8–9. See also his 'Proiekt Konstytutsii Ukrainy u Verkhovnii Radi', and Rostyslav Pavenko, 'Skilky palat potribno Parlamentu Ukrainy?' (How Many Houses Does the Ukrainian Parliament Need?), *Nova Polityka*, No. 5 (1996), p. 37.

60 The Materials of the Constitutional Commission, Fourth Meeting, Archives of the Constitutional Commission (March 1991), p. 8.

61 *Kommunist*, No. 49, December 1995, p. 4.

62 Author's interview with Galina Starovoitova, the member of the MDG faction, Kyiv, July 1997. The regional elites also favoured the formation of the Senate on the principle of proportionality. See, for example, the views of Mykhailo Pozhyvanov, a deputy and head of the Mauriopol city council, in *Holos Ukrainy*, 19 March 1996, p. 5.

63 *Holos Ukrainy*, 16 September 1994.

64 Tomenko, *Ukrainska perspektyva: istoryko-politolohichni pidstavy*, pp. 62–3. The head of the Parliamentary commission on culture and spirituality Mykhailo Kosiv, asserted that 'Ukraine is the homeland of the Ukrainian people, who implement their sacred right to self-determination, by creating the Ukrainian state, in which there are national minorities'. *Holos Ukrainy*, 16 September, 1994, p. 4.

65 *Programme of Rukh*, Kyiv, 1989. It was also published in Lindheim and Luckyi (eds.), *Towards an Intellectual History of Ukraine*, pp. 341–362.

66 Tomenko, *Ukrainska perspektyva: istoryko-politolohichni pidstavy*, pp. 62–3.

67 *Programme of Rukh*, Kyiv, 1989.

68 Oleksandr Trubushnyi, 'Movna polityka v Ukraini: problemy i priorytety (Language Policy in Ukraine: Problems and Priorities)', *Viche*, Vol. 9 (1997), p. 100.

69 An article by the head of the Parliamentary Commission on Culture and Spirituality Mykhailo Kosiv published in *Holos Ukrainy*, 16 September, 1994.

70 *Vechirnyi Kyiv*, 15 March 1996, p. 3.

71 *Holos Ukrainy*, 16 September, 1994.

72 *Ibid.*

73 The exact English-language translation of the opening verse of the anthem '*Shche ne vmerla Ukraina'* is technically 'Ukraine Has Not Yet Died'. However, this does not bring across the defiant tone of the hymn. Thus a better translation is 'Ukraine Has Not Yet Perished'. The text of the anthem was published as a patriotic poem in 1863 by Pavlo Chubynsky, a Ukrainian ethnographer and civic leader. The music was written by Verbytsky and it was published with the score in 1885. The song was recognised in 1917 as the anthem of the Ukrainian National Republic and banned under the Soviet Union.

74 The notion of the political community advocated by the national-democrats represented a juxtaposition of two conceptions: communitarian and pluralistic. In that respect, the national-democrats diverged from the mainstream East–Central European nationalist stance, as they championed both the rights of ethnic minorities and the titular nation, and at no point did they advocate 'Ukraine for Ukrainians', something Wilson implies in *Ukrainian Nationalism in the 1990s,* pp. 149–150.

75 Wilson argues that the civic notion of nationhood is more suited to Ukraine. However, civic nationhood with its stress on equal political and socio-economic rights—which is epitomised by the so-called French model—does not presuppose any particular legal, institutional guarantees and provisions for minorities.

76 Tomenko, *Ukrainska perspektyva: istoryko-politolohichni pidstavy*, pp. 62–63.

77 *Kommunist*, No. 11, March 1996, p. 3.

78 *Holos Ukrainy,* 21 March 1996, p. 3.

79 *Kommunist*, No. 49, December 1995, p. 5.

80 Author's interview with Volodymyr Moiseienko, a member of the Communist faction, Kyiv, November 1995.

81 Rogers Brubaker, *Nationalism Reframed* (Cambridge: Cambridge University Press, 1996), p. 60.

82 *Holos Ukrainy*, 21 March 1996, p. 9.

83 *Ibid.*

84 *Kommunist*, No. 11, March 1996, p. 3.

85 For an example of non-left views advocating the official status of Russian in Ukraine see an article by Ivan Shapovalov and Volodymyr Aleksiiev in *Holos Ukrainy*, 27 July 1995, p. 9. On the liberal views on nationhood in Ukraine see Yevhen Bystrytskyi, 'The National Idea, Civil Society and Political Nation', in Oleksandr Dergachov (ed.), *Ukrainian Statehood in the Twentieth Century* (Kyiv: Political Thought, 1996), pp. 323–32.

86 Paradoxically, Kravchuk's emphasis on the historical continuity with the Ukrainian People's Republic (1917–1921), of which Hrushevskyi was the president, relegated Kravchuk to the role of the second president of Ukraine, as Hrushevskyi was proclaimed the president of the UNR in April 1918 (see chapter 2). However, this 'problem' was dealt with by referring to Kravchuk as the 'first *elected* president of Ukraine'.

87 Kuchma's inaugural speech was published in *Uriadovyi Kurier*, 21 July 1994, p. 2.

88 *Ibid.*

89 Kuchma's speech commemorating the fifth anniversary of Ukrainian independence, the text of which was published in *Holos Ukrainy*, 28 September 1995, pp. 2–3.

90 See Kuchma's speech in *Uriadovyi Kurier*, 8 June 1996.

91 On language policies under Kravchuk see D. Arel, 'Ukraine: The Temptation of the Nationalising State', in V. Tismaneanu (ed.), *Political Culture and Civil Society in Russia and the New States of Eurasia* (Armonk, New York: M.E. Sharpe, 1995), pp. 157–88. See also Wilson, *Ukrainian Nationalism in the 1990s,* pp. 110–114. Under Kravchuk efforts were made to create a national united Orthodox Church independent of Russia under the umbrella of the Ukrainian Orthodox Church of the Kyiv Patriarchate.

92 In contrast to Kravchuk, under Kuchma the government favoured neutrality in church–state relations. The events of 'Black Tuesday' in July 1995, when police attacked mourners of the nationalistic orthodox Patriarch, demonstrated the state's aloofness from religious issues. Kuchma announced that the state is devoted to equal treatment of all concessions and can only act as a conciliator in the conflict between them. In other words, the state refrained from promoting the 'patriotic' Ukrainian Orthodox Church of the Kyiv Patriarchate as a 'national' church. For Kuchma's views on state–church relations see *Holos Ukrainy*, 27 July 1995, p. 2.

93 *Uriadovyi Kurier*, 23 December 1995, p. 4.

94 Kuchma's speech commemorating the 400th anniversary of the birth of Bohdan Khmelnytskyi was published in *Uriadovyi Kurier*, 23 December 1995 and *Holos Ukrainy*, 22 December 1995.

95 Kuchma's speech commemorating the fifth anniversary of Ukrainian independence, the text of which was published in *Holos Ukrainy*, 28 September 1995, pp. 2–3.

96 See D. Arel and A. Wilson, 'Ukraine under Kuchma: Back to "Eurasia"?', *RFE/RL Research Report*, Vol. III, No. 32 (1994).

97 See Dmytro Vydryn and Dmytro Tabachnyk, *Ukraina na porozi XXI stolittia (Ukraine on the Brink of the XXIst Century)'*, Kyiv, 1996, and Hryniov, *Nova Ukraina: yakoiu ya yi bachu.* While holding the post of presidential adviser, Hryniov was effectively marginalised, and Vydryn and Tabachnyk's book was withdrawn from circulation before it was widely distributed. On the national-democrats' critique of those views see Viacheslav Chornovil, 'Natsionalna inteligentsiia i ukrainska polityka (The National Inteligentsia and Ukrainian Politics)', *Slovo I Chas,* No. 2(422) (February 1996), pp. 24–27.

98 *Demokratychna Ukraina*, 30 January 1996.

99 The right-wing political parties, however, intensified their calls for state cultural and linguistic policies to revive a Ukrainian identity. One of the initiatives to put pressure on the government to support Ukrainian language and culture was the National Congress of Ukrainian Intelligentsia, which was held in Kyiv in November 1995. The Petition of the Congress of Ukrainian Intelligentsia was published in *Uriadovyi Kurier*, 16 July 1996 and *Ukraina Moloda,* 12 July 1996. See also Anatoliy Pohribnyi, 'Yaka Ukraina buduietsia? (What Kind of Ukraine Is Being Built?)', *Slovo I Chas*, No. 2(422) (February 1996), pp. 24–7. More generally on the interactions between the cultural intelligentsia and the Ukrainian state see Marko Pavlyshyn, 'Culture and National Identity: Ukrainian Developments 1991–1996', in Vladimir Tikhonov (ed.), *In Search of Identity* (Melbourne: CRE–AS Publication Series No. 1, 1996), pp. 79–91.

100 See Andrew Wilson, 'The Ukrainian Left: Still a Barrier to Reform?', *The Ukrainian Review*, Vol. 44, No. 1 (Spring 1997), pp. 30–7.

CHAPTER SIX

THE PASSAGE OF THE CONSTITUTION: PROCESS, ACTORS, AND STRATEGIES

Three years after the proclamation of the Act of Independence, the Ukrainian state lacked a firm constitutional basis, something which led to a political paralysis that engulfed Ukraine in the summer of 1993. While tinkering with the 1978 constitution during Kravchuk's presidency, Ukrainian elites failed to pass the new constitution, and the drafting of the most fundamental law of the polity was postponed until after the pre-term elections in 1994.

Taking into account the highly disputed conceptions of statehood held by the key actors after the 1994 elections, constitution making, which was resumed soon after the elections, was expected to be anything but straightforward. Therefore, to speed up the process, the president attempted to deal with the division of powers at the centre in a stop-gap constitution, which took the form of a Constitutional Agreement of June 1995. Although the Agreement reduced mounting tensions, it nevertheless failed to reconcile the differences and suffered from a lack of procedural legitimacy. At the same time, the Agreement established a deadline of twelve months for the passage of the fully-fledged constitution. As the constitution had to resolve the highly disputed issues of the 'national question', the territorial–administrative model, and socio-economic issues, aside from the contentious issue of the form of government, the prospect for the completion of the process within the prescribed time limit looked dim. However, within twelve months parliament adopted the constitution by a constitutional majority after a tense stand off between the president and parliament.

While the newly adopted Basic Law was permeated with compromises, the resolution on some issues favoured particular actors. Kuchma emerged victorious from his struggle to preserve most of the powers assigned to the presidency in 1995, even if the parliament passed the constitution 'against' the will of the president. The resolution of the 'national question' in the constitution most closely reflected the preferences of the national-democrats, despite them being in minority on this issue. This chapter aims to untangle the contingency of factors, that allowed the president, the national-democrats and, to a considerably lesser extent, the centrists to shape the blueprint of Ukrainian statehood enshrined in the new constitution.

This outcome can be attributed to a circumstantial configuration of factors. The multiplicity of issues to be resolved, strategies of actors and a dense matrix of cross-cutting institutional and partisan divisions all played a role. So did the lack of clearly formulated and agreed rules governing the passage of the constitution. Constitution making consisted of two parallel processes: the elaboration of the constitutional norms, and the improvised elaboration of procedures to approve the constitution. These processes were closely interwoven, as the actors' subjective perceptions of their abilities to determine the outcome affected their preferences on the promulgation procedure and vice versa. Overall, a corollary of the prevailing procedural uncertainty was that it created opportunities for actors, most of all the president and the national-democrats, to apply a variety of tactics and manoeuvres to steer the outcome of the process in a preferred direction, despite being in numerical minority on some issues.

The chapter consists of two parts. The first provides a chronological overview by breaking the two years between 1994–1996 into key stages, according to the dominant actors and outcomes. It charts the progress of constitution making from the creation of the Constitutional Commission in autumn 1994, through the Little Constitution in June 1995 to the passage of the fully-fledged constitution in June 1996. The second part of the chapter analyses the main actors involved in the process—the president and the three blocs in parliament: national-democrats, left wing and the centre—in terms of their resources, hierarchy of preferences, and strategies in order to determine whether and to what extent they shaped the conception of the state enshrined in the new constitution. The content of the document will be examined in chapter 7.

FROM A 'LITTLE' TO A 'BIG' CONSTITUTION

THE UNPROMISING RE-LAUNCH OF CONSTITUTION MAKING (JULY–DECEMBER 1994)

Immediately after the elections, president Kuchma publicly demonstrated his exasperation with the existing amorphous and contradictory constitutional framework by arguing that the 1978 constitution had outlived its usefulness and obstructed economic reforms. He decided to 'remedy' the situation immediately by issuing two decrees (*ukazy*) in August 1994, which restored the executive chain of command subordinated to the president which had been dismantled in early 1994 (see chapter 4). According to the first *ukaz* the president as the head of the executive branch directed the activities of the cabinet of ministers. The second *ukaz* subordinated elected heads of *radas* at oblast and *raion* levels (who were simultaneously the heads of *vykonkomy*) directly to the president, and made them personally responsible for the execution of state powers.[1] The second *ukaz*, which was in breach with Kuchma's electoral slogan of decentralisation of power to the regions, limited democratically elected local authorities. Shortly after, however, as a kind of counterbalancing gesture, he created a Council of Regions (*Rada Regioniv*). This advisory-consultative body was headed by the president and consisted of the heads of oblasts, the mayors of Kyiv and Sevastopol, and the Deputy Prime-Minister of the Republic of Crimea.

Soon after being elected, Kuchma announced the long awaited intensification of reforms and to this end demanded the strengthening of the presidency (something which was to be repeated after his re-election in 1999). In October 1994, he succeeded in obtaining parliamentary approval for his policy programme 'The Road to Radical Economic Reform'. Within three months of the elections, the seeds of conflict between Kuchma and the leftist factions in the Supreme Council, which advocated a different path for institutional reform and mode of economic recovery, had been planted. In particular, the strengthening of the presidency towards an executive type envisaged the transformation of the Supreme Council into an ordinary legislature and its powerful chairman into an ordinary speaker. Such plans clearly contradicted the agenda of the left wing, which dominated parliament. The *ukazy* marked the end of the post-election honeymoon between the parliamentary Left and president, both of which were elected by votes of Eastern and Southern Ukraine.

Amidst the inconclusive scholarly debate on what kind of body ought to draft the new constitution,[2] the new Constitutional Commission was formed in October 1994. Rather than being a parliamentary commission as was its predecessor, the new body was a 'state commission' consisting of 'subjects with the right of legislative initiative'. Such a formula allowed for the inclusion of the two directly elected representatives of the electorate—the president and parliament. As a result, Kuchma and the new chairman of the Supreme Council, Oleksandr Moroz, co-chaired the 40-strong body consisting of 15 representatives of the Supreme Council (representing the parliamentary factions on a proportional basis), 15 representatives of the president, 1 representative of the Supreme Council of Crimea, and 7 members from the Judicial branch (Supreme, Arbitrary, and Constitutional Courts and the Procuracy). Thus, the Commission was a large and all-inclusive forum for political actors (both institutions and partisan groupings). The contradictory preferences of its heads and members soon came to the fore. At the very first meeting, the Constitutional Commission got bogged down in the highly contentious issue of the description of the sovereign people and did not even agree on internal procedures. The work of this all-inclusive Commission (which held meetings only once a month) was marred by scepticism about the whole endeavour both at the elite level and society at large.

THE 'LITTLE CONSTITUTION' (DECEMBER 1994–JUNE 1995)

To ease the deepening constitutional crisis and the impasse within the Constitutional Commission, the president decided to propose a temporary solution. In December 1994 he tabled the draft 'Constitutional Law on Power and Local Self-Government' in parliament, which was to provide a 'stop-gap constitution' until the new one was ready.[3] The law envisaged a radical shift to presidentialism; the form of government was modelled on the new Russian Constitution adopted in December 1993.

A number of considerations underlay this decision. Firstly, the draft counteracted the left wing's initiative to reinstate the system of soviets. From the beginning of the new parliamentary term in the spring of 1994, the self-assured left wing led by the Communist Party of Ukraine took the leading role in parliament and adopted a series of resolutions.[4] Even before the presidential elections, in order to reverse the constitutional reforms initiated by Kravchuk, the Left proposed the draft law

'On Local Radas of People's Deputies', according to which the system of soviets would be reinstated with the Supreme Council as the highest state organ, while the president would be deprived of means of control over the executive structure and ultimately would be limited to ceremonial functions. Secondly, the president hoped that by excluding other contentious issues such as the 'national question' or private property, and focusing only on the division of powers, the 'Law on Power' had greater chances of being adopted than a fully-fledged constitution. Thirdly, the Law as a hybrid between an ordinary law and a constitution could circumvent the requirement of the constitutional majority. The distribution of votes within parliament meant that the prospect of obtaining a constitutional majority was remote. The situation was exacerbated by simple mathematics: the changes to the existing constitution required at least two thirds of the total number of the mandates (i.e. 300 out of 450). Yet as approximately 50 seats were vacant at the end of 1994,[5] in practice the constitutional majority was close to three quarters of sitting members. As a large group of deputies rarely attended parliamentary sessions, and only about 350 deputies participated regularly, the requirement of a two-thirds majority in reality meant four fifths of the actual number of active deputies. The Law offered a chance of introducing changes to the constitution disguised as an ordinary law (which only required a simple majority of 226). Fourthly, it would be a harbinger of the new constitution and strengthen the argument that the form of government ought not to be very different from the 'Law on Power', and thereby would provide for a powerful presidency. Once adopted, the Law would set a precedent for the work of the Constitutional Commission, as by December 1994 the Commission had not yet decided in favour of the form of government in general and the role of the president in particular.

Even if the Supreme Council approved the draft for further consideration with the support of the six centre-right factions (176 deputies voted in favour, 135 against and 30 abstained), the prospects of the Law being adopted were dim. However, the first reading led to a path-breaking institutional innovation within parliament to deal with the anticipated deadlock. Rather than delegate the revision of the draft to one of the parliamentary standing commissions (which were often dominated by one ideological orientation), a special *ad hoc* conciliatory commission was created to deal with the areas of dispute. Not only did the debates move from the parliamentary floor to a smaller room. Moreover, one faction was granted one vote, according to the rules that the conciliatory commission adopted. This arrangement favoured the smaller centre and right-wing factions, and disadvantaged the left-wing bloc with its large communist faction (Table 6.1). The commission soon trimmed some of presidential power and elaborated the procedures on the dissolution of parliament and impeachment of the president,[6] but it did not depart from presidentialism.[7] Despite the Left's numerous procedural objections designed to sabotage the draft, in May 1995 the draft law mustered a simple majority in the second reading (224 in favour, 93 against, 14 abstained). Yet, in order to come to force, the left- wing insisted, the bill necessitated the suspension of a number of articles of the 1978 Soviet Ukrainian Constitution and this required a constitutional majority. Thus, the last word belonged to the leftist faction, which voted against such a constitutional revision on the 30 May 1995.[8]

Kuchma did not accept defeat and embarked on confrontation. On 28 May he decreed a referendum on the populace's confidence in the president and parliament on the basis that 'on many occasions a large section of deputies demonstrated a lack of will and an inability to work constructively, [and] provoked confrontation within parliament and between parliament and the president'.[9] Opting for a referendum Kuchma gambled on his popularity, as the referendum was to force the electorate to choose its favourite institution by answering positively to one of the two questions: 'Do you trust the president? and 'Do you trust the Supreme Council'; ballots with both answers 'negative' would be invalidated.[10] In retaliation, the parliament declared the decree on referendum unconstitutional on 1 June (with only 9 votes against) and attempted to block it by refusing to authorise funding to carry it out. Even the national-democrats feared a plebiscite in view of the Belarussian referendum held at the same time, which endangered Belarussian sovereignty. Yet Kuchma was not to be deterred and confirmed his intention to go ahead with the referendum.

To resolve the deadlock, an extraordinary form of a Constitutional Agreement (*Konstytutsiinyi Dohovir*) was resorted to.[11] As a special political settlement between the branches of power, the *Dohovir* was conceived as a way of justifying the by-passing of the requirement of a two-thirds majority in the legislature. The legislature and president, representing the two branches of power, would not only 'agree' to obey the temporary set of rules regulating their interactions until a fully-fledged constitution was adopted, but also specify the procedure for the passage of the new constitution. Six right-centre parliamentary factions agreed to this formula and, after intensive negotiations, Oleksandr

Moroz, the chairman of the Council, who until then opposed the 'Law on Power', also conceded to the Agreement. The *Dohovir* was voted in and signed personally by 240 deputies on the 7 June 1995 (see Table 6.1). In a special ratification ceremony in Marinskyi Palace, Moroz and Kuchma signed an extraordinary 'Constitutional Agreement on Temporary Organisation and Functioning of State Powers and Local Self-government in Ukraine until the Passage of the New Constitution'. The *Dohovir* stipulated a suspension of certain sections of the 1978 Constitution and the adoption of the 'Law on Power' for twelve months, that is, until the new constitution was sanctioned in a nation-wide referendum.

Table 6.1. Breakdown of Voting on the Constitutional Agreement (7 June 1995)

Faction	*For*	*Against*	*Abstained*	*Did Not Vote/ Absent*
Left				
Communists	3	64	4	19
Socialists	7	8	3	9
Peasants	37	1	0	10
Centre				
MDG	23	1	1	5
Unity	26	0	0	5
Centre	23	0	0	7
Independents	25	1	0	4
Right				
Rukh	27	0	0	1
Reforms	28	2	0	5
Statehood	26	1	0	1
Non-affiliated Deputies	15	4	0	10
Total	*240*	*81*	*8*	*74*

Source: Laboratory F-4

The 'Law on Power', which was an integral part of the *Dohovir,* moved Ukraine towards a semi-presidential system similar to that introduced in Russia in December 1993. According to the Agreement, the president had the authority to (1) appoint a government without parliamentary approval, (2) issue decrees on economic reform providing that matters were not regulated in existing laws, (3) veto parliamentary bills, which could be overridden with a two-thirds parliamentary majority, (4) place the executive structure of councils at oblast and *raion* level under presidential jurisdiction (while councils at those levels were to be abolished). In turn, the legislative branch had the right (1) to reject the government programme (and take a no-confidence vote in the new government), (2) to hold a vote of no confidence in the government but no sooner than one year after the formation of the government, (3) to veto presidential decrees by a qualified majority. However, the president could not dissolve the parliament, which in turn could not impeach the president. Also, the *Dohovir* stated that no referenda be carried out until the adoption of the constitution unless they concerned the new constitution. Effectively, Kuchma was afforded powerful prerogatives, with the only major limitations being that he was denied the right to dissolve parliament (while parliament could not impeach the president). However, a time limit was imposed on the president by parliament as the *Dohovir* was only to be in force for a year (that is till June 1996).

THE CONSTITUTIONAL COMMISSION (SUMMER 1995–FEBRUARY 1996)

Although the *Dohovir* mitigated the confrontation, it was only a momentary cease-fire in the unfolding conflict between the president and parliament rather than its resolution. As a little constitution, the *Dohovir* dealt predominantly with the institutions at the centre. However, not only did it leave other pivotal issues unresolved, it even failed to clearly define the legislative–executive relations. Being a sketchy, hastily prepared piece of legislation, it contained some contradictory norms. For example, the diverging interpretations of articles 46 and 53, which concerned the local administration, soon resulted in the 'war of laws' between the Supreme Council and the president over the right to determine the administrative structure of the state in the autumn 1995. The legality of the *Dohovir* was questioned as it amended the 1978 constitution by a simple majority vote (240 voted in favour rather than the minimum 300 required); the communists dubbed it a constitutional putsch. While the *Dohovir*'s heavily pro-presidential nature somewhat alienated the reformers from the presidency, it greatly fuelled leftists' abhorrence of Kuchma and his desire for a strong presidency. So while the *Dohovir* delayed the final resolution, it also reinforced already held preferences; the left wing became even more deeply entrenched in their anti-presidential position. The lifespan of the *Dohovir* was thus finite, so much that one of its authors, a national-democratic deputy Roman Bezsmertnyi, suggested that 'by October [1995] the Constitutional Agreement outlived itself and to rely on it any longer was a mistake'.[12]

While the one-year deadline mobilised the parliament and the president, no agreement on the general principles of the new constitution was forthcoming in general, or on the role of *Dohovir* in the process in particular. The glacial pace of progress in the Constitutional Commission prompted the formation of a smaller body; in September 1995 a group of legal experts was delegated the task of preparing the first draft. The experts were selected by the subjects with legislative initiative: 4 presidential, 4 parliamentary and 2 representatives of the 'judicial branch'. Once this small working group embarked on the drafting, the process acquired momentum, and in October 1995 a full draft was ready. It was the third full draft prepared since the onset of the constitutional process in 1990 (after the 1992 and 1993 drafts).

Being the product of the furtive co-operation between the working group and the Presidential Administration, the draft contained the form of government, which bore a striking resemblance to the *Dohovir*. The cornerstone of the institutional framework was a strong executive branch subordinated to the president. The latter, however, was named only 'head of state', rather then 'chief executive'. Where the draft most diverged from the *Dohovir* was the bi-cameral legislature (*Natsionalni Zbory*), and the structure of local government and the executive institutions at the intermediate level.[13] Ukrainian was defined as the state language. However, in line with the 'Declaration of Minority Rights' of 1992, in compact settlements of national minorities, the language used by the majority of the population could be used in public sphere. In other words, Russian could be granted 'official status' at the regional level. The highly controversial issue of the national symbols (i.e. flag, emblems and the anthem) was left out and was to be determined by ordinary law. Therefore, while the form of government in the November 1995 draft reflected presidential preferences, the resolution of the 'national question' made concessions to the deputies on the left-centre flanks of the ideological spectrum.

Even if in November 1995, the Constitutional Commission tentatively approved the draft as a baseline for further work (by 22 votes in favour out of 40), this was not out of any sense of satisfaction with the draft. Rather the Commission itself had no other 'output' to show for twelve months' work. In order to further 'improve' the draft, another body was created, the so-called working sub-committee of the Constitutional Commission, which, this time, was composed of the 'judicially literate' members of the Constitutional Commission.[14] Yet, as the formula of appointment was the same as used with the experts' working group, the members who favoured a strong presidency dominated also this body. Although the sub-committee introduced extensive changes to the November draft, the system of government, which centred on a strong presidency, remained a blueprint of the new, so-called March draft.

To this end, the inability to compromise within the large and inclusive Constitutional Commission led to narrow bodies of experts taking over constitution drafting. Despite being convened on the principle of proportional representation, these bodies squeezed out ideological diversity, as parliament—the key forum for the ideological contest—was allocated 4 out of 10 seats. The president was put on an equal footing with the legislature before his role in the polity was asserted. This biased membership made it possible to prepare the March draft (under the close guidance of the presidential entourage), which subsequently served as a template for the new constitution.

THE MARCH DRAFT

The March draft deserves attention as a milestone in the constitutional process. Not only did it serve as a constant point of reference for the drafters of the constitution until June 1996, but also one of its prominent features, the idea of bi-cameralism, was brought back onto the political agenda by president Kuchma after his re-election in 1999. The March draft, as the president put it, was intended 'to end Soviet rule in Ukraine once and forever' and envisaged a form of government based on the principle of the separation of powers. Its distinctive—and most controversial—feature was the bi-cameral legislature (*Natsionalni Zbory*). The lower chamber (*Palata Deputativ*) had legislative and budget functions, while the upper chamber (*Senat*), the popularly elected representation of the regions, was given extensive nominative authority mostly to approve presidential candidates for highest state posts.[15] Most importantly, the draft envisaged a strong executive presidency, which had the right to:

- appoint and dismiss from (most) judicial, military, and state posts, (though in some cases only with the approval of the Senate);
- appoint the prime minister and Cabinet on approval of the House of Deputies and dismiss the prime minister and ministers unilaterally;
- issue decrees with the power of laws;
- initiate legislation;
- veto parliamentary bills, a decision which could only be overruled by a qualified majority of 2/3 of both the House of Deputies and the Senate;

- personally endorse the vertical state administration (by nominating heads of oblast and *raion* state administrations);
- dissolve the legislature (if the House of Deputies were to reject the program of government twice within 60 days).

The extensive powers of the presidency contrasted with those of the lower chamber of the legislature that were mainly limited to law making. Parliament could not easily veto presidential decrees.[16] It could however, impeach the president, although only through a cumbersome procedure involving the Constitutional Court. According to the draft, the cabinet of ministers would be approved by parliament and would exist for the duration of the president's term in office. The cabinet would not have the right of legislative initiative, as law making initiatives would be the prerogative of the president. According to the chapter on local government, while local self-government was guaranteed at the community level (cities and villages), the oblast and *raion radas* were to be indirectly elected and dominated by their heads, who simultaneously served as presidential representatives and heads of regional state administration. The decisions of local self-government bodies could be suspended by heads of the appropriate state administration, who were subordinated both to the cabinet of ministers and the president. When analysing the text of the draft, one observer sarcastically commented that 'the system of "checks and balances" in the draft constitution was actually transformed into a "system of checks" for parliament and "system of power" for the president'.[17] At the same time, the article on the symbols was revised in line with the national-democrats' preferences. While the article on language remained unchanged (and allowed the use of Russian in the public sphere), the national symbols were defined as the 'Trident', the 'Blue and Yellow' flag and the anthem 'Ukraine Has Not Yet Perished'. This way both the president and national-democrats became the most ardent supporters of the draft.

THE PARLIAMENTARY COMMISSION (MARCH–MAY 1996)

In February, the March draft was approved by the Constitutional Commission by a majority of 20 votes (out of 40), although the representatives of the parliamentary Left uniformly voted against it. Although the draft, the third one after the 1992 and 1993 drafts, was officially tabled in parliament in March 1996,[18] it appeared to fare no better than its predecessors in terms of its chances of becoming the Basic Law of Ukraine.

The Left, which had consistently voted against the draft in the Constitutional Commission, attempted to stall the ratification process. This was greatly facilitated by the absence of an agreed procedure governing the passage of the constitution,[19] as it opened a floodgate for proposals for ways to pass the constitution, which changed as frequently as actors' perceptions of their chances to shape the content of the constitution. Moreover, the question was not only 'how' but also 'what' should the Supreme Council consider, as at the same time as the draft of the Constitutional Commission was presented, a number of alternative drafts were tabled, including the draft of the CPU.[20]

The Left vehemently criticised the March draft, and the communists flatly refused to debate it.[21] At the same time, despite the nominal approval of the March draft by the Supreme Council for further consideration, there was only lukewarm enthusiasm for the March draft across the centre-right part of the political spectrum. Both the autocratic spirit of the constitution and many specific provisions in the draft sparked a wide-ranging condemnation. Amongst the numerous provisions of the draft, the bi-cameral legislature evoked the most zealous and uniform resistance.[22] Thus, even the most ardent supporters of the draft soberly realised that it would not obtain even a simple majority in parliament. At the same time, however, there was some relief that at least there was now a complete draft to work on. Even if the March draft excessively favoured the presidency, it was, nevertheless, of a higher quality and more representative than the alternative drafts tabled by political parties or individual deputies at that time.

In order to ensure the draft's approval in parliament, an informal conciliatory group headed by a little known, centrist deputy, Mykhailo Syrota, was convened within parliament (the precedent was established during the approval of the *Dohovir*). The group included all centre-right factions, with peasants and socialists as 'observers', while the communists refused to participate. The conciliatory group set about crafting a more balanced form of government, and the article on the upper chamber was one of its first victims. When it was evident that this informal group—driven by the imperative to compromise against the Left's opposition—made fast progress, in early May 1996, on Oleksandr Moroz's initiative, the group was transformed into a formal 'Temporary Extraordinary Commission on the Preparation of the Draft Constitution'. However, despite the intention of the Left, the Commission continued with the previous voting arrangements: 'one faction—one vote', which, once again, turned the Left into a minority. Facing the determination of the right-centrist factions to push forward the process, the moderate Left failed to radically alter the content of the March draft.[23]

At the end of May 1996, the Extraordinary Commission produced an amended version of the March draft, the so-called 'Syrota draft'. Even if the draft did not fundamentally alter the form of government envisaged by the March draft, the conciliatory group and the Commission improved the system of 'checks and balances' by weakening the presidential powers and strengthening the position of the legislature and the cabinet of ministers. Yet, the Left remained unrepentant: 'an unbiased analysis [of the Syrota draft] leads to the conclusion that ... it amounted to "cosmetic surgery", which did not change the anti-national nature of this document. The rejection of bi-cameralism hardly changed anything'.[24] As a result, the Syrota draft was only approved by 17 out of 28 members of the Temporary Extraordinary Commission (all but one representatives of the leftist factions voted against it).

PLENARY DEBATES IN PARLIAMENT (JUNE 1996)

While the Extraordinary Commission was making progress on the draft, the procedure for the passage of the constitution remained undecided. Thus, the plenary debates started in June 1996 again with the hotly debated procedural issues and a show-down between the Moroz-led left-wing factions and the centre-right in the Supreme Council (on the breakdown of parliament see Table 6.2). When the draft finally underwent its first reading, it obtained, as was expected, only a simple majority (258 in favour, 106 against, 19 abstained, 9 did not vote). This result was to a large extent due to the efforts of the group and Commission led by Syrota, which won over a greater number of the centrist deputies. The likelihood of a successful passage by a two-thirds majority was still perceived as negligible. Satisfied with such parliamentary 'blessing', the national-democrats urged the president to unilaterally set a date for the referendum to by-pass the Left's resistance.

Despite the fact that the Left attempted to forestall the process, the parliament moved on to the second reading of the draft on 19 June 1996. However, with mundane debates on each article progress was glacial and the second reading appeared to drift into a stalemate. A number of key articles did not muster a constitutional majority (including the text of the Preamble, the articles on the language, national symbols and private property), and the resolution of the main bones of contention was simply deferred to the third (and final) reading. The highly charged polemics and protracted deliberations fuelled a deep scepticism about the whole endeavour and a growing conviction that the Supreme Council could not adopt the constitution in the third reading by a qualified majority of 300.

Table 6.2. Breakdown of the Ukrainian Parliament (May 1996)

Left	
The Communist Party of Ukraine	87
The Socialist Party of Ukraine	28
The Peasant Party of Ukraine	25
Centre	
Inter-Regional Bloc for Reforms	26
Independents	26
Unity (*Yednist*)	28
The Agrarians for Reforms	25
Centre	28
Social Market Choice	26
Right	
Rukh	29
Reform	31
Statehood	29
Non-affiliated	27
Total	*415 of 450*

Source: Holos Ukrainy, 31 May 1996.

THE CONSTITUTIONAL NIGHT (27–28 JUNE 1996)

At this point, president Kuchma re-emerged as the dominant force in constitution making. On 26 June 1996, he dispensed with legal niceties and announced that with no prospect of the constitution being adopted by the Supreme Council, a nation-wide referendum on the constitution would be held in September 1996.[25] Most importantly, it was to be on the earlier, more pro-presidential March draft, rather than the Syrota draft, which had already been passed by a simple majority in parliament. In a one-fell move president Kuchma side-stepped the cumbersome compromises worked out within the Supreme Council over four months on grounds that the Syrota draft was 'approved' within the parliament, but not officially 'agreed' with the president (despite the fact that the Syrota Commission held weekly meetings with the president and the presidential administration to discuss any revisions). The March draft was viewed by the majority of the factions, even those allied with the president, as inferior to the Syrota draft already approved in the first reading and the decree caused uneasiness and consternation, even amongst the national-democrats, who had urged the president to take the Syrota draft to a referendum.

Table 6.3. Voting Results from the Adoption of the Ukrainian Constitution (28 June 1996)

Faction	*For*	*Against*	*Abstained*	*Did Not Vote*
Left				
The Communists	20	29	10	20
The Socialists	17	6	2	0
The Peasants	21	0	0	2
Centre				
Inter-Regional Bloc for Reforms	23	0	0	1
Independents	22	0	0	0
Social Market Choice	23	0	0	3
Unity (*Yednist'*)	24	0	0	1
Centre (*Tsentr*)	26	0	0	1
Agrarians for Reforms	25	0	0	0
Right				
Reforms	29	0	0	1
Rukh	26	0	0	1
Statehood (*Derzhavnist*)	25	0	0	0
Non-affiliated	34	1	0	0
Total	*315*	*36*	*12*	*30*

Source: The Supreme Council of Ukraine.

Kuchma's decree induced a profound legitimacy crisis: the Supreme Council was failing to carry out its duties by not being capable of passing a fundamental law. By decreeing on a referendum and undermining the role of parliament, the president claimed to act in line with the 'popular will', frustrated with the deadlock within parliament. This strategy leant heavily on the high level of popular support for the president compared to that for parliament. Yet parliament was not to be easily dismissed. The decree and the threat of an imminent referendum acted as catalysts in forging some sense—even if short-lived—of collective solidarity of parliament as the highest representative body with responsibility for the adoption of the constitution. Fears lingered that not only might the less desirable draft be ratified in the referendum, but also that the subsequent dissolution of parliament would be a mere formality, as Kuchma was bending backward and forward to discredit the legislature in the state-controlled media. One observer neatly attributed the radical change in the attitudes of the deputies to the fact that: 'nothing concentrates the mind more wonderfully than the premonition of a hangman's noose or a firing squad'.[26] Sensing its imminent dissolution, the parliament sharply accelerated its work-rate, led by its socialist chairman Moroz, who until then had actively hindered the passage. Moroz arranged a non-stop debate, which turned into a 23-hour marathon of frantic negotiation and repetitious voting. Throughout that crucial night, the issues, such as the status of Russian language, symbols, property rights or the status of Crimea, which proved to be the greatest obstacle to the passage of the constitution, were tackled by repeated voting (10–20 times on some articles). The issues were also voted on as 'packages' to force reluctant factions to vote in favour (see below). In a highly tense and emotional atmosphere a constitutional majority (300 votes) was achieved when 315 deputies voted in favour of the constitution, while 36 voted against, 12 abstained while 30 did not vote (Table 6.3).

This result was met with astonishment by all sides. When taking the decision on the referendum, the president presumed that the ideological cleavages within parliament made a settlement impossible and would prevent the legislature from acting unanimously. Yet by submitting a draft to a referendum which was viewed by all factions in parliament as worse than the already approved Syrota draft and, moreover, by putting a question mark over the future of parliament, the decree had a powerful and—taking into account the presidential intentions—unintended consequence of recreating a conflict between the institutions, similar to that in the Russia of 1993. Having achieved his main goal through the efforts of parliament, the president, even if visibly puzzled by this unexpected 'attainment', congratulated the parliamentarians, apologising for his tactics and calling off the referendum. But even if unwittingly, the president acted as a midwife, delivering the constitution under the trying conditions of a divided parliament unable to master a constitutional majority. Symbolically, Ukraine succeeded in ratifying the new constitution, and hence gained the pivotal attribute of sovereignty, before the decisive second round of the 1996 Russian presidential elections, when Yeltsin's victory and Ziuganov's defeat seemed far from certain.

ACTORS' PREFERENCES, STRATEGIES AND INSTITUTIONAL RESOURCES

The chronological overview provided an account of the two years (1994–1996) of intense constitutional reform, which despite the difficulties, resulted in the 1995 'Little Constitution', and was followed by a proper constitution a year later. The chronological overview raised a number of questions, which have so far remained unanswered. Were the preferences of actors, as described in the previous chapter, fixed and static or did they change in the process? What strategies did the actors adopt to realise their preferences? What institutional resources did they employ? To what extent did the actors shape the content of the constitution? Why did some of them succeed whereas others failed? The next section, thus, will examine in more detail the preferences, strategies and institutional resources of main actors in the process (the presidency, the national-democrats, the Left and the centrists). Although the focus will be on these collective actors, attention will be drawn to individuals whenever their actions affected the course of events.

THE PRESIDENCY

The president's dominant role in the constitutional process stemmed from both a clearly and narrowly defined set of preferences and the institutional resources, which the president had at his disposal. Without the baggage of ideological convictions from the outset, the focus of the president and his administration was on the form of government, and he threw all resources at the constitution making to secure the desired outcome.[27] In pursuit of institutional advantage, Kuchma pushed to the brink of embarking on a confrontation with parliament.

As pointed out in chapter 5, the president favoured a strong, executive presidency with legislative power and control over the cabinet of ministers and the regions. At the same time, the president paid little attention to the 'national question'. Yet, even if focused on the institutional goals, Kuchma and his entourage took advantage of the fact that the national question was of 'principal importance' for the Right, while as far as Kuchma was concerned it was 'tradable'. Hence, the issue of symbols and language were utilised to attract the support of the national-democrats. While in the November draft, the national symbols (flag, emblems and the anthem) were to be determined by an ordinary law, Kuchma later firmly backed the national-democrats in their insistence that the constitution specifies the 'yellow and blue' flag, trident and the anthem ('Ukraine Has Yet Not Perished') as the national symbols. The president swiftly adopted the 'rhetoric of statehood' to win over the support of the right wing, arguing that: '[the March draft is] quite European in its letter and spirit and reflects the traditions of Ukrainian state building'.[28] Kuchma equated support for the March draft with support for sovereignty and depicted those who opposed it as the enemies of the national interest and traitors of the 'people'.

With the *Dohovir* 1995 as a milestone in the consolidation of presidential powers, the primary objective of the president was to copy the chapters on the division of powers from the *Dohovir* into the new constitution. Working to Kuchma's advantage, was the fact that the *Dohovir* not only 'swung the pendulum' towards presidentialism, it also introduced a crucial change to the ratification procedure. Even if tentatively, the *Dohovir* authorised the role of the president as equal to that of parliament and opened the door for ratification in a referendum, in contrast to the 1978 constitution, which only allowed for changes to the constitution to be approved by parliament. Although the president had no right to request a referendum on the constitution on his own initiative, the *Dohovir* envisaged a referendum after the text of the constitution had been agreed between the president and parliament. On the basis of this provision, Kuchma insisted on keeping the ratification of the constitution unconstrained by any rules, and objected to parliamentary initiatives to elaborate the detailed procedure. By specifying the meaning of the term 'agreed', the president's room for manoeuvre would be considerably narrowed. Taking into account the popular legitimacy of the president, the *Dohovir*, even if hampered by procedural illegitimacy, provided the president with an instrument with which to pressurise parliament, namely the plebiscite, which he was only too keen to exploit.

Apart from initiating the *Dohovir,* the presidency seized a crucial institutional advantage at the outset of the process. When the second Constitutional Commission was set up in October 1994, it differed from its predecessor in that it was not a *parliamentary* commission. Instead, it included 'representatives of subjects with legislative initiative'—the legislature, the executive and the judicial branch. Taking into account that the principle of the separation of powers was the bone of contention in Ukraine, the formation of the Constitutional Commission according to this principle was a path-breaking event. Not only did it introduce the principle through the back door, but also created the institutional setting, which favoured the president. The application of the principle of the separation of powers put the president on an equal footing with parliament: he appointed almost half of the members of the Constitutional Commission. Moreover, as 2–3 out of the 4 representatives of parliament sided with Kuchma in his views on the form of government, he gained a competitive edge over the anti-presidential forces. This advantage became even more pronounced in the experts' working group.[29] Indeed, the November draft closely resembled the *Dohovir,* except for the bi-cameral legislature. Overall, the composition of the Constitutional Commission and the working group proved crucial in determining the outcome of the constitutional process, in particular with regard to the form of government.

The presidency resorted to a variety of tactics to prevent such changes greatly helped by the institutional resources available to it. When the draft was prepared in the Constitutional Commission in 1994–1995, the president was directly involved in the debates. However, once parliament took over the draft in March 1996, the president's role was reduced to that of an observer. But Kuchma and his Administration continued to play a key role in the process, as he commanded impressive know-how and human resources in comparison to parliament in general, and individual parliamentary factions in particular. All the institutional resources available within the Presidential Administration and the cabinet of ministers were thrown at the problem to secure the passage of the constitution.[30] The Presidential Administration embarked on intensive behind-the-scenes lobbying, negotiations, promises and deals with factions and individual deputies to minimise the changes to the form of government as outlined in the March draft. In particular, it ensured it gained support within the Supreme Council, by dwelling on the dependency of some deputies on the presidency. Some deputies combined parliamentary mandates with posts in the executive branch at the central and local level (the so-called *sumisnyky*), and, as such, were ultimately subordinated to the president. Thus, a group of approximately 40 deputies consistently defended the presidential position, and effectively acted as the president's 'fifth column' in parliament. Aware of those loyalties, Moroz attempted to purge parliament of *sumisnyky* in November 1995, but failed to obtain the necessary support in parliament. Moreover, while parliament was debating the constitution, the president recruited some prominent deputies from the volatile centrist factions, with which he found it difficult to negotiate, into the executive branch.

The ideological diversity in parliament and the bitter strife between the Left and the Right prevented an anti-presidential alliance in parliament, yet smaller bodies such as the informal conciliatory group and the Temporary Extraordinary Commission could pose a greater challenge. These were small groups of committed deputies, who worked intensively on a 'voluntary basis' driven by the need to work out a compromise both within the group and within their factions. Several members of the Commission commented in interviews that they developed a collective identity and their common goal was to prepare a draft, which would be passed by the Supreme Council. The president, however, sought to undermine their determination and unity by bringing up demands in weekly meetings, which were impossible to accept by the informal group without jeopardising the fragile consensus and hard-won compromises. Often those demands were designed to exacerbate the internal cleavages within the factions (mainly centrist ones), and, as such, played havoc with the progress of work and created delays.

One of the most controversial, but decisive events of the process was the president's decision to put to referendum the more pro-presidential March draft rather than the Syrota draft. As this was inconsistent with Kuchma's earlier actions, this came as a surprise even to the pro-presidential deputies. In late May 1996 the president declared his unconditional support for the Syrota draft and during the first reading in early June 1996, all *sumisnyky*-deputies were instructed (because of their usual high level of absenteeism) to attend the session in order to counter-act the Left's attempt to boycott the first reading by refusing to register. However, after the first reading, the president and the Presidential Administration radically changed their rhetoric and tactics, and began to boycott the parliament's efforts, despite the fact that the form of government in general and the presidential powers in particular remained essentially unchanged between the readings. During the second reading, the *sumisnyky* were instructed not to participate.[31] The presidential side expected that without the *sumisnyky*, the centre-right deputies would not cobble together a constitutional majority, and this would only strengthen the case of the president to put the draft constitution to a referendum. The two national-democratic factions, Rukh and *Derzhavnist'*, were also persuaded to take up this strategy although they did so with less consistency (see below).

This inconsistency and change of tactics can be attributed to the internal workings of the Presidential Administration, where internal factions competed for influence in determining the institutional strategy.

The moderates, headed by the presidential adviser Oleksandr Rozumkov, favoured the 'lawful' passage of the constitution in the Supreme Council; initially they had the upper hand. As a contingency plan, preparations were made for a referendum.[32] Yet, between the first and second reading in June 1996, the 'hard-liners', led by the head of the Presidential Administration, Dmytro Tabachnyk, gained the upper hand and disposed of all niceties. They unleashed an uncompromising assault on the Supreme Council and advised the president to submit the March draft to a referendum.

The weak legal basis for holding a referendum was not a deterrent for Kuchma, as a precedent had been established prior to the *Dohovir*. Kuchma attempted to offset any legal shortcomings by emphasising his popular mandate and posing as a popular champion forced to counteract the paralysis within parliament. On numerous occasions, Kuchma stressed that it was recommended that he resorted to a referendum to complete the process; for example, the Council of National Security and Defence asked him to act decisively on the grounds that further delays in passing the constitution would pose a serious threat to Ukraine's national security.

In sum, the president and his entourage was the driving force in the constitutional process, propelled by clearly defined institutional interests and bolstered with considerable institutional resources. The presidential initiative in the early stages of the constitutional process proved decisive for suppression of the spectrum of views represented in the Supreme Council, and resulted in a draft skewed in favour of the presidency. As Moroz admitted: '[when appointing the Constitutional Commission] there was an attempt to include all views and positions. With the benefit of hindsight [it can be concluded that] it was a mistake. The constitution should have been drafted by the Supreme Council'.[33] As a result of this initial decision, parliament worked to amend the pro-presidential drafts against the clock and mounting tension from the presidency. While the ideological divisions within parliament protected the presidential interests in the constitutional process, the threat of a referendum 'finished the job' by forcing parliament to submit.

THE LEFT

The Left's strategy in the constitutional process was that of an unmitigated series of rejections of compromises and a staunch opposition to the drafts, which did not fully take into account its preferences. Thus the Left resorted to a mix of blocking manoeuvres to slow down the constitutional process while hoping that, at some point, it would be able to mould the content of the constitution to its liking. However, the Left's orthodoxy and rigidity alienated its potential allies—the centrist deputies. As a result, despite being the largest ideological orientation in parliament, the Left failed to gain the initiative, and eventually crumbled under the pressure during the final night.

The Left in general and the communists in particular rejected both the November and the March drafts, because they included the following provisions:

- the abolition of the structure of radas with the Supreme Council as the highest authority;
- the bi-cameral legislature;
- the dominance of the president over the legislature with prerogatives more extensive than in the *Dohovir*;
- inadequate protection of the state and collective property in contrast to that of private property;
- the introduction of 'capitalist social relations';
- insufficient social guarantees to preserve 'socialist achievements';
- 'nationalistic' state symbols;
- the elevation of the Ukrainian nation (national state) and Ukrainian as the sole state language; and
- the abolition of *prokuratura's* function to oversee legality.[34]

In particular, on the 'national question' the communist leader, Petro Symonenko, was outspoken in his criticism of the March draft:

> The constitution aims to allow the domination of a nationalistic and anti-human (*liudyno-nenavysnytskoi*) ideology, symbols of Petliura-Bandera, which are rejected by the majority of the population, and the linguistic discrimination against tens of millions of people who do not belong to the so-called 'indigenous nation'.[35]

The Left condemned the form of government based on the principle of the separation of powers embedded in the draft constitution on the grounds that 'having formally declared the principle of separation of powers, the authors seriously invalidated the principle by putting the president above the other branches of power and practically beyond the reach of minimal control by the society and the citizens, who elected him.'[36] The Left declared that all of the above objections were of 'principal importance' and it would not ratify a draft that did not take them on board. The left-wing factions declared that 'they cannot agree to the brutal imposition of the Fundamental Law, the basic principles of which break both the articles of the Declaration of Sovereignty … and the Concept of the Constitution approved by the Supreme Council [in July 1991'].[37] As a result, the Left rejected outright the November, March and then the Syrota draft, and took a range of steps to ruin the process.

The Left questioned the authority of the Constitutional Commission to draft the constitution because its working group consisted only of pro-presidential specialists, and members of the left-wing factions were marginalised in the Constitutional Commission.[38] The communist leader—Petro Symonenko—depicted the constitution as the result of a plot hatched by presidential cronies.[39] Similarly, the Socialist Oleksandr Moroz referred to the March draft as 'an extremely contradictory draft, born in the womb of one of the branches of power by individual apparatchiks'.[40] At the beginning of 1996 the Communist Party had launched a campaign to collect 3 million signatures in support of a referendum. As the most legitimate way to draft the constitution, the communists advocated a referendum on the principles of the constitution, such as the language, symbols, the status of private property, before the constitution could be drafted by the Supreme Council. However, the petition was ruled illegal by the Minister of Justice, the Electoral Commission and the General Procurator. The communists declared the campaign a 'moral crusade'.[41] Being unable to resort to instruments of direct democracy, the communists tabled their own draft the 'Constitution of the Ukrainian Soviet Socialist Republic' signed by 125 members of parliament in the hope that it would become an alternative to the March draft (see above). In the meantime, they attempted to stall the ratification of the March draft by strictly adhering to the *Reglament*, a set of parliamentary rules of the legislative process, which were not only vague but also did not elaborate the procedure for the passage of the constitution. The Left repeatedly refused to register so that a quorum could not be reached.[42] Between the first and second reading, they tried to 'jam the system' by proposing several thousand changes to the Syrota draft. In sum, the Left championed procedural legality and relied on its numerical strength to halt the ratification process.

Although more moderate in their rhetoric, the socialists and peasants backed the communists in the attack on the March and Syrota drafts.[43] Oleksandr Moroz acted as a powerful spokesman of the Left. Although he signed the *Dohovir*, he stressed its temporary nature, and emphasised that the provisions of the *Dohovir* remained totally separate from and in no way contiguous with the new constitution. He praised the communist draft: 'it is a presentable draft, in which all functions of the branches of power are clearly specified, the guarantees of social welfare of citizens are strengthened, the chapter of the judicial power and, especially, local government are reasonable'.[44] Nevertheless, while the communists adopted a strategy of non-cooperation, Moroz proved more amenable to compromise. Thus, his faction, the socialists, participated in the conciliatory group headed by Syrota as 'observers'. Moroz then attempted to exercise greater control and bring the Left into the process by giving a formal recognition to the Syrota commission. However, as the revision of the March draft was almost complete by that time, his initiative came too late to radically alter the content of the draft before the first reading.

Even if Moroz used his position as chairman to torpedo the ratification of the March and Syrota drafts in parliament, his institutional role made him rise above his ideological convictions. Entrenched in their opposition, the communists favoured a referendum as a means of ratification. In contrast, Moroz insisted on the passage of the constitution by the Supreme Council and condemned the referendum on the grounds that it would polarise society, fearing that it would side-track the parliament. He expected that the communists' draft would be considered parallel to that of the Temporary Extraordinary Commission and that the two drafts would eventually be amalgamated into a single draft. This way the Left's preferences would be incorporated into the constitution. While Moroz remained torn between the ideological preferences, the need to secure his power base in parliament, and his institutional role as chairman of parliament, Kuchma's decree on the constitutional referendum tipped the balance in favour of the latter. Having obstructed the passage until then, Moroz overnight turned into an ardent supporter of the Syrota draft. He set out to persuade the centre-left deputies opposing the constitution of the danger of their strategy—namely, that without the passage of the constitution, the Supreme Council would cease to exist. He convened a non-stop session of parliament arguing 'that we can't stop the session, because the momentum would then be gone'.[45] Overnight, Moroz's status changed from that of a side-tracked politician to that of a statesman, as he gained the aura of a politician who was prepared to sacrifice his own partisan convictions for the sake of higher considerations—reconciliation and stability of the country. Eventually, he succeeded in winning over those socialists, peasants and even some communists who feared the ramifications of the failure to pass the constitution by the *Verkhovna Rada*. The inevitable result was a split of the Left into hard-liners and moderates, although the division did not follow neatly factional lines (see Table 6.3). The left-wing bloc, renowned for its voting discipline up till that point, splintered under pressure during the final night, in which Moroz's role was highly instrumental.

Overall, despite having a clearly defined set of preferences and being the largest bloc in parliament with over one third of all seats, the Left emerged as the loser. This can be attributed to three main factors. Firstly, the Left flatly rejected the whole conception of statehood proposed by the centre-right, and the sheer number of the disputed issues made compromise with other factions practically impossible. Secondly, the leftist strategy relied on its relative numerical strength in the Supreme Council to control the outcome of the constitutional process. By embarking on a strategy of non-cooperation, boycotting the process, and waiting for an opportunity to introduce radical changes to the draft constitution before it was passed, the Left's ideological preferences isolated it from other actors. The Left's uncompromising stance in its opposition to the March draft acted as a catalyst in drawing the fragmented centre-right factions and the president together in support of the constitution, despite the profound differences between the preferences of those actors. Thirdly, the internal rifts within the Left were decisive. The hard-line communists rejected compromise and opted for confrontation rather than accepting a 'nationalist, authoritarian constitution'. In contrast, the moderate Left's readiness to embrace at least some of the ideas propagated by other factions, such as the right of private property, made them more open to compromise. While the internal cleavage within the leftist bloc initially remained narrow, it widened radically after the president decreed on the referendum, especially as the leader of the moderate socialists, Moroz, put premium on his institutional role. Ultimately, however, the content of the constitution was influenced neither by the moderates, who sanctioned the constitution, nor the hard-line communists, who did not.

THE NATIONAL-DEMOCRATS

The stance of the national-democrats in the constitutional process amounted to a wholesale rejection of the Soviet legacy in post-Soviet Ukraine. But as the process progressed, they encountered fierce opposition from the Left, they found themselves unable to realise their vision of statehood. By necessity, they found an unlikely ally in the president, a coalition that allowed them to instil their conception of nationhood in the constitution, but caused some confusion on other issues, and their overall strategy.

In order to turn Ukraine into a modern, democratic and 'fully European' state, they advocated the abolition of the system of soviets, a change in the definition of the political community to assert the role of the titular majority, and the creation of the institutional framework to ensure the territorial integrity of Ukraine. The national-democrats, however, most of all abhorred the idea of the restoration of the Soviet Union, which was the professed goal of hard-line communists. The referendum on the constitutional principles, which the Communist Party of Ukraine attempted to organise in the winter-spring of 1996, was to include a question on 'attitudes toward the voluntary Union of Independent States created on the territory of the ruined Soviet Union'.[46] Moreover, the Left's attempt to block the March draft acquired a particular dimension in light of the upcoming Russian presidential elections in June 1996, in which the communist candidate Genadii Ziuganov challenged the incumbent president Boris Yeltsin. The national-democrats feared that the latter's victory would give a new lease of life to communist forces across the former Soviet Union and boost the standing of the Communist Party of Ukraine in its drive to re-integrate Ukraine with Russia.[47] As a win for Ziuganov would present a tangible threat to Ukraine's sovereignty, as far as the national-democrats were concerned, the schedule of the presidential elections in Russia dictated the 'constitutional timetable' in Ukraine.

Those considerations determined the priorities of Rukh and the *Derzhavnist'* factions, and to a lesser extent, Reforms. At the end of 1995 Viacheslav Chornovil, the leader of Rukh, commented on the November draft: 'familiarity with the draft constitution ... fills me with deep sadness, and even deeper fear', and he criticised the draft constitution as 'anti-national, anti-party and anti-parliamentary'.[48] However, by the spring 1996, as the CPU launched its offensive (see above), the quick ratification of the constitution became the utmost priority. The Left's outright rejection of the March draft and the resulting stalemate in parliament convinced the right-wing that mustering a constitutional two-thirds majority would be nothing short of miracle, and thus the procedural hurdles had to be circumvented, 'because of the attempt of the communo-bolshevik majority to delay the debates on the draft constitution'.[49] They urged the president to set a tight deadline for the passage of the constitution in the Supreme Council, which, if not met, would result in the constitution being submitted to referendum. But the national-democrats advocated only a referendum on the full draft of the constitution, and opposed the communists' suggestion for a referendum on the general principles, which—as they feared—would not only delay the process, but might not have resulted in the electorate supporting the national-democrats' preferences. Believing that the full draft could be ratified only with presidential backing, they looked to the president as a vital ally in the task of sanctioning their vision of the Ukrainian state. Unwilling to concede on any principal point the national-democrats, *a priori* rejected the compromise with the Left and profoundly distrusted any of its initiatives. As Chornovil commented: 'it was impossible to consolidate pro-statehood (*derzhavnytski syly*) and anti-statehood (*anty-derzhavnytski*) forces'.[50] For example, the formalisation of the special conciliatory group, which actually conferred the Syrota draft greater legitimacy, was interpreted as a plot by the socialist Moroz to torpedo the whole process. The fear of a 'red encroachment' (*kommunistychna navala*) made the national-democrats exclude the Left rather than woo it into co-operation.

The national-democrats placed the 'national question' and protection of Ukraine's territorial integrity at the top of their constitutional agenda. As one participant in the process from the presidential side commented: 'Crimea, language, symbols and the constitution as a symbol—all of these were sacred (*sviate*) for the right wing'.[51] Even if the passage of the constitution was the highest priority, the national-democrats themselves boycotted the debates by refusing to register (so that a quorum of two thirds could not be obtained), when there was a threat that the centre and leftist deputies could close ranks to ensure that the Russian language was granted the 'official status'.[52] During the constitutional night, the Right voted against granting Crimea the status of 'Autonomous Republic' even at the risk of jeopardising the whole ratification process. The 'national question' and 'territorial integrity' was not to be sacrificed for the sake of quick and lawful passage of the constitution by parliament.[53]

As regards the form of government, for the national-democrats the significance of the constitutional process was more than a matter of securing institutional advantage through the creation of either a presidential or parliamentary system. For them the overarching goal was the protection of the sovereignty of Ukraine. Serhiy Holovatyi, the Minister of Justice, commented on the institutional framework in the March draft: 'these are only details. Because, today, what concerns me the most is the problem of survival. And that very much depends on whether or not Ukraine will have its own constitution before the elections in Russia'.[54] Paradoxically, by the end of Kuchma's first term in office, Holovatyi became one of the most ardent critics of the incumbent's use of his presidential prerogatives. As long as the system of soviets was abolished and the principle of separation of powers was upheld in the constitution the specific presidential powers were open to negotiation. The Right's willingness to accommodate presidential demands on the form of government rose proportionally to its perception of the difficulty in mustering a constitutional majority for the articles on the language, symbols and the Preamble. As a result, when on 28 June 1996 the president decreed on taking the March draft to a referendum, some of the national-democrats faced a conundrum: while overall they preferred the Syrota draft to the March draft, they were undecided over whether to back the president's bold (and unconstitutional) move or to continue the search for a compromise within parliament. Unable to work out a coherent strategy, the bloc remained divided during the constitutional night. In effect, the head of Rukh—Viacheslav Chornovil—abstained from the voting in the pivotal second reading.

Like all other collective actors involved in constitution making, the right wing faced the problem of internal dissent. Some national-democrats refused to support the president at any cost. Several deputies in *Derzhavnist'* (the members of the Ukrainian Republican Party) left their faction in protest at the pro-presidential stance of other members. Nevertheless, the opponents of Kuchma were in a minority amongst the national-democrats. With truly revolutionary fervour, Rukh's leader, Viacheslav Chornovil, called for unity, and outlawed any dissent: 'The next few months will be decisive for the fate of Ukraine. In a struggle between imperialism and independence, communism and civilisation there is no room for "free critics" in opposition to anybody or anything'.[55] Although the faction *Reformy*, which grouped younger deputies with liberal leanings, was far from unanimous in its support of the March draft, nevertheless, it also conceded that the urgent adoption of the Basic Law was of the highest priority for Ukraine.

Overall, in terms of preferences, as long as the system of soviets was abolished, the actual powers of the presidency were considered ultimately of the less importance than the 'national' credentials of Ukraine (the state language and symbols, and the definition of the political community as the 'Ukrainian people'). This made it possible for the majority of the national-democrats to co-operate closely with the president, and despite being in a minority to ensure that the 'national question' was resolved in line with their preferences.

THE CENTRE

The motives and strategies of the centrist factions during the final stages of the constitutional process differed so widely that only a broad generalisation can be provided, despite the large numbers of centrist deputies. After the elections, many independent deputies, mainly from Left bank constituencies with loose or no ideological affiliation, grouped around the leftist bloc attracted by its sheer size, and the fact that the centrists had little in common with the nationalist right wing. After noting that Kuchma's presidency was decisive, pragmatic, and free of ideological phraseology, they loosened their links with the Left and became more inclined to support the reformist camp, although not necessarily sharing the president's views on the form of government. Overall, the majority of the centrist factions were tentatively united in their preference for a devolution of power to the regions (most of all through the preservation of directly elected oblast councils), a parliament-centred form of government and the inclusion of the right to private property in the constitution. They opposed strengthening the presidency at the expense of the emasculation of the Supreme Council and the cabinet of ministers. In particular, the preservation of the unicameral legislature generated almost a uniform support. Yet while supporting a more parliamentary system, the centrists did not favour the restoration of the 'arch-parliamentary' system of soviets. This combined with their support for private property put them in opposition to the communists.

Nevertheless, despite some shared preferences, there was little unity amongst the centrist factions. In the case of the 'Centre', its affiliation with the cabinet of ministers dictated its loyalty to the president. However, they were divided on the national question. The Inter-Regional Group of Deputies (MDG)—with its many deputies from Crimea—was united in its opposition to Ukrainian becoming the only state language, and to national symbols. It supported granting far-reaching powers to the Crimean Autonomous Republic. The MDG's position threatened the compromise within the conciliatory group as it was at loggerheads with Rukh and 'Statehood' over the 'national question'. Yet the MDG lacked a clear stance on other issues.[56] Other factions, such as the 'Social Market Choice', 'Independents' and 'Unity', which represented the Russophone regions of Ukraine, remained divided on the 'national question'. Significantly, despite representing mainly Russophone regions, the centrists did not create a supra-factional coalition on the language question. Remaining loose groupings out of convenience, the centrist factions did not adopt a coherent set of preferences and pursue them. Often two deputies representing the same centrist faction voted differently in the Syrota group and commission. Despite the fact that the centrists overwhelmingly agreed on the need for a new constitution, their motives and priorities remained volatile and unpredictable, which impaired their chances of becoming a leading force in the process.

Moreover, even when members of the centrist factions showed some initiative, they were prevented from playing a constructive role (in the early stages) in forging a compromise, as neither of the ideological blocs trusted them.[57] The national-democrats in particular feared the potential alliance between the Left and centrists on the 'national question', which would allow the changes to the articles on Crimea, the state language and national symbols to take place.

However, despite being divided on many issues, once the president decreed on the constitutional referendum the centrists hardly needed any persuasion—for them the referendum was an unmistaken harbinger of the dissolution of parliament. To save the day, they took on the role of a mediator between the Left and Right in order to persuade them to abandon their ideological trenches. The centrists devised a strategy of coupling the most contested issues. For example, the articles on the national symbols were coupled with the chapter on the Crimean Autonomous Republic, as the Right opposed the 'Crimean Republic' and the Left opposed the 'nationalist' symbols. This provided the right- and left-wing deputies with an incentive to vote positively, so that a constitutional majority could be garnered on these issues.

Overall, the sheer mass of centrists made them a critical component in parliament, accounting, as they did, for nearly half of all deputies. Yet they played a highly ambiguous role in the constitutional process. On the one hand, the fragmentation and weak organisation of the centre further hampered the constitutional process by compelling tedious and time-consuming negotiations not only between the president and parliamentary factions, but even between individual deputies.[58] On the other hand, however, it was precisely the volatility of centrist deputies, which left room for manoeuvre between the two hostile ideological blocs, and so allowed the constitution to be adopted despite all the odds. The threat of a referendum only reinforced the centrists' propensity to compromise. Nevertheless, no overall discipline, apart from the final vote on the constitution, was ever worked out in this bloc. Ultimately, the centre's weak organisational structures and nebulous ideological commitments meant that it punched below its weight in terms of shaping the content of the constitution, despite some gains in balancing out the powers of parliament and president. The constitution process turned into a zero-sum game between the president and national-democrats on the one side, and the left-wing factions on the other.

CONCLUSION

While the matrix of preferences (such as presented in Table 5.4) gives an overview of preferences, it does not reveal the internal hierarchy of preferences from the actors' point of view. During constitution making in Ukraine, the existence of such hierarchies was fully recognised by the participants themselves. In their own words, there were 'issues of principle' (*pryntsypovi pytannia*) and 'political issues' (*nepryntsypovi/politychni pytannia*). While the former were concerned with various types of interest and such were open to at least some negotiation and bargaining, the 'issues of principle' denoted the deepest normative convictions, which could not be the subject of bargaining and trade-offs. These 'internal' hierarchies of preferences that provide vital clues in accounting for strategies that each of the key actors resorted to in the constitutional process.

For the national-democrats, the 'historically correct' definition of the nationhood mattered more than the prerogatives of parliament. In a similar vein, the hard-line Left risked the dissolution of parliament in which they were represented, rather than concede to the 'nationalistic' state symbols. During the constitutional night, it was not the institutional prerogatives which jeopardised the compromise (indeed, the articles on the form of government were hardly changed at all), but the highly emotional questions of collectivity and its attributes, which overshadowed the issue of the division of powers and threatened the constitutional compromise. The deeply held beliefs of the national-democrats or the communists proved largely impervious to rational calculations of personal and group institutional advantages. The Right and Left clung to an exclusive, absolute style of thinking, which can be best conceptualised by Carl Schmitt's notion of the 'politics of us against them'. The national-democrats viewed the Left as the fifth column of the external 'foe', the imperialist forces in Russia. With the 'foe' being defined in a sweeping way (even if only part of the Left actually questioned the legitimacy of the new polity), the threat to the state's integrity and sovereignty was perceived as imminent. The defence of collective integrity against 'the other' became the highest political order.[59] Until the polity was fenced off from the endangering forces, Easton's politics of 'who get what, when, and how' (even if in the constitutional process this meant the redistribution of *kompetentz*) could not be casually resumed.[60] Thus, for some of the national-democrats the division of powers between the presidency and legislature remained 'only details'.

However, the politicisation of constitution making with its juxtaposition of deeply held ideas, institutional and personal interests ultimately provided a framework for the mediation between two opposing visions of the polity. The less 'ideologised' actors, the president and the centrist deputies, who were primarily driven by institutional and/or group interests, intersected the ideological blocs. In particular, the involvement of the centrist factions explains the propensity to organise conciliatory groups, which greatly facilitated the compromise reached on the constitutional night. Their efforts to force the national-democrats and the Left to renege on their 'issues of principle' required, as one participant put it, 'Such diplomacy takes place only once in a lifetime'.[61]

The final factor, which accounts for the outcome, was the institutional context in which constitution drafting took place, characterised by the presence of two directly elected representatives of the electorate with competing claims to popular legitimacy. Throughout most of the process the main cleavage cut across institutions and ran between the 'restorationists' and the 'reformers': the parliamentary centre-right sided with the president (albeit rather tentatively and reluctantly in the case of some centrists). However, the presidential decree on the referendum radically shifted the cleavage so that it began to run between the institutions: the parliament and the president. Undoubtedly informed by the Russian example, the deputies, especially from the centrist factions, recognised that the costs of embarking on confrontation would be too high to incur for them personally and for the country at large. The fate of the Supreme Council (and their careers as deputies) was at stake, and the consequences of a failed referendum were hard to predict and could be potentially disastrous indeed: a spiral of conflict between the Supreme Council and the president. The prospect of aggravating political tensions and even a fear of civil war created pressure to settle the conflict. Under such conditions a 'compromise' and eventually a constitutional majority were attained. By exerting pressure on the parliament, the president achieved his main aims. Yet, nevertheless, the parliament was able to preserve its status as an autonomous institution.

To this end, the shifting and cross-cutting ideological and institutional cleavages explain the fact that despite its content, the constitution was passed by a constitutional majority in parliament as 'a lesser evil'. The long-standing line of conflict (prior to the presidential decree) determined the text of the constitution, which—to a large extent—excluded the views of the Left. It provided for a strong presidency and incorporated the national-democratic resolution on the 'national question' (see chapter 7). However, the passage of the constitution took place in a radically different context: the president and parliament were at loggerheads, and the president was determined to bring in 'the people' as the arbiter in the intra-elite conflict. To prevent such a scenario, the pro-presidential constitution was adopted 'against' the president, not so much by the national-democrats, as by the centrists and the moderate left, that is the Socialists and Peasants.

Undoubtedly, the politico-ideological cleavages characterised by a deep-seated mutual distrust and an *a priori* rejection of compromise resulted in an antagonistic style of politics. However, a collorary of the ideological nature of the conflict was the fact that, despite the lack of recognised rules, the stringent procedural legitimacy was respected within parliament (i.e. each individual article of the constitution was approved by the two-thirds majority). On the one hand, the mistrust between the Left and Right made them insist on an adherence to high procedural requirements in order to prevent being outmanoeuvred by the ideological 'foe'. On the other hand, with no shared set of values, there was no other principle validating the new constitution apart from the procedural legitimacy derived from the achievement of the constitutional majority.

NOTES

1 The institution of the presidential representative at the regional and local level was abolished in law 'On the Formation of Local Power and Self-Governing Organs'. See *Holos Ukrainy*, 16 February 1994.

2 There were some debates on the Constitutional Assembly, as the optimal institution to pass the new constitution, but it was never considered seriously. For arguments in favour of the Constitutional Assembly see, Anatoliy Tkachuk, 'Noviy derzhavi novu

konstytutsiu (The New Constitution for the New State)', *Polityka i Chas*, No. 10 (October 1995), pp. 30–7. The major impediment was a lack of agreement on the mode of formation of the Assembly (elections or appointment).

3 The idea of the law originated in early 1994, when during a meeting of the Constitutional Commission Kravchuk proposed the adoption of a 'Law on Power' as a 'Little Constitution' until a new one was adopted. At that time, the proposal was discarded and no further action was taken. See the Materials of the Round Table organised by the Ukrainian Legal Foundation in December 1994.

4 See Volodymyr Lytvyn, *Politychna arena Ukrainy (The Political Scene of Ukraine)* (Kyiv, 1994), p. 275.

5 Due to the above-mentioned defects of the electoral law such as the requirement of 50 percent turnout and a 50 percent 'winning threshold' (see chapter 5).

6 According to the original draft (December 1994) the president would have the right to resolve parliament, if parliament rejected the budget law submitted by the cabinet of ministers twice or rejected its programme twice.

7 If anything the commission proposed a streamlined form of government, that is a pure presidential model, in which there was no post of the prime minister and the cabinet of ministers was directly subordinated to the president. The president, however, demanded restoration of the post of prime minister.

8 The results of the voting were: 221 in favour, 103 against and 17 abstained (*Ukrainska Perspektyva*, No. 1, 1995).

9 Kuchma's address to the nation, *Holos Ukrainy*, 2 June 1995, p. 2.

10 The decree was published in *Holos Ukrainy*, 2 June 1995, p. 2.

11 The notion was put forward by two lawyers, Serhiy Holovatyi and professor Leonid Yuz'kov, in December 1994, who believed that with no prospects for a constitutional majority in parliament, the impasse could lead to 'undesirable tragic results as in Russia in October 1993'. The authors expressed a hope that: 'there is a Russian version, and there could be a Ukrainian way of searching for agreement'. Materials of the Round Table on Constitutional Agreement held at the Ukrainian Legal Foundation on 14 December 1994.

12 Four months after the signing of the Constitutional *Dohovir* around 10 deputies requested that their signatures under it be crossed out. (Author's interview with Roman Bezsmertnyi, member of faction 'Statehood', Kyiv, November 1995.)

13 According to the *Dohovir*, the heads of the oblast and regional level simultaneously performed functions of heads of state administration, and, as such, were subordinated to the president. In the November draft, however, these functions were separated and the head of state administration existed alongside the directly elected heads of councils.

14 The sub-commission included 4 parliamentary, 4 presidential representatives and 2 of the 'judicial branch'. It could be argued that the composition of this working subcommittee was the most decisive movement in the constitutional process. The first choice of the representatives of the Supreme Council were Volodymyr Stretovych, Serhiy Hmyria (Communist), Mykola Dudchenko (Agrarian faction), and Volodymyr Marchenko (Socialist). As the latter refused to participate on ideological grounds, he was replaced by Ivan Zaiets (Rukh). The group adopted rules that 7 out of 10 in favour were needed to pass a decision. Zaiets with strong national-democratic views sided with 4 presidential and 2 judicial representatives, and his vote was crucial in the final approval of the draft by the working sub-committee. Au-

thor's interview with Volodymyr Stretovych, the Head of the Commission on Legal Polity and Reform, Birmingham, November 1996.

15 Between November and March, the mode of elections was changed. The Senate was to be elected in direct elections. However, as was pointed out above, the main candidates in direct elections tended to be regional state officials, who according to the draft would be nominated by the president. Thus, the Senate would still be likely to consist of individuals dependent on the president.

16 Only the ruling of the Constitutional Court, which was to be nominated by the Senate and president, could suspend presidential decrees.

17 *Holos Ukrainy*, 3 February 1996.

18 It was published in *Uriadovyi Kurier*, 21 March 1996.

19 According to the 1978 constitution, any changes to the Fundamental Law lay exclusively within the competencies of the Supreme Council and require a qualified majority of two thirds. The *Dohovir*, in turn, stated that the text of the draft constitution agreed between the president and parliament would be subject to a referendum. As the meaning of the 'agreed text' was unclear, it was widely interpreted by the right-centre as having to be first passed in parliament; however, there was also no consensus as to whether the term implied a simple or constitutional majority. The communists emphasised the binding power of the Concept of the New Constitution adopted in 1991, according to which the form of government, the socio-economic system, the symbols and the name of the state would be decided in a referendum. (*Kommunist*, No. 17, April 1996, p. 1).

20 There were several alternative drafts including one proposed by the Communist faction and the 1993 draft proposed by a social-democratic deputy. On the alternative drafts see Volodymyr Butkevych, 'Proiekt Konstytutsii Ukrainy u Verkhovnii Radi (Draft Constitution in the Supreme Council)', *Nova Polityka*, No. 3(5) (May–June 1996), pp. 10–19. The Christian-Democratic Deputies presented their draft in *Holos Ukrainy*, 16 March 1995, p. 3. According to Butkevych, either the status or authorship of those alternative drafts was unclear. See *The Rukh Insider*, Vol. 2, No. 4, 25 March 1996 and Butkevych, 'Proiekt Konstytutsii Ukrainy u Verkhovniy Radi', p. 12.

21 The Left was only 2 votes short of the number needed to reject the March draft at the very onset of its consideration in the Supreme Council (*Ukrainske Slovo*, 5 May 1996).

22 In a survey in the Supreme Council only 82 deputies (Rukh and *Derzhavnist* members featured prominently on the list) supported the bi-cameral legislature. *Chas–Time*, 29 March 1996, p. 3.

23 Unable to make much impact on the work of the Commission, the communists 'revised' their own draft constitution, which they had proposed in March 1996, by taking the draft of the Commission and grafting onto it their main constitutional preferences.

24 *Kommunist*, No. 24, June 1996, p. 3.

25 The decree was in breach of the *Dohovir*, which stipulated the rules for setting up a referendum specified in the 'Law on National and Local Referenda'. According to the law, the president could call for a referendum if at least half of deputies voted in favour.

26 Markian Bilynskyi, 'Finally, a constitution is born', *The Ukrainian Weekly*, 7 July 1996, p. 2.

27 As one of the deputies involved in the constitutional process commented 'the presidential side was only interested in 3–4 chapters of the constitution, dealing with the system of government'. Kuchma was essentially interested in the chapters on 'The Presidency',

'the Supreme Council', 'the Judicial System' and 'the Cabinet of Ministers'. Interview with Serhiy Soboliev, head of faction 'Reforms', Kyiv, September 1996.

28 *Demokratychna Ukraina*, 23 March 1996, p. 1.

29 Many of the lawyers shared Kuchma's belief in the merits of the 'Law on Power'. For example, Volodymyr Shapoval, one of the authorities on constitutional law argued, 'the people who write the constitution, should follow the content of the "Law on Power". We can assume that it is a ready-made chapter for the new constitution'. *Uriadovyi Kurier*, 16 May 1995, p. 7.

30 For example, the Department of Internal Affairs in the Presidential Administration worked full time on the passage of the constitution and more appointments were made. Oleksandr Yemets', a skilful politician, was appointed as vice-prime minister in charge of Politico-Legal Affairs whose portfolio effectively meant ensuring 'the passage of the constitution' by lobbying factions and individual deputies.

31 Prime minister Lazarenko arranged a meeting of the cabinet of ministers away from Kyiv at the Cherkasy Spirit Distillery (*sic*). Nevertheless, some of the ministers—*sumisnyky* were present in parliament during the constitutional night. In order to severe their links with the Presidential Administration, telephones were switched off in the governmental section in the plenary hall. Artur Bilous, 'Do i pislia Konstytutsii (Before and after the Constitution)', *Nova Polityka*, No. 3(5) (May–June 1996), p. 5 and author's interview with Serhiy Soboliev, Kyiv, September 1996.

32 Thus, the media, which were controlled by the executive branch, launched a campaign designed to erode the already low level of public support for the Supreme Council. Also, the influential Council of Regions worked on 'raising public awareness on the constitutional question' at the local level. *The Ukrainian Weekly*, 5 May 1996.

33 Interview with Oleksandr Moroz, *Visnyk programy spryiannia Parlamentovi Ukrainy (Newsletter of the Parliamentary Development Programme*), No. 7, June 1997, p. 12.

34 *Holos Ukrainy*, 26 December 1995. See also the views of the radical communist, Volodymyr Moisieienko in *Holos Ukrainy*, 3 February 1996, p. 3.

35 *Kommunist*, No. 24, June 1996, p. 3.

36 *Kommunist*, No. 11, March 1996, p. 3.

37 *Kommunist*, No. 17, April, 1996, p. 3.

38 Author's interview with member of the Socialist faction, Mykola Lavrynenko, Kyiv, November 1995. See also the views of Petro Symonenko—the leader of the CPU—in *Kommunist*, No. 17, April 1996, p. 3.

39 *Kommunist*, No. 24, June 1996, p. 3.

40 *Demokratychna Ukraina*, 21 May 1996, p. 1.

41 *Kommunist*, No. 13, March 1996, p. 1.

42 See *The Rukh Insider*, Vol. 2, No. 4, 25 March 1996. As the Left did not register there was no quorum to open the debates. This method, called 'constructive destruction', was first used by the national-democrats in order to block the Left getting its way in parliament in 1994.

43 In particular, the socialists were in favour of a weak presidency, but not the abolition of the institution. Unlike the communists, they supported limited privatisation of the means of production, so-called small privatisation. As a hard-line communist deputy commented: 'They [socialists and peasants] argue that they cannot support the Communist Party and that we have to become more progressive'. (Authors' interview with Volodymyr Masenko, member of the communist faction, Kyiv, November 1995.)

44 *Demokratychna Ukraina*, 21 May 1996, p. 1.

45 Author's interview with Roman Bezsmertnyi, Kyiv, September 1996.

46 *Kommunist,* No. 6, February 1996, p. 1.

47 However, only approximately 20 percent of all deputies favoured the restoration of the USSR and the abolition of the sovereignty of Ukraine. The ranks of the most hard-line 'internationalists' included the head of the CPU, Petro Symonenko.

48 *The Ukrainian Weekly*, 31 December 1995, p. 21.

49 Rukh's petition to the president was published in *Chas-Time*, 15 March 1996, p. 1.

50 *Molod' Ukrainy*, 22 March 1996, p. 2.

51 Author's interview with Oleksandr Reimer, Senior Consultant in the Department of Internal Affairs of the Presidential Administration, Kyiv, July 1997.

52 *Molod' Ukrainy*, 28 June 1996, p. 1. Such an alliance would be possible if the rules for the passing of the constitution were changed in line with the suggestion of the centrist factions, that is, that a simple majority would be enough to pass individual articles in the second reading, and in the third reading the constitution would be voted on 'as a whole'. As the Social Market Choice, *Yednist, Nezalezhni* and MDG were split on the issue, they were more likely to vote together with the left-wing factions.

53 This was one of the questions that divided the president and the national-democrats. Another was article 17.7 forbidding the stationing of foreign military bases on the territory of Ukraine. While the constitution was drafted, the president was involved in negotiations on the Friendship and Co-operation Treaty with the Russian Federation, and the issue of the base for the Russian part of the Black Sea Fleet in Sevastopol was one of the major bones of contention. Thus, Kuchma categorically refused to accept art. 17.7. See Materials of Temporary Extraordinary Commission on the Preparation the Draft Constitution, Minutes of the Meeting on 18 and 24 June 1996.

54 *The Ukrainian Weekly*, 17 March 1996.

55 *Ibid.*

56 According to Oleksandr Reimer, Senior Consultant in the Department of Internal Affairs of the Presidential Administration, there was no stable leadership in MDG as the official head of the faction controlled only approximately one third of members of the faction. Author's interview with Oleksandr Reimer, Kyiv, July 1997.

57 The MDG, the 'Independents', and the 'Social Market Choice' proposed an interpretation of the *Reglament* (Rules of Procedures), which would lower the voting threshold in order, speed up the ratification process in the second reading. Each article was to be approved by a simple majority and only the final vote for the constitution as a whole would require a two-thirds majority. Yet, entrenched in their opposition both the Right and Left rejected this proposal fearing that the simplification of rules would benefit its opponent.

58 Author's interview with Oleksandr Reimer, Senior Consultant in the Department of Internal Affairs of the Presidential Administration, Kyiv, July 1997.

59 Carl Schmitt, *The Concept of the Political* (Chicago and London: The University of Chicago Press, 1996).

60 Gianfranco Poggi, *The Development of the Modern State: A Sociological Introduction* (London: Hutchinson, 1978), pp. 5–9.

61 Author's interview with Vasyl Kostytskyi, member of the 'Reforms' faction, Kyiv, September 1996.

CHAPTER SEVEN

UKRAINE AS A NATION-STATE: THE CONCEPTION OF STATEHOOD IN THE 1996 CONSTITUTION

The new 1996 constitution finally provided a blueprint for the Ukrainian state: it described the new polity in institutional, territorial, national and socio-economic terms. Firstly, it established the parameters of the 'political community' by defining the nature and attributes of the 'nation'. Secondly, the political framework of the state—the institutions, rules and procedures—was specified both between the branches of power at the centre and at the sub-national level. Thirdly, by deciding the status of private property and the role of the state in the socio-economic sphere, the socio-economic profile and goals of the state were established. The purpose of this chapter is to analyse the conception of statehood that was embedded in the new constitution of Ukraine. Each of the three clusters of issues will be examined in more detail in order to highlight the extent to which different conceptions of statehood found their way into the constitution. The chapter will illuminate how the document reflected the overarching imperative of the consolidation of the Ukrainian state. This agenda, however, detracted attention from the need for detailed, legalistic scrutiny of the Basic Law, especially in the sphere of institutional design, something that proved to have dear consequences for the quality of institutional interactions, that is the development of the 'political constitution'.

THE POLITICAL COMMUNITY

As argued above, constitutions in new states, in addition to the goal advocated by liberal constitutionalism, such as the creation of instruments of governmental accountability and the protection of human rights and liberties, have more fundamental functions, such as defining the political community and establishing a collective identity. As Offe points out 'at the most fundamental level a "decision" must be made on who "we" are, i.e. on identity, citizenship, and the territorial as well as social and cultural boundaries of the nation-state'.[1] International practice has not been much of a guide. Since 1918 new states have invoked a powerful Wilsonian doctrine of self-determination to justify the formation of new polities. Taking into account the diversity within Western tradition, the type of collectivity, which can legitimately exercise the right to self-determination, has never been satisfactorily defined in international law and practice.[2] This question—the most fundamental for any polity—thwarted the progress of the constitution-making process in Ukraine, as radically different concepts of the political community prevailed in the constitutional debates.

Nevertheless, despite the deeply polarised views held by the Left and Right, the definition that was finally hammered out in the first sentence of the Constitution's Preamble, 'The Ukrainian people—citizens of Ukraine of all nationalities', seemed to reconcile the difference in a compromise which satisfied both protagonists.[3] The national-democrats incorporated the sacred concept of 'Ukrainian people', while the polyethnic composition was alluded to in 'citizens of all nationalities'. The two concepts of nationhood—civic and ethnic—were synthesised by stating that the right to self-determination was exercised by the eclectic 'Ukrainian ethnic nation (*natsiia*), all-Ukrainian nation (*narod*)'. Being wider than *natsiia*, *Ukrainskyi narod* made it possible to encompass 'citizens of all nationalities'. Yet, the role of the Ukrainian *natsiia* as the nucleus of the 'Ukrainian people' is reflected in a number of the constitutional provisions, such as article 11 which obliges the state 'to support the consolidation and development of the Ukrainian *natsiia*, its historical consciousness, tradition, and culture'.[4] In particular, the symbiotic link between the Ukrainian *natsiia* and the state emanates from the norms on the state language and symbols.

The provisions on the state language turned into a battleground for the assertion of the Ukrainian credentials of the state and the circumvention of the dominance of Russian. Although none of the official draft constitutions between 1992—1995 granted Russian official status, in the final text Ukrainian was declared the sole state language, while Russian (despite being explicitly referred to in the constitution) was defined only as the language of the Russian minority. Paradoxically, this was an unintended consequence of the Left's insistence on enhancing the position of Russian. The March 1996 draft envisaged that:

> In areas of *dense* population of citizens of one or several national minorities, the language accepted by the *majority of the population* of a certain location may be used in the activities of bodies of state power and state organisations, along with the state language (art. 10). (emphasis added)

This was in line with the progressive Declaration of the Rights of Nationalities of November 1991, according to which Russian could become the language of the local administration, if it was used by the majority of the population (and presumably not necessarily only ethnic Russians—see chapter 3). In other words, the March draft opened the door for the effective recognition of Russian in the public sphere at the regional level, especially in Eastern and Southern Ukraine, where this language dominated. Still, the Left remained unsatisfied and demanded more explicit recognition of, and guarantees for, the status of Russian to outlaw potential acts of forced linguistic Ukrainisation in Russophone regions.

In comparison with the March draft, the final June version of the constitution, although more vague, and thus open to various interpretations, turned out to be a Pyrrhic victory for those who sought to upgrade the status of Russian language. The Ukrainian language remained the only state language, while 'the free development, use of and protection of Russian, [along with] other languages of national minorities of Ukraine, is guaranteed' (art. 10).[5] While the left-wing's demand for the inclusion of the word 'Russian' in the article was satisfied, the status of Russian was effectively reduced to that of a language of the Russian minority. Moreover, the same article stipulates that the state 'ensures the comprehensive development and functioning of the Ukrainian language in all spheres of social life throughout the *entire territory* of Ukraine' (emphasis added). In other words, Russian *can* develop freely, yet Ukrainian has to be promoted by the state.[6] The constitution defined the aims of the state in the sphere of language as a progressive Ukrainisation of public life. The highly contentious issue of language policies shifted into the sphere of constitutional obligations and, thus, became immune to the vacillation of day-to-day politics at the level of central, and especially, regional governments. This was reflected in the controversial ruling of the Constitutional Court on the interpretation of article 10 in December 1999, which confirmed the role of Ukrainian in public sphere by obliging state officials to use the language in the conduct of their duties.

In a similar manner a compromise on state symbols emerged: the flag, emblem and anthem, despite some concessions to placate the Left, reflected the preference of the Right. While the 'blue-and-yellow' flag was approved relatively smoothly during the constitutional night, the emblem stirred immense controversy. The search for an acceptable, non-aggravating formula is reflected in the elaborate wording of article 20, which avoids the word 'trident' at all cost:

> The Great State Emblem of Ukraine shall be established with the consideration of the Small Emblem of Ukraine and the Emblem of the Zaporizhian Host, by the law adopted by no less than two-thirds of the constitutional composition of the Supreme Rada of Ukraine.
>
> The main element of the Great State Emblem of Ukraine is the Emblem of the Royal State of Volodymyr the Great (the Small State Emblem of Ukraine).

Yet, the trident, disguised as the Small State Emblem of Ukraine, became the state symbol of Ukraine. In their only major concession to the Left, the Right agreed to drop the 'provocative' text of the national anthem 'Ukraine Has Not Yet Perished' (*Shche Ne Vmerla Ukraina*), which alludes to *Moskali* (a derogative term for Russians) though retaining the original Verbytskyi score. The new lyrics of the anthem were to be decided by competition.[7] To this end, the iconographic symbols and vocal representation of the Ukrainian state were derived from the historical, cultural reservoir of the titular majority.

Nevertheless, while asserting the role of the titular majority through language and symbols, the constitution also granted collective minority rights to indigenous people (*korinni narody*) and national minorities: 'the state ... guarantees ethnic, cultural, linguistic and religious self-preservation (*samobutnist*) of all indigenous nations and national minorities of Ukraine' (art. 11). Article 10 states that, beside Russian, free development of 'other languages of the national minorities' is guaranteed in Ukraine and the extensive rights to education in minority languages are listed in article 53. Moreover, in places of the compact residence of indigenous people and national minorities, the state administrations are to 'ensure that programmes for their national and cultural development are implemented' (art. 119.3).[8] Nevertheless, while the constitution upheld collective minority rights, Ukraine's stance on this issue has evolved between 1990–1996 from a vague but explicit promise of territorial autonomy in the 1991 'Declaration of Minority Rights' to a narrower right to cultural autonomy (although still in line with 'European standards').

Ukrainians are not depicted as the 'sole owners' of the state and national minorities have been recognised as 'state-constituting communities', as expressed in the first sentence of the constitutional Preamble. As the constitution does not imply that political and national identities have to be congruent, it allows a divergence between ethnicity and citizenship. However, in Connor's terms, Ukraine was conceived as a 'unihomeland, multi-national state': inhabited by many ethnic groups but homeland of the titular majority—Ukrainians.[9] The term 'people' (*Ukrainskyi narod*) consists of several components: the *Ukrainska natsiia* (ethnic Ukrainian nation), *korinni narody* (indigenous minorities with no homelands outside Ukraine), and other national minorities (ethnic groups which have their respective homelands outside Ukraine). The emergent hierarchy of constituent communities differentiates between the 'more' and 'less' indigenous groups (and ethnic Ukrainians belong to the former), and the rights and citizens depend on their degree of 'indigenous' attachment to Ukrainian land.[10]

Such a multi-layered construction of political community may have diverse implications for various groups in society, especially those that do not fit into any of the categories of the constituent communities sanctioned in the constitution. While the ethnic factor has been given full accreditation, the ethno-linguistic category of Russophone Ukrainians, which cut across constituent ethnic communities (ethnic Ukrainians and Russians), has not been granted constitutional recognition. Because they cannot be regarded as a minority, Russian-speaking Ukrainians, who account for at least one third of the population, were denied the constitutional right to demand the provisions to ensure the use of Russian in the public sphere (even if in everyday life Russian prevails in Ukrainian oblasts east of the Dnieper).[11]

While the concept of the 'Ukrainian people' incorporates both civic/territorial and ethnic criteria, the weight of respective 'elements' in this precarious, but not untypical, juxtaposition remains unclear. Each polity contains a variety of groups, which have distinctive needs and interests to be protected and promoted; the terms of recognition and accommodation of diversity in the constitutional framework vary enormously. Even if the constitution implies nation building through the homogenisation of the titular ethnic majority by rallying around symbols and language,[12] the practical implications of the constitutional norms are still to be determined.

The competing pressures, on the one hand, to create a pluralistic multi-cultural Ukrainian political community, and on the other, to assert the 'leading role of the titular majority' have moulded the concept of the political community in the new constitution. This community was constructed as a hierarchical framework of ethnic communities with differentiated rights. The struggle of constitution makers with the 'national question' underscores the difficulties of justifying 'national self-determination' according to which 'the state should be constituted as a nation' in a multi-ethnic society. As no notion of a 'unitary people' existed in Ukraine, the constitution created the 'people' as an indispensable element of a nation-state. As an ethusiastic journalist explained the significance of the new constitution:

> We have the "Ukrainian people", and not the "people of Ukraine", we have the State blue-and-yellow flag, State Emblem—Trident, and State Anthem (even if only music), the State Language (although with some concessions in favour of the language of the big brother). All this allows us to assert that an independent, Ukrainian nation-state was constitutionalised, or, if you want, canonised.[13]

Overall, the 'national question' proved the most vexed in the constitutional process. It led to dramatic tensions, which overshadowed the constitutional debate from the outset and remained a bone of contention until the very night of the adoption of the constitution. It evoked emotions, which 'reason' could not easily subdue. The opposing stances, accompanied by deeply felt passions, prevented cool-headed bargaining and a satisfactory compromise. When the 'national question' emerged as the very last point of dispute during the final night, the anti-nationalist forces capitulated under the immense pressure to adopt the constitution. As a result, the constitution asserted Ukraine to be a nation-state implying homogeneity and uniformity, without an underlying consensus on what binds the citizens of Ukraine into 'the people' amongst the 'founding fathers'.

PRIVATE PROPERTY, RIGHTS AND LIBERTIES

In the constitutional debates, the Left was adamant that the constitution offered protection of all (including collective) forms of property, and not only the right to private property, as the Right, president and the centrist factions insisted. Article 13 fully satisfied this demand 'the state ensures the protection of the right to property and economic management of all subjects, as well as the social orientation of the economy'. All subjects of the right of property are equal before the law'. Moreover, the Left's concern about capitalist exploitation was echoed in moralistic statements, such as 'Property entails responsibility. Property shall not be used to the detriment of the person and society' (art. 13). But despite this concession to the 'socially responsible use of property', the Left continued to oppose the constitutional recognition of the right to private property until the constitutional night. A compromise was only reached when the additional hurdle, that 'the right of private property is acquired by a procedure determined by law' (art. 41), was added, and ensured the crucial extra votes from the left wing. Although the final wording of the article was interpreted by each side differently,[14] a basis for the transition to the market economy, however circuitous, was provided in the constitution.

The communist-era constitutions were saturated with 'negative' liberties and rights such as freedom of speech, thought and association, which the regime repeatedly infringed. All post-communist constitutions extensively re-stated 'negative' rights, aiming to turn them into a meaningful instrument of protection against the government's interference in the private sphere, in accordance with the normative directives of liberal constitutionalism. Accordingly, the Ukrainian constitution incorporated an array of human rights and political freedoms, including the right to life (art. 27), dignity (art. 28), privacy (art. 31), and personal freedoms of movement (art. 33), thought and speech (art. 34), personal philosophy and religion (art. 35), association (art. 36) and so forth. Not only was the list of rights and freedoms copied from the European Convention of Human Rights and Fundamental Freedoms of 1950, but so was the wording of some of the articles. There was hardly any disagreement on that issue. Also, a special institution was created, the Authorised Human Rights Representative of the *Verkhovna Rada* of Ukraine, who exercises parliamentary control over the observance of constitutional human and citizens' rights and freedoms (arts. 55 and 101).

The communist constitutions were also renowned for their incorporation of an array of 'positive' socio-economic guarantees of housing, work, holidays, health care, free education etc., which placed a duty on the state to deliver socio-economic benefits. The new Ukrainian constitution did not depart from that tradition and is a lawful descendent of the 1978 constitution with its taxonomy of rights to: 'a decent standard of living' (art. 48), 'an environment that is safe for life and health' (art. 50), 'work' (art. 43), 'rest' (art. 45), 'housing' (art. 47) and so forth.

The preservation of such entitlements in post-communist constitutions has been criticised by Western, especially American, observers who adhere to the ideal of a minimalist constitution on the grounds that 'If a government is to be effective, few rights of its citizens can be stated in absolute form'.[15] Moreover, burdening the state with excessive commitments to socio-economic welfare is perceived as an obstruction in the transition to a market economy by authorising and legitimising the state's interference with the market. Vaguely defined socio-economic rights, i.e. to 'a decent standard of living', or to 'safe environment' are teleological statements which cannot be realistically enforced in the legal system.[16] The saturation of the constitution with declarative statements and promises erodes its credentials as a legal document, which it has to become in order to properly perform its 'limiting' function defined in terms of liberal constitutionalism. Thus, being a vestige of the communist past, they merely devalued the role of the constitution as a marker of a genuine 'fresh start'.[17]

In such a context, the inclusion of socio-economic pledges in the new Ukrainian constitution suggested a victory for the opponents of the socio-economic transition to a market economy. However, while the Left staunchly opposed omitting the references to the 'socialist achievements', the Right not only did not push that hard to exclude them, but even added more 'unenforceable' pledges, such as the state's duty to ensure 'the preservation of historical monuments and other objects of cultural values and takes measures to return to Ukraine the cultural treasures of the nation that are located beyond its borders' (art. 54). Although the Right longed for a 'civilised' constitution free of promises that cannot be realistically fulfilled, it did appreciate the symbolic dimension of such guarantees for society at large. (Also, as the Right was preoccupied with the 'national question', the issue of scaling down the socio-economic rights was assigned to a lower priority.) This opened the door to a relatively easy compromise. Thus, while positive, socio-economic rights were preserved, the victory of the defenders of the 'socialist achievements' was more apparent than real.

The Ukrainian constitution belongs to a family (together with many other post-communist constitutions) of what Sartori describes as 'bad constitutions, technically speaking', because 'they have come to include unrealistic promises and glamorous professions of faith on the one hand, and numberless frivolous details on the other'.[18] However, the 'imperfection' of the Ukrainian constitution is not accidental. As Elazar points out, a sketchy 'frame-of-government' constitution works best in political systems where there exists a basic consensus on the character of the polity.[19] In 'old' states, 'frame-of-government' constitutions symbolised the advent of the rule of law, which enhanced the legitimacy derived from historical continuity. Their succinct constitutions were concerned with the machinery of government, bill of rights and the provisions for amendments.[20] In the age of constitutions, the (secular) power of the modern state was derived from the procedural legitimacy, which became the reason used to justify the citizens' duty to obey the state.[21] However, the authority of the new states rarely rests solely on the procedural compliance of the fundamental law. The passing of procedural hurdles, however difficult they may be, is unlikely to elicit the commitment of the people to the new state of which they are citizens. Poggi, echoing the argument by Carl Schmitt, argues that:

> The motivating force of such a notion [procedural legitimacy] is relatively weak because it does not evoke a substantive ideal, a universally shared standard of intrinsic validity, but instead refers to purely formal, contentless considerations of procedural correctness. [22]

In this context, a long taxonomy of positive and negative rights, freedoms and guarantees in the new Ukrainian constitution did not only reflect deep running ideological cleavages and a disagreement on the axiological foundation of the new state, but also a desperate search for a formula to bind and integrate society.[23] To compensate for Ukraine's fragile historical legitimacy, the new constitution contains an array of teleological aims, goals, aspirations, values and basic beliefs.

As pointed out above, constitutions perform various functions in different polities and the content of the constitution should not be regarded as *une idée fixe*. According to Elazar, the constitution establishes and describes the triangular links between the 'moral basis of polity', 'socio-economic map' and the 'frame of government'.[24] The inclusion of a 'socio-economic map' should be viewed not in terms of efficacy, legality and rationality, but rather in terms of its integrative role. Preuss argued that placing 'social fields of action' under state protection can serve to compensate for the lack of an organic nation-state, as was the case in (post-war) Germany; constitutional pledges to socio-economic security and welfare consolidate the nation.[25] Liberal, 'negative' constitutionalism cannot be easily transplanted onto, and take root in, arid soil; other 'irrigative' techniques have to be used to cultivate and nourish it. In Ukraine, hindered by a fragile popular legitimacy, the promise of the continuation (from the Soviet era) of welfare provisions, even if declarative and symbolic, was a much too vital link between the state and its citizens to be disrupted by excluding socio-economic entitlements from the constitution.

THE INSTITUTIONAL FRAMEWORK

INSTITUTIONS AT THE CENTRE

The constitution, which finally dismantled the remnants of the system of soviets, did not transplant into Ukraine any particular tested foreign model. The configuration of powers between state institutions, although falling into the category of semi-presidential system, is novel. The form of government resulted from a contingency of forces. During six years of chronic tinkering with the division of powers, the form of government gradually evolved from the system of soviets to a system dominated by an executive presidency in the *Dohovir* (albeit with some hiccups in the final stages of Kravchuk's presidency—see chapter 3). Undoubtedly, Kuchma's driving role in constitution making paid off, as parliament sanctioned a strong presidency, although not to the extent the incumbent hoped for. Such a major leverage of power as the right to dissolve parliament was effectively denied to the president. However sceptical parliament was of its own ability to overcome its internal polarisation and work constructively, it stopped short of relinquishing all power to the president and introduced what was perceived as a number of 'checks and balances' into the early pro-presidential draft (November 1995). Therefore, the final six months of the constitutional process witnessed numerous *ad hoc* deletions, additions and revisions to the draft constitution, which account for a novel distribution (and, as it soon turned out, overlap) of institutional powers.[26]

According to the Ukrainian constitution, 'state power is exercised on the principle of its division into legislative, executive and judicial power' (art. 6). The uni-cameral parliament is the 'sole body of legislative power' (art. 75), whereas the president is 'the head of state' and 'guarantor of state sovereignty and territorial indivisibility of Ukraine, the observance of the Constitution of Ukraine and human and citizens' rights and freedoms' (art. 102) and the cabinet of ministers is 'the highest body in the system of bodies of executive power' (art. 113), the judicial branch consists of courts of general and special jurisdiction, (Chapter VIII) as well as the Constitutional Court (Chapter XII).

Semi-presidentialism, as enshrined in the constitution, combined with self-government at the local level, sounded the death knell for the institutional basis of Soviet *narodovladia*. In spite of its retained name, the Supreme Council lost the 'supreme' position it enjoyed in the system of soviets. As the powers of state institutions were 'positively' proscribed, the authority of parliament was delineated: it cannot take over or delegate prerogatives to other state institutions, such as the government or local councils, unless positively authorised to do so in the constitution. The parliament was transformed into a professional institution, in which deputies worked on a 'permanent basis' (art. 78). The 'imperative mandate' was replaced with a free, 'representative' mandate, and the instruments of direct democracy, such as referenda, were relegated to secondary importance *vis-à-vis* the representative institutions (in marked contrast to the 1991 Concept of the New Constitution where the former played a prominent role—see chapter 3).

According to the constitution, Ukraine has two agents of the electorate, the legislature and the president, but there is no fusion of head of state and head of government, something that is characteristic of pure presidential systems. Instead, the executive branch is bifurcated: the presidency co-exists with the cabinet of ministers. Despite being named the 'head of state', the actual powers of the president turn him into a chief executive rather than a figurehead limited to performing ceremonial functions.[27]

According to the constitution, the authority of the Supreme Council includes the right to:

- adopt laws and the budget of Ukraine (arts. 85.3 and 85.4);
- approve the prime minister, as proposed by the president (art. 85.12);
- approve the programme of socio-economic development proposed by the cabinet of ministers (art. 85.6);
- determine the principles of domestic and foreign policy (art. 85.5);
- determine the organisation and activities of the agencies of the executive (art. 92.12);
- dismiss the cabinet in a no-confidence vote, although this right can be exercised only once a session and not within one year following the approval of its programme (art. 87);
- determine the organisation and activities of the bodies within the executive powers (art. 92.12);
- hear annual and special messages of the president of Ukraine on the domestic and foreign situation of Ukraine (art. 85.8);
- impeach the president in the event of treason or some other crime (art. 111).

The president was granted an extensive array of appointive, policy-making powers as well as some limited law making prerogatives:

- appoint the prime minister with the agreement of the Supreme Council (art. 106.9);
- appoint members of the cabinet of ministers and heads of central bodies of executive power proposed by the prime minister (without parliamentary consent) (art. 106.10);
- appoint one third of the Constitutional Court, the Council of the National Bank, as well as the Prosecutor General, and other central executive organs (in most cases the consent of parliament is required);
- create, restructure, and abolish the executive agencies of the state (art. 106.15);
- revoke acts of the cabinet of ministers of Ukraine and the Council of Ministers of the Autonomous Republic of Crimea (art. 106.16);
- dismiss the prime minister and ministers (art. 106.9);
- initiate legislation (art. 93);
- have presidential draft laws considered by parliament as a priority (art. 93);
- veto parliamentary bills, although the veto can be overridden by a qualified majority of two thirds of parliament (arts. 94 and 106.30);
- issue decrees on economic issues (not regulated by laws) for three years (until 1999) on the condition that they are signed by the prime minister and that the draft laws are simultaneously submitted to parliament (art. 4 of the Transitional Provisions);[28]
- dissolve parliament if it cannot convene for thirty days during a plenary session. (However, according to art. 106.8, the president cannot dissolve the Supreme Council during the last six months of his term, and one year after the pre-term elections.)

The cabinet of ministers, which is composed of the prime minister, the first vice-prime minister, three vice-prime ministers and the ministers, was allocated power to:

- ensure state sovereignty and the economic independence of Ukraine (art. 116.1);
- implement domestic and foreign policy (art. 116.1);
- carry out the execution of the constitution, the laws of Ukraine and the acts of the president (art. 116.1);
- ensure the implementation of state policies, such as fiscal, investment, employment, education, etc. (art. 116.3);
- draft the state budget (art. 116.6);

- implement the state budget of Ukraine and submit a report on its implementation to the Supreme Council (art. 116.6);
- issue resolutions and orders, within the limits of its competence, which are mandatory for the execution on the territory of Ukraine (art. 117).

According to Shugart and Carey's classification, the constitution created a president-parliamentary system, which is characterised by two key features: asymmetrical control over the cabinet (the president nominates and recalls it but parliament can take a vote of no-confidence in it) and law making authority granted to the president.[29] Moreover, in the Ukrainian case, the semi-presidential form of government is characterised not only by the functional separation of powers (although, as was argued above, there is actually a significant overlap in prerogatives), but also by the separation of the membership, as, according to the new constitution, deputies of the Supreme Council cannot hold posts in the executive branch.[30] At the same time, as the above description suggests, in the attempt to balance out the authority of the president and parliament, the powers of those institutions were duplicated rather than separated. Thus, the system is characterised by overlapping authority between the president and the Supreme Council.

The constitution provides a basis for building a multiparty democracy, as it states that 'political parties in Ukraine promote the formation and expression of the political will of citizens, and participate in elections' (art. 36). The article demonstrated an underlying change in the view of the role of political parties as compared to the 1991 Concept of the New Constitution, which expressed distrust in the institution (see chapter 3). However, the new constitution does not outline the role of parties in structuring the executive–legislative relations.[31] This lack cannot be put down to an omission, especially when the noticeable tendency to provide detailed outlines of state institutions is taken into account. Rather it resulted, firstly, from the lack of an agreement on other fundamental institutions of the political system such as the electoral system (which is not described in the constitution), and, secondly, from the uncertainty as to how precisely the political parties would fit into the machinery of such a semi-presidential system. Because as the written constitution was drafted under time pressure, there was no time to reflect on, and assess, its impact on the actual functioning of the state institutions. Apart from a lack of reflection on the role of the (fledging) party system in structuring the interactions between the branches of power, this general lack of foresight has proved to have grave consequences for executive–legislative relations, which deteriorated, rather than stabilised, under the new constitution (see chapter 8).

The principle of the separation of powers was vindicated in the provision of the Constitutional Court, which has given sole authority to constitutional jurisdiction, despite the objections of the Left, which viewed it as a usurpation of the powers of the Supreme Council. The Court consists of 18 judges, who are nominated for 9 years. The president, parliament and the Council of Judges appoint six each.[32] The Court decides on the issue of conformity of laws to the constitution and interprets the constitution and laws (art. 147). Ukraine took a decisive step towards the judicialisation of political power, subjecting political disputes to judicial decisions, in order to resolve the power conflict (see chapter 8). As Ludwikowski put it, the introduction of the judicial review was 'the greatest novelty in the post-socialist world'.[33] However, the legal system in Ukraine was also tainted by an institutional leftover from the Soviet system, namely the *prokuratura*, which in Chapter VII was allowed to retain its general function of 'supervision of the observance and application of laws' in the 'transitional provisions' until the laws regulating this matter are passed. The lack of an expiry date for this provision means that the *prokuratura* can continue to exercise its Soviet-era functions, and as such, become a useful tool in presidential hands to control political opponents.[34]

Shugart and Carey argue that the president-parliamentary form of government is not a hybrid between parliamentarism and presidentialism, but a distinct form of government in its own right (even if a relatively rare one). However, even if the end product conforms to the ideal type of a system, Ukraine's form of government is clearly eclectic in terms of its origin. The Western principle of 'separation of powers' served as a body on which home-grown institutions woven of ideas, values and interests were grafted. In other words, borrowing amounted to an emulation of principles rather than any specific institutional arrangements from the West. Neither did the Ukrainian pre-communist past inspire the constitution makers to opt for pure parliamentarism, as professed by the leaders of the Ukrainian People's Republic (UNR). If anything, the form of government copied by the pro-presidential experts was that of the Russian 1993 constitution, both in the 1995 *Dohovir* and also the November draft. Then the 'Russian model' was altered in an attempt to strengthen the Supreme Council's control over the government and to protect parliament from the potential authoritarian leanings of the presidency. As a corollary of the preoccupation with equalising powers, no effective instruments were provided to stimulate co-operation between the two agents of the electorate and to resolve potential deadlocks between the president and parliament over legislation and appointments.

As was argued in chapter 5, the constitutional debates symbolised the clash between the incompatible ideals of the Soviet system of *narodovladia* favoured by the Left and Montesquieu's classical system of the separation of powers advocated by the centre, the Right and the president. Despite the opposition of the Left, the remnants of the Soviet system were dismantled in the constitution and the Left only 'won' on the uni-cameral form of parliament against the wishes of Kuchma (this added the crucial votes of the centrist deputies). The form of government was the result of a complex matrix of ideals and interests contested in prolonged negotiations, which account for the innovative institutional design, the inconsistency in the distribution of 'checks and balances', and the overlap of powers in order to temper the excesses of the presidential authority. Nevertheless, the resulting president-parliamentary system with a strong, executive presidency was the heaviest loss incurred by the proponents of the *status quo ante*.

THE TERRITORIAL–ADMINISTRATIVE MODEL OF THE STATE

In contrast to the elaborated chapters on the central authority, the brevity of the chapter on the territorial model of the state is striking. In general, constitutions in unitary states either regulate local self-government in detail or outline only the basic framework. In the case of Ukraine, the latter path was opted for. However, it was not for a fear of rigidity and over-regulation, but rather the lack of a coherent conception of the territorial distribution of power and centre–periphery relations, something that was evident in the half-hearted debate on the merits and perils of centralised and decentralised models of the state.[35]

As was argued in chapter 5, federalism was discarded as too dangerous to a new Ukrainian state and, more controversially, at odds with 'indigenous tradition' of statehood. At the same time, the devolution of power to the regions remained on the agenda insofar as none of the key actors openly favoured a centralised model. Yet, despite the prevailing rhetoric, decentralisation proved an empty promise. Article 132 of the new constitution stated:

> The territorial structure of Ukraine is based upon the principles of unity and individual state territory and is based on the principle of centralisation and decentralisation in the exercise of state power.

The Soviet-era administrative division was upheld in the constitution and the country's grid of oblasts, districts, cities and villages was retained (art. 133). Local government was guaranteed at the community level of the village and city (arts. 7 and 140). Article 140 'de-statised' the soviets by defining local government as 'the right of a territorial community ... to resolve independently issues of local character within the limits of the Constitutions and the laws of Ukraine'. However, the constitution is unclear in its provisions on the *meso* level (oblast and district). For example, when describing the mode of elections, the constitution only mentions local self-government (village and city), and does not stipulate how oblast and district councils are formed. It only says that the chairpersons of district and oblast councils are elected by the respective councils and lead the executive staff of the council (art. 141). (The norm on the indirect mode of elections to those bodies, as favoured by the Right and the president, was excluded during the constitutional night in order to appease the Left.) Moreover, the prerogatives and resources of self-governing bodies were defined in an incoherent and convoluted way.

At the same time, despite the opposition of the Left and some centrist factions, the rigid vertical executive pyramid of the 'regional state administration', which was first introduced by Kravchuk in early 1992 and then reinstated by Kuchma in 1994 (see chapters 4 and 6) was retained in the constitution. The heads of the local state administration (oblast and district level) are appointed by the president on the recommendation of the prime minister and are subordinated to heads of administration at higher levels (art. 118). Regional and local state administrations were vested with wide-ranging powers listed in art. 119, including the preparation and implementation of oblast and district budgets. However, the oblast or district councils obtained a degree of leverage against the centre as under certain circumstances they can force the president to recall the head of the respective state administration (art. 118).

In general, the constitution did not clarify centre–periphery relations: not only is the model of regional and local self-government ill defined but also the division of powers of self-governing institutions *vis-à-vis* the state administration remained unclear (art. 142-4). A clear description of the legal status of sub-national institutions is a precondition of effective local/regional autonomy and decentralisation of the unitary state.[36] Without an explicit constitutional description of the scope of the autonomy, the model of the state may more easily veer toward a unitary centralised state. This has been the case in Ukraine.

In the case of Ukraine, the need to compromise resulted in vague provisions, vulnerable to conflicting interpretations. The final confrontation over the system of local government was merely postponed, rather than finalised with the passage of the constitution (see chapter 8). Nevertheless, instruments for the domination of the centre over the periphery were placed in the constitution, as neither the president nor the national-democrats were willing to devolve power from the centre to directly elected representative bodies at the intermediate level. Nevertheless, the vestige of the past—the system of soviets, uniting the representative and state administration functions as an institutional framework for *narodovladia*—was finally dismantled.

The only region of Ukraine which was granted territorial autonomy was Crimea; it was defined as an Autonomous Republic of Crimea (ARC) in an otherwise unitary state. The resolution of the 'Crimean question' was the biggest concession on the part of the Right. The ARC was granted the right to its own constitution, a parliament with the right to issue 'normative acts', and a Council of Ministers. Nevertheless, Kyiv's authority on the peninsula was asserted and Crimean autonomy circumscribed in a number of ways. First of all, the ARC was declared 'an inseparable constituent part of Ukraine and [it] decides on the issues ascribed to its competence within the limits of authority determined by the Constitution of Ukraine' (art. 134).[37] Secondly, the Constitution of the ARC has to be approved by Ukrainian parliament in Kyiv (art. 135). Thirdly, the prime minister of the ARC can be appointed and dismissed by the Supreme Council of ARC only with the consent of the president of Ukraine (art. 136). The Supreme Council of ARC can issue 'normative' or 'legal' (as opposed to legislative) acts only in specified areas, and even then they have to comply not only with the Constitution of Ukraine but also with laws passed by the Supreme Council of Ukraine. In case of their 'nonconfirmity' the president has the right to suspend and file a case to the Constitutional Court to determine their constitutionality (art. 137). Thirdly, the decisions of the Council of Minister of the ARC have to comply with the acts of the president and the cabinet of ministers of Ukraine (art. 135). Fourthly, the court system of Crimea belongs to a unified system of courts of Ukraine (art. 136). And finally, the ARC was refused the right to raise taxes and to have separate (or dual, Russian) citizenship. The chapter on the ARC served as a basis for the drafting of the Crimean Constitution, which was approved by the Supreme Council of Ukraine in December 1998.

The experience of the centralised model of communist states, which allowed for the subordination of local needs and interests to those of the centre, inspired calls for a shift from 'regional administration' to 'regional government' after the collapse of communism.[38] In Ukraine, the idea of decentralisation was in principle widely supported by the 'reformers' not only in order to eradicate the legacy of Soviet centralism, but also—as the national-democrats argued—to restore the indigenous pre-communist traditions of the decentralised model of state (see chapter 2). However, those considerations ultimately gave way to the overriding political objective of territorial integrity and unification.[39] The upsurge of centrifugal forces provided justification for a unitary centralised model of state, with the exception of Crimea where autonomy was opted for as a more suitable model for containing centrifugal tendencies. Ukraine emerged as an independent state following the breakup of the USSR, but was soon after haunted by a spectre of internal centrifugal forces. This experience was a formative experience for a new polity. A unitary territorial model was designed to facilitate integration by providing a framework for imposing and pursuing uniform policies across the territory, and subordinating sub-state, regional interests to those of the centre.

CONCLUSION

An analysis of the constitution illustrates the extent to which the final constitutional reconciliation was the result of painstaking negotiation and enforced compromises between conflicting ideas, beliefs and interests. Undoubtedly, compromise forms an integral part of any political decision making in general, and constitution drafting in particular, but the nature of that settlement is of special interest in Ukraine, where diametrically different conceptions of statehood and cohorts of rules and institutions were pursued. Like in other post-communist states, the task of reconciling different ideas and interests was compounded in Ukraine by the sheer range of issues that needed to be addressed in the constitution. In line with Soviet legal tradition, the constitution was drafted as a comprehensive and rigid code. This form of fundamental law was borrowed by the Soviet regime from the German *Rechtsstaat*, the constitution of which set out precise responsibilities, rules and procedures, as opposed to the minimalist Anglo–Saxon frame-of-government constitutions. The legitimacy of the constitution as a code depends on the achievement of a formalised consensus in the body representative of popular sovereignty.

This requirement was met in Ukraine. Yet the achievement of a constitutional majority should not detract attention from the very limited extent to which the left-wing forces shaped the content of the constitution, despite controlling approximately half of all seats in parliament. Even the gains, such as keenly fought over socio-economic entitlements and the specific reference to the Russian language, were more apparent than real. Therefore, in terms of the preferences of the left-wing forces, the constitution was the product of exclusion, rather than of reconciliation and compromise. The latter concepts, however, can be more readily applied to the nature of settlement between the centre-right forces, including the president, especially insofar as the distribution of powers between the president and parliament was concerned. At the same time, the compromise amongst the centre-right forces did not extend to the domain of centre-periphery relations; these were left ill-defined in the constitution.

The functions the constitution performs are those of constituting, organising, and limiting. Yet, as was argued in chapter 1, the extent to which any constitution can perform these functions depends on the particular circumstances of the polity it applies to. Hence the adoption of a new constitution in a country such as Ukraine was a qualitatively different act from cases where constitutional reform is a matter of a (relatively) straightforward re-organising or just refining an institutional framework within existing states. Such types of constitutional reforms are well evidenced in France, which has had a string (at least 15) of constitutions since 1789, and where, as Jennings put it, 'constitutional tinkering … has been something of a national pastime'.[40] Undoubtedly, in the 1996 Ukrainian constitution the three functions coincided. The liberal, 'limiting' elements are embedded in the comprehensive chapter of Human Rights and Freedoms and in the regulated framework of government, which sets legal limits on the arbitrary use of state powers. However, the pivotal role of this constitution lies in its constituting and organising functions: the aim of the constitution is not so much the protection of a pre-existing structure of the economic, political and cultural life but the creation of this very structure.[41] In order to provide a basis for a 'sovereign and independent, democratic, social, law-based' (art. 1) nation-state, the content of the constitution is determined by the intention to integrate and unify. This intention shaped the provisions on the institutional framework of the state, the notion of the 'sovereign people' and the socio-economic commitments of the state.

Not only did the passage of the constitution itself symbolise a critical threshold in the formation of a polity, but also the content of the constitution was driven by the imperatives of state building. The constitution, by removing the ideological and institutional residuals of the particularistic Soviet model, was designed to turn Ukraine into a modern 'European nation-state' embodying national sovereignty with its homogenising undertones and uniformist institutional set-up. Its paramount aim was to integrate. The constitution 'covers up' much of Ukraine's diversity, disunity and disagreement by locating popular sovereignty with the 'Ukrainian people', when the latter category has little shared meaning in Ukrainian society. The constitution becomes an instrument of state building: it purports to instil a sense of belonging and allegiance by pointing out the nation's individual name, public symbols, official language and tradition of 'centuries-old history of Ukrainian state building', as well as socio-economic pledges. The legacy of being ruled by different states—pronounced regional differences—was to be managed by the semi-presidential form of government at the centre and through domination of the centre over regional concerns (though granting autonomy to Crimea as a recognition of its special profile amongst the Ukrainian regions).

In order to develop such an eclectic and yet integrative constitution, the constitution-makers tailored the universalistic constitutional principles to particular Ukrainian circumstances. Universalistic aspirations of creating a nation-state entailed the recognition of a particularistic path of Ukrainian state building. In the course of constitution drafting, the review of the 'Western traditions' was guided by the paramount criterion of their suitability 'to the current stage and peculiarities of the national and socio-economic development in Ukraine'.[42] This consideration mitigated against wholesale, indiscriminate imports of any particular Western model, while, at the same time, Ukraine aspired to emulate 'Western traditions'. If anything Ukraine's form of government was originally to be modelled on that of Russia, although it underwent significant modification during constitution drafting.

The rejection of the Soviet model (even in the absence of an unmitigated declaration of breaking with the Soviet past) posed the pertinent question of the legitimate historical roots of the state. The symbolic continuity of 'centuries of Ukrainian state building' was asserted in the constitution's Preamble. The historical genealogy of the state was established in public discourse through the invoking of Hrushevskyi and Khmelnytskyi as the father figures of the modern Ukrainian state by both presidents, Kravchuk and Kuchma.[43] Yet, despite the symbolic assertion of continuity, the constitution did not restore the pre-communist models. This was at least partially because of the difficulty of reconciling the disparate interpretations of the 'indigenous tradition'. And even in places where it was relatively unambiguous, such as a decentralised territorial model of the UNR, the indigenous tradition was critically screened for its suitability for the renewed state-building project, which above all—as was believed—required national and territorial consolidation.

The by-product of these efforts to reconcile the assertion of the universalistic constitutional principles with the particularistic imperatives of state building was the multi-faceted assertion of nationhood, as well as a novel organisation of executive–legislative relations, an institutional design that lacked transparency and coherence in many places, with grave consequences for political stability in the post-constitutional period. The eclectic nature of the finally approved conception of statehood was hardly surprising; as Geertz pointed out: 'to an extent, this is true for virtually all the new states, which tend to be bundles of competing traditions gathered accidentally into concocted political frameworks rather than organically evolving civilisations'.[44]

In sum, the 1996 constitution dressed Ukraine in modern and universal clothes (sovereign people, rights and freedoms, governmental institutions, local government), although with some creases and a fair bit of patchwork. And it must be remembered that such an 'outfit' was neither readily available from a reservoir of Ukraine's history, nor could it be easily tailored in 1991. The new Ukrainian constitution, however, was far from an 'innovative leap' or 'conceptual revolution'; it predominantly aspired to match and conform to uniform standards (albeit by tailoring them to 'indigenous circumstances') rather than to invent new ones. The main goal the constitution served was to include Ukraine in the dominant, authoritative forms of constitutional recognition and to lift the paradigm of 'stateness' to a new, dialectically higher level. At the same time, the imperative of state building took priority over efforts to embrace constitutionalism.

NOTES

1 Claus Offe, 'Capitalism by Democratic Design', *Social Research,* Vol. 58, No. 4 (Winter 1991), p. 886.

2 See, for example, Margaret Moore, 'On National Self-determination', *Political Studies*, Vol. XLV, No. 5 (December 1997), pp. 900–13.

3 The Preamble is an introductory passage of the constitution, often written with pathos and explaining the subject and the axiological basis of the new constitution. There is no agreement as to whether the Preamble is an integral part of constitution, and as such, acquires the status of a legal norm, or whether its value is primarily symbolic-expressive (i.e. facilitates the interpretation of constitutional norms, but it does not contain any itself). See, for example, Piotr Winchorek, *Dyskusje konstytucyjne (Constitutional Discussions)* (Warsaw, 1996), pp. 111–117.

4 The national-democrats insisted on the so-called right of people to rise up to defend the state (*pravo narodu na povstania*). The March draft contained the following article: 'The people have the right to resist anyone attempting to subvert the Ukrainian state, or constitutional system, violate its territorial integrity or perform activities aimed at seizing state power, if measures provided by the Constitution cannot be used' (art. 14 of the March draft). This norm would enable people to resort to extra-constitutional means in the case of any threat to the Ukrainian state, including, for example, a decision to enter a union with Russia even if made in a referendum. However, the norm did not even get a simple majority in June 1996 and was excluded from the final draft. However, article 65 states that 'Defence of the Motherland, of the independence and territorial indivisibility of Ukraine, and respect for its state symbols, are the duties of citizens of Ukraine'.

5 Article 13 in the Ukrainian language original text actually reads 'the free development, use of and protection of Russian, other languages of national minorities of Ukraine, are guaranteed'. The awkward wording was opted as the national-democrats would not allow an 'and' between the word 'Russian' and the phrase 'other minority languages'. This, in their opinion, would emphasise the special status of Russian in Ukraine, whereas they wanted to emphasise its 'minority status'.

6 A national-democratic deputy, Roman Bezsmertnyi, commented on such an outcome: 'The Left must have suffered an intellectual blackout when they voted on this article' (Author's interview in September 1996, Kyiv).

7 However, as by end of 1998 no suitable lyrics were submitted, it was decided to retain the first phrase of the original text.

8 Moreover, art.138.9 refers to 'the development and implementation of state programmes for the return of deported peoples', which was particularly aimed at the Crimean Tatars—the largest group of indigenous people in Ukraine.

9 Walker Connor, *Ethnonationalism: the Quest for Understanding* (Princeton University Press: Princeton, 1994), p. 78.

10 Louise Jackson and Kataryna Wolczuk, 'Defining Citizenship and Political Community in Ukraine', *The Ukrainian Review*, Vol. 44, No. 2 (Summer 1997), pp. 16–27.

11 *Ibid.*

12 However, religion was not recognised as one of the defining attributes of a political community. Article 35 explicitly prevents such a possibility: 'The Church and reli-

gious organisations in Ukraine are separated from the State, and the school—from the Church. No religion shall be recognised by the State as mandatory'. There was hardly any debate on this provision, in contrast, for example, to Poland, where this was one of the most hotly disputed issues.

13 *Vechirniy Kyiv*, 2 July 1996, p. 1.

14 While interpreting the article on private property as a defeat of the Left, Vadym Het'man anticipated that the Left would aim to take revenge after losing the constitutional battle on that issue [Vadym P. Het'man, *Yak prynymalas Konstytutsiia Ukrainy* (*How the Ukrainian Constitution Was Adopted*) (Kyiv, 1996), p. 59]. In contrast, Serhiy Soboliev from pro-market faction 'Reforms' concluded that 'we lost the article on property as the references to laws means that acquiring it can be limited by ordinary laws' (Author's interview in September 1996, Kyiv).

15 K. C. Wheare, *Modern Constitutions*, 2nd ed. (London: Oxford University Press, 1966). p. 38.

16 Of special interest is article 49 in the constitution which states that the existing health service provisions cannot be reduced, something which was incorporated into the constitution as one of the 'contributions' of the Socialist faction. Taken literally, the article implies that even the closure of a small local surgery will be in breach of the constitution.

17 For a criticism of their inclusion see Cass Sunstein, 'Why Social and Economic Rights Don't Belong in the New Constitutions of Post-Communist Europe', *East European Constitutional Review,* Vol. 2, No. 1 (Winter 1993).

18 Giovanni Sartori, 'Constitutionalism: A Preliminary Analysis', *American Political Science Review*, Vol. 56, No. 4 (December 1962), p. 862.

19 Daniel J. Elazar, 'Constitution Making: The Pre-Eminently Political Act', in Keith G. Banting and Richard Simeon (eds.), *The Politics of Constitutional Change in Industrial Nations* (London and Basingstoke: Macmillan, 1985), pp. 232–448.

20 Elster, *Introduction to Constitution Making in Eastern Europe*, p. 465.

21 Ulrich K. Preuss, 'Patterns of Constitutional Evolution and Change in Eastern Europe', in Joachim Jens Hesse and Nevil Johnson (eds.), *Constitutional Policy and Change in Europe* (Oxford: Oxford University Press, 1995) p. 100. However, since the second World War, the commitment to the procedural aspects of constitutionalism was combined with the pursuit of social justice and welfare in European constitutional practice and theory (although not so much in written constitutions). As a result, socio-economic benefits came to be regarded as an integral part of citizens' portfolio of rights, and this portfolio became an integral and distinctive characteristic of the Western European state model. In that respect, the new Ukrainian constitution (similarly to other post-communist constitutions) by making those pledges more explicit and generous, broadly adheres to the European strand of constitutional practice.

22 Gianfranco Poggi, *The Development of the Modern State: A Sociological Introduction* (London: Hutchinson, 1978), p. 132.

23 As Preuss pointed out 'there seems to be a significant correlation between the dearth of a long-standing and firm constitutional tradition and the preference for a teleological constitution'. Preuss, 'Patterns of Constitutional Evolution and Change in Eastern Europe', p. 103. Indeed, the twentieth-century constitutions that began to include substantive, material rights, such as the German (Weimar Republic) (1918 and

1923), Yugoslavian (1921), Polish (1921), Romanian (1922), were, as a rule, adopted in new or reconstituted states with weak liberal traditions.

24 Elazar, 'Constitution Making', pp. 232–448.

25 Preuss, 'Patterns of Constitutional Evolution and Change in Eastern Europe', p. 102.

26 The chapters describing the form of government resulted from deliberations in the constitutional commission and working groups; the plenary session of parliament hardly introduced any changes. Indeed, apart from changing the name of parliament (from *Narodni Zbory* to Soviet-era Supreme Council) the articles on central authority were not amended during the eventful constitutional night, when language, symbols, private property and Crimea remained the 'bones of contention'. During the constitutional night, the prime minister, Pavlo Lazarenko, tried to strengthen his position by proposing a last minute change requiring that the prime minister not only be appointed but also dismissed by the president *with* the consent of parliament. The idea was, as expected, favourably looked on by the Left, yet was discarded as a recipe for constitutional deadlock in the event of the prime minister gaining enough independent support in parliament to remain *in situ* despite his dismissal by the president.

27 There have been some attempts to devise a measurement of presidential powers. Shugart and Carey divided presidential powers into legislative powers to issue decrees and nonlegislative powers (cabinet formation, dissolution of assembly, etc.). Each power was weighted on a scale of 1–4 on the basis of how comprehensive it was. See Matthew S. Shugart and John M. Carey, *Presidents and Assemblies: Constitutional Design and Electoral Dynamics* (Cambridge: Cambridge University Press, 1992). p. 150. McGregor divided presidential powers into symbolic powers (without immediate political importance), ceremonial (awarding honours), procedural (such as opening of parliament), appointive powers (for example, to appoint prime minister), and political powers (vetoing legislation). The weighting assigned to each power was then adjusted in the light of the extent to which the power was shared with other bodies. See James McGregor, 'The Presidency in East Central Europe', *RFE/RL Research Report*, Vol. 3, No. 2 (14 January 1994), pp. 23–31. However, as was argued in chapter 4, the arbitrary element and legalistic nature of such measurements renders them something of an academic exercise. While they assist in the comparison of constitutional frameworks of different states, they do not shed much light on the actual weight of the institutions in specific national contexts.

28 The decree comes into force if the Supreme Council does not adopt a law on the same issue or does not reject the presidential draft law within 30 days.

29 Shugart and Carey, *Presidents and Assemblies*, pp. 24–5.

30 As a result, the so-called *sumisnyky*, that is those who combined the two positions, had to either quit their deputy mandate or resign from the executive branch after the 1998 elections. (*Eastern European Constitutional Review*, Vol. 7, No. 3, p. 38).

31 While the majority of constitutions are silent on the role of political parties in representing the views of the electorate and executive–legislative relations, the scarcity of provisions on the role of political parties is according to Loewenstein 'indicative of the existing cleavage between constitutional nominalism and political reality. Thus, he refers to norms such as 'deputies represent the entire nation' as 'a piece of undiluted semantics'. Karl Loewenstein, 'Reflections on the Value of Constitutions in

Our Revolutionary Age', in Harry Eckstain and David E. Apter (eds.), *Comparative Politics: A Reader* (London: The Free Press of Glencoe, 1963), p. 158.

32 The even number of judges in the Constitutional Court was a 'leftover' from an earlier proposal which was based on the principle of rotation of a third of the total number of the judges every three years (6 out of 18).

33 Rett R. Ludwikowski, *Constitution Making in the Region of Former Soviet Dominance* (Durham and London: Duke University Press, 1996), p. 231.

34 In the March draft the *prokuratura* was deprived of its function of overseeing legality; yet the conciliatory group and the Temporary Extraordinary Commission on the Preparation the Draft Constitution reinstated this function as a concession to the Left and some centrist deputies. On the debates on the judicial reform see *Biuletyn Verkhovnoi Rady Ukrainy*, 1992 (Fifth Session), No. 54 and 59.

35 The reform of local government was the most difficult part of reform even in the countries which launched their institutional reforms earlier and in a more systematic manner, such as Poland, where the reform was finalised only in 1998. See H. Wollman, 'Institution building and decentralisation in formerly socialist countries: the cases of Poland, Hungary, and East Germany', *Environment and Planning C: Government and Policy*, Vol. 15, No. 4 (November 1997), pp. 463–80 and J. Regulska, 'Decentralisation or (re)centralization: struggle for political power in Poland', *Environment and Planning C: Government and Policy*, Vol. 15, No. 2 (May 1997), pp. 187–207.

36 Daniel J. Elazar, *Exploring Federalism* (Tuscaloosa, AL: the University of Alabama Press, 1987), p. 48. According to Elander, decentralisation includes the following dimensions: 1) the range of functions carried out at local level; 2) the degree of autonomy about how these functions are carried out; 3) the degree to which local government is funded from its own resources rather than from central grants. I. Elander, 'Between centralism and localism: on the development of local government in postsocialist Europe', *Environment and Planning C: Government and Policy*, Vol. 15, No. 2 (May 1997), pp. 143–59.

37 As Oleksandr Lavrynovych, a deputy head of Rukh, commented: 'The chapter on the Crimean Republic is the worst in the constitution'. (Author's interview, Kyiv, September 1996.)

38 The case for decentralising the state was made for a number of reasons: locally elected institutions offer representative, accessible and responsible government, foster direct participation in public decision making, develop a sense of community and civic ties (political rationale); devolution in spending and revenue-raising responsibilities result in efficiency gains (economic rationale); and improvements in collection of information (administrative rationale). K. Zsamboki and M. Bell, 'Local self-government in Central and Eastern Europe', *Environment and Planning C: Government and Policy*, Vol. 15, No. 2 (May 1997), pp. 177–86. However, some scholars warned about uncritical captivation with decentralisation as a case could be made for (reformed) centralisation. Elander, argues that 'Neither centralism nor localism are inherently good or bad', and points out that centralisation offers the following advantages: 1) promotion of the public and national interest, 2) helps to minimise inequality amongst different parts of the country and equal socio-economic conditions for the citizens, 3) allows the co-ordination and control. I. Elander, 'Between centralism and localism', pp. 143–59.

39 For a general debate on territorial models of state and the underlying justifications see Ronan Paddison, *The Fragmented State: The Political Geography of Power* (Oxford: Basil Blackwell, 1983).

40 Jeremy Jennings, 'French Constitutional Tradition', in Richard Bellamy, Victorio Bufacchi, and Dario Castiglione (eds.), *Democracy and Constitutional Culture in the Union of Europe* (London: Lothian Foundation Press, 1995), p. 22.

41 Preuss, 'Patterns of Constitutional Evolution and Change in Eastern Europe', p. 104.

42 Materials of the Special Conciliatory Group, Minutes of the Meeting on 5 April 1996.

43 Kataryna Wolczuk, 'History, Europe and the "National Idea": the Official Narrative of National Identity in Ukraine', *Nationalities Papers*, Vol. 28, No. 4 (December 2000), pp. 672–94.

44 Clifford Geertz, *The Interpretation of Cultures* (London: Fontana, 1973), p. 244.

CHAPTER EIGHT

UKRAINE UNDER THE NEW CONSTITUTION: THE ANATOMY OF A CRISIS

The passage of the Basic Law constituted only the first, albeit pivotal, step in the process, of erecting the institutional edifice of the state; to complete the process numerous laws needed to be adopted on the basis of constitutional norms. It is believed that the 'downstream' process of learning to live under the new fundamental law is easier than the 'up-stream' process of drafting the constitution:[1] the expectations are that once the constitutional norms regulating inter-institutional relations were created, the ideological conflict would be contained by rules and procedures and, as a result, its intensity would be reduced. As such conflicts would be less destabilising than the struggle over *kompetentzkompetentz*, or, especially, than the emotion-arousing issues of nationhood. As the new constitution 'constitutionalised' the 'national question' by containing it in a set of constitutional rules, the 'question' was effectively taken out of day-to-day politics. However, hopes that the passage of the constitution would mark the advent of a new era in Ukrainian politics were soon dashed: the post-1996 period was characterised by an escalation of the conflict between the branches of power. The high point of the conflict was the referendum on the constitutional amendments in April 2000, initiated by Kuchma to emasculate the parliament. Even though this initiative failed, the relations have remained strained and unsettled. The inter-institutional strife, which became a feature of the post-constitutional scene, crippled the legislative process and effective policy-making.

The conspicuous failure of the constitution to bring constitutionalism to Ukraine, at least in the sphere of inter-institutional relations, tends to be attributed to the low level of political culture and the legal nihilism of the political elites.[2] Political actors—with their notorious and habitual scoring of rules—conducted politics with disregard for the set of constitutional rules they themselves adopted. By focusing on the psychological and cultural predisposition of the elites, this explanation, however, implies that the constitution—as a set of constraining and enabling norms—was totally or largely ignored. Yet the constitution mattered. Far from being irrelevant, the constitution to a large extent induced inter-institutional competition by creating an array of constraints and opportunities, which guided the actors' aims and strategies. This conflict-inducing propensity of the constitution was an unintended outcome of the constitution-making process. The desperate search for a form of government, which would satisfy the diverse agenda of the actors involved in constitution making, resulted in the poorly thought-out delineation of authority between the president and parliament. In particular, the lack of foresight and precision in the design of the presidency, which was conceived as a hybrid between the figurehead 'head of state' and the chief executive, fuelled intense competition over control of the executive branch. By creating a web of overlapping prerogatives of the president and the legislature, the constitution provided an impetus for these institutions to expand and consolidate their respective spheres of authority. Kuchma has taken the initiative in this contest. Even if the presidency did not succeed in permanently weakening the legislature in constitutional terms, its control of the administrative structure of the state and arbitrary interpretations of the constitution means that the institution has come to overshadow other state institutions.

The chapter illuminates the way that the institutional framework, designed in the 1996 constitution, structured the political conflict in such a way that it brought about the challenges to the constitutional order itself. But even if institutional factors are prioritised in explaining political outcomes, the complex knot of social life can rarely be untied by using only one type of analytical instrument. Undoubtedly, beside the constitutional norms, the cross-sectional divisions in parliament, which persisted despite the introduction of a mixed, majoritarian–proportional system in 1998, accounted for the problems in clarifying the nature of executive–legislative relations. In particular, the 'centre' of the political spectrum, which throughout the 1990s did not develop into a coherent political orientation, was captured by powerful business interests. Having a vested interest in close co-operation with the executive branch, the so-called oligarchic factions have had a corrosive effect on Ukrainian parliament and politics in general. But while the importance of social cleavages, and the political culture of elites' are not to be glossed over, the analysis of the post-constitutional developments vividly demonstrates the extent to which the particular distribution of institutional prerogatives outlined in the constitution contributed to the perpetuation of political instability in Ukraine.

The first part of the chapter demonstrates how, after the passage of the constitution, the process of state building became a hostage in the 'war at the top', as the president and parliament neutralised each others' actions. The second section examines the results of the 1998 parliamentary elections, the reasons for the perpetuation of the Supreme Council's fragmentation, and the parliamentary crisis in early 2000. In the third section it is argued that, despite the creation of a parliamentary majority, the prospects for the reduction of inter-institutional strife by consensual means were ill fated after the re-election of the incumbent. Kuchma held a referendum to try to force the legislature into submission. It was called on moot constitutional grounds and was characterised by a gross abuse of the administrative structures of the state. Even though it failed to bear fruit, no resolution to the inter-institutional strife is in sight. It is concluded that in light of post-constitutional developments, the case of Ukraine can be seen as a powerful indictment of systems with directly elected, executive presidencies.

'THE MORNING AFTER': EXECUTIVE–LEGISLATIVE RELATIONS UNDER THE NEW CONSTITUTION

The adoption of the 1996 constitution was marked by a shift of the main political cleavage in Ukraine. While the ideological conflict between the Right and Left did not lose its intensity, it came to be overshadowed by the institutional confrontation. Undoubtedly, the inter-institutional cleavage developed as a result of circumstances under which the constitution was promulgated. During constitution making the most important cleavage ran between the Left and 'the rest'. The former blocked the passage of the constitution, while the centre-right deputies together with the president pushed the process forward. But the anti-Left, pro-constitutional coalition in the 1994–1998 parliament was only a situational alliance of convenience and hence short-lived; it splintered once its main objective was achieved. Soon the particular form of government, president-parliamentary, adopted in the constitution fuelled the inter-institutional conflict over remits of power.

This was a paradoxical outcome taking into account that Ukraine's form of government was relatively balanced, especially in comparison to other post-Soviet states, including Russia. During constitution making, the pro-presidential spirit of the March draft induced the deputies to re-address the balance between the presidency and parliament resulting in a more even distribution of powers in the May, so-called Syrota, draft (see chapter 6). However, despite an apparent improvement on the autocratic March draft, the hastened pace of work prevented in-depth deliberations on the consequences of the particular distribution of powers in the final stages of constitution making. The more balanced form of government was achieved by the duplication rather than clear-cut separation of some areas of power between the president and legislature. In particular, their competencies overlapped in the following spheres:

- oversight of the cabinet of ministers;
- dismissal of the cabinet of ministers;
- organisation of other bodies within the executive branch;
- defining the general direction of the internal and foreign policy;
- law making (although the presidential right to issue decrees in economic matters not regulated by laws was granted to the president for 3 years only and hence expired in June 1999).

As was argued in chapter 7, despite defining the president as 'the head of state', the constitution allocated the president far-reaching executive powers. The discrepancy between the formal wording and the actual scope of prerogatives soon became apparent. The overlap in powers between the parliament and the president, combined with the vagueness of some of the constitutional norms, opened the door to diametrically diverging interpretations of the Basic Law. Oleksandr Lavrynovych, a member of parliament who was closely involved in drafting the constitution, commented 'Even in their worst nightmares the constitution makers could not anticipate the present interpretations of the constitution [by the president]'.[3] And yet such diverse interpretations shaped the president and parliament's objectives and strategies. Kuchma attempted to usurp the powers that were denied to him during constitution making by biased interpretation of the constitution, presidential decrees and a plebiscite. At the same time, apart from the adjudication of the Constitutional Court, the constitution did not offer any tension-defusing devices, because of the independence of the presidency and legislature in terms of their survival (see chapter 7).

The constitutional norms needed to be developed in a series of laws. Many of those laws, such as 'On the Accounting Chamber of the Supreme Council', 'On the State Property Fund', 'On Local Self-government', 'On the Cabinet of Ministers', or 'On the Local State Administration', were to further elaborate and clarify the constitutional prerogatives of the branches of power. Yet soon the legislative process was marred by the conflict between the president and parliament, both of which fiercely defended any encroachments onto what they came to view as their own constitutional prerogatives. This was most vividly demonstrated by the embroil surrounding the draft 'Law on the Cabinet of Ministers' in late 1997. It turned into a tug-of-war in which the prize was the strengthening of the 'presidential' and 'parliamentary' spheres of authority in the president-parliamentary form of government.

The draft 'Law on the Cabinet of Ministers' was designed by the parliamentary Committee on Legal Reforms to clarify the structure of the executive branch by limiting the role of the president to that of a figurehead and defining the role of the cabinet of ministers as that of the supreme executive organ dependent on a parliamentary majority. The deputies relied on the wording of the constitution, according to which, as the then chairman of parliament Moroz emphasised, 'the president is the head of state'; this meant, by implication, 'He is *not* the chief executive'.[4] Through the law on the cabinet of ministers, for the first time the parliament endeavoured to institutionalise the parliamentary majority. According to the law, the president was to submit a candidate for the post of prime minister for parliament's approval, after the candidate had been agreed on by the chairman of parliament and the parliamentary groups and factions. If the Supreme Council did not approve the agreed on president's candidate, then it was required to nominate the prime minister by a two-thirds majority; if it failed, the president could appoint the prime minister without parliament's consent. Although, according to the constitution, the president could dismiss the prime minister unilaterally, the draft stipulated that he had to inform parliament of the reasons for such a dismissal. As Volodymyr Stretovych, the head of the parliamentary commission for legal reform, explained: 'Drafting the law, we counted on the fact that any prime minister will be a person of the parliamentary majority. Thus parliament must be told why the prime minister whom it supports failed to execute his duties properly'.[5] Although that draft did not break the norms of the constitution *per se*, it elaborated on procedures unanticipated by the Fundamental Law. By allocating a key role to the parliamentary majority, the institution that was absent in the constitution, parliament endeavoured to assert its control over the cabinet of ministers by obliging the president to respect the preferences of the parliamentary majority. Yet, without presidential consent, legislative measures to raise the profile of the parliamentary majority were doomed to fail. Not unexpectedly, Kuchma vetoed the law. Despite repeated efforts, the law has not been enforced, and, as a result, the status and procedures governing the functioning of the cabinet of ministers have remained unclear and by 2001 are still regulated by presidential decrees and the internal acts of the government.

The fate of the 'Law of the Cabinet of Ministers' was symptomatic of any attempts to delineate the spheres of responsibility and procedures for exercising constitutional powers of the president and the Supreme Council. Virtually each major law, which was adopted by the Supreme Council to develop the constitutional norms has been objected to (mostly through a formal veto or filing a case in the Constitutional Court) by the president. The 'Law on Local Self-government' was vetoed three times and returned to parliament before the president finally capitulated and signed it.[6] The 'Law on Local State Administration' had not been enacted for two years, despite the fact that the parliament overrode the presidential veto by a two-thirds majority on no fewer than four occasions, although, as Kuchma pointed out, this was achieved by violating the constitution and *Reglament,* something he, the guarantor of the constitution, could not tolerate. Unable to force the parliament to include his proposals, Kuchma exploited loopholes in the constitution: even if a presidential veto is overridden by a constitutional majority, the law still needs to be signed by the president to come into force. So the president did not sign the document for two years (the law came into force only in April 1999). The 'Law on the Accounting Chamber of the Supreme Council' was vetoed by Kuchma three times, then signed and subsequently challenged by him in the Constitutional Court. The 'Law on Privatisation of State Property', which was adopted by parliament in February 1997, subordinated the State Property Fund to the Supreme Council. On the basis that it impinged on president's constitutional powers, Kuchma challenged the law in the Constitutional Court, which ruled in favour of the president and invalidated the relevant section of the law.

As can be seen, the Constitutional Court turned into an arbiter between the legislature and presidency. Its creation was a major success story after the passage of the constitution, although it did not happen without violating the 3-month deadline stipulated in the 'transitional provisions'. The 'Law on the Constitutional Court' was adopted on 16 October 1996 after renewed opposition from the left-wing factions, which continued to uphold the supremacy of the Supreme Council and oppose the removal of parliament's Soviet-era right to interpret the constitution. According to the constitution and the 'Law on the Constitutional Court', Ukraine adopted what could be defined as the 'European model' of constitutional review: concentrated, abstract, *ex post* and final. The prerogative of constitutional review was vested in one body, the Constitutional Court, which was given sole authority not only to interpret the constitution, but also to rule on the unconstitutionality of laws and normative acts; such a ruling brought about a default sanction of the invalidation of the relevant sections of the act in question. Apart from special matters, the Court can only consider laws and normative acts in force. The Court performs abstract reviews of laws and legal acts, while the consideration of the legality of decisions of bodies of state power and local government fall under the authority of courts of general jurisdiction. The Court's rulings are final and are binding on the territory of Ukraine. The Court consists of 18 judges nominated for 9 years, without the possibility of re-appointment for a second term. The president, parliament and the Congress of Judges appoint six judges each.

Like in other post-communist states, despite, or rather because of, the lack of tradition of judicial review, in Ukraine the Constitutional Court was conceived as a powerful institution. Yet, the power of the Ukrainian Constitutional Court was a double-edge sword: while it was granted power to deliver a final resolution in disputes between state institutions, the ill-conceived design of the constitutional framework led to the flooding of the Constitutional Court with cases which were essentially not judicable in purely legal terms. Although the Court has portrayed itself as a humble interpreter and defender of the constitution, its rulings were concerned with the most pivotal and controversial political and social issues.[7] Therefore, since its creation in 1996, the Court has come to play a pivotal stone in the institutional arch of Ukrainian politics by assuming the role of an adjudicator in inter-institutional conflict. The Constitutional Court came to compensate for the lack of a majority in parliament and in congruence between the political profile of the legislative and executive branches. At the same time, the Court found itself in a highly precarious and vulnerable position. To avoid challenges from any sides, the Court's adjudication strategy was characterised by moderation, restraint, and a degree of 'judicial reluctance' as the

Court tended to refrain from issuing rulings on the most difficult issues unless it was forced to take a stance. Despite the frequent invalidation of, at least some provisions of, legal acts, the Court often strove to limit the impact of its rulings by carefully seeking out the middle ground. Nevertheless, this strategy still did not protect it from criticism, especially by parliament, which found itself at the receiving end of the Court's reluctant adjudication, instigated by the president who was proactive in filing cases in the Court. This 'middle ground' strategy, however, began to fail when the presidential offensive on the powers of parliament curtailed the Court's room for manoeuvre. In fact, the Court only mitigated the worst excesses of the presidency but did not use its powers to prevent the onslaught on the legislature. By the fourth year of the Court's existence, its rulings began to bear more clear signs of concession to political expediency (see below).

Overall, the rulings of the Court calmed but did not eliminate inter-institutional strife and the relations between the president and parliament remained tense. Both institutions engaged in mutual incriminations and accusations of usurpation of powers. Volodymyr Lytvyn, the then presidential adviser blamed the parliamentarians for the on-going conflict:

> If only some people's deputies finally find the courage to realise that they have not only a lot of power but also a big responsibility; they should not avoid responsibility or usurp competencies depending on what is going on.[8]

The parliament, in turn, imputed the personality of the president. One of the authors of the constitution, Volodymyr Stretovych, put the blame on the personal qualities of the incumbent:

> When preparing the Constitution of 1996, we started with the premise that the president is head of state, who stands above the branches of power, is a superior arbiter and a guarantor of the Constitution. Today, our problem lies in the purely subjective factor of the [current] president of Ukraine, and not the presidency as an institution, which exists in many countries.[9]

According to Stretovych, the incumbent's disregard for the constitutional delimitation of his role as 'head of state' lay at the root of the tensions. Symptomatically, the presidential entourage has not challenged the assertion that the president was merely the 'head of state', it simply imbued the term with a different meaning. Rather than being an apolitical figurehead, the presidency was at the centre of politics as the supreme political institution of the state. According to Vasyl Kremen', the head of the Internal Affairs Department of the Presidential Administration, 'in terms of his prerogative, he [the president] does not belong to any branch of power, but *plays an important role in functioning of each of them'* (emphasis added).[10] Hence, the ill-conceived, hybrid role of the 'head of state' (according to the formal wording of the constitution), and the 'head of the executive branch' (in the light of the president's actual constitutional prerogatives) allowed the presidency to double as the 'guarantor of the constitution' and the 'chief executive'.

THE 1998 PARLIAMENTARY ELECTIONS

The 1998 parliamentary elections, which took place under the new, mixed electoral system, raised hopes for a breakthrough in the structurisation of parliament, hopes, which, despite some initial advances, remained unrealised. When, however, a concerted effort was made to create a majority, it was overshadowed by Kuchma's determination to win the upper hand over the volatile legislature.

According to the 'Law on the Elections', which was passed in autumn 1997, half of the deputies (225) were elected in single mandate districts using a 'first past the post' formula, and the other half from national party lists in accordance with the principle of proportional representation for those parties which cleared the 4 percent threshold. The deliberation on the electoral law took place amidst a political struggle between the president and the non-party based factions, on the one hand, and the party-based factions, such as Rukh and the CPU, on the other. The law was challenged in the Constitutional Court, which ruled that 21 provisions of the law were unconstitutional, mainly those that privileged political parties over candidates in single mandate constituencies. Despite lingering fears, the Court did not strike down the principle of proportional representation.[11]

Overall, 30 parties and electoral blocs registered for the elections. With the exception of well-known players with clearly identifiable ideological platforms, such as Rukh and CPU, the elections prompted much re-shuffling on the political spectrum. The Socialists and Peasants formed the 'For Truth, People and Ukraine' bloc, while the Progressive Socialist Party of Ukraine remained as a political outcast and competed alone. The centre of the political spectrum was reshaped by the appearance of several reincarnated parties. The parties that until then had lingered on the edges of the political life, turned their marginal position into an electoral asset by portraying themselves as 'clean', that was untainted by collaboration with the power structures. The Green Party, which had been created in the hey-day of perestroika, but then led a dormant existence, became a haven for business people interested in gaining a parliamentary mandate (this was an important consideration for many business people seeking a mandate which offered parliamentary immunity from prosecution at a time when the deputies of regional and local radas were being deprived immunity). *Hromada* (Community), which was created in 1993, was taken over by Pavlo Lazarenko in 1996, when he was still a prime minister. As relations with Kuchma worsened, Lazarenko used *Hromada* as his independent powerbase. Another party, which emerged from obscurity, was the Social Democratic Party of Ukraine (United), one of many offshoots of the original Social-Democratic Party of early 1990s. It was used as an electoral vehicle by such well-known statesmen as Leonid Kravchuk and Yevhen Marchuk, and two prominent businesspeople, who sponsored the campaign, Viktor Medvedchuk and Hryhoriy Surkiz. There were also relatively new arrivals on the political landscape, such as the People's Democratic Party, which was formed in February 1996. Closely associated with the presidential administration and nicknamed the 'party of power', it was to become the main pro-presidential force in the new parliament in order to boost Kuchma's chances of being re-elected in the 1999 presidential elections. While the centre of the political spectrum reached a low level of institutionalisation during the term of the 1994–1998 parliament (see chapters 5 and 6), the introduction of the mixed electoral system spawned frantic attempts to enter this previously almost uncharted territory, but the new 'centre' has proven anything but a stabilising factor in Ukrainian politics in general, and in executive–legislative relations in particular.

Nevertheless, while the mixed system had a noticeable mobilising effect, it failed to deliver a clear-cut winner. Only eight of the parties and blocs cleared the threshold of 4 percent (amongst those only 5 passed the threshold in at least two thirds of oblasts, whereas *Hromada*, PSPU and SDP(U) benefited from high popularity in certain oblasts only, namely Dnipropetrovsk, Sumy and Zakarpattia, respectively). Many more parties got in on the majoritarian list. The majoritarian pool of seats was divided between 22 parties and blocs, 9 of which had only 1 deputy. Hence, the 1998 parliament became populated by more parties than its predecessor (Table 8.1). In terms of the structurisation and transparency of the party system, the preservation of the majoritarian system for 225 seats offset the gains from the introduction of the proportional representation.

Table 8.1. Results of the March 1998 Parliamentary Elections

	Party Lists		Majoritarian	
Party/Electoral Bloc	*Percentage of Votes*	*Number of Seats*	*Number of Seats*	*Total*
Communist Party of Ukraine	24.7	84	39	*123*
Rukh	9.4	32	14	*46*
Bloc of the Socialist Party of Ukraine and the Peasant Party of Ukraine	8.6	29	5	*34*
Green Party	5.4	19	–	*19*
People's Democratic Party	5.0	17	11	*28*
Hromada	4.7	16	7	*23*
Progressive Socialist Party of Ukraine	4.1	14	–	*14*
Social-Democratic Party of Ukraine (United)	4.0	14	–	*14*
Agrarian Party of Ukraine	3.7	–	8	*8*
Christian-Democratic Party	1.3	–	3	*3*
National Front	2.7	–	3	*3*
Reform and Order Party	3.1	–	3	*3*
Soiuz Party	0.7	–	2	*2*
Party of Regional Rebirth	0.9	–	2	*2*
Independent Candidates	–	–	114	*114*

Source: The Central Electoral Commission of Ukraine.

At first sight, the winner was the CPU and, more generally, the left-wing parties, including the anti-presidential *Hromada*, which controlled approximately 42–44 percent of seats. Yet the Left emerged with plurality but not majority. In a far cry from the threats of the 'red revenge', the CPU managed to obtain 24.68 percent of the vote, far below the expected 35 percent. The Socialists, despite being in tandem with the Peasants, obtained fewer seats (8.54 percent) than they did alone in 1994. Moreover, in contrast to the 1994 parliament, by 1998 the left-wing was far less united, as the passage of the constitution deepened the cleavage between the CPU and SPU/SelPU, especially as the SPU continued edging towards a social-democratic platform. The conspicuous losers, however, were those who failed to climb over the threshold of 4 percent, which included 'Reforms and Order', the party, based on the parliamentary faction 'Reforms', which won 3.13 percent, the pro-reform and pro-presidential Agrarian Party of Ukraine (3.67 percent), or the bloc 'National Front', which included, amongst others, the Republican Party of Ukraine (2.72 percent). Nevertheless, even those who did clear the barrier could hardly consider the elections a victory. Despite coming second in the elections, Rukh's 10 percent of seats signified its inability to reach out beyond its stronghold in Western Ukraine, while the People's Democratic Party's performance with 5 percent amounted to a dismal failure of the 'party of power', which enjoyed the backing of the state structures in the electoral campaign. If anybody could be crowned the winners, it would be the 'reincarnated' parties, especially, the Greens and the Social-Democrats, which, despite their relatively low score (5.4 and 4.01 percent, respectively), emerged from almost total obscurity to parties with a nation-wide profile, and, as it turned out, exerted considerable influence in the Supreme Council, thanks to their close links with the executive branch and financial resources.

Despite the elections of a large contingent of independents (114 deputies), the parties set the tone in the new legislature. According to the change to the *Reglament* of 13 May 1998, factions could only be created on the basis of parties which cleared the 4 percent barrier on the party list (as 4 percent was equivalent to 14 seats, the latter number became minimum for registering a faction), and only formally registered factions had the right to participate in the formation of internal bodies. This decision allowed the party-based factions to compete for hearts of non-party deputies (often by lining their pockets). The ranks of the PDP swelled four times, and *Hromada*'s—two-fold. The 'Left-centre' faction of the SPU and SelPU initially attracted 35 deputies (May 1998), but already in October a separate faction of SelPU of 15 deputies was formed ('Left-centre' retained 3 SelPU deputies amongst its 24 members) (Table 8.2).

A FUTILE SEARCH FOR A PARLIAMENTARY MAJORITY

Initially the formation of eight party-based factions in the newly elected *Verkhovna Rada* suggested a marked improvement compared to the 1994–98 parliament (see Table 8.2). Yet, despite official proclamations in early 2000, a consolidated parliamentary majority failed to emerge in parliament by 2001. This failure can be explained by three factors: the hanging balance of power because of the 'fuzzy bi-polarity', the ruling of the Constitutional Court, and the lack of a structural incentive to form such a majority.

Table 8.2. The Composition of the Ukrainian Parliament (1998–2001)

Party/Bloc	*March 1998*	*October 1998*	*April 1999*	*April 2000*	*June 2001*
Left					
Communist Party of Ukraine	*123*	*122*	*122*	*115*	*112*
'Centre-Left' (Socialists and Peasants)	*34*	*25*	*24*	–	–
'Centre-Left' (Socialists)	–	–	–	*19*	*16*
Peasant Party of Ukraine*	–	*14*	*15*	–	–
Progressive Socialist Party of Ukraine*	*14*	*14*	*13*	–	–
Solidarity (*Solidarnist'*)	–	–	–	*21*	*21*
Centre-Right					
Green Party	*19*	*26*	*24*	*17*	*17*
People's Democratic Party	*28*	*84*	*53*	*24*	*16*
*Hromada**	*23*	*45*	*17*	–	–
Fatherland (*Batkivchyna*)	–	–	*24*	*35*	*26*
Social-Democratic Party of Ukraine (SDPU)	*14*	*23*	*27*	*34*	*35*
Faction of Independents*	–	*26*	*18*	–	–
Revival of the Regions/Democratic Union	–	–	*27*	*36*	*27*
Regions of Ukraine	–	–	–	–	*20*
Yabluko	–	–	–	–	*15*
Labour (*Trudova Ukraina*)	–	–	–	*38*	*46*
Reforms–Centre/Reforms–Congress	–	–	*14*	*14*	*16*
People's Movement of Ukraine (Rukh)	*46*	*48*	–	–	–
People's Movement of Ukraine (Rukh–Chornovil/Udovenko)	–	–	*16*	*18*	*14*
Ukrainian People's Movement (Rukh–Kostenko)	–	–	*30*	*24*	*22*
Non-affiliated Deputies	*114*	*23*	*18*	*45*	*46*
Total	*450*	*448*	*446*	*440*	*449*

* Factions of the Progressive Socialist Party, the Peasant Party of Ukraine, Independents and *Hromada* were struck off the register because the size fell below 14 deputies in February 2000.

Source: Verkhovna Rada of Ukraine, Romyr Report (Spring 1999), *Post-Postup*, 20 April 2000, BBC Monitoring Global Newsline Former Soviet Union Political File, 6 June 2001.

Firstly, in contrast to the 1994 parliament, which was characterised by the presence of two ideological blocs, the Left and the national-democrats, and a large amorphous centre, initially the 1998 parliament, was characterised by the 'fuzzy bi-polarity', that is the presence of two loose and unstable multi-party coalitions. Although both left-centre and centre-right had about 210 votes, each bloc lacked the strength to adopt laws (which still required a 226 majority under the 1994 *Reglament*),[12] but could block each others initiatives. Attitudes to economic reforms constituted the main, but not the only, cleavage within the new parliament. The centre-right parties, such as Rukh, Social-Democrats (United), the People's Democratic Party and the Greens favoured a market economy, whereas the left-centre, that is the communists, Socialists/Agrarians, Progressive Socialists, and to a lesser extent, *Hromada*, advocated the restoration of the command economy. However, *Hromada's* anti-reformist stance stemmed from its abhorrence of the president rather than from a coherently elaborated ideological programme. Hence, the pro- and anti-reform cleavages cut across president Kuchma's support within parliament. President Kuchma's confrontational style of politics tended to alienate even the most ardent reformers in parliament. Although the main pro-presidential faction, centred on the People's Democratic Party, grew in strength by attracting many non-affiliated deputies, it failed to become a beacon of the structured majority, because of its image of the 'party of power' serving the interests of presidential and governmental circles, as well as the ongoing power struggle within the party between the 'nomenklatura' and 'ideological' wings, which advocated divergent goals for the party.

The hanging balance of power stifled the competition for posts, which resulted in the prolonged elections of the chairman of parliament. Despite 18 rounds of voting over two months, neither candidates of the left, such as Moroz, Symonenko, nor from the centre-right, such as Ivan Pliushch, could master the requisite 226 votes. Finally, with the consent of the presidential side (which, above all, feared the election of Oleksandr Moroz), Oleksandr Tkachenko, the deputy head of the SelPU, was elected thanks to the crucial extra votes from the PDP, Greens and the SDP(U). Victor Medvedchuk from the Social-Democratic Party of Ukraine (United) and Adam Martyniuk from the CPU became the deputy speakers. Rather than the expected figurehead, Tkachenko turned out to be a highly problematic ally of the president. Even if the second half of 1998 witnessed an unprecedented degree of co-operation between the two (undoubtedly smoothed by the writing-off of the debt of Tkachenko's company *Zemlia i Ludy*), the Tkachenko–Kuchma tandem fell apart. Tkachenko pushed his own policy line, especially on foreign affairs,[13] and developed leadership ambitions (in a self-aggrandising manner, he named himself the 'head of the legislative branch of power').[14] At the same time, Tkachenko's heavy-handed style of leadership antagonised the deputies of the centre-right, who grew increasingly frustrated with his treatment of parliament as a personal fiefdom and rampant violations of the parliamentary *Reglament*. The chairman's elections revealed the presidential strategy towards the parliament: rather than fostering unity in the centre-right bloc and building a majority through the 'party of power', the People's Democratic Party, the president pitched the centre-right factions against each other by striking separate deals with individual factions or even their members.

The second reason, which explains why an emergence of a majority was thwarted, was that the early gains of a more structured parliament were nullified by a ruling by the Constitutional Court in December 1998. The Court ruled on the unconstitutionality of the changes to the 'Rules of Procedures' of the Supreme Council (*Reglament*) of May 1998, according to which only factions which cleared the 4 percent barrier on the party lists had the right to form a faction. The relaxation of rules on faction-formation spawned a rapid proliferation of new factions and *en masse* movement of deputies (see Table 8.2). In March 1999, the powerful oligarch and Kuchma's close ally, Oleksandr Volkov, created a new faction 'Revival of the Regions', which later became the basis for two separate factions, 'Ukrainian Regions' and 'Democratic Union'. The PDP, torn between its pro-presidential and pro-reformist wings, began to lose deputies to both 'oligarchic' and 'ideological' factions. The split affected Rukh, the second largest party, in early 1999. Because of the disagreement on the leadership role of Chornovil and priorities of the party, most importantly for relations with the president, Rukh split into two factions: one led by Yuriy Kostenko, the former Minister of Environment, and the other by Viacheslav Chornovil. Despite the fact that neither faction departed from the national-democratic ideological platform, the split deepened after Chornovil's death in a road accident, when Udovenko, the former Minister of Foreign Affairs, replaced him; this move cemented rather than helped to overcome the split, especially as Udovenko and Kostenko threw their hats into the ring for the 1999 presidential elections. In the aftermath of Lazarenko's detention in Switzerland on money laundering charges, *Hromada*'s ranks were decimated by the outflow of deputies to the 'Fatherland' faction headed by Yulia Tymoshenko. *Hromada* was subsequently struck off the official register of factions in early 2000. In addition, at that time three other factions, the Progressive Socialist Party, the Peasant Party of Ukraine, and Independents, were also struck off because their size fell below the required minimum of 14 deputies. A new, left-of-centre faction, 'Solidarity', headed by Ivan Chyzh, attracted some deputies from the faction of Socialists, thereby meeting the presidential aim of weakening the Socialists. In the autumn of 2000, another small 'oligarchic' faction, the so-called Yabluko, was created by Mykhailo Brodskyi, a businessman who fell out of favour with Kuchma. The proliferation of factions perpetuated the chaotic parliamentary politics. While the strongest party-based factions, the CPU and to a lesser extent, the right-wing factions, maintained their ideological cohesion and voting discipline,[15] the voting patterns of most centrist factions reflected the fact that, despite their nominal party membership, they were groupings bonded most of all by corporate interests rather than ideological closeness.

The third reason for the poor structurisation of parliament was that the Supreme Council lacked a strong incentive to form a majority in light of parliament's weak appointive powers *vis-à-vis* the president. The Council only had the constitutional right to approve the prime minister and had no say in the appointment of vice-prime ministers and ministers. Moreover, while parliament's right to dismiss the prime minister unilaterally was qualified (see chapter 7), the president's equivalent prerogative was not only unconstrained by any constitutional qualifications, but he could also dismiss individual ministers as well as the prime minister. The institutional separation of powers was demonstrated when, in line with the constitutional rules, the creation of the new parliament was not followed by the automatic resignation of the cabinet. Hence, the government headed by Valerii Pustovoitenko, Kuchma's loyal ally (who replaced Pavlo Lazarenko under the previous parliament in 1997), stayed in office after the 1998 elections. The president's promise to include some nominees of the parliamentary factions in the cabinet came to nothing, not only because of the lack of agreement on the parties' role in the formation of the cabinet but also because of the parties's reluctance to associate themselves with the unpopular government on the eve of the presidential elections. The overall continuity in membership of the cabinet after the elections emphasised the lack of constitutional instruments for the parliament to effectively oversee the executive branch.[16] Two years after the parliamentary elections, the expectation that the introduction of the new electoral system would stabilise the composition of the parliament and lead to a formation majority-backed cabinet proved unfounded.

The hanging balance of power between the two broad, multi-party blocs in parliament, the left and centre-right, culminated in a dramatic stand-off in January 2000. Upon announcing the creation of a parliamentary majority, deputies from the 11 centre-right factions attempted to dismiss Tkachenko as parliamentary chairman. As Tkachenko resisted by violating parliamentary rules, the majority (243 deputies from a 450-deputy house) walked out and assembled in a separate session in another building. It left behind the minority with the chairman but no quorum. During the two weeks of parallel existence, the majority elected a new speaker, Ivan Pliushch, and replaced the left-wing heads of all the parliamentary committees. It also amended its *Reglament* to give recognition to the institutions of the parliamentary majority and opposition. By storming into the building on the 1 February, the majority (by that time consisting of 259 deputies) took over the parliament's premises. The 'new' Council adopted a series of symbolic gestures, such as renaming itself the Rada of the 3rd convocation (instead of the Supreme Council of the 14th convocation, which symbolised the continuity with Soviet-era Councils) and voted to remove Soviet-era symbols from the façade of the building of the Council. Despite the abuses of its position (including the removal of left-wing heads of parliament's committees), the proclamation of the formation of a parliamentary majority appeared to be a milestone along the road towards a more structured and transparently organised legislature.

Nevertheless, the majority's role and hence survival could not be taken for granted in light of the distribution of power between the legislature and presidency and intra-parliamentary cleavages. The parliament's basic problem of volatility did not go away, as the newly formed majority was crippled by the internal cross-cutting divisions between the pro-reform and pro-presidential factions, which broadly coincided with the party- and business-factions. One of the strongest proponents of the formation of the majority was actually the faction the 'Revival of the Regions' controlled by Volkov, a powerful oligarch with close connections to Kuchma; the majority was to serve as a powerbase of the presidency. Yet the support of other factions, such as the two Rukhs or Reforms-Centre was not automatic, as it depended on their support of the specific pro-reform measures of the executive branch. They insisted that the parliamentary majority could only support a cabinet over which they had some degree of control, rather than the presidency, which was an entirely autonomous institution, and hence unaccountable to parliament. Both the unreformed Left and, especially, the disintegrating Right could not lead the parliament single-handedly. Yet co-operation with the 'centre' was frustrated by the latter's prioritisation of the immediate interests of its leaders-cum-business persons. In particular, the oligarchs' drive to 'privatise the state' required close association with the presidency.

FROM THE PRESIDENTIAL ELECTIONS TO A CONSTITUTIONAL CRISIS

In Ukraine's third presidential elections in the autumn of 1999, the incumbent, Leonid Kuchma, was re-elected for a second term. In the aftermath of his comfortable victory, Kuchma brought the question of the constitutional division of power straight back to the top of the political agenda. Hence, the completion of the electoral cycle not only failed to reduce the inter-institutional conflict, but actually intensified it when the president staged an assault on the Supreme Council under the smokescreen of 'satisfying the popular will'. By launching an attack on the Council under the cover of a plebiscite, the president tried to emasculate the legislature.

Rather than focussing on the president's record in office and examining his ideological platform, the run up to the elections was a replication of the presidential elections in Russia of 1996 in Ukraine. Like Yeltsin, Kuchma started the campaign with less than a 10 percent popularity rating, yet successfully neutralised his toughest opponents and distracted attention from Ukraine's dire economy by invoking the fear of a 'red menace'. Like Yeltsin, Kuchma won by staging the final contest between himself and the hard-line leader of the Communist Party. As the incumbent faced the greatest challenge from the Left, Kuchma's strategy was to split the left-wing bloc into competing camps, and to block Oleksandr Moroz, the leader of the Socialist Party of Ukraine, from getting to the second round. As a moderate left candidate, Moroz was capable of appealing to a considerably wider section of the electorate than the hard-liner Symonenko, who campaigned on the radical platform of stopping or partly reversing the privatisation of state property; reverting to central economic planning and resource allocation; and repudiating the Ukraine–NATO Charter of Distinct Partnership. Kuchma's strategy succeeded because the divisions between the Left and Right thwarted a broad anti-incumbent alliance. In August 1999, four of Kuchma's opponents—Moroz, Tkachenko, Marchuk and, the mayor of Cherkasy, Oliynyk—teamed up with the aim of nominating one candidate. Yet, despite the amount of publicity it gained, the so-called 'Kaniv four' failed to deliver a joint candidate. At the last minute, Tkachenko withdrew, but not in favour of any of his Kaniv allies but the leader of the Communist Party, Petro Symonenko.

Kuchma's strategy bore fruit. While collectively, the left-wing candidates won nearly 50 percent of the vote (Moroz, Tkachenko, Vitrenko, Symonenko and other candidates), it was Symonenko with 22.24 who got to the second round, along with Kuchma, who scooped 36.49 percent. Before the second round, all the left-wing candidates threw their votes behind Symonenko, who also made a belated attempt to shift to the centre of the political spectrum, in particular by expressing his support for Ukraine's independence. Yet, Symonenko's platform proved too radical for many voters and his score of 37.8 percent in the second round was lower than for the leftist candidates in the first round, despite the fact that the candidates mobilised the rural votes in the central Ukrainian oblasts in support of Symonenko. In turn, Kuchma, who was reluctantly supported by Rukh and centrist candidates, enjoyed a comfortable victory with 56.25 percent.

The elections demonstrated the radically altered political geography of Ukraine, as the ethno-linguistic cleavage did not seem to determine voters' preferences, something which bodes better for the long-term ethnic truce in Ukraine. The elections challenged the traditional view of the political geography of Ukraine. In 1994 the election was marked by a clear-cut split into the Left- and Right-bank Ukraine. The line of division almost coincided with the line of partition of Ukraine in the mid-17 century. Kravchuk won in the West and Kuchma in the East, meaning that the political orientation correlated the ethno-linguistic divisions in Ukraine. However, the 1999 elections blurred this cleavage. The 'red belt' ran north to south from Chernihiv through Central Ukraine, Zaporizhia to the Crimea, that is through the agricultural oblasts of Ukraine. Russophone Ukraine voted for Kuchma, rather than Symonenko, despite the fact that he promised to grant Russian official status.

However, in terms of the general progress of democracy, the elections did not inspire optimism, because of widespread media intimidation, biased coverage in the state-controlled media, and interference in the campaign by the state apparatus at the regional and local level.[17] The experience of running a heavy-handed electoral campaign was soon put into successful use for a referendum, when Kuchma embarked on strengthening the presidential powers in Ukraine's president-parliamentary form of government.

Out of 13 opponents of Kuchma in the elections all but one held parliamentary seats. Hence during the campaign, Kuchma did not spare harsh criticism of parliament and sent a clear warning signal: 'either the parliament will be different or there will be no parliament'.[18] In the autumn of 1998, during the crusade against his electoral opponent, the former prime minister Pavlo Lazarenko, Kuchma called for a referendum on the abolition of the immunity mandate of the deputies on the grounds that 'some deputies belong not in parliament but behind bars'.[19] During the electoral campaign, one of his pledges was to seek 'the redistribution of power' through a referendum. After his re-election, Kuchma refused to take the oath of allegiance in the building of the parliament as a way of symbolising that he was not bound by the legislature's authority (The constitution was vague on this issue. Parliament reluctantly acceded to the president's wish to take the oath in the Palace of Ukraine only hours before the ceremony was to start.) When after the presidential elections, parliament refused to re-confirm Valerii Pustovoitenko in the post of prime minister, Kuchma announced that if there was no pro-presidential majority in the Supreme Council, the country did not need such a parliament. Thereby, the president assumed the role of an arbiter on the utility of the Ukrainian legislature, using as the main criterion whether or not parliament supported the president. The parliament 'passed the test', when the centre-right deputies backed Kuchma's pro-reform measures, by approving the chairman of the National Bank, Viktor Yushchenko, as prime minister with a 296 strong majority (out of 450) in December 1999, even if the largest faction, the communists, abstained from voting. However, the legislature 'failed' when it rejected the draft budget law in mid-January 2000.

While the Supreme Council got entangled in an internal struggle (see above), on 15 January the president pushed for an expansion of presidential powers, by decreeing on a nation-wide referendum to be held on 16 April 2000. Despite the appearance of an act of 'popular initiative', the campaign of collecting signatures was initiated and closely co-ordinated by the local and regional state apparatus subordinated to the president. In a highly efficient process, over 3-million signatures were collected by January 2000 so that the president could decree on a referendum initiated by a 'popular initiative'. According to the decree, the population was to be requested to approve a number of points:

1. no-confidence in the current parliament and changes to art. 90 of the constitution giving the president the right to dissolve the legislature if a popular referendum votes on no-confidence in parliament;
2. changes to art. 90 of the constitution granting the president the right to disband the parliament if it does not form a majority within one month after the elections, or approve the state budget within three months;
3. the limitation of the immunity of deputies (and the appropriate changes to the art. 80 of the constitution);

4. a reduction of the size of the lower chamber from 450 to 300 (and appropriate changes to art. 76);

5. the creation of an upper chamber of legislature in order to represent regional interests; and

6. consent to the constitution being amended in a nation-wide referendum.

The legislative basis for the referendum was so inconsistent (the outdated 1991 law of referendum stayed in force only insofar as it did not contradict the 1996 constitution) that it could not function as a guide for conducting a referendum. The issue of the decree coincided with the intensification of the anti-parliamentary campaign in the state-controlled media. Amongst other indictments, Kuchma claimed that the Supreme Council was unrepresentative on the grounds that only 2 percent of the population were members of political parties, yet parties were allocated 50 percent seats in the 1998 parliament.[20]

The decree led to consternation on the domestic scene and international condemnation of Ukraine. The parliamentary factions, ranging from Rukh to the CPU, condemned the idea of the plebiscite and the Supreme Council issued a moratorium on any plebiscites until the new law was passed. The president simply ignored it. The Council of Europe expressed its concern over the referendum, and, in particular, the lack of an appropriate legislative basis, and the encroachment on the parliament's powers. Despite the ruling of the Constitutional Court (see below), in early April 2000 the Council of Europe recommended that Ukraine postpone the referendum until the new bill on referendum was adopted, and threatened to suspend Ukraine's membership of the Council if the referendum was conducted unconstitutionally or the results were implemented in breach of the constitution. The recommendation was widely criticised in the state-controlled media by the presidential entourage, as an act of interference in Ukraine's internal matters. Kuchma was not to back off on this occasion (as he did in 1995 and 1996). Yet, as on previous occasions, the president insisted that he only obeyed the 'sovereign will of the people' (see chapter 6).

The legal consternation was reflected in the ruling of the Constitutional Court, which was drawn in as an adjudicator after a group of 108 deputies filed a case in the Court on the unconstitutionality of Kuchma's decree. In the face of mounting tension and international critique, the Constitutional Court issued its pivotal ruling on 27 March 2000. The ruling endeavoured to square the circle by attempting to reconcile the principle of popular sovereignty (expressed in art. 5 'the people are the bearers of sovereignty and the only source of power in Ukraine'), on the one hand, with the doctrine of constitutionalism, according to which the 'popular will' was subject to constitutional limitations, on the other. The Court's decision prioritised the former principle over the latter, although the power of the 'popular will' was somewhat curtailed. The Court decided to uphold four out of the six questions, despite the fact that the constitution specifies a procedure for the enactment of amendments to the constitution (according to article 156, the referendum is specified as one of the procedural requirements for changes to some chapters of the constitution, but takes place *after* the Supreme Council voted in favour of changes by a constitutional majority). The ruling, sketchy and contradictory in its spirit, nevertheless struck off the two questions which if supported by the population would have allowed for amendments to the constitution to be enacted on the sole basis of the referendum (hence by-passing the legislature altogether) and would have granted the president the right to dissolve the Supreme Council. The Court also stated that any changes to the constitution could only be made in accordance with Chapter XIII 'Introducing Amendments to the Constitution'.

Undoubtedly, the exclusion of the two questions eliminated the imminent and gravest threat to the constitutional order and principles of constitutionalism in Ukraine, and hence was welcome by the parliamentarians, who feared the onset of autocratic, presidential rule in Ukraine. Oleksandr Moroz, the leader of the Socialist Party of Ukraine, proclaimed it as a 'victory of rule of law'. Serhiy Holovatyi, the most ardent anti-referendum campaigner in the Ukrainian delegation to the Council of Europe, reckoned that:

> The possibility of introducing a new constitution of Ukraine by using this referendum has been eliminated. That's a blow against those forces that wanted to put Ukraine on the same track as [Belarussian president Aleksander] Lukashenka ... By its decision, the Constitutional Court has supported parliament as an institution.[21]

The ruling, however, did not eliminate the doubts over the constitutionality of the referendum. In particular, the Court's insistence that the results of the referendum were 'binding' for all state institutions was difficult to square with its assertion that only parliament can change the constitution; in accordance with the principle of the separation of powers, no court or any other institution can order the legislature, as a sovereign branch of power, to approve any law. By 'informing' the legislature of its duties, the Court overstepped its authority. The Court's arbitration on the referendum was an example of the precarious task of taming the power conflict by subjecting it to a judicial decision, when the legislative framework was patchy and hence open to conflicting interpretations. By being implicated and issuing a controversial ruling which tempered the worst excesses of the decree but essentially did not prevent the abuse of the contradictory legislative framework by the president, the Court did not escape the damning of its reputation, from which its dented image of a neutral arbiter is not likely to recover in the nearest future.

The results of the referendum on the 16 April 2000 exceeded the most optimistic expectations of the presidential circles and hence indirectly confirmed the widespread interference of the state administration or even the outright falsification of results in some oblasts. Prior to the referendum, the opinion polls indicated that the Ukrainians would give approval to all the questions, yet, the turn-out would be low. Yet, the application of the 'administrative measures', that is various forms of pressure and intimidation by the state administration at the local level, secured the turn-out of 78.99 percent. According to the official results, the electorate gave overwhelming approval to all four proposals, with the reduction of the number of deputies from 450 to 300 gaining the highest rate of approval, 90 percent (Table 8.3).

Table 8.3. The Results of the Referendum in April 2000

Issue	*Yes*	*No*	*Spoiled Ballots*
Lifting of the immunity mandate	*89.2*	*9.8*	*1.2*
The creation of the bi-cameral parliament	*81.8*	*16.7*	*1.4*
The reduction of the number of deputies from 450 to 300	*90.0*	*8.7*	*1.2*
The right of the president to dissolve the Supreme Council if it does not form a majority within one month or approve a budget in three months	*85.0*	*13.6*	*1.3*

Source: Postup, 18 April 2000.

The announcement of the results instantly sparked debates on how the results should be acted upon. The questions not only provided poor directions for constitutional amendments, despite the fact that their wording included what looked like ready-made phrases to amend the constitution, but a number of pivotal issues were remained unresolved.

The question on bi-cameralism did not specify the powers, mode of creation and size of the upper chamber. The question about the reduction of the number of deputies did not specify which chamber that number applied to: the lower one or both. The question regarding the immunity mandate did not stipulate if immunity was to be abolished or only limited. In the light of the limited role of the Supreme Council in the appointment of the cabinet of ministers, it was unclear what role of parliamentary majority was to be apart from preventing the president from dissolving the legislature. Oleksandr Lavrynovych, a prominent deputy, commented:

> Regarding the question of the dissolution of the parliament if the Supreme Council cannot form a permanently functioning majority or approve a budget in three months, it is doubtful if such words can pretend to become legal norms. A majority can be created the day after the new parliament convenes, and 450 deputies can join it. And then this majority will not be capable of electing a speaker for a whole year or approve a prime minister, despite the fact that it formally exists.[22]

The referendum vividly demonstrated the overwhelming domination of the presidency on the political landscape of Ukraine. Apart from evidencing the weakness of institutions such as the Central Electoral Commission, which proved a docile being in the president's hands, the referendum also exposed the impotence of other actors. While many parties, ranging from the Communists, Socialists to Rukh and 'Reforms and Order', criticised the referendum, they not only failed to build an inclusive anti-referendum alliance, but even within individual parties internal dissent prevented them from adopting coherent strategies.[23] The newly formed parliamentary majority was crippled by conflicts between the more principled, party-based factions, and factions advancing the interests and ambitions of the oligarchs, such as the 'Revival of Regions' and SDPU(U). Their diverse objectives came out into the open after the plebiscite. Factions, such as the two Rukhs and Reforms-Centre, conceded only to the limiting of the parliament immunity. The 'Revival of Regions' faction, in contrast, insisted that the president had a moral right to dissolve the Supreme Council in the event that it does not adopt all the changes to the constitution.[24] It appeared that the 'oligarchic' factions adopted a course on the dissolution of parliament in the expectation that pre-term elections would provide a chance for stronger representation in the Supreme Council.

Nevertheless, there were some positive steps taken. Pro-reform factions responded to the initiative of the cabinet headed by Victor Yushchenko by signing a memorandum on mutual responsibility (*solidarna vidpovidalnist*) in April 2000. The memorandum envisaged closer co-operation between the government and parliament, including extra-constitutional instruments such as consultations and the presence of deputies at meetings of commissions of the cabinet in order to agree on a common position prior to tabling of draft laws. Yet, Yushchenko's cabinet failed to win the support of the oligarchic factions, which found his reformist drive in the energy sector in particular, harmful to their business interests.

TIPPING THE BALANCE TOWARDS SUPER-PRESIDENTIALISM?

Notwithstanding the flawed legitimacy of the referendum, it appeared to open the door to piecemeal constitutional reform. Yet a scandal which broke in the autumn 2000 weakened the president to the extent that his plans *vis-à-vis* the legislature has been floundered. However, while popular pressure has not been strong enough to oust Kuchma, neither has the parliament been capable of acting unanimously to bring about his downfall. While the international image of Ukraine has been given a serious blow by the fact that its head of state has been implicated in a murder of a journalist, the president survived, not least because of the determined use of the instruments of control over the media, judiciary, procuracy, as well as the support of the oligarchic factions in parliament.

The ruptured Supreme Council seemed easy prey for the president's hunt for more powers. This was especially so as Kuchma enjoyed the tacit backing of the Constitutional Court, the approval of which was crucial for any changes to the constitution to be enacted. In summer 2000, two alternative draft constitutional amendments were prepared by the president and parliamentary left wing. While the president sought to enact the changes approved in the referendum, the Left aimed at a more fundamental shift of the balance of power between the legislature and executive in favour of the former. The Court's decision that the presidential draft satisfied the criteria of article 157,[25] without announcing its decision on the second draft, revealed overtly political motives for the way the Court prioritised the cases. Under pressure from the parliament, the Court issued a ruling on the opposition's draft in which it approved only the provisions that coincided with the narrow proposals in the president's draft, on the grounds that other proposed amendments were not directly related to the questions addressed in the referendum.[26] By insisting that only changes initiated in the president's referendum could be incorporated into the constitution, the Court's stance contravened the parliament's power to initiate changes to the constitution at any time.

The parliament's fortunes were rescued by the temporary weakening of the presidency in the aftermath of the so-called Gongadze scandal. The release of audiocassettes by a former security guard, Mykola Melnychenko, of recordings allegedly from Kuchma's office, implicated the president in the death of a opposition journalist critical of the regime, Hryhoriy Gongadze. He disappeared in September 2000 and his body was found two months later. The revelations sparked popular anti-Kuchma protests and prompted the creation of a number of anti-president oppositional organisations, such as the 'National Salvation Forum' and 'For the Truth' (*Za Pravdu*), aimed at pressuring Kuchma into resignation. While Kuchma succumbed to the pressure to remove some state officials discredited for their interference in the investigation of the Gongadze scandal, such as Yuriy Kravchenko, the Minister of Internal Affairs, he refused to step down himself. After a couple of months, the strength of mass demonstrations waned away, as the fragmented opposition proved unable to unite, let alone to galvanise the disillusioned and cynical Ukrainian citizenry into mass protests against the discredited head of state. Most importantly, the oppositional movements did not find the necessary backing amongst the parliamentarians. The legislature failed to initiate coherent steps against the president, because the oligarchic factions stood firmly behind Kuchma, linked by intricate business ties to the presidential administration. Impeachment procedures turned out too difficult to initiate not only because of the problems with mustering a sufficient number of votes but also because of the lack of an appropriate legislative framework. By the spring of 2001 as relations between the parliament and Yushchenko's cabinet became the focus of attention, it appeared that Kuchma weathered the political storm. However, the issue of constitutional amendments to emasculate the parliament was removed from the parliamentary agenda as there was no prospect for a constitutional, two-thirds majority under the circumstances.

The events of winter and spring 2001 revealed not only the extent of Kuchma's control of the law enforcement forces in Ukraine but also his symbiotic relations with the oligarchic factions. The ousting of Yushchenko's cabinet, the most reformist government Ukraine has had since independence, amply demonstrated the corrosive influence of the oligarchic factions on the parliament's actions and the progress of economic reforms in Ukraine. While officially the centre-right majority, proclaimed in early 2000, still existed, the 'centrist' factions, such as the Social-Democratic Party of Ukraine, the Labour Ukraine, Yabluko, and the Democratic Union, allied with the Communists in their opposition to Yushchenko. As only the two Rukhs and the faction of the party 'Reforms and Order' stood behind the embattled prime minister, he was voted out of office with 263 votes in favour and 59 against. Even if the president refrained from dismissing Yushchenko himself, he swiftly acted upon his removal by the communist–oligarchic coalition and—as it turned out—scooped the benefits of the prime minister's departure. Not only did he install a more compliant figure, Anatoliy Kinakh, the head of the Ukrainian Union of Industrialists and Entrepreneurs, in charge of government, but also assured more direct control over the cabinet.

The role of the cabinet of ministers and its relations with the president and the parliament remained ill-defined, because of the president's refusal to sign the 'Law on the Cabinet of Ministers'. Still the Soviet-era notion of the government as a technocratic collective body in charge of the implementation of socio-economic policies was difficult to sustain for much longer. The cabinet's political accountability not only to the president but also to the parliament made its role a pivotal bone of contention between the parliament and the president since the passage of the constitution. While continuing to block the parliament's legislation, the president once again decided to take the lead and tip the balance in his favour. By strengthening his control over the administrative structures of the cabinet and shifting the balance of power within the cabinet in favour of the administrative component of the cabinet, the president wanted to counteract the ongoing process of 'politicisation' of the cabinet. This process resulted from the tendency for the prime ministers to develop their political agenda irrespective of the president and for the parliament to exercise its control, however limited, over the government. In the decree 'On Measures to Continue Carrying out Administrative Reform in Ukraine', the president created a new institution of a state secretary, a post which was designed to provide greater stability in government 'regardless of the political and economic situation'. According to the decree, state secretaries were to be appointed by the president for his term of office, five years, and their job was not to terminate with the change of government. By usurping the parliament's right to regulate the organisation of the cabinet of ministers, the president's decree readily exploited the loopholes in the constitution, blatantly disregarding the corresponding rights of the parliament (see above).

With the implementation of the pro-presidential amendments to the constitution halted in late 2000, the prospects for constitutional reform leading to a creation of a super-presidential system have rescinded. This is despite the fact that Kuchma did not change his views and bemoaned his 'limited' powers:

> I believe there must be a totally presidential form of rule during the transition period. [W]hy does the USA not reject the presidential form of rule and no one speaks about any sort of attacks on anything there? It appears that only the Ukrainian president has no opportunity to dissolve the parliament even when it is completely inefficient.[27]

Yet even though he failed to expand his constitutional prerogatives, the informal distribution of power continues to make the president an unrivalled force on the Ukrainian political arena. There is no sign of the president voluntarily relinquishing his existing powers over the executive branch, which is a *sine qua non* for the gradual evolution of the political system in Ukraine towards a parliamentary form of government. Without a solution in sight, it appears that the shadow of the ill-thought institutional framework is bound to hunt Ukraine for the foreseeable future.

CONCLUSION

In the aftermath of the collapse of the Soviet Union, the region witnessed a proliferation of powerful presidencies.[28] That the institution came under the scrutiny is hardly surprising in light of the claims made regarding Latin America, where presidentialism was held responsible for the breakdown of nascent democracies because of its inherent structural problems, which had tended to trigger conflict and instability.[29] Amongst post-Soviet states, Ukraine provides powerful ammunition for the critiques of systems with directly elected, executive presidencies.

While considering the arguments that presidential democracy is prone to breakdown and leads to abuses of power in contrast to 'benevolent' parliamentarism, Shugart and Carey stress the need for a clear distinction between two different types of 'presidentialism': firstly those with 'presidential constitutions that are formally democratic but fail', and secondly 'those in which formal presidential dominance over other actors precludes workable checks and balances to begin with'.[30] It is clear that the majority of the former Soviet republics, such as Belarus, Azerbaijan or Kazakhstan, fall into the second category. In those countries the constitutions were devised for particular office holders and never meant to provide a normative framework for genuinely pluralistic politics. Ukraine, however, belongs to the first category: its democratic 'presidential constitution' was lawfully passed by the country's legislature and endeavoured to strike a balance between a desire for decisive leadership and asserting the role of the legislature. Yet soon such a design led to a crippling conflict between the legislature and president. To decisively tip the balance in his favour, the president launched an attack on the constitutional order. The most grave assault took the form of a constitutional plebiscite, during which Kuchma exploited his popular mandate and abused control over the administrative structures. Although the initiative failed to bear fruit, there are clear warning signals that Ukraine is on a slippery slope moving towards a system in which, even if it does not appear super-presidential in constitutional terms, the accumulation of informal mechanisms of pressure and populist instruments in the hands of the presidency contradicts the constitutional principle of limited government. Therefore, despite the overall positive balance sheet of the first couple years of Kuchma's first presidency when the institution provided a much-needed sense of direction and impetus for reforms,[31] the experience of Ukraine provides a powerful indictment of executive presidencies. The incumbent's incessant drive to increase presidential powers rather than voluntarily relinquish them suggests that without a careful revision of the constitutional distribution of powers, the conflict is unlikely to abate. However, prospects for any constitutional revisions of that type are remote, to say the least. In this context, the strife between the president and parliament will continue to be a trademark of Ukrainian politics under the 1996 constitution.

NOTES

1 The terms of 'upstream' and 'downstream' were coined by Jon Elster in 'Afterward: the making of postcommunist presidencies', in. Ray Taras (ed.), *Postcommunist Presidents* (Cambridge: Cambridge University Press, 1997), p. 225.

2 Mykola Tomenko, *Samovyznachenia Ukrainy: vid istorii do polityky (The Self-Determination of Ukraine: from History to Politics)* (Kyiv: Zapovit, 1998), p. 129.
3 Author's interview, London, December 1998.
4 *Zerkalo Nedeli*, 27 July 1996.
5 *Ukrnews*, 23 January 1997.
6 The law was published in *Uriadovyi Kurier*, 14 June 1997.
7 Kataryna Wolczuk, 'The Constitutional Court in Ukraine' in Wojciech Sadurski (ed.), *Constitutional Justice, East and West* (Oxford: Oxford University Press, forthcoming).
8 *Holos Ukrainy*, 18 November 1998, p. 3.
9 *Visnyk Programmy Spryiania Parlamentovi Ukrainy*, Nos. 2–3 (37–8), 9 June 1999, p. 11.
10 Vasyl Kremen', 'Resurs vlady (Resources of Power)', *Uriadovyi Kurier*, 8 July 1997.
11 As a result the system became less preferential for the political parties. However, as the ruling was announced when the campaign was in full swing and after the registration of all the candidates was completed, the parliament decided that the ruling could not be applied retrospectively, hence, it would apply to the future elections.
12 The Supreme Council failed to adopt the new Rules of Procedures (*Reglament*), so the old *Reglament* of July 1994, despite the fact that it was not passed as a law, was outdated and in many places contradicted the constitution, remained in force.
13 This was most vividly demonstrated in the vote Tkachenko orchestrated on Ukraine's entry to political arm of the CIS, the Inter-Parliamentary Assembly in April 1999, in spite of the stance of the presidential administration.
14 Oleksiy Haran' and Oleksandr Maiboroda, *Obrannia Oleksandra Tkachenka spiker-om i perehrupyvannia livykh syl (The Election of Oleksandr Tkachenko to the Post of the Speaker and the Reshuffle of Left-wing Forces),* Mimeo, Centre for Studies of National Security, Kyiv, (September 1999).
15 *Visnyk Programmy Spryiania Parlamentovi Ukrainy*, No. 1(36) (10 February 1999), p. 8.
16 See 'Kontrolni funktsii Parlamentu (The Overseeing Functions of the Parliament)', *Visnyk Programmy Spryiannia Parlamentovi Ukrainy*, Nos. 2–3, (9 June 1999).
17 The conduct of the elections was observed by the OSCE, the Council of Europe and European Institute of Media. The OSCE condemned violations which took place on the voting days, such as multiple voting, the presence of security forces, falsification of voting attendance so in some electoral polling states it showed over 100 percent and so forth. But according to the OSCE, such violations were not widespread. The Organisation reserved the harshest criticism for what it called 'comprehensive interference' in the electoral campaign by the state apparatus and the heavy media bias. At the regional and local level, state employees were in charge of Kuchma's campaign. Access to non-partisan information was limited, while state-controlled media were biased in favour of the incumbent, but others worked for a specific candidate as well (the private STB station harassed). Some analysts describe this situation as 'mediated violation': there were no gross violations on the polling day; everything happened in the run-up to the elections. However, the international organisations which monitored the elections did not challenge the results. See the OSCE report on the presidential elections (November 1999).

18 Oleksandr Holovko, 'Winter Storms Ahead', *The Ukrainian Observer*, Issue 27, No. 1 (23 December 1999).
19 *Kyiv Post,* 3 November 1998.
20 Ukrainian TV, UTN1, 14 April 2000.
21 *RFE/RL Poland, Belarus, Ukraine Report*, 31 March 2000.
22 *Den',* 18 April 2000, p. 4.
23 For example, Udovenko's Rukh was torn apart between the outright boycott and 'negative answers' to 3 questions and a positive one to the question of lifting the immunity mandate.
24 A statement by a member of the 'Revival of Regions' faction, Oleksiy Kucharenko on STB Channel, 17 April 2000.
25 See the decision of the Constitutional Court of Ukraine, Re: Changes to Articles 76, 80, 90, 106 of the Constitution of Ukraine, 27 June 2000, (N 1–38/2000).
26 See the decision of the Constitutional Court of Ukraine, Re: Changes to the Constitution upon the Initiative of the People's Deputies of Ukraine, 11 July 2000, (N 1–39/2000).
27 Ukrainian Television Second Programme, 12 June 2001 cited in BBC Monitoring Global Newsline—FSU Political, 12 June 2001.
28 On post-communist presidencies see Timothy J. Colton and Robert C. Tucker (eds.), *Patterns of Post-Soviet Leadership* (Boulder: Westview Press, 1995) and Ray Taras, 'Separating power: keeping presidents in check', in. Ray Taras (ed.), *Postcommunist Presidents.*
29 See, for example, J. J. Linz and A. Valenzuela (eds.), *The Failure of Presidential Democracy: Comparative Perspective* (Baltimore & London: The Johns Hopkins University Press, 1994); A. Lijphart, 'Constitutional Choices for New Democracies', *Journal of Democracy*, Vol. 2, No. 1 (Winter 1991), pp. 73–84; A. Lijphart, 'Democracies: Forms, Performance, and Constitutional Engineering', *European Journal of Political Research*, Vol. 25, No. 1 (January 1994), pp. 1–16; S. Mainwaring, 'Presidentialism, Multipartism, and Democracy: the Difficult Combination', *Comparative Political Studies*, Vol. 26, No. 2 (July 1993), pp. 198–222.
30 Matthew S. Shugart and John M. Carey, *Presidents and Assemblies: Constitutional Design and Electoral Dynamics* (Cambridge: Cambridge University Press, 1992), p. 36.
31 Kataryna Wolczuk, 'Presidentialism in Ukraine: A Mid-Term Review of the Second Presidency', *Democratization*, Vol. 4, No. 3 (Autumn 1997), pp. 152–71.

CONCLUSION

Ukraine began its independence in 1991 able to draw on very limited experience of independent statehood and no experience of having to abide by a legitimate, effective and *limiting* constitutional framework. Hence constitution making after the demise of communism embodied both aspirations to build a polity capable of surviving, as well as the desire to encode a set of rules that would effectively govern the polity. As such, Ukraine's constitutional process was not only inspired by a longing for constitutionalism, reflected in the idea of limited government, but also by the need to build a strong state. In other words, constitution making had multiple aims. This made the case of Ukraine qualitatively different from cases of established states, where constitution making aimed, above all, to provide the basis for the development of constitutionalism. This multiplicity of aims shaped the outcome of the process in Ukraine. The lack of a shared understanding of independence was reflected in the profound disagreement on the fundamental questions of statehood. This disagreement, illuminated by prolonged and hotly contested constitution drafting, cast a shadow over the legitimacy and viability of the state. Under such circumstances, state building became the main objective of the constitutional process. The evolution of the conception of statehood over time symbolised the gradual distancing by the elites from the Soviet constitutional model and a move towards a model of a European nation-state. Thus, upon its passage in 1996, the constitution was proclaimed a milestone in the process of state formation. The constitution was to assume a boundary-setting function: it set the parameters of political discourse on the fundamental questions of the polity, which, it was hoped, would either cease to be an object of contestation, or at least confine the contestation within clearly delineated rules and procedures. It was envisaged that stability would be the result of such boundary setting. However, ten years after independence and five after the passage of the constitution, Ukraine can hardly be regarded as a more stable and orderly country, either in the eyes of its own citizenry, the elites or the international community. This prolonged crisis grossly affected Ukraine's chances of asserting its 'Europeanness' in institutional terms, as the European Union has kept Ukraine at arms' length, abhorred by its internal turmoil. Thus the question emerges of why the passage of the constitution, despite the lofty declarations and high expectations, has failed to mark a breakthrough in the way politics are conducted in Ukraine. These concluding remarks will try to shed light on this question. This will be done, first of all, by reflecting on the evolution of thinking on statehood over 1990–1996 and the state-building role of the constitution, and, secondly, by considering why the constitution has not put an end to the debilitating pattern of political instability.

The conception of statehood enshrined in the 1996 constitution differed radically from the one prevailing at the onset of the constitutional process. In 1990–1991, the system of soviets, reinforced by elements of presidentialism, was preferred. The political community was defined in territorial–political and not ethno-cultural terms, and the 'socialist choice' remained the cornerstone of the ideological superstructure of the state. Over 1990–1996, constitution making amounted to a gradual shift away from a vision of statehood anchored in the Soviet dogmas to the conception of a nation-state, described in the Western *lingua franca* of constitutional theory.[1] What had been 'radical' and 'nationalist' views propagated by the opposition in 1990 had, by 1996, become the views of the majority (even if, in the case of some issues, only situational). In the shifting domestic and international context, the ideas of the previous opposition gained wider resonance and acceptance, while the Soviet-era models and concepts have loosened their pervasive grip on the key sections of the political elites.[2] Constitution making represented an intensely ideological period of large-scale and fiercely contested change of the worldview of the key section of the elites (albeit without any outbreaks of violence). The constitution amounted to a landmark for the 'European option' in Ukrainian politics. This was despite the fact that the evolution from a 'Soviet' to a 'European' perspective was not achieved by all actors at the same time. A considerable proportion of the political elite with communist leanings never fully embraced an ideal of sovereign statehood, a 'return to Europe', and the 'superiority' of Western principles over the 'indigenous Soviet' tradition. Yet, the peaceful passage of the constitution, despite all the odds, was presented as yet more evidence of Ukrainians' European provenience:

> Ukraine yet again proved that it is not Russia. Even in the most difficult of times, [Ukrainian] politicians are capable of finding lawful solutions, without resorting to the use of tanks. And such a civilised route meant that we are, nevertheless, Eastern Europe and not Western Asia.[3]

Undoubtedly, the idealised conception of Ukraine as a nation-state was filtered through and 'enriched' by various individual, institutional and group interests. But even if the interests gave shape to many specific institutional solutions, in general, they tended to reinforce, rather than weaken, the shift away from the Soviet legacy, the interests of the presidency were especially instrumental in that respect. Even though the proponents of the old order remained numerous and vocal, they failed to reach across the ideological gap to co-operate with those centrist forces, which opposed the ethno-national assertion of statehood. Coerced by the president, a critical mass in favour of the new constitution was mastered, even if the merits of specific constitutional norms were questioned by some deputies.

The passage of the constitution crystallised the situation in fundamental terms: those in favour and those against a sovereign Ukraine. The group of parliamentarians, who voted for the constitution and then swore an oath of allegiance to it, effectively came to symbolise the strength of the pro-statehood orientation in Ukrainian politics.[4] An overarching consensus on the primacy of Ukrainian sovereignty was symbolically sanctioned in the formalised procedure of voting by a constitutional majority in parliament. Arguably, Ukraine required six years of a constitutional process to finalise its passage to independence; that is to come to terms with the meaning of independence and hammer out a conception of statehood.

Therefore, the passage of the constitution was instantly proclaimed as the most important event in Ukraine since the referendum on independence in 1991. The constitution has been canonised in public discourse, public holidays, anniversaries of independence, the school curriculum and so forth.[5] It acquired the status of a symbolic attribute of sovereignty and a 'secular catechism of the state'. This celebrated status reflected the constitution's perceived role in state building, something which was expressed by a Ukrainian constitutional lawyer on the eve of its passage:

> There is no state without a constitution. The construction of statehood begins from the time of the adoption of a constitution. What we have now—is a transitional period. To finish that period, we have to adopt a constitution and to resolve all political issues among parties, political convictions, and political values within the frameworks of a national state, which will be built.[6]

To this end, the role of the constitution in post-Soviet Ukraine was predominantly viewed through the prism of state building. This preoccupation was hardly new or surprising. Attainment of statehood constituted the Ariadne's thread of Ukraine's history in the twentieth century:

> The motives for national self-determination through a constitution animated the actions of the authors of the [constitutional] documents of UNR, ZUNR, Hetman Skoropadskyi and Directory, and the leaders of the national-liberation movement and dissidents. The constitutional debates of the contemporary Ukrainian state also took place under the banner of national liberation, while the content of the document and its legal justification was of secondary importance ... The historic struggle for the constitution was most of all a struggle for a national ideology, a national idea, and not for the Basic Law of the state and its citizens.[7]

In the context of the prioritisation of state formation, the limiting function of the constitution stemming from the original *telos* of constitutionalism did not inspire the minds of the drafters to the same degree that state- and nation-building did. The idea of the constitution as a fundamental set of principles and correlated institutional arrangements that would restrict the arbitrary use of state power was put on the backburner. That the role of the constitution as an embodiment of constitutionalism was assigned a lower priority was evidenced in two ways. Firstly, under the acutely felt pressure of time, the profound ideological rift prevented systematic, detailed, legalistic deliberations on the consequences of particular norms adopted. This omission was especially evident when Ukraine is compared with other post-communist countries, such as Poland where constitution making took place almost simultaneously and culminated in 1997. In Poland, the tedious debates on the exact distribution of powers between the branches of power were inspired by the desire to craft a constitution that would safeguard constitutionalism. In particular, the experience of law-twisting excesses that characterised Lech Wałęsa's presidency in the early 1990s prompted thorough deliberations on the possible interpretations and potential consequences of any particular norm.[8] Yet, in Ukraine, politicians rather than lawyers had the final say over the content of the constitution with the result that the quality of the final product as the legal foundation of the polity, as opposed to a political manifesto, was much more dubious. Secondly, as the elites struggled to develop a conception of statehood out of diverse ideas and interests, the prioritisation of state building made the elites opt for an institutional framework, including the centralised territorial–administrative model and an executive presidency, which—as it soon turned out—was not necessarily conducive to promote the principles of constitutionalism.

When it came to the institutional choices, the proclaimed focus on state building concealed an important divergence between aims of the various actors involved in the process. Under the banner of consolidation of the state, members of the post-communist elites succeeded in acquiring institutional prerogatives, which may have been otherwise denied to them. That the notion of the state building was exploited to pursue the narrow agenda of office holders was most amply demonstrated by president Kuchma. For the incumbent the passage of the constitution was merely a stage in the pursuit of unconstrained political domination on the political landscape. The poorly delineated executive powers of the presidency enabled him to consolidate power by exploiting constitutional loopholes in addition to other non-constitutional means. Therefore, the prioritisation of state building during constitution making facilitated not only the retention but the expansion of power by some members of the former nomenklatura elites.

Many constitution drafters made a tacit, hopeful assumption that once the constitution had been adopted, the principles of constitutionalism, including structured and regulated interactions between the branches of power within their respective constitutional boundaries of authority, would follow suit. And yet as was demonstrated in the final chapter of this study, the dearth of legalistic foresight soon proved to have dire consequences for regulating executive–legislative relations. The design of the legislative–executive relations put the branches of government on a collision course, something, which jeopardised the constitutional order by inducing conflict and uncertainty. The ill-designed constitutional framework, beside all other factors, has contributed to the perpetuation of inter-institutional strife in Ukraine, which has crippled the country's capacity to advance its political and economic transformation. With little progress made in the transformation, ten years after the proclamation of independence Ukraine remains weak and unstable.

NOTES

1 Incidentally, there were some linguistic hurdles to be passed. There was no agreed Ukrainian translation of the 'separation of powers' which was translated as *podil* and *rozpodil*, and in the spring of 1996, while the constitution was drafted, linguistic experts stipulated that the *podil* should be used.

2 The dominant discourse on 'normality', 'civilised practices' and 'universal models' in the constitutional process forced even the Left to adjust its language; as a result they attempted to present the Soviet model in terms of 'universal' values of democratic accountability, human rights, prevention of dictatorship, popular sovereignty etc. See, for example, *Holos Ukrainy*, 26 December 1995.

3 *Molod' Ukrainy*, 2 July 1996, p. 1.

4 Whereas 90 deputies refused to take an oath of allegiance to the new constitution in July 1996, by December only 57 communists and 6 other deputies had not sworn their allegiance (*Den*, 20 December 1996).

5 A public holiday was established on 28 June to mark the day of the passage of the constitution. The study of the constitution became a compulsory part of the national curriculum in secondary schools and higher education.

6 Comments by professor Petro Martynenko, a constitutional law expert who participated in the drafting of the constitution, during the TV Youth Political Talk Shaw organised to publicise the constitutional process in the spring of 1996. Transcripts of the show were kindly provided by the International Foundation of Electoral Systems, Kyiv.

7 Mykola Tomenko, *Samovyznachenia Ukrainy: vid istorii do polityky*, pp. 127–8.

8 On constitution making in Poland see Mark Brzezinski, *The Struggle for Constitutionalism in Poland* (Houndmills and London: Macmillan, 1998).

BIBLIOGRAPHY

PRIMARY SOURCES

ARCHIVAL MATERIALS AND DOCUMENTS

Central State Archive of Civic Organisations of Ukraine (CSACOU) (the former archive of the CPU);

The Materials of the Constitutional Commission (1990–1994). The materials were kept by Mr Anatolii Zaiets of the Secretariat of the Supreme Council, who was responsible for the technical support of the Constitutional Commission between 1990–1994. Mr Zaiets made the Materials available to the author in the summer of 1997. At the time when the fieldwork was conducted, they were not catalogued. In 1999 the Materials were deposited in the Central State Archive of Civil Organisations of Ukraine (CSACOU);

The Materials of the Special Conciliatory Group and Temporary Extraordinary Commission on the Preparation of the Draft Constitution of the Supreme Council. The Materials were kept by Ms Valentyna Dorhozhkina, who provided secretarial support to the Group and Commission. She provided access to them in the summer of 1997;

Stenographic Records of the Session of the Supreme Council (25–28 June 1996) (the electronic version was provided by Mr. Ihor Koliushko);

Kontseptsia Novoi Konstytutsii Ukrainy z chervnia 1991 (The Concept of the New Constitution of Ukraine of June 1991);

Proiekt Konstytutsii z chervnia 1992 (Draft Constitution of June 1992);

Proiekt Konstytutsii z zhovtnia 1993 (Draft Constitution of October 1993);

Konstytutsiinyi Dohovir (The 'Constitutional Agreement on the Temporary Organisation and Functioning of State Powers and Local Self-government in Ukraine until the Passage of the New Constitution' of 8 June 1995);

Proiekt Konstytutsii z lystopada 1995 (Draft Constitution of November 1995);

Proiekt Konstytutsii z lutoho 1996 (Draft Constitution of February 1996);

Proiekt Konstututsii z travnia 1996 (Draft Constitution of May 1996, the so-called Syrota draft);

Konstytutsiia Ukrainy (The Constitution of Ukraine adopted on 28 June 1996);

*Biuletyn Verkhovnoi Rady (*Bulletins of the Supreme Council which contain stenographic records of parliamentary debates);

Kontseptsia Derzhavotvorenia v Ukraini (2–4 December 1992). (The 'Conception of State-Building' adopted by the Fourth All Ukrainian Congress of Rukh);

Oleksandr Burakovsky (ed.), *The Council of Nationalities, Popular Movement of Ukraine (Rukh), 1989–1993* (University of Alberta: Canadian Institute of Ukrainian Studies, 1995) (in Ukrainian);

Konstytutsiini Akty Ukrainy (Constitutional Acts of Ukraine), 1917–1920 (Kyiv, 1992).

Texts of the Declaration of Nationalities' Rights and 'Law on National Minorities' (published in *Informatsiinyi Biuletyn,* No. 2, June 1995, the Ministry for the Affairs of Nationalities, Migration and Cults;

Materials of the International Symposium 'Project of the Constitution of Ukraine' (The Ukrainian Legal Foundation), 20–22 June 1993 (in English);

Materialy Kruhloho Stola (Materials of the Round Table organised by the Ukrainian Legal Foundation in December 1994);

Transcripts of the TV Programme 'Youth Political Talk Show' broadcast in the spring of 1996, the International Foundation for Electoral Systems (in English);

Vidomosti Verkhovhoi Rady, which contain the normative acts adopted by the Supreme Council;

VI Vseukrainski Zbory Narodnoho Rukhu Ukrainy, 15–17 December 1995, (6th Congress of People's Rukh of Ukraine, Stenographic Records);

Zakon pro Prezydenta UkrSSR (The 'Law on the Creation of the Presidency of the Ukrainian Soviet Socialist Republic and Changes to the Constitution of UkrSSR' of 5 July 1991);

*Zakon pro Predstavnyka Prezydenta Ukrainy (*The Law on the Representative of the President of Ukraine, February 1992);

Zakon pro Vybory Narodnykh Deputativ Ukrainy (The 'Law on the Elections of People's Deputies of Ukraine' of 18 December 1993).

INTERVIEWS CONDUCTED BY THE AUTHOR

Valerii Bebyk, consultant, the Presidential Administration, Kyiv (November 1995).

Roman Bezsmertnyi, member of the 'Statehood' and then Constitutional Centre factions and the presidential representative in the Supreme Council, Kyiv (November 1995 and September 1996).

Fedir Burchak, professor of law, vice-president of the Academy of Legal Science, advisor to the President of Ukraine, Kyiv (April 1997).

Mykola Dudchenko, member of the 'SelPU' faction, Kyiv (September 1996).

Vadym Het'man, head of the faction 'Independents', Kyiv (September 1996).

Ihor Koliushko, member of the 'Reforms' faction, Kyiv (November 1995 and September 1996), Birmingham (November 1996).

Vitalii Kononov, head of the Green faction, Kyiv (September 1998).

Albert Kornieiev, the secretary of the Constitutional Commission, 1994–1996, Kyiv (April 1997).

Vasyl Kostytskyi, member of the 'Reforms' faction, Kyiv (September 1996).
Serhiy Kyrychenko, member of the 'Social-Market Choice' faction, Kyiv (July 1997).
Mykola Lavrynenko, member of the Socialist faction, Kyiv (November 1995).
Oleksandr Lavrynovych, deputy head of Rukh and deputy head of the Commission on Legal Policy and Reform, Kyiv (November 1995 and September 1996) and London (December 1998).
Volodymyr Masenko, member of the Communist faction, Kyiv (November 1995).
Valerii Mishura, member of the Communist faction, Kyiv (June 1999).
Viktor Musiaka, member of the 'Reforms' faction, representative of the President in the Supreme Council until June 1996, Kyiv (September 1996).
Volodymyr Moiseienko, member of the Communist faction, Kyiv (November 1995).
Serhiy Odarych, president of the 'Ukrainska Perspektyva' foundation, Kyiv (September 1996).
Viktor Pohorilko, professor of law, the Institute of State and Law, member of the working group of the Constitutional Commission, Kyiv (November 1995).
Ivan Popesku, member of the MDG faction, Kyiv (July 1997).
Oleksandr Reimer, senior consultant in the Department of Internal Affairs of the Presidential Administration, Kyiv (April and July 1997).
Serhiy Soboliev, head of the faction 'Reforms', Kyiv (September 1996).
Galina Starovoitova, member of the MDG faction, Kyiv, (July 1997).
Volodymyr Stretovych, head of the parliamentary Commission on Legal Policy and Reform, Kyiv (November 1995) and Birmingham (November 1996).
Mykhailo Syrota, head of the Special Conciliatory Group and Temporary Extraordinary Commission on the Preparation the Draft Constitution, Kyiv (September 1996).
Serhiy Teleshun, head of the Department of Home Affairs, the Presidential Administration, Kyiv (November 1995).
Anatoliy Tkachuk, parliamentary deputy in the 1990–1994 Supreme Council, Kyiv (April 1997).
Bohdan Yaroshynskyi, head of the Ukrainian Republican Party in 1995–1996, Kyiv (September 1996).
Anatoliy Zaiets, deputy head of the Legal Department of the Secretariat of the Supreme Council, Kyiv (July 1997).

UKRAINIAN NEWSPAPERS AND PERIODICALS USED FOR THE RESEARCH

Chas-Time
Demokratychna Ukraina
Demos
Den'
Eastern Economist
Holos Ukrainy
Kommunist
Molod' Ukrainy
Narodna Armia

Post Postup
Pravda Ukrainy
Rukh Insider
Slovo I Chas
Tovaryshch
Ukraina Moloda
The Ukrainian Weekly
Ukraina-Centre
Ukrainske Slovo
UNIAN-Polityka
Uriadovyi Kurier
Vechirniy Kyiv
Visnyk Prohramy Spryiannia Parlamentovi Ukrainy
Zerkalo Nedeli

SECONDARY SOURCES

GENERAL

Amstrong John A., 'The Ethnic Scene in the Soviet Union: The View of the Dictatorship', in Eric Godhagen (ed.), *Ethnic Minorities in the Soviet Union* (New York: Praeger, 1968), pp. 4–21.

Amstrong John A., *Ideology, Politics and Government in the Soviet Union*, 3rd ed. (London: Nelson, 1974), pp. 176–80.

Arato Andrew, 'Constitution and Continuity in the East European Transitions. Part 1: Continuity and its Crisis', *Constellations*, Vol. 1, No. 1 (1994).

Andrews William G., *Constitutions and Constitutionalism* (Princeton: D. Van Nostrand Company, Inc., 1968).

Beetham David, *The Legitimation of Power* (Houndmills and London: Macmillan, 1991).

Bellamy Richard, 'The Political Form of the Constitution: the Separation of Powers, Rights and Representative Democracy', *Political Studies*, Vol. XLIV (1996), pp. 436–456.

Bellamy Richard (ed.), *Constitutionalism, Democracy and Sovereignty: American and European Perspectives* (Vermont: Avebury, 1996).

Bellamy Richard, Castiglione Dario, and Bufacchi Victorio (eds.), *Democracy and Constitutional Culture in the Union of Europe* (London: Lothian Foundation Press, 1995).

Berman H. J., 'The Rule of Law and the Law-Based State (*Rechtsstaat*) (with special reference to development in the Soviet Union)', *The Harriman Institute Forum*, Vol. 4, No. 5 (1991), pp. 5–6.

Bicanic Ivo, 'The Economic Causes of New State Formation during Transition', *East European Politics and Societies*, Vol. 9, No. 1 (Winter 1995).

Billing Michael, *Banal Nationalism* (London: Sage, 1997).

Bottomore T. and Goode P. (eds.), *Austro–Marxism* (Oxford: Claredon, 1978).

Breuilly John, *Nationalism and the State*, 2nd ed. (Manchester: Manchester University Press, 1993).

Brubaker Rogers, *Nationalism Reframed* (Cambridge: Cambridge University Press, 1996).

Brzezinski Mark, *The Struggle for Constitutionalism in Poland* (Houndmills and London: Macmillan, 1998).

Buchanan James M., 'Federalism as an Ideal Political Order and an Objective for Constitutional Reform', *Journal of Federalism*, Vol. 25, No. 2 (Spring 1995), pp. 20–27.

Bunce Valerie and Csanadi Maria, 'Uncertainty in the Transition: Post-communism in Hungary', *East European Politics and Societies*, Vol. 7, No. 2 (Spring 1993), pp. 240–275.

Canovan Margaret, *Nationhood and Political Theory* (Cheltenham: Edward Elgar, 1996).

Castiglione Dario, 'The Political Theory of the Constitution', *Political Studies*, Vol. XLIV, No. 3 (1996).

Colton Timothy J. and Tucker Robert C. (eds.), *Patterns of Post-Soviet Leadership* (Boulder: Westview Press, 1995).

Connor Walker, *Ethnonationalism: the Quest for Understanding* (Princeton University Press: Princeton, 1994).

Dallin Alexander and Lapidus Gail W. (eds.), *The Soviet System: From Crisis to Collapse*, revised ed. (Boulder, San Francisco, Oxford: Westview Press, 1995), pp. 405–10.

Dearlove John, 'Bringing the Constitution Back in: Political Science and the State', *Political Studies*, Vol. 37 (1989), pp. 521–539.

Dogan Mattei, 'Political Science and the Other Social Sciences', in Goodin Robert E. and Kligemann Hans-Dieter (eds.), *A New Handbook of Political Science* (Oxford and New York: Oxford University Press, 1996), pp. 97–130.

Dogan Mattei and Pelassy Dominique, *How to Compare Nations* (New Jersey: Chatham House Publishers, Inc., 1984).

Duchacek Ivo D., *Power Maps: Comparative Politics of Constitutions* (Santa Barbara: ABC–Clio Press, 1973).

Dunleavy Patrick and O'Leary Brian, *Theories of the State* (London and Basingstoke: Macmillan, 1987).

Duverger Maurice, 'A New System Model: Semi-Presidential Government', *European Journal of Political Research*, Vol. 8 (1980), pp. 165–87.

Dyson Kenneth, *The State Tradition in Western Europe: A Study of an Idea and Institutions* (Oxford: Oxford University Press, 1980).

Easton D., *The Political System* (New York: Knopf, 1953).

Elander I., 'Between Centralism and Localism: on the Development of Local Government in Postsocialist Europe', *Environment and Planning C: Government and Policy*, Vol. 15, No. 2 (May 1997), pp. 143–59.

Elazar Daniel J., 'Constitution-Making: The Pre-eminently Political Act', in. Keith G. Banting and Richard Simeon (eds.), *The Politics of Constitutional Change in Industrial Nations* (London and Basingstoke: Macmillan, 1985), pp. 232–448.

Elazar Daniel J., *Exploring Federalism* (Tuscaloosa, AL: The University of Alabama Press, 1987).

Elster Jon and Slagstad Rune (eds.), *Constitutionalism and Democracy* (Cambridge: Cambridge University Press, 1988).

Elster Jon, 'Constitutionalism in Eastern Europe: an Introduction', *The University of Chicago Law Review*, Vol. 58 (1991), pp. 445–82.

Elster Jon, 'On Majoritarianism and Rights', *East European Constitutional Review*, Vol. 1, No. 3 (Summer 1992).

Elster Jon, 'Constitution Making in Eastern Europe: Rebuilding the Boat in the Open Sea', *Public Administration*, Vol. 71, No. (Spring/Summer 1993), pp. 169–217.

Finer E., Bogdanor V., and Rudden B., *Comparing Constitutions* (Oxford: Clerendon Press, 1995).

Franklin Daniel P. and Baun Micheal J. (eds.), *Political Culture and Constitutionalism* (Armonk and London: M.E.Sharpe, 1995).

Galtung Johan, *Theory and Methods of Social Research* (New York: Columbia University Press, 1969).

Geertz Clifford, *The Interpretation of Cultures* (London: Fontana, 1973).

Giddens Anthony, *Central Problems in Social Theory: Action, Structure and Contradiction in Social Analysis* (Houndmills and London: Macmillan, 1979).

Giddens Anthony, *The Nation-State and Violence* (Cambridge: Polity, 1985).

Goodin Robert E., 'Designing Constitutions: the Political Constitution of a Mixed Commonwealth', *Political Studies*, Vol. XLIV (1996), pp. 635–46.

Goodin Robert E. and Kligemann Hans-Dieter (eds.), *A New Handbook of Political Science* (Oxford and New York: Oxford University Press, 1996).

Grey Thomas C., 'Constitutionalism: an Analytical Framework', in Pennock J. Roland and Chapman John W. (eds.), *Constitutionalism* (New York: New York University Press, 1979), pp. 189–209.

Habermas J., Facticity and Validity: *Contributions to a Democratic Theory of Law and the Constitutional State* (Cambridge, Mass., 1993).

Hall John A. and Ikenberry G. John, *The State* (Buckingham and Philadelphia: Open University Press, 1989).

Hall Peter A. and Taylor Rosemary C. R., 'Political Science and the Three New Institutionalisms', *Political Studies*, Vol. XLIV (1996), pp. 939–57.

Harper Samuel N. and Thompson Ronald, *The Government of the Soviet Union,* 2nd ed. (Toronto: D. Van Nostrand Company, 1952).

Hay Colin, *Re-stating Social and Political Change* (Buckingham and Philadelphia: Open University Press, 1996).

Heller Ágnes, 'Phases of Legitimation in Soviet-type Societies', in Rigby T. H. and Fehér Ferenc (eds.), *Political Legitimation in Communist States* (London and Basingstoke: Macmillan, 1982), pp. 45–63.

Hellman Joel, 'Constitutions and Economic Reform in the Postcommunist Transitions', *East European Constitutional Review*, Vol. 5, No. 1 (Winter 1996), pp. 46–56.

Hoffman J., *Beyond the State: an Introductory Critique* (Cambridge: Polity, 1995).

Holmes Stephen, 'Precommitment and the Paradox of Democracy', in Jon Elster and Rune Slagstad (eds.), *Constitutionalism and Democracy* (Cambridge: Cambridge University Press, 1993).

Holmes Stephen, *Passions and Constraint: on the Theory of Liberal Democracy* (Chicago and London: University of Chicago Press, 1995).

Holmes Stephen, 'Conceptions of Democracy in the Draft Constitutions of Post-Communist Countries', in. Beverly Crawford (ed.), *Markets, States and Democracy: The Political Economy of Post-Communist Transformation* (Boulder, San Francisco, Oxford: Westview Press, 1995).

Howard Dick A. E. (ed.) *Constitution Making in Eastern Europe* (Johns Hopkins University Press, 1993).

Inoue K., *MacArthur's Japanese Constitution: A Linguistic and Cultural Study of Its Making* (Chicago: University of Chicago Press, 1991).

Jennings Jeremy, 'French Constitutional Tradition', in Richard Bellamy, Victorio Bufacchi, and Dario Castiglione (eds.), *Democracy and Constitutional Culture in the Union of Europe* (London: Lothian Foundation Press, 1995), pp. 21–36.

Jordan Bill, 'Constitutionalism and Social Rights', in Richard Bellamy, Victorio Bufacchi, and Dario Castiglione (eds.), *Democracy and Constitutional Culture in the Union of Europe* (London: Lothian Foundation Press, 1995), pp. 121–36.

Judge David, 'East Central European Parliaments: the First Steps' in Attila Ágh (ed.), *The Emergence of East Central European Parliaments: The First Steps* (Budapest: Hungarian Centre of Democracy Studies Foundation, 1994).

Kommers Donald P. and Thompson W. J., 'Fundamentals in the Liberal Constitutional Tradition', in Hesse Joachim Jens and Johnson Nevil (eds.), *Constitutional Policy and Change in Europe* (Oxford: Oxford University Press, 1995).

Krasner Stephen D., 'Approaches to the State: Alternative Conceptions and Historical Dynamics', *Comparative Politics*, Vol. 16, No. 2 (January 1984), pp. 223–246.

Kubicek Paul, 'Delegative Democracy in Russia and Ukraine', *Communist and Post-Communist Studies*, Vol. 27, No. 4 (1994), pp. 423–41.

Lane Jan Erik, *Constitutions and Political Theory* (Manchester and New York: Manchester University Press, 1996).

Lijphart Arend (ed.), *Parliamentary versus Presidential Government* (Oxford: Oxford University Press, 1992).

Lijphart Arend, 'Constitutional Choices for New Democracies', *Journal of Democracy*, Vol. 2, No. 1 (Winter 1991), pp. 73–84.

Lijphart Arend, 'Democracies: Forms, Performance, and Constitutional Engineering', *European Journal of Political Research*, Vol. 25, No. 1 (January 1994), pp. 1–16.

Linz Juan J., 'Presidential or Parliamentary Democracy: Does It Make a Difference', in Juan J. Linz and Arturo Valenzuela (eds.), *The Failure of Presidential Democracy: Comparative Perspective* (Baltimore, London: The Johns Hopkins University Press, 1994), pp. 3–90.

Loewenstein Karl, 'Reflections on the Value of Constitutions in Our Revolutionary Age', in Eckstain Harry and Apter David E. (eds.), *Comparative Politics: A Reader* (London: The Free Press of Glencoe, 1963), pp. 149–63.

Los Maria, 'Legitimation, State and Law in the Central Return to Democracy', in Volkman Gessner *et al.* (eds.), *European Legal Cultures* (Aldershot: Avebury, 1996), pp. 473–81.

Ludwikowski Rett R., *Constitution-Making in the Region of Former Soviet Dominance* (Durham and London: Duke University Press, 1996).

MacCormick Neil, 'Constitutionalism and Democracy', in Richard Bellamy (ed.), *Theories and Concepts of Politics: an Introduction* (Manchester: Manchester University Press, 1993), pp. 124–47.

MacCormick Neil, 'Liberalism, Nationalism and the Post-Sovereign State', *Political Studies*, Vol. XLIV (1996), pp. 553–67.

Maddox G., 'Constitution', in T. Ball, J. Farr, and R. L. Hanson (eds.), *Political Innovation and Conceptual Change* (Cambridge: Cambridge University Press, 1989).

Mainwaring S., 'Presidentialism, Multipartism, and Democracy: the Difficult Combination', *Comparative Political Studies*, Vol. 26, No. 2 (July 1993), pp. 198–222.

Mann Micheal, 'The Autonomous Power of the State: Its Origins, Mechanisms and Results', in John A. Hall (ed.), *States in History* (Oxford: Basil Blackwell, 1986), pp. 109–36.

Mann Micheal, *The Sources of Social Power* (Cambridge: Cambridge University Press, 1995), Vols. 1 and 2.

McGregor James, 'The Presidency in East Central Europe', *RFE/RL Research Report*, Vol. 3, No. 2 (14 January 1994), pp. 23–31.

Moore Margaret, 'On National Self-determination', *Political Studies*, Vol. XLV, No. 5 (December 1997), pp. 900–13.

Motyl Alexander J., *Sovietology, Rationality, Nationality: Coming to Grips with Nationalism in the USSR* (New York: Columbia University Press, 1990).

O'Donnell Guillermo, 'Delegative Democracy', *Journal of Democracy*, Vol. 5, No. 1 (January 1994), pp. 55–69.

Offe Claus, 'Capitalism by Democratic Design', *Social Research,* Vol. 58, No. 4 (Winter 1991), pp. 865–892.

Offe Claus, 'Designing Institutions for East European Transitions', in Jerzy Hausner, Bob Jessop, and Klaus Nielsen (eds.), *Strategic Choice and Path Dependency in Post-Socialism: Institutional Dynamics in the Transformation Process* (Aldershot: Edward Elgar, 1995), pp. 47–65.

Offe Claus, *Varieties of Transition: The East European and East German Experience* (Cambridge: Polity Press, 1996).

O'Neil Patrick, 'Presidential Power in Post-Communist Europe: The Hungarian Case in Comparative Perspective', *The Journal of Communist Studies*, Vol. 9, No. 3 (September 1993), pp. 177–201.

Paddison Ronan, *The Fragmented State: The Political Geography of Power* (Oxford: Basil Blackwell, 1983).

Parekh Bhikhu, 'The Concept of National Identity', *New Community*, Vol. 21, No. 2 (April 1995), pp. 255–68.

Parekh Bhikhu, 'Ethnocentricity of the Nationalist Discourse', *Nations and Nationalism*, Vol. 1, No. 1 (1995), pp. 25–52.

Pickvance C. G., 'Decentralization and Democracy in Eastern Europe: a Sceptical Approach', *Environment and Planning C: Government and Policy*, Vol. 15, No. 2 (May 1997), pp. 129–42.

Pipes Richard, *The Formation of the Soviet Union: Communism and Nationalism, 1917–1923* (Cambridge, Mass.: Harvard University Press, 1957).

Pogány István, 'Constitution Making or Constitutional Transformation in Post-Communist Societies?', *Political Studies*, Vol. XLIV, No. 3 (1996), pp. 568–91.

Poggi Gianfranco, *The Development of the Modern State: A Sociological Introduction* (London: Hutchinson, 1978).

Preuss Ulrich K., 'Feature: Constitution-Making and Nation-Building: Reflections on Political Transformations in East and Western Europe', *European Journal of Philosophy,* Vol. 1, No. 1 (April 1993), pp. 81–92.

Preuss Ulrich K., 'Patterns of Constitutional Evolution and Change in Eastern Europe', in Hesse Joachim Jens and Johnson Nevil (eds.), *Constitutional Policy and Change in Europe* (Oxford: Oxford University Press, 1995).

Preuss Ulrich K., 'Prospects of a Constitution for Europe', *Constellations*, Vol. 3, No. 2 (1996), pp. 209–24.

Preuss Ulrich K., 'The Political Meaning of Constitutionalism', in Bellamy Richard (ed.), *Constitutionalism, Democracy and Sovereignty: American and European Perspectives* (Aldershot: Avebury, 1996).

Preuss Ulrich K., Elster Jon, and Offe Claus, *Institutional Design in Post-Communist Societies* (Cambridge: Cambridge University Press, 1998).

Przeworski Adam, *Democracy and the Market* (Cambridge: Cambridge University Press, 1991).

Preece Jennifer Jackson, 'National Minority Rights vs. State Sovereignty in Europe: Changing Norms in International Relations', *Nations and Nationalism*, Vol. 3, No. 3 (1997), pp. 345–64.

Rakowska-Harmstone Teresa, 'Communist Constitutions and Constitutional Change', in Keith G. Banting and Richard Simeon (eds.), *The Politics of Constitutional Change in Industrial Nations* (London and Basingstoke: Macmillan, 1985), pp. 203–31.

The Rebirth of Democracy. 12 Constitutions of Central and Eastern Europe, 2nd ed. (Strasbourg: Council of Europe Publishing, 1996).

Regulska J., 'Decentralisation or (Re)Centralization: Struggle for Political Power in Poland', *Environment and Planning C: Government and Policy*, Vol. 15, No. 2 (May 1997), pp. 187–207.

Roeder Philip G., 'Soviet Federalism and Ethnic Mobilization', *World Politics*, Vol. 43, No. 2 (January 1991), pp. 196–232.

Roeder Philip G., 'Varieties in Post-Communist Authoritarian Regimes', *Post-Soviet Affairs,* Vol. 10, No. 1 (1994), pp. 61–101.

Rousseau Jean-Jacques, *The Social Contract* (London: Penguin Group, 1968).

Safran W., 'State, Nation, National Identity, and Citizenship: France as a Test Case', *International Political Science Review*, Vol. 12 (1991), pp. 219–38.

Sakwa Richard, 'The Struggle for the Constitution in Russia and the Triumph of Ethical Individualism', *Studies in East European Thought*, Vol. 48, (1996), pp. 115–157.

Sartori Giovanni, 'Constitutionalism: A Preliminary Analysis', *American Political Science Review*, Vol. 56, No. 4 (December 1962), pp. 853–864.

Sartori Giovanni, 'Neither Presidentialism nor Parliamentarism', in J. J. Linz and A. Valenzuela (eds.), *The Failure of Presidential Democracy* (Baltimore, London: The Johns Hopkins University Press, 1994), Vol. 1.

Schmitt Carl, *The Concept of the Political* (Chicago and London: The University of Chicago Press, 1996).

Schochet Gordon J. and Chapman John W., 'Introduction: Constitutionalism, Liberalism, and the Study of Politics', in Roland J. Pennock and John W. Chapman (eds.), *Constitutionalism* (New York: New York University Press, 1979).

Schuppert Gunnar Folke, 'On the Evolution of a European State: Reflections on the Conditions of and the Prospects for a European Constitution', in Joachim Jens

Hesse and Nevil Johnson (eds.), *Constitutional Policy and Change in Europe* (Oxford: Oxford University Press, 1995), pp. 329–70.

Sharlet Robert, *Soviet Constitutional Crisis: From De-Stalinization to Disintegration* (Armonk, New York: M. E. Sharpe, 1992).

Sharlet Robert, 'Legal Transplants and Political Mutations: the Reception of Constitutional Law in Russia and the Newly Independent States', *East European Constitutional Review*, Vol. 7, No. 4 (Fall 1998), pp. 59–68.

Shugart Matthew S., 'Of Presidents and Parliaments', *East European Constitutional Review*, Vol. 2, No. 1 (Winter 1993), pp. 30–32.

Shugart Matthew S. and Carey John M., *Presidents and Assemblies: Constitutional Design and Electoral Dynamics* (Cambridge: Cambridge University Press, 1992).

Slider Darrell, 'Political Elites and Politics in the Republics', in David Lane (ed.), *Russia in Flux* (London: Edward Elgar, 1992).

Squires Judith, 'Liberal Constitutionalism, Identity and Difference', *Political Studies*, Vol. XLIV (1996), pp. 620–34.

Surazska W. *et al.*, 'Towards Regional Government in Central Europe: Territorial Restructuring of Postcommunist Regimes', *Environment and Planning C: Government and Policy*, Vol. 15, No. 4 (November 1997), pp. 437–462.

Sunstein Cass, "Why Social and Economic Rights Don't Belong in the New Constitutions of Post-Communist Europe", *East European Constitutional Review,* Vol. 2, No. 1 (Winter 1993).

Suny Ronald Griogor, *The Revenge of the Past: Nationalism, Revolution and the Collapse of the Soviet Union* (Stanford, California: Stanford University Press, 1993).

Taras Ray (ed.), *Postcommunist Presidents* (Cambridge: Cambridge University Press, 1997).

Thelen Kathleen and Stainmo Sven, 'Institutionalism in Comparative Politics', in Sven Stainmo, Kathleen Thelen, and Frank Longstreth (eds.), *Structuring Politics: Historical Institutionalism in Comparative Analysis* (Cambridge: Cambridge University Press, 1992), pp. 1–32.

Tilly Charles (ed.), *The Formation of National States in Western Europe* (Princeton: Princeton University Press, 1975).

Tully James, *Strange Multiplicity: Constitutionalism in the Age of Diversity* (Cambridge: Cambridge University Press, 1995).

Unger L. Aryeh, *Constitutional Developments in the USSR: a Guide to the Soviet Constitutions* (London: Methuen, 1981).

Vile M. J. C., *Constitutionalism and the Separation of Powers* (Oxford: Claredon Press, 1967).

Vincent Andrew, *Theories of the State* (Oxford and New York: Blackwell, 1987).

Weiler J. H. H., 'European Neo-constitutionalism: in Search of Foundations for the European Order', *Political Studies*, Vol. XLIV (1996), pp. 517–33.

Wheare K. C., *Modern Constitutions*, 2nd ed. (London: Oxford University Press, 1966.

Whinney Edward, *Constitution Making: Principles, Process and Practice* (University of Toronto Press, 1981).

Winchorek Piotr, *Dyskusje konstytucyjne (Constitutional Discussions)* (Warsaw, 1996).

Wollman H., 'Institution Building and Decentralisation in Formerly Socialist Countries: the Cases of Poland, Hungary, and East Germany', *Environment and Planning C: Government and Policy*, Vol. 15, No. 4 (November 1997), pp. 463–80.

Zielonka Jan, 'New Institutions in the Old East Block', *Journal of Democracy*, Vol. 5, No. 2 (April 1994), pp. 87–104.

Zsamboki K. and Bell M, 'Local Self-government in Central and Eastern Europe', *Environment and Planning C: Government and Policy*, Vol. 15, No. 2 (May 1997), pp. 177–86.

BOOKS AND ARTICLES ON UKRAINE (IN ENGLISH)

Arel Dominique, 'Language Politics in an Independent Ukraine: Towards One or Two State Languages', *Nationalities Papers*, Vol. 23, No. 3, (September 1995).

Arel Dominique, 'Ukraine: The Temptation of the Nationalising State', in V. Tismaneanu (ed.), *Political Culture and Civil Society in Russia and the New States of Eurasia* (Armonk, New York: M.E. Sharpe, 1995), pp. 157–88.

Arel Dominique and Khmelko Valeri, 'The Russian Factor and Territorial Polarization in Ukraine', *The Harriman Review*, Vol. 9, Nos. 1–2 (Spring 1996), pp. 81–91.

Arel Dominique and Wilson Andrew, 'The Ukrainian Parliamentary Elections', *RFE/RL Research Report*, Vol. 3, No. 26 (1994).

Arel Dominique and Wilson Andrew, 'Ukraine under Kuchma: Back to "Eurasia"?', *RFE/RL Research Report*, Vol. III, No. 32 (1994).

Baltarovych Yevhen, 'Ukraine: A Federal or Unitary State', *Demos*, 1(7) (28 Nov 1994).

Bilinsky Yaroslav, 'Mykola Skrypnyk and Petro Shelest: An Essay on the Persistence and Limits of Ukrainian National Communism', in *Soviet Nationality Policies and Practices* (1981), pp. 105–42.

Bilinsky Yaroslav, 'Shcherbytsky, Ukraine and Kremlin Politics', *Problems of Communism*, Vol. 32, No. 4 (July–Aug. 1983), pp. 1–26.

Bilous Artur, 'Ukraine's Parliament: Who's in Power', *Demos*, Vol. 2, No. 1 (1995), pp. 36–43.

Birch Sarah, 'Nomenklatura Democratization: Electoral Clientelism in Post-Soviet Ukraine', *Democratization*, Vol. 4, No. 4 (Winter 1997), pp. 40–62.

Birch Sarah, 'Electoral Systems, Campaign Strategies, and Vote Choice in the Ukrainian Parliamentary and Presidential Elections of 1994', *Political Studies*, Vol. XLVI, No. 1 (March 1998), pp. 96–114.

Borys Jurij, 'Political Parties in the Ukraine', in Taras Hunchak (ed.), *The Ukraine, 1917–1921: A Study in Revolution* (Cambridge, Mass.: Harvard University Press, 1977), pp. 128–59.

Boshyk Yurii (ed.), *Ukraine During World War II: History and Its Aftermath* (Edmonton, Ont.: CIUS, 1986).

Bremmer Ian, 'Ethnic Issues in Crimea', *RFE/RL Research Report*, Vol. 2, No. 18 (Apr. 1993).

Brown Micheal, *Ferment in the Ukraine* (London and Basingstoke: Macmillan, 1971).

Ciuciura Theodore Bohdan, 'Galicia and Bukovina as Austrian Crown Provinces: Ukrainian Experience in Representative Institutions, 1861–1918', *Studia Ucrainica*, Vol. 5 (1984), pp. 175–95.

Dąbrowski Marek, 'The Ukrainian Way to HyperInflation', *Communist Economics and Economic Transformation*, Vol. 6, No. 2 (1994), pp. 215–137.

Dergachov Oleksandr *et al.*, *Ukrainian Statehood in the Twentieth Century* (Kyiv: Politychna Dumka, 1996).

Dzyuba Ivan, *Internationalism or Russification?* (London: Wiedenfeld and Nicholson, 1968).

Farmer Kenneth C., *Ukrainian Nationalism in the Post-Stalin Era: Myth, Symbols and Ideology in Soviet Nationalities Policy* (The Hague–Boston–London: Martinus Nijhoff Publishers, 1980).

Futey Bohdan A., 'Ukraine's Draft Constitution Meets Political Reality', *East European Constitutional Review*, Vol. 2, No. 1 (Winter 1993).

Futey Bohdan A., 'Comments on the Constitution of Ukraine', *East European Constitutional Review*, Vol. 5, Nos. 2–3 (1996), pp. 29–34.

George G. Grabowicz, 'Province to Nation: Nineteenth-Century Ukrainian Literature as a Paradigm of the National Revival', *Canadian Review of Studies in Nationalism*, Vol. 16, Nos. 1–2 (1989), pp. 117–32.

Guthier S., 'The Popular Basis of Ukrainian Nationalism in 1917', *Slavic Review*, Vol. 38, No. 1 (March 1979), pp. 30–47.

von Hagen Mark, 'The Dilemmas of Ukrainian Independence and Statehood, 1917–1921', *The Harriman Institute Forum*, Vol. 7, No. 5 (January 1994), pp. 7–11.

Himka John-Paul, *Galician Villagers and the Ukrainian National Movement in the Nineteenth Century* (Alberta: Canadian Institute of Ukrainian Studies, 1988).

Himka John-Paul, 'Western Ukraine between the Wars', *Canadian Slavonic Papers*, Vol. 34 (December 1992), pp. 391–412.

Hodnett Grey, 'The Views of Petro Shelest', *The Annals of the Ukrainian Academy of Arts and Sciences in the United States*, Vol. XIV, Nos. 37–38 (1978–1980), pp. 209–43.

Horak Stephan M., 'Soviet Historiography and the New Nationalities Policy, a Case Study: Belorussia and Ukraine', in Jane P. Shapiro and Peter J. Potichnyi (eds.), *Change and Adaptation in Soviet and East European Politics* (New York: Praeger, 1976).

Hunchak Taras (ed.), *The Ukraine, 1917–1921: A Study in Revolution* (Cambridge, Mass.: Harvard Ukrainian Research Institute, 1977).

Jackson Louise and Wolczuk Kataryna, 'Defining Citizenship and Political Community in Ukraine', *The Ukrainian Review*, Vol. 44, No. 2 (Summer 1997), pp. 16–27.

Kohut Zenon E., 'The Development of a Little Russian Identity and Ukrainian Nation-building', *Harvard Ukrainian Studies*, Vol. 10 (1986), pp. 559–76.

Kohut Zenon E., *Russian Centralism and Ukrainian Autonomy: Imperial Absorption of the Hetmanate 1760s–1830s* (Cambridge MA: Harvard Ukrainian Research Institute, 1988).

Kornienko Mykola, 'Regional Autonomy: Federation or Decentralization', *Ukrainian Law*, No. 3 (1996), pp. 139–145.

Krawchenko Bohdan, 'The Impact of Industratalisation on the Social Structure of Ukraine', *Canadian Slavonic Papers*, Vol. 22, No. 3 (September 1980), pp. 338–57.

Krawchenko Bohdan, *Social Change and National Consciousness in Twentieth-Century Ukraine* (Houndmills and London: Macmillan, 1985).

Krawchenko Bohdan, 'The Social Structure of Ukraine in 1917', *Harvard Ukrainian Studies,* Vol. 14, No. 1/2 (June 1990), pp. 97–112.

Krawchenko Bohdan, 'Ukraine: the Politics of Independence', in Ray Taras and Ian Bremmer (eds.), *Nations and Politics in the Soviet Successor States* (Cambridge: Cambridge University Press, 1993).

Kulchytskyi Yarpolok (ed.), *Presidential Election Guide* (Kyiv: International Foundation for Electoral Studies, 1994).

Kuzio Taras (ed.), *Dissent in Ukraine under Gorbachev* (London: Ukrainian Press Agency, 1989).

Kuzio Taras, 'An Independent Ukraine—but Still Communist?', *Soviet Analyst* (28 August 1991).

Kuzio Taras and Wilson Andrew, *Ukraine: Perestroika to Independence* (London: Macmillan, 1994).

Kuzio Taras, 'The Multi-Party System in Ukraine on the Eve of Elections', *Government and Opposition,* Vol. 29, No. 1 (Winter 1994).

Kuzio Taras, 'Radical Nationalist Parties and Movements in Contemporary Ukraine before and after Independence: The Right and Its Politics, 1989–1994', *Nationalities Papers,* Vol. 25, No. 2 (1997), pp. 211–42.

Laba Roman, 'The Russian–Ukrainian Conflict: State, Nation and Identity', *European Security,* Vol. 4, No. 3 (Autumn 1995), pp. 457–87.

Liber George, *Soviet Nationality Policy, Urban Growth and Identity Change in the Ukrainian SSR, 1923–1934* (Cambridge: Cambridge University Press, 1992).

Lindheim Ralph and Luckyi George S. N. (eds.), *Towards an Intellectual History of Ukraine: An Anthology of Ukrainian Thought from 1710 to 1995* (Toronto—Buffalo—London: University of Toronto Press, 1996).

Luckyi George S. N., 'Polarity in Ukrainian Intellectual Dissent', *Canadian Slavonic Papers,* Vol. 14, No. 2 (Summer 1972), pp. 269–79.

Mace J. E., *Communism and the Dilemmas of National Liberation: National Communism in Soviet Ukraine, 1918–1933* (Cambridge, Mass.: Harvard University Press, 1983).

Mace J. E., 'Famine and Nationalism in Soviet Ukraine', *Problems of Communism*, Vol. 33, No. 3 (May–June 1984), pp. 37–50.

Magocsi Paul Robert, 'A Subordinate or Submerged People: The Ukrainians of Galicia under Habsburg Empire', in Richard L. Rudolph and David F. Good (eds.), *Nationalism and Empire: The Habsburg Empire and the Soviet Union* (New York: St. Martin's Press, 1992), pp. 95–108.

Magocsi Paul Robert, *A History of Ukraine* (Toronto–Buffalo–London: University of Toronto Press, 1996).

Mark Rudolf, 'Social Questions and National Revolution: The Ukrainian National Republic in 1919–1920', *Harvard Ukrainian Studies*, Vol. XIV, No. 1/2 (June 1990), pp. 114–31.

Markov Ihor, 'The Role of the President in the Ukrainian Political System', *RFE/RL Research Report*, Vol. 2, No. 48 (3 Dec. 1993).

Markovits Andrei and Sysyn Frank (eds.), *Nationbuilding and the Politics of Nationalism: Essays on Austrian Galicia* (Cambridge, Massachusetts: Harvard University Press, 1982).

Marples David R, *Stalinism in Ukraine in the 1940s* (London: Macmillan, 1986).

Marples David R., 'The Ukrainian Election Campaign: The Opposition', *Soviet Analyst,* Vol. 2 (9 March 1990).

Marples David R, 'The First Session of the Ukrainian Parliament', *Report on the USSR,* Vol. 2, No. 39 (28 September 1990), pp. 15–7.

Marples David R., 'A Sociological Survey of Rukh', *Report on the USSR,* Vol. 2, No. 2 (1990).

Martynenko Petro, 'Parliamentarism: the World Practice and Ukraine's Searches', *The Ukrainian Quarterly,* Vol. LII, No. 4 (Winter 1996), pp. 309–21.

Martyniuk Jaroslav, 'The Shifting Political Landscape', *Transition* (28 July 1995), pp. 9–11.

McDonald David, 'Nationhood and Its Discontents: Ukrainian Intellectual History at Empire's End. A Review Article', *Journal of Ukrainian Studies*, Vol. 23, No. 2 (Winter 1998), pp. 105–16.

Mihalisko K., 'Public Confidence in the Ukrainian Leadership', *RFE/RL Research Report,* Vol. 1, No. 43 (1992).

Mihalisko K., 'Ukrainians and Their Leaders at a Time of Crisis', *RFE/RL Research Report,* Vol. 2, No. 31 (30 July 1993), pp. 54–61.

Motyl Alexander J., *The Turn to the Right: The Ideological Origins and Development of Ukrainian Nationalism, 1919–1929* (Boulder: East European Monographs, 1980).

Motyl Alexander J., *Dilemmas of Independence: Ukraine after Totalitarianism* (The Council on Foreign Relations, 1993).

Motyl Alexander J. and Krawchenko Bohdan, 'Ukraine: From Empire to Statehood', in Ian Bremmer and Ray Taras (eds.), *New States, New Politics: Building the Post-Soviet Nations* (Cambridge: Cambridge University Press, 1997), pp. 235–75.

Nahaylo Bohdan, 'Ukrainian Party Plenum: Stagnation Wins out over Talk of Restructuring', *Radio Liberty Report,* No. 481 (25 October 1988).

Nahaylo Bohdan, *The Ukrainian Resurgence* (London: C.Hust & Co., 1997).

Nemiria Grigorii, Regionalism and Ukrainian Nation-State Building, Unpublished Conference Paper, CREES, June 1996.

Palvyshyn Marko, 'Culture and National Identity: Ukrainian Developments 1991–1996', in Vladimir Tikhonov (ed.), *In Search of Identity* (Melbourne: CRE–AS Publication Series No. 1, 1996), pp. 79–91.

Pirie Paul S., 'National Identity and Politics in Southern and Eastern Ukraine', *Europe–Asia Studies,* Vol. 48, No. 7 (November 1996), pp. 1079–104.

Potichnyj Peter J. (ed.), *Ukraine in the 1970s* (Oakville, Ont: Mosaic Press, 1975).

Pritsak Omeljan, 'Prolegomena to the National Awakening of the Ukrainians during the Nineteenth Century', in Roland Sussex and J. C. Eade (eds.), *Culture and Nationalism in Nineteenth Century* (Columbus, Ohio: Slavice Publishers, Inc., 1983), pp. 96–110.

Resheter John, *The Ukrainian Revolution, 1917–1920* (Princeton: Princeton University Press, 1952).

Riabchuk Mykola, 'Authoritarianism with a Human Face?', *The East European Reporter,* Vol. 5, No. 6 (November–December 1992).

Rudnytsky Ivan L. (ed.), *Mykhaylo Drahomanov. A Symposium and Selected Writings* (New York: The Annals of the Ukrainian Academy, 1952).

Rudnytsky Ivan L., 'The Fourth Universal and Its Ideological Antecedents', in Taras Hunchak (ed.), *The Ukraine, 1917–1921: A Study in Revolution* (Cambridge, Mass.: Harvard University Press, 1977), pp. 186–219.

Rudnytsky Ivan L., 'The Ukrainians in Galicia under Austrian Rule', in Andrei Markovits and Frank Sysyn (eds.), *Nationbuilding and the Politics of Nationalism: Essays on Austrian Galicia* (Cambridge, Massachusetts: Harvard University Press, 1982), pp. 23–68.

Rudnytsky Ivan L., *Essays in Modern Ukrainian History* (Alberta: Canadian Institute of Ukrainian Studies, 1987).

Rudolf Mark A., 'Social Question and National Revolution: The Ukrainian National Republic in 1919–1920', *Harvard Ukrainian Studies,* Vol. XIV, No. 1/2 (June 1990), pp. 114–31.

Sasse Gwendolyn, 'The Crimean Issue', *Journal of Communist Studies and Transition Politics,* Vol. 12, No. 1 (March 1996), pp. 83–100.

Saunders David, *The Ukrainian Impact on Russian Culture* (Edmonton, Ont: CIUS, 1985).

Saunders David, 'Modern Ukrainian History', *European History Quarterly*, Vol. 21, No. 2 (1991), pp. 81–95.

Sekarev Alexei, 'Ukraine's Policy Structure', *RFE/RL Research Report*, Vol. 1, No. 32 (14 August 1992), pp. 60–3.

Shandor V., *Carpatho–Ukraine in the 20th Century* (Harward: Ukrainian Research Institute, 1996).

Shapoval Volodymyr, 'The State System of Ukraine: Political and Legal Aspects', *Ukrainian Law*, No. 3 (1996), pp. 130–8.

Shevelov George, 'The Language Question in the Ukraine in the Twentieth Century (1900–1941)', *Harvard Ukrainian Studies,* Vol. X, No. 1/2 (June 1986), pp. 71–170.

Solchanyk Roman, 'Moulding the "Soviet People": The Role of Ukrainians and Belorussians', *RFE/RL Research Report,* No. 382 (9 November 1982).

Solchanyk Roman, 'The Uncertain Road to Independence', *Report on the USSR,* Vol. 3 (4 January 1991), pp. 22–24.

Solchanyk Roman, 'Ukrainian Communist Party on the Offensive', *Report on the USSR,* Vol. 3 (8 March 1991), pp. 13–4.

Solchanyk Roman, 'The Changing Political Landscape in Ukraine', *Report on the USSR,* Vol. 3 (14 June 1991).

Solchanyk Roman, 'Ukraine and the New Union Treaty', *Report on the USSR,* Vol. 3 (26 July 1991), pp. 22–4.

Solchanyk Roman, 'Ukraine: Political Reform and Political Change', *RFE/RL Research Report*, Vol. 1, No. 21 (22 May 1992), pp. 1–5.

Solchanyk Roman and Kuzio Taras, 'Democratic Political Blocs in Ukraine', *RFE/RL Research Report,* Vol. 2, No. 16 (16 April 1993), pp. 14–7.

Subtelny Orest, *Ukraine. A History* (Toronto: University of Toronto Press, 1988).

Sullivant Robert S., *Soviet Politics and the Ukraine 1917–1957* (New York: Columbia University Press, 1962).

Sysyn Frank E., 'The Reemergance of the Ukrainian Nation and Cossack Mythology', *Social Research*, Vol. 58, No. 4 (Winter 1991), pp. 845–64.

Sysyn Frank E., 'The Khmelnytsky Uprising and Ukrainian Nation-Building', *Journal of Ukrainian Studies*, Vol. 17, Nos. 1–2 (Summer–Winter 1992), pp. 141–70.

Szporluk Roman, *Ukraine. A Brief History* (Detroit MI: Ukraine Festival Committee, 1979).

Szporluk Roman, 'Ukraine: From an Imperial Periphery to a Sovereign State', *Daedalus*, Vol. 126, No. 3 (1997), pp. 85–119.

Tillett L., 'Ukrainian Nationalism and the Fall of Shelest', *Slavic Review*, Vol. 34, No. 4 (1975), pp. 752–68.

Tolstov Serkhiy, 'Dimensions of Inter-Ethnic Relations in Ukraine', *The Ukrainian Review,* Vol. XL, No. 2 (Summer 1993).

Velychenko Stephen, *National History as Cultural Process* (University of Alberta: Canadian Institute of Ukrainian Studies, 1992).

Velychenko Stephen, *Shaping Identity in Eastern Europe and Russia: Soviet and Polish Accounts of Ukrainian History, 1914–1991* (New York: St Martin's Press, 1993).

Vorndran Oliver, 'The Constitutional Process in Ukraine: Context and Structure', *Research Papers in Russian and East European Studies*, REES97/3, The University of Birmingham.

Wanner Catherine, 'Historical Narratives, Personal Narratives: Ethnographic Perspectives on Nationess in Post-Soviet Ukraine', *The Harriman Review*, Vol. 9, No. 2 (Spring 1996), pp. 11–5.

Wilson Andrew, 'Crimea's Political Cauldron', *RFE/RL Research Report*, Vol. 2, No. 2 (12 Nov 1993).

Wilson Andrew, 'The Ukrainian Left: In Transition to Social Democracy or Still in Thrall to the USSR', *Europe–Asia Studies*, Vol. 49, No. 7 (1997), pp. 1293–1316.

Wilson Andrew, 'The Ukrainian Left: Still a Barrier to Reform?', *The Ukrainian Review,* Vol. 44, No. 1 (Spring 1997), pp. 30–7.

Wilson Andrew, 'Myths of National History in Belarus and Ukraine', in Geoffrey A. Hosking and George Schopflin (eds.), *Myths and Nationhood* (London: Hurst and Co, 1997), pp. 182–97.

Wilson Andrew, *Ukrainian Nationalism in the 1990s. A Minority Faith* (Cambridge: Cambridge University Press, 1997).

Wilson Andrew, 'Ukraine: Two Presidents and Their Powers', in Ray Taras (ed.), *Postcommunist Presidents* (Cambridge: Cambridge University Press, 1997).

Wilson Andrew, *The Ukrainians: Unexpected Nation* (New Haven and London: Yale University Press, 2000).

Wolczuk Kataryna, 'Presidentialism in Ukraine: A Mid-Term Review of the Second Presidency', *Democratization*, Vol. 4, No. 3 (Autumn 1997), pp. 152–71.

Wolczuk Kataryna, 'The Politics of Constitution-Making in Independent Ukraine', in Taras Kuzio (ed.), *Contemporary Ukraine. Dynamics of Post-Soviet Transformation* (Armonk and New York: M. E. Sharpe, 1998), pp. 118–38.

Wolczuk Kataryna, 'Constituting Statehood: The New Ukrainian Constitution', *The Ukrainian Review*, Vol. 45, No. 3 (Autumn 1998), pp. 17–38.

Wolczuk Kataryna, 'History, Europe and the "National Idea": the Official Narrative of National Identity in Ukraine', *Nationalities Papers*, Vol. 28, No. 4 (December 2000), pp. 672–94.

Wolczuk Kataryna, 'The Constitutional Court in Ukraine' in Wojciech Sadurski (ed.) *Constitutional Justice, East and West* (Oxford: Oxford University Press, forthcoming).

Zolotariov Volodymyr, 'Constitutional Process in Ukraine', *Demos*, No. 1(3) (28 October 1994).

Zolotariov Volodymyr, 'A Federative System of Government as a Means of Resolving the Present Crisis in Ukraine', *Demos*, No. 1(7) (28 November 1994).

BOOKS AND ARTICLES ON UKRAINE (IN UKRAINIAN, POLISH OR RUSSIAN)

Andrusiak Ivan and Petrenko Yevhen, *Blysk i zlydennist' ukrains'koi natsional-demokratii (The Bright and Dark Days of Ukrainian Social-Democracy)* (Kyiv, 1999).

Bezsmertnyi Roman, 'Konstytutsiia garantuie samovriaduvania (The Constitution Guarantees Local Self-Government)', *Nova Polityka*, No. 5 (1996), pp. 25–8.

Bilous Artur *et al.*, *Proiekt Konstytutsii Ukrainy: stan, problemy, perspektyvy (The Draft Constitution of Ukraine: the Current Situation, Problems, Prospects)* (Kyiv, 1996).

Bilous Artur, 'Do i pislia Konstytutsii (Before and after the Constitution)', *Nova Polityka,* No. 3(5) (May–June 1996), pp. 3–5.

Bruski Jan Jacek, 'Miedzy sobornoscia a separatyzmem: funkcjonowanie i rozpad Ukrainiskiej Federacji Galicyjsko-Naddnieprzanskiej, 1918–1919 (Between Sobornist' and Separatism: the Functioning and Fall of the Galician–Dnieper Federation, 1918–1919)', in Irena Stawowy-Kawka and Wojciech Rajka (eds.), *Ku zjednoczonej Europie* (Towards a United Europe) (Krakow: Wydawnictwo Uniwersytetu Jagiellonskiego, 1997), pp. 37–52.

Butkevych Volodymyr, 'Proiekt Konstytutsii Ukrainy u Verkhovnii Radi (Draft Constitution in the Supreme Council)', *Nova Polityka,* No. 3(5) (May–June 1996), pp. 10–19.

Chornovil Viacheslav, 'Natsionalna inteligentsiia i ukrainska polityka (The National Intelligentsia and Ukrainian Politics)', *Slovo I Czas,* No. 2(422) (February 1996), pp. 24–7.

Chyzh Ivan, 'Ukrainski sotsialisty zavzhdy budut' livishymy vid evropeiskykh (The Ukrainian Socialists Will Always Be More to the Left Than Europeans)', *Viche*, No. 6, (1997), pp. 112–122.

Domoroslyi Valentyn, 'Deklaratsia pro derzhavnyi suverenitet Ukrainy: vytoky i naslidky (The Declaration of the State Sovereignty of Ukraine: the Origins and Consequences)', *Viche*, No. 51 (June 1996).

Gortat Radzislawa, *Ukrainskie wybory (Ukrainian Elections)* (Warsaw: Fundacja Polska Praca, 1998).

Haran'Oleksiy and Maiboroda Oleksandr, 'Obrannia Oleksandra Tkachenka spikerom i perehrupuvannia livykh syl (The Election of Oleksandr Tkachenko to the Post of the Speaker and the Re-shuffle of Left-wing Forces)', Mimeo, Centre for Studies of National Security, Kyiv (September 1999).

Haran' Oleksiy *et al.* (eds.), *Stanovlenia vladnykh struktur v Ukraini (The Creation of Power Structures in Ukraine)* (Kyiv, 1996).

Het'man Vadym, *Yak prynymalas Konstytytsiia Ukrainy (How the Ukrainian Constitution Was Adopted)* (Kyiv, 1996).

Holovatyi Serhiy and Yuz'kov Leonid (eds.), *Konstytutsiia Nezalezhnoi Ukrainy (The Constitution of Independent Ukraine)* (Kyiv, 1995).

Hor'ovyi Leonid and Shvets' Mykola, 'Informatsia i zakonotvorchyi protses (Information and the Legislative Process)' *Viche*, No. 5 (May 1996).

Hryniov Volodymyr, *Nova Ukraina: yakoiu ya yi bachu (New Ukraine: How I See Her)* (Kyiv, 1995).

Hrytsak Yaroslav, *Narys istorii Ukrainy: formuvania modernoi ukrains'koi natsii XIX–XX stolittia (A Brief History of Ukraine: the Formation of a Modern Ukrainian Nation, 19–20 Century)* (Kyiv, 1996).

Kachkovskyi Oleksiy, 'Idea derzhavnosti v ukrainskomu mentaliteti (The Idea of Statehood in the Ukrainian Mentality)', *Nova Polityka*, No. 2(4) (March–April 1996), pp. 61–4.

Kopieichnikov Volodymyr and Medvedchuk Viktor, 'Nova Konstytutsiia Ukrainy: realnist' i myfy (The New Constitution of Ukraine: Reality and Myths)', *Nova Polityka*, No. 3(5) (May–June 1996), pp. 6–9.

Kovtun Volodymyr, *Istoria narodnoho rukhu Ukrainy (A History of the People's Movement of Ukraine)* (Kyiv, 1995).

Kravchenko Valeriy, 'Ne magiia sliv a vse-taki vidrodzhenia (Not the Magic of Words, but a Rebirth Nevertheless', *Viche*, No. 6(51) (June 1996), pp. 68–79.

Kubijovych Volodymyr (ed.), *Encyklopedia ukrainoznavstva (The Encylopedia of Ukrainian Studies),* Reprint of the 1949 ed. (Kyiv, 1994).

Lytvyn Volodymyr, *Politychna arena Ukrainy (The Political Scene of Ukraine)* (Kyiv, 1994).

Medvedchuk V. V., *Konstytutsiinyi protses v Ukraini i organizatsia derzhavnoi vlady ta mistsevoho samovriaduvannia (The Constitutional Process in Ukraine and the Organisation of State Power and Local Self-Government)* (Kyiv, 1996).

Moroz Oleksandr, 'Interview', *Viche*, No. 8(53) (August 1996), pp. 3–8.

Olszanski Tadeusz A., 'Jak powstawala Konstytucja Ukrainy (How the Ukrainian Constitution Was Created)', *Eurazja*, Rok IV, No. 1, (1997), pp. 43–54.

Pavenko Rostyslav, 'Skilky palat potribno Parlamentu Ukrainy? (How Many Houses Does the Ukrainian Parliament Need?)', *Nova Polityka*, No. 5 (1996).

Podhorodecki Leszek, *Dzieje Kijowa (A History of Kyiv)* (Warszawa, 1982).

Pohorilko Viktor, *Nova Konstytutsiia Ukrainy (The New Constitution of Ukraine)* (Kyiv, 1996).

Pohribnyi Anatoliy, 'Yaka Ukraina buduietsia? (What Kind of Ukraine is Being Built?', *Slovo I Chas,* No. 2(422) (February 1996), pp. 24–7.

Popesku Ivan, 'Nova Konstytutsiia i prava natsionalnykh menshyn v Ukrainii (The New Constitution and the Rights of National Minorities in Ukraine)', *Nova Polityka*, No. 5 (1996), pp. 29–31.

Porokhniavyi Yuriy, 'Problema kordoniv Ukrainy (Problems with Ukraine's State Borders)', *Nova Polityka*, Vol. 2 (November–December 1995), pp. 42–4.

Shevchuk Valerii, *Kozats'ka derzhava: etiudy do istorii ukrains'koho derzhavotvorenia (The Cossack State: Essays on the History of Ukrainian Statebuilding)* (Kyiv, Abrys, 1995).

Sliusarenko A. and Tomenko, Mykola (eds.), *Istoria ukrains'koi konstytutsii (A History of Ukrainian Constitutions)* (Kyiv, 1997).

Tkachuk Anatoliy, 'Noviy derzhavi novu konstytutsiiu (The New Constitution for the New State)', *Polityka i Chas*, No. 10 (October 1995), pp. 30–7.

Tomenko Mykola, *Ukrainska perspektyva: istoryko-politolohichni pidstavy suchasnoi derzhavnoi stratehii (A Ukrainian Perspective: the Historical-Political Foundation of Contemporary State Strategy)* (Kyiv, 1995).

Tomenko Mykola, *Yaku Ukrainu buduie komanda Prezydenta Leonida Kuchmy? (What Kind of Ukraine Is Being Built by Kuchma's Team?)* (Kyiv, Ukrainska Perspektyva, 1996).

Tomenko Mykola *et al.*, *Khto i yak ukhvaliuvav Konstytutsiu Ukrainy (How Was the Constitution of Ukraine Adopted)* (Kyiv, Ukrainska Perspektyva, 1996).

Tomenko Mykola *et al.*, *Rossiiska Konstytutsiia Ukrainy (The Russian Constitution of Ukraine)* (Kyiv: Ukrainska Perspektyva, 1996).

Tomenko Mykola *et al.*, *Konstytutsiinyi referendum: yednist chy rozkol Ukrainy (The Constitutional Referendum: the Unity or Division of Ukraine)* (Kyiv: Ukrainska Perspektyva, 1996).

Tomenko Mykola, Iryna Kosonotska, and Serhkiy Odarych, *Shostyi uriad Ukrainy (The Sixth Government of Ukraine)* (Kyiv, Ukrainska Perspektyva, 1996).

Tomenko Mykola, Orobets Yuriy, and Odarych Serkhiy, *Konstytutsiina mifolohia suchasnoi Ukrainy (The Constitutional Mythology of Contemporary Ukraine)* (Kyiv, Ukrainska Perspektyva, 1996).

Tomenko Mykola, *Somovyznachenia Ukrainy: vid istorii do polityky (The Self-identification of Ukraine: From History to Politics)* (Kyiv, Zapovit, 1998).

Trubushnyi Oleksandr, 'Movna polityka v Ukraini: problemy i priorytety (Language Policy in Ukraine: Problems and Priorities)', *Viche*, Vol. 9 (1997), pp. 99–107.

Vybory v Ukraini (Kiev: International Foundation for Electoral Studies, 1994).

Vydryn Dmytro and Tabachnyk Dmytro, *Ukraina na porozi XXI stolittia (Ukraine on the Brink of the XXXst Century)* (Kyiv, 1996).

Zolotariov Volodymyr, 'Zakon pro vladu—seria drukha ale ne ostannia (The Law on Power, The Second, but Not Last, Series)', *Demos*, No. 8(17) (1995), pp. 3–7.

Zolotariov Volodymyr, '1996: Perekhid do organizovanoho khaosu (The Passage to Organised Chaos)', *Demos*, No. 1 (1996), pp. 3–10.

Zaitsev V., 'Konflikt mizh hilkamy vlady v protsesi iikh stanovlenia, 1991–1996 (Conflict between the Branches of Power in the Process of Their Creation, 1991–1996)', in. O. Haran' *et al.* (eds.), *Stanovlenia vladnykh struktur v Ukraini* (Kyiv, 1996), pp. 5–29.

INDEX

For Product Safety Concerns and Information please contact our EU representative GPSR@taylorandfrancis.com Taylor & Francis Verlag GmbH, Kaufingerstraße 24, 80331 München, Germany

Batch number: 10725853

Printed by Printforce, the Netherlands